➢ FIRST EDITION ◄

A COMPLETE GUIDE TO GUN LAW IN ILLINOIS

ILLINOIS GUN LAW

Armed And Educated

Written by Attorney Michael A. Johnson and published in the
United States of America.

U.S. LawShield, LLP
ISBN 978-1-7333432-1-3

To order additional books by phone or
for wholesale orders call (877) 448-6839.

TABLE OF CONTENTS

PREFACE

U. S. and Texas LawShield would like to thank its members and others who made this edition of Armed and Educated possible.

As a lawyer with years of representing law-abiding gun owners in cases all over the State of Illinois, I have seen how well-intended folks exercising their Second Amendment rights get mixed up in the legal system.

The law can be complicated, overlapping, hard to understand, and in some cases, completely arbitrary to the point of confusion. Laws are often written by lawyers for lawyers or are the result of political compromises generating confusing laws that the courts are left to interpret. After years of legal work in the arena of firearms law, I found there did not exist a resource that explained gun law in a manner that was easy for everyone to understand—because understanding the law goes far beyond just reading statutes or regulations. If you do not know either the process by which the law is being administered or how the courts are interpreting the meaning of the law, then you don't understand the full legal story.

That is why I wrote and will continue to revise Illinois Gun Law: Armed And Educated. It is a one-volume guide to the minimum law every gun owner needs to know to stay legal. Whenever appropriate, I tried to present useful analysis and real world applications. My goal was to explain the "law" so gun owners could inform and educate themselves. Hundreds of hours have gone into producing this resource, always with the goal in mind of education. Many people firmly believe that "it" can't happen to them. Even people who have never been in trouble before, find themselves in the world of law, lawyers, and law enforcement through ignorance of the law.

I am committed to helping protect Second Amendment rights for all legal gun owners. It is my passion and my mission. I want people to know the law, because only through eternal vigilance will we protect our cherished right to bear arms. If you own a gun, the laws concerning firearms and their use apply to you. Ignorance of the law is not a valid legal excuse. Therefore, if you want to stay legal, know the law. I hope you enjoy reading it as much as I enjoyed writing it!

I need to thank the lawyers at U.S. and Texas LawShield for all the support and experience in helping put this book together. I would also be remiss if I did not thank my administrative assistant Barbara Wright for all her hard work and dedication in helping me navigate the complexities invlolved in producing this edition. Finally, I thank my wife Dawn for her patience and understanding when I was not present for long periods of time while I was working to complete this task.

CHAPTER ONE

BRIEF LEGAL HISTORY OF
THE RIGHT TO BEAR ARMS
And The Laws Regulating Firearms

I. INTRODUCTION AND OVERVIEW

To fully understand gun rights today in Illinois or the United States, one should start first at the beginning: the formation document for our federal government, the United States Constitution. The Constitution was written without any enumerated guaranteed individual rights. The Founding Fathers thought it obvious and apparent that individuals had rights; therefore, there was no reason to elucidate them in a document that was supposed to control the government. James Madison also thought that by naming certain rights, it would imply that those were the only rights an individual possessed. After much discussion, and a complete change of opinion by Madison, the lack of enumerated rights was remedied in the first Congressional session and the state ratification process. When the dust settled, ten amendments were added to the Constitution; these ten amendments are the Bill of Rights. It is the Second Amendment that concerns firearms specifically, though throughout this book we will reference many others, including the Fourth and Fifth Amendments that both affect your right to bear arms and the fundamental rights for us all.

II. DO I HAVE A CONSTITUTIONAL RIGHT AS AN INDIVIDUAL TO KEEP AND BEAR ARMS?

Yes. The United States Supreme Court has decided that an individual has a constitutional right to keep and bear arms that flows from the Second Amendment, which states simply:

> A well-regulated Militia, being necessary to the security of a free State, the right of the people to keep and bear Arms, shall not be infringed.

From a plain reading, there are two important parts to this amendment: first, that a well-regulated militia is necessary to the security of a free state, and second, that there is a right of the people to keep and bear arms. For years before the issue was decided, anti-gun activists have tried to argue that the Second Amendment only applied to "militias" and not to individuals. Luckily, this argument is not the law. Nevertheless, despite the Supreme Court rulings stating otherwise, this myth seems to persist. What do these parts of the Second Amendment mean? Are they the same, or are they different?

A. What is a "well-regulated militia?"

As we discussed earlier, the first part of the Second Amendment references a "well-regulated militia." What is a well-regulated militia? The U.S. Supreme Court has held what this phrase does and does not mean. In 1939, in the case of *United States v. Miller*, 307 U.S. 174 (1939) (ironically, a ruling that upheld firearms regulation), the Court defined a "militia" as comprising "all males physically capable of acting in concert for the common defense." Based on how the amendment was drafted, the Court stated, it was clear that the militia pre-dated Article I of the Constitution, because unlike armies and navies, it did not have to be created by Congress. What then is "well-regulated" per the Court? It is exactly what it sounds like: the imposition of discipline and training. So, is this just the National Guard? No.

In the case of *D.C. v. Heller*, 554 U.S. 570 (2008), the Supreme Court stated that the well-regulated militia is not the state's military forces, but a separate entity altogether. The Supreme Court stated that the word "militia" referred to the body of the people, and they—the people—were required to keep a centralized government in check. The Supreme Court considered and rejected the position that the National Guard is the current militia under the Second Amendment.

B. How has the phrase "right to keep and bear arms" been interpreted by the courts?

One of the first cases to directly deal with the Second Amendment was *United States v. Miller.* In *Miller*, the Supreme Court found that the National Firearms Act ("NFA"), which imposed registration requirements on machine guns, short-barreled weapons, destructive devices, and other similarly unique firearms, did not violate the

Second Amendment. The Court used the reasoning that possession of weapons regulated by the NFA did not reasonably relate to the preservation or efficiency of a well-regulated militia, therefore, the NFA was upheld as constitutional.

UNITED STATES v. MILLER, 307 U.S. 174 (1939)

THE FACTS

Defendants, Miller and Layton, transported a double barrel 12-gauge shotgun with a barrel length of less than 18 inches from Oklahoma to Arkansas, and were being prosecuted under the National Firearms Act (which required certain types of firearms to be registered and a tax to be paid). Defendants challenged the NFA as an unconstitutional violation of the Second Amendment.

THE LEGAL HOLDING

Upheld the National Firearms Act as constitutional and not a violation of the Second Amendment.

An interesting quirk of history in the *Miller* case (and not a shining moment for the legal system) is that Miller's attorney never appeared at the arguments before the U.S. Supreme Court because he was court-appointed and had not been paid. There was no written brief and no legal representation at oral arguments by the party arguing that the law was unconstitutional. The Court only heard the government's side. To make matters worse, Miller was shot to death before the decision was rendered.

C. 69 years later, the Supreme Court interprets the Second Amendment again: *D.C. v. Heller*

It would be 69 years after *Miller* until the U.S. Supreme Court addressed the Second Amendment directly again, except this time the Court would hear both the Government's and the Defendant's arguments. Fortunately, freedom and Second Amendment rights prevailed in court that day. The Court held that individuals have a right to keep and bear arms.

DISTRICT OF COLUMBIA v. HELLER, 554 U.S. 570 (2008)

THE FACTS

Heller applied for a handgun ownership permit and was denied; without such a permit, D.C. required that all firearms (including rifles and shotguns) be kept unloaded and disassembled, or bound by a trigger lock, even in a person's own home.

THE LEGAL HOLDING

1. The Supreme Court found that the Second Amendment protects an individual right of firearms ownership for the purpose of self-defense and is not connected with any militia or military purposes; it further elaborated that individual self-defense is "the central component" of the Second Amendment. Further, handguns are the primary defensive weapon of choice and are protected by the Second Amendment.

2. A well-regulated militia is not the state's military forces.

3. The Court also discussed what the phrase "bear arms" meant: "wear, bear, or carry... upon the person or in clothing or in a pocket, for the purpose... of being armed and ready for offensive or defensive action in a case of conflict with another person."

4. The D.C. regulation was held to be unconstitutional.

5. The Court concluded that like other rights, the right to bear arms is not completely absolute. Reasonable provisions and restrictions have been upheld.

Keep in mind *D.C. v. Heller* was a split 5–4 decision; only one Justice away from a completely different outcome, where the

Second Amendment (according to the dissent) had "outlived its usefulness and should be ignored."

D. Can states ignore the Second Amendment? *McDonald v. City of Chicago*

D.C. v. Heller was fantastic, but there was a slight quirk: the District of Columbia is under the exclusive jurisdiction of Congress and is not part of any state. Therefore, the case shed no light on the question of what states can do when it comes to regulating or banning firearms. How do state constitutions interact with the Second Amendment? Can states ban guns outright? Two years after *Heller*, *McDonald v. City of Chicago* sought to answer these questions.

McDONALD v. CITY OF CHICAGO, 561 U.S. 742 (2010)

THE FACTS

A Chicago ordinance banned handgun possession (among other gun regulations). McDonald was a 76-year-old retired maintenance engineer who wanted a handgun for self-defense. Chicago required that all handguns had to be registered, but refused all handgun registration after a 1982 citywide handgun ban.

THE LEGAL HOLDING

The Supreme Court held that the Second Amendment is fully applicable to the States and that individual self-defense is "the central component" of the Second Amendment. Therefore, the Second Amendment prohibits states from enacting bans on handguns for self-protection in the home.

E. Legal limitations of the right to keep and bear arms

The U.S. Supreme Court has stated: "Of course the right [to keep and bear arms] was not unlimited, just as the First Amendment's right of free speech was not." Courts may have struggled over the years with what the Second Amendment means, but they have been resolute that there is an element of self-defense. The *Heller* Court stated that, "The Second Amendment does not protect the right to carry arms for any sort of confrontation," focusing their decision on self-defense. Further, the *Miller* Court stated that the weapons protected were those "in common use at the time" of the decision. This is supported by historical traditions of prohibiting the carry of "dangerous and unusual weapons" that are commonly used by criminals offensively, as opposed to by law-abiding citizens for defensive purposes.

The Second Amendment does not protect against legislative prohibitions on firearm possession by felons and the mentally ill. *Heller* made this point in its decision, and many circuit court cases such as *U.S. v. Everist* had previously used the same reasoning prior to *Heller*. The Fifth Circuit Court of Appeals in *U.S. v. Everist* stated that the Second Amendment is subject to, "limited narrowly tailored specific exceptions or restrictions for particular cases that are reasonable; it is clear that felons, infants and those of unsound mind may be prohibited from possessing firearms." *U.S. v. Everist*, 368 F.3d 517, 519 (5th Cir. 2004). Along this same train of thought, the U.S. Supreme Court did not want to eliminate laws that imposed conditions and qualifications on the commercial sales of firearms.

It also does not mean that the Second Amendment includes the right to carry anywhere a person wants. The *Heller* Court stated that their opinion was not meant to allow the carrying of firearms in sensitive places, such as schools and certain government buildings.

Currently, the two most important court decisions fortifying our gun rights are *Heller* and *McDonald*. But those cases were very, very close to going the other way! Both were decided by a 5–4 majority, meaning that if only one other Supreme Court Justice had decided differently, our individual right to possess and carry firearms could have been severely limited. -Michael

F. The future of the Second Amendment

How will the Second Amendment be treated going forward? With the passing of Supreme Court Justice Antonin Scalia, one of the key supporters and author of the 5–4 decision that was *Heller*, the split-down-the-middle Supreme Court truly seemed poised to either continue protecting firearms rights, or backslide to the position that the Second Amendment only applied to militia activity. When the dust settled, Justice Scalia's empty seat ended up going to Neil Gorsuch. How Justice Gorsuch has treated the Second Amendment in the past will be a central component of its future. The Court's newest Justice, Brett Kavanaugh, is a tried and true supporter of the right to bear arms. His appointment and confirmation bodes well for the future of the Second Amendment.

Although Justice Scalia's opinion in *Heller* established the right for individuals to bear arms, it includes the famous caveat: "Like most rights, the right secured by the Second Amendment is not unlimited." *D.C. v. Heller*, 554 U.S. at 595. That sentence left open the possibility that some gun regulations could pass muster, without spelling out the criteria for constitutionality. Overall, these regulations can be generalized into three major archetypes: those that impose registration requirements on firearms or their owners, those that ban certain types of firearms or firearm accessories, and those that prohibit the carrying of firearms in public (be it through impossible-to-obtain licensing schemes, or piecemeal prohibition).

The sheer volume of such cases allowing the erosion of the Second Amendment is alarming, but not as alarming as how many are denied certiorari.

In the years since *McDonald*, there have been more than 70 U.S. Circuit Court opinions upholding state restrictions on the Second Amendment that the U.S. Supreme Court has refused to review. These restrictions include requiring the registration of firearms, prohibiting "large capacity" magazines, banning certain firearms as "assault rifles," and creating classes of individuals who are restricted from owning firearms.

A Ninth Circuit case that many observers thought the U.S. Supreme Court would review is *Peruta v. County of San Diego*, 742 F.3d 1144 (9th Cir. 2014). On June 26, 2017, the Supreme Court again denied certiorari. However, Justice Thomas along with newly appointed Justice Gorsuch issued an opinion decrying the Court's decision and stated therein:

> The Court's decision to deny certiorari in this case reflects a distressing trend: the treatment of the Second Amendment as a disfavored right. ... The Constitution does not rank certain rights above others, and I do not think this Court should impose such

a hierarchy by selectively enforcing its preferred rights. ... For those of us who work in marbled halls, guarded constantly by a vigilant and dedicated police force, the guarantees of the Second Amendment might seem antiquated and superfluous. But the Framers made a clear choice: They reserved to all Americans the right to bear arms for self-defense. I do not think we should stand by idly while a State denies its citizens that right, particularly when their very lives may depend on it. *Peruta v. California*, 198 L.E.2d 746 (Mem) (2017) (THOMAS, J., dissenting from denial of certiorari).

III. MAJOR FIREARMS STATUTES EVERY GUN OWNER NEEDS TO KNOW

At the federal level, there are plenty of laws and regulations that concern firearms, but this section will focus on some of the more major legislative actions that all gun owners need to know.

A. Gun Control Act of 1968

The Gun Control Act of 1968 ("GCA") was enacted by Congress to "provide for better control of the interstate traffic of firearms." This law is primarily focused on regulating interstate commerce in firearms by generally prohibiting interstate firearms transfers except among licensed manufacturers, dealers, and importers; however, interstate commerce has been held by the courts to include nearly everything. It also contains classes of individuals to whom firearms should not be sold. For the specifics of who can and can't purchase a firearm, please refer to Chapter 3. Among other things, the GCA created the Federal Firearms License ("FFL") system, imposed importation restrictions on military surplus rifles (adding a "sporting purpose test" and a "points system" for handguns), and marking requirements.

B. The Brady Handgun Violence Prevention Act

The Brady Handgun Violence Prevention Act, commonly referred to as the Brady Law, instituted federal background checks (the National Instant Criminal Background Check System or "NICS") for firearm purchasers in the United States. It also prohibited certain persons from purchasing firearms. (*See* Chapter 3 for more information on who can or can't purchase a firearm).

C. The Firearm Owners' Protection Act

The Firearm Owners' Protection Act ("FOPA") revised many provisions of the original Gun Control Act, including "reforms" on the inspection of FFLs. This same Act updated the list of individuals prohibited from purchasing firearms that was introduced by the GCA. The FOPA also banned the ownership by civilians of any machine gun that was not registered under the NFA as of May 19, 1986. FOPA created what is called a "safe passage" provision of the law, which allows for traveling across states with a firearm. Finally, FOPA prohibited a registry for non-NFA items that directly linked firearms to their owners.

D. The Public Safety and Recreational Firearms Use Protection Act

The Public Safety and Recreational Firearms Use Protection Act, commonly referred to as the Federal Assault Weapons Ban, was a subsection of the Violent Crime Control and Law Enforcement Act of 1994. It banned outright the manufacture and transfer of certain semi-automatic firearms and magazines. This ban grandfathered-in previously legally owned weapons, but no prohibited firearm could be acquired or manufactured after September 13, 1994. With great foresight, the drafters of this law included a so-called "sunset provision" which stated that the ban would expire ten years later unless renewed. The ban expired in 2004, and all attempts to renew it have been unsuccessful.

E. The National Firearms Act

The National Firearms Act ("NFA") regulates and imposes a statutory excise tax on the manufacture and transfer of certain types of firearms and weapons: machine guns, short-barreled weapons, suppressors, explosive devices, and "any other weapons" ("AOWs") (AOWs can range from everyday objects that are actually firearms, such as an umbrella that can fire a round, to other weapons the ATF decides to place in this category). The tax is $200 if you make or transfer an item other than the transfer of AOWs; the tax for transferring AOWs is $5. The NFA is also referred to as Title II of the federal firearms laws. (*See* Chapter 14 for more information on how to navigate the NFA while remaining legal).

IV. DO ILLINOIS RESIDENTS HAVE A RIGHT TO KEEP AND BEAR ARMS IN THE ILLINOIS CONSTITUTION?

Yes. The Illinois Constitution Article 1, Section 22 reads:

> Subject only to the police power, the right of the individual citizen to keep and bear arms shall not be infringed.

The more observant will notice that, as opposed to the Second Amendment of the United States Constitution, this description specifically allows for regulation by police powers. The courts in Illinois have acknowledged that Section 22 allows the legislature to create laws to prohibit certain types of weapons, and have upheld "unlawful carrying" laws and license requirements. *People v. Aguilar,* 2 N.E.3d 321 (Ill. 2013).

A. Can Illinois prohibit local municipalities from making certain gun laws?

Yes. With a few exceptions. Traditionally, Illinois had broadly permitted the local regulation of firearms. A law adopted by the General Assembly in 2013, however, significantly curtailed this broad authority in several areas. (2013 ILL. ALS 63, 2013 Ill. Laws 63, 2013 P.A. 63, 2013 ILL. HB 183.) In *McDonald v. Chicago*, 561 U.S. 742 (2010), the U.S. Supreme Court reversed a U.S. Seventh Circuit Court of Appeals decision that affirmed the dismissal of Second Amendment challenges to handgun bans in Chicago and Oak Park, Illinois. This right, as first delineated in *District of Columbia v. Heller*, 554 U.S. 570 (2008), guarantees the individual right of law-abiding citizens to possess a firearm in the home for self-defense. *McDonald* effectively rendered unconstitutional handgun possession bans in Chicago, Oak Park, and other Illinois communities, to the extent that their bans restricted gun possession in the home for self-defense. *Heller* and *McDonald* also implicitly overruled (or at least diminished the impact of) *Kalodimos v. Village of Morton Grove*, 470 N.E.2d 266 (Ill. 1984), a key Supreme Court of Illinois decision that held when the state enacts statutes relating to the ownership, possession, or sale of firearms, it does not preempt the field of firearms regulation but permits local laws further regulating or restricting firearms.

The Firearm Owners Identification ("FOID") Card Act of 2013 requires an individual to obtain a license called a FOID card before acquiring or possessing any firearm or ammunition. The amended FOID Card Act states:

> ... The regulation, licensing, possession, and registration of handguns, and the transportation of any firearm and ammunition, including but not limited to the delivery of ammunition by the United States Postal Service or other courier, by a holder of a valid Firearm Owner's Identification Card issued by the Department of State Police under this act are exclusive powers and functions of this State. ILL. COMP. STAT. 65/13.1(b).

According to the amended FOID Card Act, any ordinance or regulation, or portion thereof, enacted on or before the date of the Amendment (July 9, 2013) that imposed regulations or restrictions on a holder of a valid FOID card in a manner that is inconsistent with the FOID Card Act, is invalid in its application to a holder of a valid FOID card. 430 ILL. COMP. STAT. 65/13.1(b).

B. What local governments may regulate

Local municipalities under state law are empowered to and may regulate gun ownership and use only in a very limited way. Illinois, which passed Concealed Carry on July 30, 2013, has a long list of restrictions which will be discussed in detail in later chapters. The amended FOID Card Act explicitly states that its provisions are a denial and limitation of home rule powers and functions under Art. VII Sec. 6(h) of the Illinois Constitution. 430 ILL. COMP. STAT. 65/13.1(e). Following these major alterations to local regulatory authority involving firearms, the permissible scope of cities and counties in Illinois to regulate firearms has narrowed. The amended FOID Card Act left in place a provision that states that, except as described above, "the provisions of any ordinance enacted by any municipality which requires registration or imposes greater restrictions or limitations on the acquisition, possession and transfer of firearms than are imposed by [the FOID Card Act], are not invalidated or affected by this Act." 430 ILL COMP. STAT. 65/13.1(a). Municipality is defined to include cities, villages, or incorporated towns, but not townships, counties, or park districts. 65 ILL. COMP. STAT. 5/1-1-2(1).

➤ CHAPTER TWO ◄

LEGAL DEFINITIONS AND
CLASSIFICATIONS
OF FIREARMS:
What Is Legal?

I. INTRODUCTION AND OVERVIEW

Before discussing the law of firearms and all its different facets, it is important first to understand what the law defines as a "firearm." Firearms laws are governed on both the federal and state levels; therefore, throughout this chapter we will explore the interactions federal and state law have on the purchase and possession of firearms.

A. What is a firearm?

FEDERAL DEFINITION

Under the federal law, a firearm is defined as "any weapon (including a starter gun) which will or is designed to or may readily be converted to expel a projectile by the action of an explosive." 18 U.S.C. § 921(a)(3). The federal definition of a firearm also includes the frame or receiver of any such weapon, any firearm muffler or silencer, or any "destructive device." This is similar to the Illinois definition, but not exactly the same.

ILLINOIS DEFINITION

In the State of Illinois, a firearm is defined in 430 ILL. COMP. STAT. 65/1.1 as any device, by whatever name known, which is designed to expel a projectile or projectiles by the action of an explosion, expansion of gas, or escape of gas excluding, however: (1) any pneumatic gun, spring gun, paint ball gun or B-B gun which expels a single globular projectile not exceeding .18 inch in diameter and which has a maximum muzzle velocity of less than 700 feet per second.

Why might it be important to know the different ways the term "firearm" is defined under federal and state law? It is because if a person finds themselves charged with a crime by federal authorities, the federal definition of a firearm will apply. Likewise, if the charge is under a violation of state law, then the Illinois definition will apply. Thus, the primary difference in the definitions and their impact on a defendant charged with a crime involving a firearm lies with how a person may be in trouble with the law. As we will see in the next section, the definitions of what does and does not constitute a firearm, although similar in many aspects, contain an array of differences that make violating the law unwittingly easy.

B. Definitions for handguns, rifles, and shotguns

In addition to defining what constitutes a firearm, federal and Illinois law further classify and define firearms into categories of handguns and long guns (rifles and shotguns). This section will provide an overview of how federal and state laws classify firearms as well as the physical requirements for a firearm to be legal.

1. What is a handgun?

Ultimately, whether looking at the federal or Illinois definition, the term handgun is defined in the same manner; it simply refers to any firearm that is designed to be fired by using only one hand. While it is true that most individuals will use two hands when firing a handgun for safety and accuracy purposes, the emphasis in the legal definition of a handgun rests purely in its design to be held or fired with a single hand.

FEDERAL DEFINITION

The United States Code of Federal Regulations defines a handgun as "(a) any firearm which has a short stock and is designed to be held and fired by the use of a single hand; and (b) any combination of parts from which a firearm described in paragraph (a) can be assembled." 27 CFR § 478.11.

ILLINOIS DEFINITION

Illinois law defines handgun in ILL. COMP. STAT. 66/5. "Handgun" means any device which is designed to expel a projectile or projectiles by the action of an explosion, expansion of gas, or escape of gas that is designed to be held and fired by the use of a single hand. "Handgun" does not include: (1) a stun gun or taser; (2) a machine gun as defined in item (i) of paragraph (7) of subsection (a) of Section 24-1 of the Criminal Code of 2012; (3) a short-barreled rifle or shotgun as defined in item (ii) of paragraph (7) of subsection (a) of Section 24-1 of the Criminal Code of 2012; or (4) any pneumatic gun, spring gun, paint ball gun, or B-B gun which expels a single globular projectile not exceeding .18 inch in diameter, or which has a maximum muzzle velocity of less than 700 feet per second, or which expels breakable paint balls containing washable marking colors.

2. What is a rifle?

Federal law defines a rifle as "a weapon designed or redesigned, made or remade, and intended to be fired from the shoulder, and designed or redesigned and made or remade to use the energy of the explosive in a fixed metallic cartridge to fire only a single projectile through a rifled bore for each single pull of the trigger." 27 CFR § 478.11. In addition, a legal rifle must have a barrel length of 16 inches or greater, and includes any weapon made from a rifle which is at least 26 inches overall in length. Illinois law does not provide a definition for a rifle, but it does classify illegal short-barreled firearms, including rifles with a barrel less than 16 inches or a shotgun having one or more barrels less than 18 inches in length. 720 ILL. COMP. STAT. 5/24-1.

Minimum lengths

In order for a rifle to not be subject to the National Firearms Act or classified as a short-barreled firearm under Illinois law, it must have a barrel of at least 16 inches in length. The ATF procedure for measuring barrel length is accomplished by measuring from the closed bolt (or breech-face) to the furthermost end of the barrel or permanently attached muzzle device. Below is an example of a rifle that does not meet the minimum barrel length requirement after measurement:

The barrel is measured by inserting a dowel rod into the barrel until the rod stops against the bolt or breech-face. The rod is then marked at the furthermost end of the barrel or permanently attached muzzle device, withdrawn from the barrel, and then measured. Any measurement of less than 16 inches will classify the rifle as being short-barreled under Illinois and federal law and subject the firearm to the NFA. (*See* Chapter 14 which discusses the NFA for short-barreled rifles and other non-compliant firearms). Note: for overall length, rifles with collapsible/folding-stocks are measured from the "extreme ends," unless the stock is "easily detachable," in which case it is measured without the stock.

3. What is a shotgun?

Federal law defines a shotgun as "a weapon designed or redesigned, made or remade, and intended to be fired from the shoulder, and designed or redesigned and made or remade to use the energy of the explosive in a fixed shotgun shell to fire through a smooth bore either a number of ball shot or a single projectile for each single pull of the trigger." 27 CFR § 478.11. Like rifles, legal shotguns have requirements for minimum barrel and overall lengths. Shotgun barrels must be at least 18 inches long and must also comply with the same 26 inch overall length requirement. Under Illinois law, shotguns are classified in the same manner as they are under federal law.

Minimum lengths

In order for a shotgun to not be subject to the National Firearms Act or classified as a short-barreled firearm under Illinois law, it must have a barrel of at least 18 inches in length. The ATF procedure for measuring the barrel length of a shotgun is the same as it is for a rifle. Below is an example of a shotgun that does not meet the minimum barrel length requirement after measurement:

Any measurement of less than 18 inches will classify the shotgun as a short-barreled weapon and illegal under Illinois and federal law unless the requirements of the NFA are satisfied. (*See* Chapter 14 for short-barreled shotguns and other non-compliant firearms). Note: the collapsible/folding-stock rule that applies to rifles applies to shotguns as well.

Numerous questions have surrounded the release of the Mossberg 590 Shockwave. The firearm has a pistol grip, shoots shotgun shell ammunition, has a barrel length of 14 inches, and an overall length of around 26½ inches. On March 2, 2017, the ATF issued a letter that states the Shockwave is not a firearm regulated by the NFA. Instead it is a GCA firearm that is regulated as any other common firearm that is available to the public. Consequently, Mossberg has marketed the 590 Shockwave as a non-NFA weapon that does not require a tax stamp for possession. The ATF determination relies on the fact that it is made without a shoulder stock and instead has a "birds head" grip. However, since the Illinois definition of a short- barreled firearm does not include the element of "intended to be fired from the shoulder" the question remains "is this legal, and can I have one in Illinois?" This firearm would be legal in Illinois. However, at this time, it would be considered illegal in the city of Chicago.

C. Antique firearms and replica firearms

When is a firearm not legally a "firearm?" It is when the law defines it as not being one, such as with "antique" firearms.

1. Federal definition of "antique firearm"

1898 or prior

The federal definition of firearm under Title 18, Section 921 of the United States Code excludes "antique firearms." Even though an antique firearm still functions ballistically similar to a "modern" firearm, under federal law, antique firearms are regulated differently. An antique firearm under federal law includes any firearm with a matchlock, flintlock, or percussion cap, or similar type of ignition system manufactured in or before 1898 or any replica of a firearm just described so long as the replica "is not designed or redesigned for using rimfire or conventional centerfire fixed ammunition, or uses rimfire or centerfire ammunition that is no longer manufactured in the United States and is not readily available in ordinary channels of commerce." 18 U.S.C. §§ 921(16)(A) and (B). So, an "antique firearm" is not a "firearm" for purposes of federal regulation; it is an "antique firearm."

Muzzle loading
In addition, federal law does not consider "any muzzle loading rifle, muzzle loading shotgun, or muzzle loading pistol, which is designed to use black powder, or a black powder substitute, and which cannot use fixed ammunition" as a firearm. Be aware, however, that the term "antique firearm" does not include any weapon which incorporates a firearm frame or receiver, any firearm which is converted into a muzzle loading weapon, or any muzzle loading weapon which can be readily converted to fire fixed ammunition by replacing the barrel, bolt, breechblock, or any combination of these parts. *See* 18 U.S.C. § 921(a)(16)(C).

2. Illinois definition of "antique firearm"
An antique firearm includes any firearm with a matchlock, flintlock, percussion cap or similar type of ignition system which is capable of being fired or discharged, or any firearm manufactured before 1898 for which cartridge ammunition is not commercially available and is possessed as a curiosity or ornament or for its historical significance or value. In *City of Chicago v. Taylor,* 774 N.E.2d (Ill. App. Ct. 2002), the court held that a firearm is not considered an antique if it is "still operable and capable of using commercially available ammunition."

3. Differences in federal and Illinois law
The area where the federal and Illinois definitions of what is not a firearm differ the most is in the use of black powder firearms. The years of manufacture for firearms that are classified as "antiques" are both the same under federal and Illinois law; antique firearms

are ones that were manufactured before 1898. However, the federal law takes things one step further by providing a separate section exempting muzzle loading firearms designed to use black powder or a black powder substitute so long as the firearm cannot be readily converted to fire fixed ammunition. Illinois law has no such exception for black powder firearms; only firearms that were produced prior to 1898 or which are replicas of weapons that were actually produced prior to 1898, are excluded.

This demonstrates one of the few examples where the federal law is less restrictive than state law. By these definitions, a person who could not otherwise legally possess a firearm, under federal law, could legally possess a muzzle loading rifle or pistol designed to use black powder that is not a replica of any weapon that was actually previously manufactured before 1898, because federal law does not consider such a weapon to be a firearm due to its mere use of black powder. However, under Illinois law, if a black powder gun is a modern black powder firearm and not a replica of an "old" pre-1898 firearm, it is considered a firearm under the Illinois Criminal Code, and it is not an "antique firearm." The possession or use of such a black powder firearm would be subject to all other Illinois laws governing the use of firearms. Illinois only excludes from its definition of firearms weapons designed to use black powder if they were actual weapons manufactured prior to 1898 or replicas of actual weapons manufactured prior to 1898.

D. What firearms are illegal?

Under Illinois law 720 ILL. COMP. STAT. 5/24-3, certain firearms are prohibited or illegal under Illinois law when they are not registered with the ATF pursuant to the National Firearms Act (*See* Chapter 14 for more information on the NFA). These firearms include:

- machine guns;
- short-barreled firearms; and
- firearm silencers or suppressors.

Note that due to this phrasing, possession of the NFA item itself is no longer inherently a crime; possessing the item without it being registered, however, is still a crime. This means a law enforcement official would need reasonable suspicion that you did not register the item to inquire about your registration status; as opposed to previously when you could theoretically be arrested and have to show up in court with your tax stamp proving registration. Functionally, however, it is always a good idea to carry around your proof of NFA compliance any time you are in possession of your weapon.

There are also zip guns (a term which includes any device which was not originally a firearm, but is adapted to become and act like one) which are illegal without exception. Zip guns are absolutely prohibited.

Under federal law, the same firearms that are prohibited weapons under state law without registration are regulated by the National Firearms Act. These firearms include:
- short-barreled shotguns;
- short-barreled rifles;
- machine guns;
- firearm silencers or suppressors;
- weapons or devices capable of being concealed on the person from which a shot can be fired;
- pistols or revolvers having a smooth bore (as opposed to rifled bore) barrel designed to fire a fixed shotgun shell;

- pistols or revolvers with a vertical handgrip;
- destructive devices; and
- weapons classified as "Any Other Weapon," or AOWs.

See 26 U.S.C. § 5845. (*See* Chapter 14 discussing the National Firearms Act for more information on these weapons).

On the surface, the prohibited firearms list is similar between both federal and state law with the primary difference existing merely in classification only (federal law classifies most of these items as firearms whereas Illinois classifies the items not as firearms but prohibited weapons). However, although these firearms and/ or weapons are prohibited by statute, it does not mean a person absolutely cannot possess one. Many of these weapons may be legally possessed with proper compliance under the National Firearms Act. (*See* Chapter 14 for more information on these prohibited weapons and the NFA).

E. How big of a gun can a person possess?

Federal law dictates that any firearm which has any barrel with a bore of more than one-half inch in diameter is a "destructive device" and is subject to the National Firearms Act. Possession of any such firearm without the proper paperwork associated with NFA firearms is illegal. Note, however, that some shotguns are regulated differently. (*See* Chapter 14 for more information on destructive devices and the NFA.)

II. AMMUNITION AND THE LAW

No discussion concerning firearms laws would be complete without examining laws concerning the ammunition that goes into a firearm. Just like firearms, the law regulates the possession, sale, and even composition of "legal" ammunition. This section addresses the essential aspects of the law concerning ammunition and what gun owners need to know, both under federal and Illinois law.

A. How does the law define ammunition?

Under federal law, the term ammunition is defined under 18 U.S.C. § 921(a)(17)(A) and means "ammunition or cartridge cases, primers, bullets, or propellant powder designed for use in any firearm." Thus, the federal definition of ammunition includes the finished product and all of the components in making a round of ammunition. However, the federal definition of ammunition does not include:

1) any shotgun shot or pellet not designed for use as the single, complete projectile load for one shotgun hull or casing; or

2) any unloaded, non-metallic shotgun hull or casing not having a primer. *See* 27 CFR § 478.11.

In other words, individual ammunition components are legally defined as ammunition themselves, even if they are simply parts, except that shotgun ammunition components, if not completely assembled, are not ammunition.

Under Illinois law, there is no statutory definition for mere "ammunition."

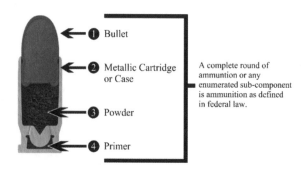

1 Bullet

2 Metallic Cartridge or Case

3 Powder

4 Primer

A complete round of ammuntion or any enumerated sub-component is ammunition as defined in federal law.

B. Is there a difference in ammunition that is used in different types of firearms?

Yes. Ammunition can be divided into two classifications: ammunition for handguns and ammunition for long guns. Long gun ammunition can be further divided into ammunition for rifles and ammunition for shotguns.

Handgun ammunition means ammunition that is meant to be fired from a handgun, and it comes in many different calibers. Rifle ammunition is meant to be fired from a rifle and is similar to handgun ammunition in that it comes in many different calibers. Shotgun ammunition, on the other hand, comes in self-contained cartridges loaded with some form of shot or a shotgun slug which is designed to be fired from a shotgun.

C. What ammunition is illegal?

Armor-piercing handgun ammunition is the only ammunition which has explicit prohibitions under both federal and Illinois law. The federal definition of armor-piercing ammunition is found in 18 U.S.C § 921(a)(17)(B) and means "[1] a projectile or projectile core which may be used in a handgun and which is constructed entirely (excluding the presence of traces of other substances) from one or a combination of tungsten alloys, steel, iron, brass, bronze, beryllium copper, or depleted uranium; or [2] a full jacketed projectile larger than .22 caliber designed and intended for use in a handgun and whose jacket has a weight of more than 25 percent of the total weight of the projectile."

Illinois prohibits the knowing manufacture, sale, purchase, possession or carrying of any armor piercing bullet, dragon's breath shotgun shell, bolo shell, or flechette shell. *See* 720 ILL. COMP. STAT. 5/24- 2(a).

FEDERAL LAW

Under federal law, while there is no blanket prohibition on the mere possession of armor-piercing ammunition, it is prohibited under four conditions:

1. Prohibition one: it is illegal to make or import armor-piercing ammunition.

Under 18 U.S.C. § 922(a)(7), it is unlawful for any person to manufacture or import armor-piercing ammunition unless:

1) the manufacture of such ammunition is for the use of the United States, any department or agency of the United States, any state, or any department, agency, or political subdivision of a state;

2) the manufacture of such ammunition is for the purpose of exportation; or

3) the manufacture or importation of such ammunition is for the purpose of testing or experimentation and has been authorized by the United States Attorney General.

2. Prohibition two: it is illegal for manufacturers and importers to sell or deliver armor-piercing ammunition.

Federal law states that it is unlawful for any manufacturer or importer to sell or deliver armor-piercing ammunition unless such sale or delivery is:

1) for the use of the United States, any department or agency of the United States, any state, or any department, agency, or political subdivision of a state;

2) for the purpose of exportation; or

3) for the purpose of testing or experimentation and has been authorized by the United States Attorney General.

See 18 U.S.C. § 922(a)(8).

3. Prohibition three: an FFL or other license-holder cannot sell or deliver armor-piercing ammunition without the proper documentation.

Under 18 U.S.C. § 922(b)(5), it is unlawful for any licensed importer, licensed manufacturer, licensed dealer, or licensed collector to sell or deliver armor-piercing ammunition to any person unless the licensee notes in his records, as required under 18 U.S.C. § 923, the name, age, and place of residence of such person if the person is an individual, or the identity and principal and local places of business of such person if the person is a corporation or other business entity.

4. Prohibition four: it is illegal to possess armor-piercing ammunition if a person is involved in a crime of violence or drug-trafficking.

Pursuant to 18 U.S.C. § 924(c)(5), it is unlawful for "any person who, during and in relation to any crime of violence or drug trafficking crime (including a crime of violence or drug trafficking crime that provides for an enhanced punishment if committed by the use of a deadly or dangerous weapon or device) for which the person may be prosecuted in a court of the United States, uses or carries armor piercing ammunition." Individuals who use or carry armor-piercing ammunition in the commission of a crime of violence or during a drug-trafficking crime are subject to heightened sentencing standards should they be found guilty.

As you can see, while possession of armor-piercing ammunition itself is not illegal, obtaining armor-piercing ammunition without violating one of the foregoing prohibitions is almost impossible.

D. Is it legal to use ammunition that works in both handguns and rifles?

Yes, except for armor-piercing ammunition that is used principally in handguns. This is because the federal and Illinois definitions of armor-piercing ammunition contemplate handguns only. Armor piercing ammunition for a rifle is perfectly legal, though it may complicate matters at trial in trying to demonstrate to the jury any differentiation. Beyond armor-piercing ammunition, it is legal to use ammunition that is available in common calibers and that functions in both handguns and rifles.

With a solid understanding of what is and is not a firearm and ammunition, as well as what firearms and ammunition a person may legally possess without the necessity of obtaining additional documentation, we are now ready to move to the next chapter discussing the purchase and possession of firearms.

CHAPTER THREE

PURCHASING, TRANSFERRING, AND POSSESSING
FIREARMS

I. LAWS OF PURCHASING AND POSSESSING: THE BASICS

The laws of purchasing, selling, gifting, or otherwise transferring a firearm are distinct and different from the laws of possessing a firearm. It may be legal for someone to possess a firearm, and it still be illegal for them to "purchase" the firearm. Further, each of these sets of laws for "purchasing" or "possessing" has a federal and a state component, both of which must be satisfied in order to stay on the right side of the law.

On the federal level, the Bureau of Alcohol, Tobacco, Firearms and Explosives ("ATF") is charged with regulating firearms including sales, purchases, and transfers through Federal Firearms Licensees ("FFLs" or "dealers"); however, a multitude of federal agencies can be involved in any given firearms law investigation or police function, most currently falling under a branch of the U.S. Department of Justice. Illinois has no direct state-level counterpart to the ATF.

A. What is an FFL?

An FFL or Federal Firearms License is a license required by federal law for those persons or entities that are engaged in the business of buying and selling firearms. A federal firearms licensee is often called an "FFL" or "dealer." When an individual purchases, sells, or transfers a firearm through a dealer, the FFL and the individual must both comply with specific federal law requirements, paperwork, and procedures concerning the buying, selling, or transferring of those firearms. These requirements will be addressed throughout this chapter.

B. Who must obtain an FFL?

Federal law requires a federal firearms license if a person is engaged in business as a firearms dealer, manufacturer, or importer. For the purposes of our discussion in this chapter, a person is engaged in the business when the person "devotes time, attention, and labor to dealing in firearms as a regular course of trade or business with the principal objective of livelihood and profit through the repetitive purchase and resale of firearms, but such term shall not include a person who makes occasional sales, exchanges, or purchases of firearms for the enhancement of a personal collection or for a hobby, or who sells all or part of his personal collection of firearms." 18 U.S.C. § 921(a)(21)(C).

C. What is a private sale?

A private sale is just what it sounds like: a sale, purchase, or transfer of a firearm by parties that are not licensed dealers. A private sale is perfectly legal for both handguns and long guns in Illinois, as long as all other legal requirements are met. We will discuss the ins-and-outs of private sales in greater detail in this chapter under Section IV.

D. What is the legal age to purchase and possess a firearm?

Federal law controls all FFL firearms transactions and requires that a person be 21 years of age or older before they may purchase a handgun or 18 for the purchase of a long gun. Under Illinois law, a handgun or long gun may be purchased in a private sale by a person who is 18 or older. In Illinois, you must be 21 or older to purchase a handgun from an FFL. 430 ILL. COMP. STAT. 65.

Under federal law, a person must be at least 18 years of age in order to possess a handgun or ammunition for a handgun. *See* 18 U.S.C. § 922(x)(2). Unlike the law on purchasing a long gun, there is no federal age requirement for the possession of a rifle or shotgun.

E. Can I buy a firearm if I have a note from my parents?

If a person finds themselves charged with selling a firearm to a minor, Illinois law does NOT provide an affirmative defense to prosecution under state law if the sale or transfer of the firearm was made to a minor whose parent or the person having legal custody of the minor had given written permission for the sale.

F. Criminal liability for allowing a minor access to firearms

Under the Illinois Criminal Code, a person may be guilty of a crime if a child (younger than 14) gains access to a readily dischargeable firearm and the person: (1) failed to secure the firearm; or (2) left the firearm in a place to which the person knew or should have known the child would gain access. 720 ILL. COMP. STAT. 5/24-9(a).

If the child discharges the firearm and causes death or great bodily harm to himself or another person and is over the age of 15, he or she can be charged as an adult and face serious felony charges.

It is unlawful for any person to store or leave, within the premises under his or her control, a firearm if the person knows or has reason to believe that a minor under the age of 14 years who does not have a valid Firearm Owner's Identification Card is likely to gain access to the firearm without the lawful permission of the minor's parent, guardian, or person having charge of the minor, and the minor causes death or great bodily harm with the firearm, unless the firearm is:

(1) Secured by a device or mechanism, other than the firearm safety, designed to render a firearm temporarily inoperable; or

(2) Placed in a securely locked box or container; or

(3) Placed in some other location that a reasonable person would believe to be secure from a minor under age of 14 years.

720 ILL. COMP. STAT. 5/24-9(c).

However, if a minor commits a crime to gain access to a firearm, the firearm's owner is not guilty of a crime. It is an affirmative defense to prosecution when a child gains access to a firearm "by entering property in violation of the Criminal Code." This means that if a child illegally breaks into a person's home or vehicle and then takes possession of a weapon illegally, the gun owner has not committed a crime.

G. When may children legally possess firearms?

Illinois law allows for the legal possession of firearms under specific exceptions. For obvious reasons, if a child uses a firearm in self-defense, or in defense of another person, there is a general public policy interest in not prosecuting those persons. 720 ILL. COMP. STAT. 5/24-9.

EXAMPLE:

One night, armed intruders break into Sally's home and hold Sally's parents at gunpoint while burglarizing the home. Sally, who is 12, covertly sees what is transpiring from the top of the stairs and knowing that her father keeps a loaded handgun in his nightstand, retrieves the weapon.

Two questions arise in this scenario: first, is Sally legally justified in shooting the armed burglar? Yes, she is. Sally is justified in defending a third person and property with deadly force under these circumstances. Second, is Sally's father in trouble legally for leaving his firearm accessible to Sally? No, he is not in trouble. Sally's access to the firearm was the result of her necessity in defending her parents who were staring down the barrel of a home invader's gun! This accessibility to a firearm is contemplated under the Illinois Criminal Code in the form of an affirmative defense. 720 ILL. COMP. STAT. 5/7-1.

Special duty of firearms dealers involving minors

Illinois law requires that a dealer of firearms post a sign in a conspicuous place on the premises where the dealer conducts his business that contains the following warning:

It is unlawful for you to: (a) store or leave an unsecured firearm in a place where a child can obtain access to it...

Federal law requires that FFLs who deliver handguns to non-licensees display at their licensed premises (including temporary business locations at gun shows) signs that customers can readily see. These signs are provided by the ATF and contain the following language:

(1) The misuse of handguns is a leading contributor to juvenile violence and fatalities.

(2) Safely storing and securing firearms away from children will help prevent the unlawful possession of handguns by juveniles, stop accidents, and save lives.

(3) Federal law prohibits, except in certain limited circumstances, anyone under 18 years of age from knowingly possessing a handgun, or any person from transferring a handgun to a person under 18.

(4) A knowing violation of the prohibition against selling, delivering, or otherwise transferring a handgun to a person under the age of 18 is, under certain circumstances, punishable by up to 10 years in prison.

In addition to the displayed sign, federal law requires FFLs to provide non-licensee customers with a written notification containing the same four points as listed above as well as Sections 922(x) and 924(a)(6) of Title 18, Chapter 44 of the United States Code. This written notification is available as a pamphlet published by the ATF entitled "Youth Handgun Safety Act Notice" and is sometimes referred to as ATF Information 5300.2. Alternatively, this written notification may be delivered to customers on another type of written notification, such as a manufacturer's brochure accompanying the handgun or a sales receipt or invoice applied to the handgun package. Any written notification delivered to a customer other than the one provided by the ATF must include the language described here, and must be "legible, clear, and conspicuous, and the required language shall appear in type size no smaller than 10-point type." 27 CFR § 478.103(c).

II. FEDERAL LAW DISQUALIFICATIONS FOR PURCHASING AND POSSESSING FIREARMS

Federal law lists categories of persons disqualified from legally purchasing and possessing a firearm. This list comprises disqualifications that come from several different pieces of federal legislation including the Gun Control Act of 1968, the Brady Handgun Violence Protection Act, and the Violence Against Women Act. If a person buys or attempts to buy a firearm from an FFL, they must not be disqualified under any of the laws. Before an FFL may sell or otherwise transfer a firearm, the purchaser must fill out an ATF Form 4473. This form has questions concerning each of the criteria that disqualify a person to purchase a firearm under federal law. These disqualifications include:

(1) If the person is not the actual purchaser of the firearm— also known as a "straw man purchaser;"

(2) If the person is under indictment or information in any court for a felony or any other crime for which the judge could imprison the person for more than one year;

(3) If the person has ever been convicted in any court for a felony or other crime for which the judge could imprison the person for more than one year;

(4) If the person is a fugitive from justice;

(5) If the person is an unlawful user of, or addicted to, marijuana, or any depressant, stimulant, narcotic drug, or controlled substance;

(6) If the person has ever been adjudicated as mentally

defective or has been committed to a mental institution;

(7) If the person has been dishonorably discharged from the Armed Forces;

(8) If the person is subject to an active protective order restraining the person from harassing, stalking, or threatening the person's child, or an intimate partner or child of such partner;

(9) If the person has been convicted in any court for a misdemeanor crime of domestic violence;

(10) If the person has ever renounced their United States citizenship;

(11) If the person is an alien illegally in the United States; and

(12) If the person is admitted under a non-immigrant visa and does not qualify for an exception.

The purchaser must legally affirm that they are not subject to any of the criteria listed above before they may purchase a firearm. If a prospective purchaser answers any question on the form in a manner that indicates they are legally disqualified, it is illegal for the FFL to sell that person the firearm, and it is illegal for the purchaser to complete the transaction or possess the firearm.

A. Understanding who is disqualified

1. Can I buy a firearm for another person?

No. This would be a "straw man" purchase. In order to legally purchase a firearm from a dealer, you must be the "actual purchaser or transferee." If you are not the actual purchaser or transferee, it is illegal for you to complete the transfer or sale under federal law. Purchases for third persons are often called "straw man" purchases and are illegal. If you are not the actual purchaser, beware!

In fact, the ATF has a campaign called "Don't Lie for the Other Guy" that is targeted at (as they term it on their website) detection and deterrence of "straw man" purchases. The ATF website lists numerous examples of prosecutions for "straw man" purchases and a United States Supreme Court case examined and upheld federal law on this matter. *Abramski v. United States*, 134 S.Ct. 2259 (2014).

So who is the "actual" buyer or transferee so as not to be a "straw man?" The ATF states that you are the actual "transferee/buyer if you are purchasing the firearm for yourself or otherwise acquiring the firearm for yourself (*e.g.*, redeeming the firearm from pawn/ retrieving it from consignment, or a firearm raffle winner)." The ATF goes on to state "you are also the actual transferee/buyer if you are legitimately purchasing the firearm as a gift for a third party."

EXAMPLE:

Jim asks his sister Crystal to purchase a firearm for him because he will be out of town during the gun sale. Jim gives Crystal the money for the firearm. Crystal then buys the firearm with Jim's money and gives him the firearm.

Crystal is not the "actual buyer" (she is legally a "straw man") of the firearm and if she indicates that she is the "actual buyer" of the firearm on ATF Form 4473, she has committed a federal crime. However, it should be noted that the Supreme Court ruling in *Abramski*, reaffirmed that "gifts" of firearms are not illegal straw man purchases. The important element in this crime is who provided the money for the purchase.

When completing ATF Form 4473, if a person checks "yes" to the box asking if the person is the "actual purchaser," then that person cannot have engaged in a separate transaction to sell or transfer the firearm privately. Please note: the Supreme Court's ruling held that a person cannot legally purchase a firearm on behalf of another even if the person receiving the firearm would not otherwise be prohibited from making the purchase themselves. So don't buy a firearm for another person no matter how good a friend, relative, or person they are—it is a crime!

FREQUENTLY ASKED QUESTION FROM ATF WEBSITE

Q: TO WHOM MAY AN UNLICENSED PERSON TRANSFER FIREARMS UNDER THE GCA?

A: A person may sell a firearm to an unlicensed resident of his State, if he does not know or have reasonable cause to believe the person is prohibited from receiving or possessing firearms under Federal law. A person may loan or rent a firearm to a resident of any state for temporary use for lawful sporting purposes, if he does not know or have reasonable cause to believe the person is prohibited from receiving or possessing firearms under Federal law. A person may sell or transfer a firearm to a licensee in any State. However, a firearm other than a curio or relic may not be transferred interstate to a licensed collector. [18 U.S.C. 922(a)(3) and (5), 922(d), 27 CFR 478.29 and 478.30]

Q: MAY A PARENT OR GUARDIAN PURCHASE FIREARMS OR AMMUNITION AS A GIFT FOR A JUVENILE (LESS THAN 18 YEARS OF AGE)?

A: Yes. However, possession of handguns by juveniles (less than 18 years of age) is generally unlawful. Juveniles generally may only receive and possess handguns with the written permission of a parent or guardian for limited purposes, *e.g.*, employment, ranching, farming, target practice or hunting. [18 U.S.C. 922(x)]

Bureau of Alcohol, Tobacco, Firearms and Explosives. (2019). Firearms - Frequently Asked Questions - Unlicensed Persons [online] Available at: https://www.atf.gov/firearms/firearms-frequently-asked-questions-unlicensed-persons [Accessed 10 July 2019].

Instead of the previous example where Jim gave Crystal money to purchase a firearm for him, if Crystal decides to buy a firearm with her own money and then give the firearm to Jim as a present, Crystal is the actual buyer/transferee of the firearm. Since Crystal is the actual buyer, there exists no sham or "straw man," and the purchase is legal.

2. A person cannot purchase a firearm if they have been convicted or are under "indictment or information" for a felony or certain misdemeanors

If a person has been convicted of a felony or other crime for which a judge may sentence, or could have sentenced the person to more than one year imprisonment, that person may not legally purchase a firearm (unless the crime was a state misdemeanor punishable by imprisonment of two years or less). *See* 18 U.S.C. § 921(a)(20)(B). Likewise, if a person is under "indictment" or "information" for a felony, or any other crime for which a judge may sentence the person to more than one year imprisonment, that person is disqualified from purchasing a firearm. An "indictment" or "information" is a formal accusation of a crime punishable by imprisonment for a term exceeding one year. It is important to point out that the actual sentence received is not the determining factor for disqualification, rather, it is the possible maximum sentence. A person may have only been sentenced to 30 days imprisonment, but if the crime for which they were charged allowed a maximum penalty of five years, then that person is disqualified. *See Schrader v. Holder*, 831 F.Supp.2d 304 (D.D.C. 2011, affd, 704 F.3d 980 (D.C. Cir. 2013)).

3. What does it mean to be a "fugitive from justice" so as to be disqualified from purchasing a firearm?

A "fugitive from justice" is a person who, after having committed a crime, flees from the jurisdiction of the court where the crime was committed. A fugitive from justice may also be a person who goes into hiding to avoid facing charges for the crime of which he or she is accused. Such individuals are not eligible to purchase or possess firearms.

4. Unlawful users of or persons addicted to drugs are disqualified from purchasing firearms

Federal law is very broad in that it disqualifies persons from the purchase of firearms if they are either users of or addicted to marijuana or any depressant, stimulant, narcotic drug, or any controlled substance. Under federal law, an "addict" is defined as a person that "habitually uses any narcotic so as to endanger the public morals, health, safety, or welfare, or who is so far addicted to the use of narcotic drugs as to have lost the power of self-control with reference to his addiction." 21 U.S.C. § 802(1). However, in using the terms "users of," no such frequency or dependence seems contemplated in the words, nor did Congress give further guidance. Illegal users and addicts are prohibited from purchasing firearms from any person under federal law, and are likewise prohibited from possessing firearms. *See* 18 U.S.C. §§ 922(d) and (g). In late 2016, the ATF felt compelled to revise its Form 4473 to include the following statement in bold lettering:

Warning: the use or possession of marijuana remains unlawful under federal law regardless of whether it has been legalized or decriminalized for medical or recreational purposes in the state where you reside.

This has caused a great amount of concern as to whether or not a person who holds a prescription or license to buy marijuana is automatically prohibited from purchasing or possessing firearms. As more and more states decriminalize marijuana this is an issue that must ultimately be resolved.

5. A person can't legally buy or possess firearms if they are "mentally defective"

What does "mentally defective" mean? A person is considered to have been adjudicated as "mentally defective" if there has been a "determination by a court, board, commission, or other lawful authority that a person, as a result of marked subnormal intelligence, or mental illness, incompetency, condition, or disease: is a danger to himself or others, or lacks the mental capacity to contract or manage his own affairs." The term "mentally defective" includes a finding of insanity by a court in a criminal case, and those persons found incompetent to stand trial or found not guilty by reason of lack of mental responsibility. 27 CFR § 478.11.

"Mentally defective" also includes a person who has been committed to a mental institution by a court, board, commission, or other lawful authority, or a commitment to a mental institution involuntarily. The term includes commitment for mental defectiveness or mental illness, and also includes commitment for other reasons, such as drug use. However, it does not include a person in a mental institution for observation or a voluntary admission to a mental institution. Individuals who have been adjudicated as mentally defective are also prohibited from possessing firearms under federal law. *See* 18 U.S.C. § 922(g)(4).

6. A person subject to a restraining order may not purchase or possess a firearm

Under 18 U.S.C. § 922(g)(8), firearms may not be sold to or received by a person subject to a court order that: (a) was issued after a hearing which the person received actual notice of and had an opportunity to participate in; (b) restrains the person from harassing, stalking, or threatening an intimate partner or child of such intimate partner or person, or engaging in other conduct that would place an intimate partner in reasonable fear of bodily injury to the partner or child; and (c) includes a finding that such person represents a credible threat to the physical safety of such intimate partner or child; or by its terms explicitly prohibits the use, attempted use, or threatened use of physical force against such intimate partner or child that a person would reasonably be expected to cause bodily injury. An "intimate partner" of a person is the spouse or former spouse of the person, the parent of a child of the person, or an individual who cohabitates with the person.

7. Domestic violence issues and disqualifications

A person who has ever been convicted of the crime of domestic violence may not purchase or possess firearms under federal law. These restrictions were passed in what is known as the Violence Against Women Act in 1994 and amended in 1996. This is an often misunderstood law, and, in fact, the ATF has numerous "Frequently Asked Questions" concerning this disqualification on its website: www.atf.gov. The ATF does a good job of explaining the scope of this subject in its FAQs. Due to the complexity of this issue, the ATF examples are included here:

FREQUENTLY ASKED QUESTION FROM ATF WEBSITE

Q: WHAT IS A "MISDEMEANOR CRIME OF DOMESTIC VIOLENCE"?

A: A "misdemeanor crime of domestic violence" is an offense that:

(1) is a misdemeanor under Federal, State, or Tribal law;

(2) has, as an element, the use or attempted use of physical force, or the threatened use of a deadly weapon; and

(3) was committed by a current or former spouse, parent, or guardian of the victim, by a person with whom the victim shares a child in common, by a person who is cohabiting with or has cohabited with the victim as a spouse, parent, or guardian, or by a person similarly situated to a spouse, parent, or guardian of the victim.

However, a person is not considered to have been convicted of a misdemeanor crime of domestic violence unless:

(1) the person was represented by counsel in the case, or knowingly and intelligently waived the right of counsel in the case; and

(2) in the case of a prosecution for which a person was entitled to a jury trial was tried, either –

(a) the case was tried by a jury, or

(b) the person knowingly and intelligently waived the right to have the case tried by a jury, by guilty plea or otherwise.

In addition, a conviction would not be disabling if it has been expunged or set aside, or is an offense for which the person has been pardoned or has had civil rights restored (if the law of the jurisdiction in which the proceedings were held provides for the loss of civil rights upon conviction for such an offense) unless the pardon, expunction, or restoration of civil rights expressly provides that the person may not ship, transport, possess, or receive firearms, and the person is not otherwise prohibited by the law of the jurisdiction in which the proceedings were held from receiving or possessing firearms.

[18 U.S.C. 921(a)(33); 27 CFR 478.11]

Editor's note: A significant number of people make the mistake of overlooking or forgetting about a court issue or family law judicial proceeding. However, if you meet the above criteria, you are federally disqualified from possessing a firearm. The fact that it may have happened a long time ago, or that you did not understand the ramifications, is legally irrelevant.

Q: MUST A MISDEMEANOR CRIME OF DOMESTIC VIOLENCE (MCDV) BE DESIGNATED AS A "DOMESTIC VIOLENCE" OFFENSE?

A: No. A qualifying offense need not be designated as a domestic violence offense. For example, a conviction for assault may qualify as an MCDV even if the offense is not designated as a domestic violence assault. [18 U.S.C. 921(a)(33) and 922(g)(9); 27 CFR 478.11 and 478.32(a)(9)]

Q: DOES THE PROHIBITION ON RECEIPT OR POSSESSION OF FIREARMS AND AMMUNITION APPLY IF THE PERSON WAS CONVICTED OF AN MCDV PRIOR TO THE ENACTMENT OF 18 U.S.C. 922(G)(9) ON SEPTEMBER 30, 1996?

A: Yes.

Editor's note: For those wondering why this is not an unconstitutional ex-post facto law, multiple federal appeals courts have ruled against that argument and the Supreme Court has consistently declined to review any of those cases, effectively accepting the ruling of the courts of appeals and upholding the law.

Q: IS AN INDIVIDUAL WHO HAS BEEN PARDONED, OR WHOSE CONVICTION WAS EXPUNGED OR SET ASIDE, OR WHOSE CIVIL RIGHTS HAVE BEEN RESTORED, CONSIDERED CONVICTED OF A MISDEMEANOR CRIME OF DOMESTIC VIOLENCE?

A: No, as long as the pardon, expungement, or restoration does not expressly provide that the person may not ship, transport, possess, or receive firearms. A restoration of civil rights, however, is only effective to remove the Federal firearms disability if the law of the jurisdiction provides for the loss of civil rights for a conviction of such a misdemeanor. [18 U.S.C. 921(a)(33); 27 CFR 478.11]

Q: IS THE RELATIONSHIP BETWEEN THE PARTIES AN ELEMENT OF AN MCDV?

A: No. The "as an element" language in the definition of "misdemeanor crime of domestic violence" only applies to the use of force provision of the statute and not the relationship provision. However, to be disabling, the offense must have been committed by someone whose relationship to the victim meets the definition in the Gun Control Act (GCA). [18 U.S.C. 921(a)(33); 27 CFR 478.11]

Editor's note: This basically means that if illegal force was used against another person, regardless of the language in the underlying statute, if the illegal force was used against a member of the protected class under the statute, federal law will deem this as satisfying the requirements and disqualify the individual from purchasing and possessing firearms.

Q: IN DETERMINING WHETHER A CONVICTION IN A STATE COURT IS A "CONVICTION" OF A MISDEMEANOR CRIME OF DOMESTIC VIOLENCE, DOES FEDERAL, STATE OR TRIBAL LAW APPLY?

A: The law of the jurisdiction determines whether a conviction has occurred. Therefore, if the law of the jurisdiction does not consider the person to be convicted, the person would not have the Federal disability. [18 U.S.C. 921(a)(33); 27 CFR 478.11]

Q: DOES THE DISABILITY APPLY TO LAW ENFORCEMENT OFFICERS?

A: Yes. The Gun Control Act was amended so that employees of government agencies convicted of misdemeanor crimes of domestic violence would not be exempt from disabilities with respect to their receipt or possession of firearms or ammunition. Thus, law enforcement officers and other government officials who have been convicted of a disqualifying misdemeanor may not lawfully possess or receive firearms or ammunition for any purpose, including performance of their official duties. The disability applies to firearms and ammunition issued by government agencies, purchased by government employees for use in performing their official duties, and personal firearms and ammunition possessed by such employees. [18 U.S.C. 922(g)(9) and 925(a)(1); 27 CFR 478.32(a)(9) and 478.141]

Q: ARE LOCAL CRIMINAL ORDINANCES "MISDEMEANORS UNDER STATE LAW" FOR PURPOSES OF 18 U.S.C. 922(d)(9) AND (g)(9)?

A: Yes, assuming a violation of the ordinance meets the definition of "misdemeanor crime of domestic violence" in all other respects.

Q: WHAT STATE AND LOCAL OFFENSES ARE "MISDEMEANORS" FOR PURPOSES OF 18 U.S.C. 922(D)(9) AND (G)(9)?

A: The definition of misdemeanor crime of domestic violence in the Gun Control Act (GCA) includes any offense classified as a "misdemeanor" under Federal, State or Tribal law. In States that do not classify offenses as misdemeanors, the definition includes any State or local offense punishable by imprisonment for a term of 1 year or less or punishable by a fine. [18 U.S.C. 921(a)(33); 27 CFR 478.11]

Q: WHAT SHOULD AN INDIVIDUAL DO IF HE OR SHE HAS BEEN CONVICTED OF A MISDEMEANOR CRIME OF DOMESTIC VIOLENCE?

A: Individuals subject to this disability should immediately dispose of their firearms and ammunition, such as by abandonment to a law enforcement agency. [18 U.S.C. 922(g)(9); 27 CFR 478.32]

Bureau of Alcohol, Tobacco, Firearms and Explosives. (2019). Misdemeanor Crime of Domestic Violence. [online] Available at: https://www.atf.gov/qa-category/misdemeanor-crime-domestic-violence [Accessed 10 July 2019].

PRACTICAL LEGAL TIP

If you or a loved one are going through court proceedings involving family issues and a restraining or protective order is entered in your case, it can suspend your ability to purchase or possess firearms. Language in the court order prohibiting any acts of family violence whether or not family violence actually occurred, make it so the person whom the order impacts is legally barred from the purchase or possession of any firearm. Believe it or not, family courts have the ability to suspend your Second Amendment rights. –Michael

8. Illegal aliens or aliens admitted under a non-immigrant visa

Persons who are illegally in the United States may not legally purchase, possess, or transport firearms. Generally, non-immigrant aliens are also prohibited from legally purchasing, possessing or transporting firearms.

EXCEPTIONS FOR NON-IMMIGRANT ALIENS

However, a non-immigrant alien who has been admitted under a non-immigrant visa is not prohibited from purchasing, receiving, or possessing a firearm if the person falls within one of the following exceptions:

(1) If the person was admitted to the United States for lawful hunting or sporting purposes or is in possession of a hunting license or permit lawfully issued in the United States;

(2) If the person is an official representative of a foreign government who is accredited to the United States Government or the Government's mission to an international organization having its headquarters in the United States;

(3) If the person is an official representative of a foreign government who is *en route* to or from another country to which that alien is accredited;

(4) if the person is an official of a foreign government or a distinguished foreign visitor who has been so designated by the Department of State;

(5) If the person is a foreign law enforcement officer of a friendly foreign government entering the United States on official law enforcement business; or

(6) If the person has received a waiver from the prohibition from the Attorney General of the United States.

See 18 U.S.C. § 922(y).

III. ILLINOIS LAW DISQUALIFICATIONS: WHO CANNOT BUY A FIREARM UNDER ILLINOIS LAW?

As mentioned earlier, Illinois has restrictions on the sale, transfer, and possession of firearms that are separate and distinct from the federal restrictions. If a person runs afoul of the law, they could potentially face prosecution in both state and federal court.

A. Illinois law disqualifications for purchasing a firearm

The disqualifications for purchasing firearms under Illinois law are contained in Section 430 ILL. COMP. STAT. 65/4 to 65/8, which apply to all transactions in Illinois. This section of the Illinois Combined Statutes makes it a crime—a class A misdemeanor or, under some circumstances, a felony for a person to:

(1) Sell, rent, lease, loan, or give a handgun to a person that the seller knows intends to commit an unlawful act;

(2) Intentionally sell, rent, lease, or give (or even offer to do so) a firearm to any child;

(3) Intentionally, knowingly, or recklessly sell a firearm or ammunition to an intoxicated person;

(4) Knowingly sell a firearm or ammunition to any person convicted of a felony; or

(5) Sell, rent, lease, loan, or give a handgun to a person knowing that the person is subject to an active protective order.

If a person falls under any of the categories (*see* full explanations below) listed in the foregoing sections, Illinois law makes it illegal for a person to sell the other person a firearm.

B. Illinois law disqualifications for possessing firearms

Similar to the disqualifications for purchasing firearms under Illinois law, Section 720 ILL. COMP. STAT. 65 also includes prohibitions on the possession of firearms. These prohibitions on possession include:

(1) Persons convicted of any felony. However, the Illinois State Police can issue a FOID card, which is required to purchase

a handgun, if the felony was a non-violent offense and it has been 20 years since the conviction or last date of imprisonment. 430 ILL. COMP. STAT. 65/l0(c)(l);

(2) Persons convicted of domestic violence punishable as a class A misdemeanor;

(3) Persons (other than law enforcement officers) who are subject to a domestic protective order and have received notice of the order and before the expiration of the order; and

(4) Any conviction for battery or assault with a firearm within the past 5 years.

Note: even though a person may not be disqualified from possession of a firearm under state law, that person may nevertheless still be disqualified to possess a firearm under federal law.

EXAMPLE:

Randy was convicted of a state crime class A misdemeanor involving domestic violence in 1992. He has a Smith & Wesson .357 Magnum in his nightstand for self-defense.

Under Illinois law, Randy may be in legal possession of his firearm because more than five years have elapsed following either his conviction or his release from community supervision. However, if push-comes-to-shove and the Feds ever care, Randy is in unlawful possession of a firearm under 18 U.S.C. § 922(g)(9) and 27 CFR § 478.32(a)(9), regardless of how legal he might be under Illinois law.

C. Understanding who is disqualified under Illinois law

Pursuant to 720 ILL. COMP. STAT. 5/24-3, Unlawful Sale or Delivery of Firearms, a person commits the offense of unlawful sale or delivery of firearms when he or she knowingly:

(1) Sells or gives any firearm of a size which may be concealed upon the person to any person under 18 years of age;

(2) Sells or gives any firearm to a person under 21 years of age who has been convicted of a misdemeanor other than a traffic offense or adjudged a delinquent;

(3) Sells or gives any firearm to any narcotic addict;

(4) Sells or gives any firearm to any person who has been convicted of a felony under laws of this or any other jurisdiction;

(5) Sells or gives any firearm to any person who has been a patient in a mental institution within the past 5 years;

(6) Sells or gives any firearm to any person with a mental disability; and

(7) Delivers any firearm of any size which may be concealed upon a person, incidental to a sale, without withholding delivery of such firearm for at least 72 hours after application for its purchase has been made, or deliver any rifle, shotgun or other long gun, for at least 24 hours after application has been made.

1. What does Illinois law define as a child for the purpose of selling a firearm?

A child refers to any person who is under 18 years of age. (*See* Section I(D) of this chapter for a discussion of age restrictions.)

2. Illegal to sell to certain felons

If a person knows that another person was convicted of a felony, they may not legally sell that person a firearm under Illinois law unless the person has been out of prison or released from community supervision for 20 years—whichever is later. Note, however, that a person may still be guilty of unlawfully transferring a firearm to a felon under federal law.

3. Differences in federal and Illinois law concerning convicted felons possessing firearms

Under federal law, a person convicted of a felony is prohibited from possessing firearms. Illinois law, however, relaxes such restrictions. Under Illinois law, a convicted felon is permitted to possess firearms in the person's home after 20 years from the date of the person's release from confinement, community supervision, parole, or mandatory supervision—whichever date is later. 430 Ill. Comp. Stat. 65/10 (c)(l).

4. Will my juvenile record prevent me from possessing or purchasing a firearm?

Generally, if any person, including a juvenile, has been convicted of a crime which carries a punishment of imprisonment for more than one year, then that person will not be permitted to purchase a firearm under either federal or Illinois law unless their firearm rights are restored. In Illinois, juvenile adjudications of delinquent conduct are not convictions and therefore are not disqualifying under Federal law. *See* 18 U.S.C. § 922(g); and *United States v. Walters*, 359 F.3d 340 (4th Cir. 2004).

IV. UNDERSTANDING "PRIVATE SALES" LAWS
A. What are the legal restrictions on "private sales" of firearms?

Private individuals may legally buy, sell, gift, or otherwise transfer firearms to another private individual in Illinois. However, when doing so, careful attention needs to be paid to not violate the laws regulating these transactions. So what are the legal restrictions? First, the ATF has an informative pamphlet entitled "Best Practices: Transfers of Firearms by Private Sellers" located on its website. This pamphlet should be a must-read before entering into a "private sales" transaction involving a firearm. So, what are the rules in Illinois regarding private sales?

1. Residency requirements

In order for the private sale of a firearm to be legal in Illinois, both parties must reside in Illinois and possess a valid FOID card. This means, for our purposes, that both the buyer and seller of the firearm must be Illinois residents. Similarly, under federal law, an unlicensed (non-dealer) may only "transfer" a firearm to another unlicensed person in the same state. This means that if a person is a resident of Illinois, federal law prohibits the person from directly (not through a dealer) selling or transferring the firearm to a resident of another state. Federal law makes these transactions illegal from both the buyer/transferee and seller/transferor perspective. It is illegal for a private individual to transport into or receive within his own state a firearm which was purchased in another state from a private seller. *See* 18 U.S.C. § 922(a)(3). Likewise, it is illegal for a private seller to sell or deliver a firearm to an individual whom the private seller knows or has reason to believe is not a resident of the seller's state. *See* 18 U.S.C. § 922(a)(5).

EXAMPLE:

Bernie, an Illinois resident, is visiting his brother-in-law, Justin in Louisiana. While visiting, Bernie and Justin decide to go hunting in the swamps around Lafayette, and Bernie borrows one of Justin's handguns to shoot snakes. Bernie is impressed with Justin's handgun. Bernie asks Justin if he could buy it from him. Since they've been in-laws for so many years, Justin agrees and gives him a good price. Bernie happily pays Justin and brings his new handgun back home to Springfield.

Has Justin committed a crime in selling the handgun to Bernie? Has Bernie committed a crime in purchasing the handgun from Justin? The answer to both questions is yes! Under federal law, Bernie is not allowed to privately purchase a handgun in another state and transport it back to his home state. Likewise, Justin is not allowed to sell a firearm legally to a person he knows lives in another state. In this example, both Bernie and Justin know that Bernie is not a Louisiana resident—the place where Justin has sold his handgun. Bernie has committed the crime of willfully receiving a firearm from an out-of-state unlicensed person while Justin has committed the federal crime of willful sale of a firearm to an out-of-state person. *See* 18 U.S.C. § 924(a)(1)(D). The penalties for these crimes include jail time up to 5 years and/or a fine of $250,000!

What if the situation is less obvious? Let's take a look at an example where "reasonable cause to believe" comes into play.

EXAMPLE:

Felicia, an Illinois resident, recently posted her Kimber 1911 for sale on an internet message board in Illinois. Felicia receives an email from a person named Thomas who would like to buy the handgun. Felicia and Thomas agree, via email, on a purchase price and arrange to meet at a place in Illinois one week later to complete the transfer. When Thomas pulls up in his 1999 Ford F-150, Felicia notices the truck's Oklahoma license plates. Nevertheless, Felicia shrugs and sells Thomas the gun anyway without going through any of the formalities of making a bill of sale, or asking for Thomas's identification. Two weeks later, Felicia finds herself at an ATF field office in Rockford answering questions about a shooting that took place in Tulsa with her (former) Kimber 1911.

Is Felicia in trouble? It is highly likely. Although Felicia is not the center of the shooting investigation, she is probably under investigation for illegally selling the firearm to an out-of-state resident under federal law. If Felicia admits to noticing the Oklahoma license plate, the ATF will assert that she had enough information to believe that she was engaging in a prohibited firearm transfer.

2. Private sales: don't knowingly sell to the "wrong" people

A private individual may sell a firearm to a private buyer in the same state so long as the seller does not know or have reasonable cause to believe that the person purchasing the firearm is prohibited from possessing or receiving a firearm under federal or state law. *See* 18 U.S.C. § 922(d). (*See also* Sections II and III of this chapter for our discussion on disqualifications).

EXAMPLE:

Gene and Jezebel are friends. Jezebel tells Gene that she has just attempted to buy a gun from a local FFL dealer and that she was denied because she was disqualified for some reason under federal law (something about a conviction or restraining order or drug use or psychiatric problems—Jezebel was too mad to remember!). Gene says, "no problem, I'll sell you one of mine," and he does.

Gene has just committed a federal and state crime, because he knew (or at least had reasonable cause to believe) that Jezebel was prohibited from purchasing a firearm under the law.

B. How does the law determine a person's residence when buying or selling a firearm?

1. Individuals with one residence

For the purpose of firearms purchases, the person's state of residence is the state in which the person is present and where the individual has an intention of making a home. 27 CFR § 478.11.

2. What if a person maintains a home in two states?

If a person maintains a home in two (or more) states and resides in those states for periods of the year, he or she may, during the period of time the person actually resides in a particular state, purchase a firearm in that state. However, simply owning property in another state does not qualify a person as a resident of that state so as to purchase a firearm in that state. To meet the residency requirements, a person must actually maintain a home in a state which includes an intention to make a particular state a residence. *See* 27 CFR § 478.11. This issue may ultimately be a fact question with evidence of residency being things like a driver's license, insurance records, recurring expenses in the state, as well as other things related to making a particular state a person's residence.

3. Members of the Armed Forces

A member of the Armed Forces on active duty is a resident of the state in which his or her permanent duty station is located. If a member of the Armed Forces maintains a home in one state and the member's permanent duty station is in a nearby state to which he or she commutes each day, then the member has two states of residence and may purchase a firearm in either the state where the duty station is located or the state where the home is maintained. *See* 18 U.S.C. § 921(b). (*See also* ATF FAQs on residency at www.atf.gov).

4. Immigrant aliens

Persons who are legally present in the United States are residents of the state in which they reside and where they intend to make a home. Such persons, provided they meet all other requirements and are not otherwise prohibited from purchasing a firearm, are lawfully permitted to purchase a firearm.

C. Suggestion on how to document a private firearms sale

Protect yourself! This is practical advice that should not be ignored. If you engage in the private sale of a firearm, here are some practical tips:

- Ask for identification whether you are the buyer/transferee or seller/transferor to establish residency.
- Get and/or give a bill of sale for the transfer and keep a copy— identify the firearm including make, model, and serial number, as well as the date and place of transfer;
- Put the residency information on the bill of sale including names, addresses, and phone numbers; and
- Do not sell or transfer a firearm or ammunition if you think the person may not be permitted or is prohibited from receiving the firearm.

Why do this? Not only will it help establish residency, but if you unfortunately happen to buy or sell a firearm that was previously used in a crime, or if you sell or transfer a gun that is later used in a crime, you want to be able to establish when you did and did not own or possess the firearm.

Further, as a matter of good course, if you are a seller or transferor in a private sale, you might ask whether there is any reason the buyer/transferee cannot own a firearm. Why? So that if there is an issue later, you can at a minimum say that you had no reason to know the buyer could not legally possess firearms. However, do not overlook behavior that may indicate the buyer is not telling you the truth, because law enforcement will not overlook facts that show you did know, or had reasonable cause to believe that the buyer/ transferee could not own a firearm at the time of the transfer if a legal issue arises later. Protect yourself!

V. BUYING, SELLING, AND TRANSFERRING THROUGH AN FFL
A. Basic procedures
Persons purchasing firearms through dealers must comply with all legal requirements imposed by federal law. These include both paperwork and appropriate background checks or screenings to ensure that the purchaser is not prohibited from the purchase or possession of a firearm under federal law.

When purchasing through a dealer, the first thing a prospective buyer will do is select a firearm. Once a selection has been made, the prospective purchaser is required to show proper identification and complete ATF Form 4473. This form requires the applicant, under penalty of law, to provide accurate identifying information, as well as answer certain questions in order to establish whether a person may legally purchase a firearm. The information provided on Form 4473 is then provided to the National Instant Criminal Background Check System ("NICS") for processing and approval in order to proceed with the transfer. An FFL dealer can submit the check to NICS either by telephone or through the online website and only after the FFL completes all of these steps successfully is a purchaser/transferee allowed to take possession of the firearm.

B. What is Form 4473?

ATF Form 4473 is the ATF's form known as a Firearms Transaction Record which must be completed when a person purchases a firearm from an FFL dealer. *See* 27 CFR § 478.124. Form 4473 requires the applicant to provide their name, address, birth date, state of residence, and other information including a government-issued photo identification. The form also contains information blanks to be filled-in including the NICS background check transaction number, the make, model, and serial number of the firearm to be purchased, and a series of questions that a person must answer. *See* 27 CFR § 478.124(c). This series of questions and the corresponding answers help determine a purchaser's eligibility under federal law. Once the form is completed, the prospective purchaser will sign the form and attest that the information provided is truthful and accurate under penalty of federal law. This means that if you lie or make false statements on this form, the Feds can and will prosecute you for a crime!

Likewise, the dealer must also sign the Form 4473 and retain it for at least 20 years. The ATF is permitted to inspect, as well as receive a copy of the Form 4473 from the dealer both during audits and during the course of a criminal investigation. The 4473 records must be surrendered to the ATF in the event the FFL dealer retires or ceases business.

C. How are background checks administered when purchasing a firearm?

1. NICS: National Instant Criminal Background Check System

Background checks by dealers when transferring firearms are completed through the National Instant Criminal Background Check System or NICS, if required, prior to the transfer of a firearm from an FFL dealer to a non-dealer. When the prospective purchaser/transferee's information is given to NICS, the system will check the applicant against at least three different databases containing various types of records. Applicants are checked against the records maintained by the Interstate Identification Index ("III") which contains criminal history records, the National Crime Information Center ("NCIC") which contains records including warrants and protective orders, as well as the NICS Index which contains records of individuals who are prohibited from purchasing or possessing firearms under either federal or state law. In addition, if the applicant is not a United States Citizen, the application is processed for an Immigration Alien Query ("IAQ") through the Department of Homeland Security's Immigration and Customs Enforcement Division.

2. Responses from NICS

NICS responses to background checks come in three basic forms: proceed, delay, or deny. The "proceed" response allows for the transfer to be completed. The "delay" response means that the transfer may not legally proceed. If the dealer receives a response of "delay," NICS has three business days to research the applicant further. If the dealer has not received a notice that the transfer is denied after the three business days, then the transfer may proceed. "Deny" means the transfer does not take place; a transferee's options after a "deny" are discussed below.

3. What transactions require background checks?

A background check is required before each and every sale or other transfer of a firearm from an FFL to a non-licensee unless an exception is provided under the law. For every transaction that requires a background check, the purchaser/transferee must also complete ATF Form 4473. This includes:

- The sale or trade of a firearm;
- The return of a consigned firearm;
- The redemption of a pawned firearm;
- The loan or rental of a firearm for use off of an FFL's licensed premises; and
- Any other non-exempt transfer of a firearm.

4. What transactions do not require a background check?

A background check is not required under the following circumstances:

- The transfer of a firearm from one FFL to another FFL;
- The return of a repaired firearm to the person from whom it was received;

- The sale of a firearm to a law enforcement agency or a law enforcement officer for official duties if the transaction meets the specific requirements of 27 CFR § 478.134 including providing a signed certification from a person in authority on agency letterhead stating that the officer will use the firearm in official duties and where a records check reveals the officer does not have any misdemeanor convictions for domestic violence;
- The transfer of a replacement firearm of the same kind and type to the person from whom a firearm was received; and
- The transfer of a firearm that is subject to the National Firearms Act if the transfer was pre-approved by the ATF.

5. If a person buys multiple handguns, a dealer must report that person to the ATF

Under federal law, FFLs are required to report to the ATF any sale or transfer of two or more pistols, revolvers, or any combination of pistols and revolvers totaling two or more to an unlicensed (non-FFL) individual that takes place at one time or during any five consecutive business days. This report is made to the ATF on Form 3310.4 and is completed in triplicate with the original copy sent to the ATF, one sent to the designated state police or local law enforcement agency in the jurisdiction where the sale took place, and one retained by the dealer and held for no less than five years.

VI. WHAT IF I'M DENIED THE RIGHT TO PURCHASE A FIREARM?
A. If I am denied the right to purchase, how do I appeal?

Persons who believe they have been erroneously denied or delayed a firearm transfer based on a match to a record returned by NICS may request an appeal of their "deny" or "delay" decision. All appeal inquiries must be submitted to the NICS Section's Appeal

Service Team ("AST") in writing, either via mail or online on the FBI's website at www.fbi.gov. An appellant must provide their complete name, complete mailing address, and NICS Transaction Number. For persons appealing a delayed transaction, a fingerprint card is required and must be submitted with the appeal, although the fingerprint card is merely recommended on appeals for denied applications. This may seem counter-intuitive, but it is required per the FBI's website.

B. What if I keep getting erroneously delayed or denied when I am attempting to buy a firearm?

Apply for a Unique Personal Identification Number ("UPIN") that is designed to solve this issue. Some individuals may have a name which is common enough (or happens to be flagged for other reasons) that it causes undue delays or denials in the background check verification process through NICS. For that reason, NICS maintains the Voluntary Appeal File database ("VAF") which allows any applicant to apply by submitting an appeal request and then obtaining a UPIN. A person who has been cleared through the VAF and receives a UPIN will then be able to use their UPIN when completing Form 4473 in order to help avoid further erroneous denials or extended delays. A person can obtain a UPIN by following the procedures outlined on the FBI's website at www.fbi.gov.

VII. ADDITIONAL CONSIDERATIONS IN FIREARMS PURCHASING AND POSSESSION LAWS

A. How can I legally purchase a firearm from someone in another state?

Any individual who wishes to purchase a firearm from a person that lives in another state than the purchaser must complete the transaction through an FFL. Sellers or transferors are legally authorized to facilitate a private transaction or transfer by shipping the firearm to the purchaser's FFL in the recipient/buyer's state, where the FFL will complete the transfer process. It is a federal crime to sell or transfer a firearm between persons who are residents of different states, or where a transfer takes place in a state other than the transferee/transferor's singular state of residence.

B. Can I purchase firearms on the internet?

Yes. However, all legal requirements for a transfer must be followed. If the buyer and seller are both residents of Illinois, then the two may lawfully conduct a private sale so long as all other legal issues are satisfied (*See* our earlier discussion on disqualifications to purchasing and possessing firearms in this chapter). However, if buyer and seller are not residents of the same state, the transaction can only be legally facilitated through an FFL.

C. Shipping firearms

1. Can I ship my firearm through the United States Postal Service ("USPS")?

Long guns: yes. Handguns: no. However, under federal law, a non-licensed individual may not transfer (and this would include shipping to someone else) a firearm to a non-licensed resident (non-FFL) of another state. However, a non-licensed individual may mail a long gun to a resident of his or her own state, and they may also mail a long gun to an FFL of another state. To that end, the USPS recommends that long guns be mailed via registered mail and that the packaging used to mail the long gun be ambiguous so as to not identify the contents. Handguns are not allowed to be mailed via USPS. *See* 18 U.S.C. §§ 1715, 922(a)(3), 922(a)(5), and 922(a)(2)(A). Rather, handguns must be shipped using a common or contract carrier (*e.g.*, UPS or FedEx).

2. Shipping handguns and other firearms through a common or contract carrier

Under federal law, a non-licensed individual may ship a firearm (including a handgun) by a common or contract carrier (*e.g.*, UPS or FedEx) to a resident of his or her own state, or to an FFL in another state. However, it is illegal to ship any firearm to a non-FFL in another state. It is a requirement that the carrier be notified that the shipment contains a firearm; however, carriers are prohibited from requiring any identifying marks on the package which may be used to identify the contents as containing a firearm. *See* 18 U.S.C. §§ 922(a)(2)(A), 922(a)(3), 922(a)(5), 922(e), 27 CFR §§ 478.31 and 478.30.

D. Can I ship my firearm to myself for use in another state?

Yes. In accordance with the law as described in the preceding section, a person may ship a firearm to himself or herself, in care of another person in another state where he or she intends to hunt or engage in other lawful activity. The package should be addressed to the owner, and persons other than the owner should not open the package and take possession of the firearm.

E. If I am moving out of Illinois, may I have movers move my firearms?

Yes. A person who lawfully possesses firearms may transport or ship the firearms interstate when changing the person's state of residence, so long as the person complies with the requirements for shipping and transporting firearms as outlined earlier. *See* 18 U.S.C. § 922(e) and 27 CFR § 478.31. However, certain NFA items such as destructive devices, machine guns, short-barreled shotguns or rifles, and so forth require approval from the ATF before they can be moved interstate. *See* 18 U.S.C. § 922(a)(4) and 27 CFR §

478.28. It is important that the person seeking to move the firearms also check state and local laws where the firearms will be relocated to ensure that the movement of the firearms into the new state does not violate any state law or local ordinance.

F. May I loan my firearm to another person?

Yes. There is no prohibition on loaning a firearm to another person, so long as the person receiving the firearm may lawfully possess one. However, under 720 ILL. COMP. STAT. 24-3 it is unlawful for a person to intentionally or knowingly sell, rent, lease, give or offer to sell, rent, lease, or give a firearm to any child younger than 18 years of age.

G. What happens to my firearms when I die?

Depending on the manner in which a person leaves his or her estate behind, firearms may be bequeathed in a customary manner like other personal property. However, firearms held in an estate are still subject to the laws of transfer and possession. Thus, careful consideration needs to be given in estate planning with consideration for firearms law of both the jurisdiction in which the estate is located as well as consideration of who is to receive the firearms.

VIII. AMMUNITION: THE LAW OF PURCHASING AND POSSESSION
A. Who is legally prohibited from purchasing ammunition under federal law?

Under federal law, there are six primary situations where a person is prohibited from buying, selling, or possessing ammunition (beyond armor-piercing ammunition which was discussed in Chapter 2).

(1) Under 18 U.S.C. § 922(b)(1), it is unlawful for a person to sell long gun ammunition to a person under the age of 18;

(2) Under 18 U.S.C. § 922(b)(1), it is unlawful for a person to sell handgun ammunition to a person under the age of 21;

(3) Under 18 U.S.C. § 922(x)(2)(B), it is unlawful for a juvenile to possess handgun ammunition;

(4) Under 18 U.S.C. § 922(d), it is unlawful to sell ammunition to a person who is prohibited from purchasing firearms;

(5) Under 18 U.S.C. § 922(g), it is unlawful for a person who is disqualified from purchasing or possessing firearms to possess firearm ammunition if such ammunition has moved in interstate commerce (which is nearly all ammunition); and

(6) Under 18 U.S.C. § 922(h), it is unlawful for a person who is employed by a person who is disqualified from purchasing or possessing ammunition to possess or transport ammunition for the disqualified individual.

For the statutes that involve juveniles, there are a couple of notable exceptions to the law. First, the law against selling handgun ammunition to a juvenile and possession of handgun ammunition by a juvenile does not apply to a temporary transfer of ammunition to a juvenile or to the possession or use of ammunition by a juvenile if the handgun and ammunition are possessed and used by the juvenile in the course of employment, in the course of ranching or farming-related activities at the residence of the juvenile (or on property used for ranching or farming at which the juvenile, with the permission of the property owner or lessee, is performing activities related to the operation of the farm or ranch), target practice, hunting, or a course of instruction in the safe and lawful use of a handgun. The law also does not apply to the temporary transfer to or use of ammunition by a juvenile if the juvenile has been provided with prior written consent by his or her parent or guardian who is not prohibited by federal, state, or local law from possessing firearms. *See* 18 U.S.C. § 922(x)(3).

Second, the law against selling ammunition to juveniles does not apply to juveniles who:

1) are members of the Armed Forces of the United States or the National Guard who possess or are armed with a handgun in the line of duty;

2) receive ammunition by inheritance; or

3) possess ammunition in the course of self-defense or defense of others in the residence of the juvenile or a residence in which the juvenile is an invited guest.

B. When is a person prohibited from purchasing or possessing ammunition under Illinois law?

The laws in Illinois pertaining to the purchase or possession of ammunition are basically the same as the laws relating to gun possessions. A person cannot purchase or possess ammunition without a valid FOID card.

EXAMPLE:

Max comes into Larry's pawn shop to browse around. Larry notices that Max has red watery eyes, slurred speech, white powder caked on his nostrils, and is staggering around. Additionally, Max is carrying a half-empty plastic baggie with a white powder. Max says that he wants to buy a .38 Special and some ammo. Larry happily obliges him and Max stumbles out the door with his new purchase. Max then gets arrested for drug possession a few blocks from the shop and the police find the gun, ammo, and a time and date stamped receipt from Larry's pawn shop. The police then show up at the pawn shop to arrest Larry for violating 720 ILL. COMP. STAT. 5/24-3.

Larry will claim that he did not know that Max was a narcotic addict, but the prosecutor will argue that Larry consciously disregarded all of the signs of Max's drug use and he therefore "knowingly" sold him the gun and ammunition.

Likewise, it is a class 3 felony if a person "knowingly sells a firearm or ammunition for a firearm to any person who has been convicted of a felony before the twentieth anniversary of the later of the following dates: (a) the person's release from confinement following conviction of the felony; or (b) the person's release from supervision under community supervision, parole, or mandatory supervision following conviction of a felony." 720 ILL. COMP. STAT. 5/24-3(d).

C. Can a person be disqualified from purchasing ammunition if they are disqualified from purchasing firearms?

Yes. Under federal law 18 U.S.C. § 922(g), it is unlawful for a person who is disqualified from purchasing or possessing firearms to purchase ammunition if the ammunition has moved in interstate commerce. Since nearly all ammunition or ammunition components move through interstate commerce in one form or another, this disqualification includes essentially all ammunition.

D. Can a person purchase ammunition that is labeled "law enforcement use only"?

Yes. Although some handgun ammunition is sold with a label "law enforcement use," such a label has no legal meaning and is only reflective of a company policy or a marketing strategy.

CHAPTER FOUR

WHEN CAN I LEGALLY USE MY GUN: PART I

UNDERSTANDING THE LAW OF JUSTIFICATION
Some Basic Legal Concepts

I. IGNORANCE OF THE LAW IS NO EXCUSE!

N ow we can start our discussion: when is it legal to use a gun as a weapon? The purpose of this chapter is to look at the essential, basic legal concepts of the law of when and under what circumstances a person is legally justified in using force or deadly force against other persons or animals. Know when you may legally shoot, because ignorance of the law holds no weight in a courtroom! That is why it is critical you know the law so that you are in the best possible situation to preserve your legal rights if you ever need them.

II. GUN OWNERS NEED TO KNOW ARTICLE 7 OF THE ILLINOIS CRIMINAL CODE

In Illinois, legal justifications appear in numerous places and areas of the law. Of particular importance to gun owners are the defenses found in Article 7 of the Illinois Criminal Code, entitled "Justifiable Use of Force; Exoneration," which we cover in detail throughout this book. The full text of relevant provisions of that article of the Illinois Criminal Code is found in the Appendix.

PRACTICAL LEGAL TIP

A defense to prosecution is not the same as a bar to prosecution. A "bar to prosecution" is where a person can't be prosecuted for engaging in certain conduct. This means the charges cannot even be filed. Whereas a "defense to prosecution" allows the charges to be filed, a jury to hear the case, and evidence produced in court, but offers the accused an opportunity to present a legal excuse called a justification that allows that person to get completely out of trouble. –Michael

III. TO LEGALLY USE FORCE OR DEADLY FORCE, YOU MUST BE "JUSTIFIED." WHAT IS LEGAL JUSTIFICATION?

A. Basic definition of justification: an acceptable excuse

So, when is it legal to use force or deadly force against another person? When is it legal to even threaten to use force or deadly force against another? The answer is when there is a legal justification, or defense. A legal justification is an acceptable reason or excuse under the law for taking an action that would otherwise be a crime.

Rick is in his suburban back yard with his faithful dog when out of nowhere, a coyote appears and is about to attack. Rick draws his handgun and shoots the coyote.

Rick has discharged his firearm in the city limits, which is ordinarily a crime. Why will Rick likely be not guilty of the crime of discharging a firearm within city limits? Because, he was legally justified in shooting the coyote! That is, the law will likely say the excuse for discharging the firearm in the city limits—protecting himself and his dog from coyotes—makes Rick's action of discharging a firearm in the city limits reasonable and, therefore, legally justified.

B. Basic requirement: you must admit your action

If a person wants the potential protection of legal justification in Illinois, in order to raise the defense of justification in court, a person is required to admit all of the elements of the crime for which they are charged. Then, the person must present "some evidence" of justification before a jury will be given an instruction that "a person is legally justified to use force if…" In plain English, a person will not be allowed to say "I didn't do it, but if I did do it, I was justified!" You must admit the underlying elements of the charge.

Jane is walking home one night, when a man jumps out of the bushes and demands her purse. Jane pulls out her handgun and points it at the man, who then runs away. Unfortunately, Jane does not call the police, but the criminal immediately does, reporting a crazy woman threatening him with a gun. Jane ends up charged with aggravated assault, even though Jane was the victim.

Because justification is a legal affirmative defense in Illinois, if Jane's case goes all the way to trial, in order to offer a legal justification for committing "aggravated assault," she must admit in court that she did pull her handgun and point it at the would-be robber. Then, in order for the jury to consider a legal justification defense (*i.e.*, receive a jury instruction from the judge), there must be some evidence of why she is legally justified under the law for having pulled her weapon (in this example, Jane believed she was being robbed). The result is that Jane is entitled to have the judge instruct the jury that they may find Jane not guilty because she was justified in her action. The jury will then decide whether Jane's belief was reasonable and whether she is guilty or not guilty of the crime of aggravated assault.

On the other hand, if Jane does not admit to the elements of the criminal offense she is charged with, she will not be allowed to offer a legal justification defense under Article 7 of the Illinois Criminal Code. Legal justification is, therefore, literally the law of "Yes, I did it, BUT…!"

IV. CATEGORIES OF FORCE FOR JUSTIFICATION UNDER THE CRIMES CODE

Anytime a person takes a physical action against another person, they have used force. Article 7 of the Illinois Criminal Code divides or categorizes uses of force into different levels. Whether or not a use of force was justified under the law often depends on how that force is categorized. These categories, which we will address throughout this book, are: 1) force, 2) deadly force, and 3) the threat of force.

A. What if a person uses greater force than the law allows?

The use of a legally appropriate level of force is important because if a person uses more force than is "reasonably believed to be necessary" (*See* Section V), that person may not be legally justified in using that level of force. It is important to understand the differences in the levels of force and the circumstances under which the law allows the use of each.

For example, if a person uses deadly force, and the law allows only for the use of force, that person will not be legally justified. Likewise, if a person uses force when no force is legally allowed, that use of force will also not be legally justified.

EXAMPLE:

Dwayne looks out his window and sees a person walking through his backyard towards his tool shed. Dwayne yells at the fellow to get off his land. The fellow in the backyard does not respond and keeps walking toward the tool shed. Dwayne rushes out to confront him and demands that he leave the backyard.

This man is clearly a trespasser! What degree of force may Dwayne use to remove the trespasser? The law, as discussed later, will show that Dwayne is only allowed to use force in response to a mere trespasser. If Dwayne uses deadly force against the trespasser, he will not be legally justified and would be guilty of unlawfully using more force than is reasonably necessary against the trespasser. Ultimately, using the correct degree of force is critical in determining whether a person has committed a crime or a legally justified action.

B. What is the legal definition of "force?"

Surprisingly, force is not defined in the Illinois Criminal Code. However, deadly force is defined. Under Article 7 of the Illinois Criminal Code, deadly force is defined as "the use of force which is intended or likely to cause death or great bodily harm." A prerequisite for being able to legally use deadly force is the requirement that deadly force may be used only if the person reasonably believes that such force is necessary to prevent imminent death or great bodily harm to himself or another, or the commission of a forcible felony.

EXAMPLE:

Mikey is being harassed and insulted by Clay, a bully at school. One day, Clay stops Mikey on the playground and suddenly clenches his fist and takes a swing at him, but misses. Mikey reacts to the swing by kicking Clay in the shin.

Clay's action was a use of force. Even though Clay missed Mikey, he placed Mikey in fear of imminent harm. Mikey's reaction of kicking Clay was likewise a use of force, and as will be discussed later, a legally justified use of self-defense.

C. What is deadly force?

1. Deadly force does not have to cause death

On the surface, the legal definition of deadly force seems simple. However, the meaning of what is and is not deadly force can be legally tricky. A particular action does not necessarily have to result in death to be legally defined as deadly force—it just needs to be intended or likely to cause death or great bodily harm. Note: great bodily harm is not precisely defined under Illinois law.

EXAMPLE:

Jim is being robbed and beaten by a group of individuals when he manages to draw his handgun and fire it at one of the most aggressive assailants. His shot misses his intended target but breaks the group up, causing the would-be robbers to flee.

In our example, even though the bullet did not kill or even strike any of his assailants, Jim legally used deadly force because his conduct fit the legal definition of "intended to or likely to cause death or great bodily harm." Thus, death is not a prerequisite for the existence of deadly force! Likewise, almost any object can be used as a weapon in a particular circumstance. Therefore, in this section of the law, the focus is on the object's intended use and not just on the object itself.

2. "Intended or likely" as a component of deadly force

Deadly force, by its legal definition, occurs when a person takes an action that is intended or likely to cause death or great bodily harm. This knowledge or intention to cause great bodily harm or death is called a person's mental state. A prosecutor must prove beyond a reasonable doubt that a person possessed a particular mental state applicable to a crime in order to meet the state's burden of proof and convict someone of a crime.

Often a person's intent is easily ascertainable by the circumstances. For example, if a person is the would-be victim of robbery, and the person resists by pulling his or her gun and firing at the robber, the law will likely find the victim used justifiable deadly force, because the victim of the crime resisted and used force that the victim intended to cause death or great bodily harm.

However, the weapon used is not always dispositive evidence of someone's intent to use deadly force. Hammers, toasters, knives, baseball bats, and almost any other object can be "intended or likely to cause" great bodily harm or death under a particular circumstance. The case legally turns, then, on how the person is using the force.

D. What are threats of force? "Stop or I will…"

A person is engaged in the "use of force" against another when he shows another a deadly weapon, such as a knife or a gun, with the intent, thereby, to cause that other person to refrain from what the defendant believed was the other person's imminent use of unlawful force against the defendant, or to prevent the commission of a robbery by threat of force. Illinois law provides that if you are legally justified to use force in any particular situation, then you may also legally threaten to use force in the same situation. Likewise, if you are justified in using deadly force in a particular situation, you may legally threaten the use of deadly force in the same situation.

Illinois courts seem to indicate (and prosecutors and trial courts follow) that a person may only legally produce a weapon as a threat in response to deadly force.

E. Warning shots

Warning shots get a lot of good folks in legal trouble! Warning shots are commonly portrayed in movies and television as a good idea—and people like to mimic what they see in movies and on TV! Leaving completely aside all practical issues of whether under a particular set of circumstances a warning shot is a good idea (and experience has taught us that very rarely are they a good idea), what does Illinois law say about warning shots?

1. Are warning shots a use of deadly force?

The term "warning shot" does not appear in the Illinois Criminal Code. But if the mere display of a weapon is the "use of force" then certainly the display and firing of a gun would be as well.

Although the firing of a warning shot is not *per se* legally forbidden, you should be aware that if you fire a warning shot, it is highly likely that your conduct will be judged under the legal standard that you have used deadly force and not just mere force. This means that a person may only be allowed the legal argument of justification if a warning shot is fired in situations in which deadly force is justified under the law. There is little appellate court case law demonstrating how Illinois courts have addressed the issue of warning shots. Every gun owner should be aware that one likely argument a prosecutor may put forth against a defendant at trial is that the simple discharge of a firearm is an action that is intended or likely to cause death or great bodily harm. Such an argument, if successful, will shift the analysis of warning shots into the use of deadly force arena, whether a person intended that action or not.

Why is it important whether the law classifies a warning shot as a use of force or a use of deadly force, even if no one is injured? Let's take a look at an example.

EXAMPLE:

Harry Homeowner looks outside during broad daylight and sees a trespasser on his property. Not knowing what the trespasser is doing, Harry grabs his firearm to investigate. Harry confronts the trespasser and demands that he leave the property, but the trespasser ignores Harry. Being both scared and agitated, Harry fires a warning shot to get the trespasser's attention and compliance.

Does Harry's discharging his gun fit the definition of the use of deadly force? Likely, yes. Harry very likely may be guilty of a crime and not have a justification available as a defense, because he used a higher degree of force than the law allows.

2. Warning shots: "But, I never meant to hurt anyone!"
Going back to our example, assume Harry will say he fired the warning shot, but that he never aimed at or even meant to hit anyone. In fact, assume Harry will say he only shot into the dirt to get the trespasser to leave. How will the law view Harry's warning shot?

Harry Homeowner was confronted in this example with a mere trespasser and under Illinois law, as we will see later, a person may legally use force, but not deadly force to remove a trespasser. Therefore, if the warning shot that was fired by Harry is legally classified as deadly force under the law, Harry will not be legally justified, and instead, a jury may decide he is guilty of a crime such as aggravated assault. So, the classification is the difference between guilt and innocence in this example.

Now, let us change the example a bit to see how things may get even more complicated.

EXAMPLE:

Harry Homeowner confronts the same trespasser, Tom, as before and fires a warning shot. This time, however, the shot startled Tom out of his zoned state of self-meditation and wandering in which he likes to contemplate the universe. Tom was so deep in his personal world, he didn't realize he had accidentally wandered onto Harry's property. In fact, Tom the trespasser was so deep in meditative strolling and enjoying the Illinois air that he didn't even hear Harry's verbal demands, but, the sound of Harry's 30.06 hunting rifle got Tom's full attention! As a result, Tom does exactly what his 25 years of police training have taught him—he draws and fires at Harry, believing that Harry's shot had meant to end his days of strolling and meditation!

Where do we start the legal analysis? First, Harry Homeowner is in what Illinois legal circles often call a "big mess!" Harry has very likely used unlawful deadly force against a mere trespasser. After Harry's shot, does this turn our absent-minded, wandering Tom into a victim who reasonably believes his life is threatened? Does this fact then allow Tom the trespasser some legal justification to return fire?

Continuing the issue, if our wandering Tom then returns fire at Harry, is Harry then legally justified in using deadly force to defend himself? Or, because Tom is an accidental trespasser, is Tom required to retreat first before he takes any action? Keep in mind that Harry knows nothing about Tom's meditation or walks—he is just confronted with a trespasser who did not respond to verbal requests, but has now responded to Harry's warning shot with muzzle flashes from a pistol. Ultimately, you can see how messy this type of scenario can become, which all started with a well-intentioned warning shot.

After the dust clears (assuming perfect knowledge), Harry likely used a higher degree of force than the law allows. But who decides if a warning shot is a warning shot and not a shot at someone that simply missed? Who decides if a response to a situation is reasonable? In the vast majority of cases in Illinois, a jury ultimately decides. There are no bright lines on warning shots, so be advised that a warning shot can potentially be viewed as a use of deadly force, whether you subjectively intended it to be or not, and, therefore, should never be used without careful consideration.

PRACTICAL LEGAL TIP

Throughout this book, we refer to juries making the ultimate determination of fact. There are, however, some limited occasions where a judge makes the determinations. For example, if the defendant waives their right to a jury, the court may conduct what is called a "bench trial." –Michael

V. WHAT DOES IT MEAN TO "REASONABLY" BELIEVE FORCE IS NECESSARY?

In Illinois law, justifiable use of force requires: (1) that force is threatened against a person; (2) that the person threatened is not the aggressor; (3) that the danger of harm is imminent; (4) that the force threatened is unlawful; (5) that the person threatened must actually believe: (a) that a danger exists, (b) that the use of force is necessary to avert the danger, and (c) that the kind and amount of force which he uses is necessary; and (6) that the above beliefs are reasonable.

But what does "reasonable" mean? Further, when is something necessary—and who decides whether it is or not? The answers to these questions are how the legal process decides guilt or justification. For all gun owners, these concepts are critical.

A. What is "reasonable?"

In determining what is reasonable, the law often uses a standard known as the "reasonable person" standard to evaluate a person's conduct. It uses a hypothetical "reasonable person." Who is a reasonable person, and how does he or she act? Ultimately, a reasonable person is whatever a jury says it is.

The legal analysis behind the reasonable person goes like this: if a person used force or even deadly force, they must act like a reasonable person would have acted under the same or similar circumstances in order to be legally justified! However, if a person fails to act like a reasonable person, their conduct will fall below the acceptable legal standard and will not be justified. The reasonable person standard is the law's attempt to make the concept of reasonableness an objective and measurable test.

Under this standard, the law does not focus on whether you subjectively (or personally) believed force was reasonable, but whether a reasonable person would have considered it reasonable, an objective standard. If the legal system (and ultimately, again, this could be a jury) determines that a reasonable person would have believed that force was necessary in response to another person unlawfully using force against you, then you will be found legally justified in using force.

Keep in mind, however, that judges, juries, and prosecutors are simply human beings, and people can have vastly different ideas of how a reasonable person should act under any given circumstances. This is particularly true if asked to decide whether force or deadly force was necessary or not.

B. What does "imminent" mean under the law?

When does someone have a reasonable belief that force is imminent? In Illinois, it ultimately may be a jury that is tasked with determining whether someone had a reasonable belief that an action was necessary or not. With that said, courts have held that "imminent" means that when a person took his action, he had to take that action right then, right there, and without delay, otherwise he may have suffered harm or injury. Clearly, imminent attempts to convey a sense of urgency for the use of force, but again, it usually falls back on the jury to decide if this standard was met in a particular case.

C. Legal presumptions: stop legal second-guessing

Self-defense is an affirmative defense, and unless the State's evidence raises the issue, the defendant must present some evidence as to each of the elements of the defense, *i.e.*: (1) that force is threatened against a person; (2) that the person threatened is not the aggressor; (3) that the danger of harm is imminent; (4) that the force threatened is unlawful; (5) that the person threatened must actually believe: (a) that a danger exists, (b) that the use of force is necessary to avert the danger, and (c) that the kind and amount of force which he uses is necessary; and (6) that the above beliefs are reasonable. Once that occurs, then the burden shifts to the prosecution to disprove, beyond a reasonable doubt, one of the elements of self-defense or the defendant must be found Not Guilty. This legal burden shifting can be a very powerful legal tool to stop legal second-guessing or "Monday morning quarterbacking" of the amount or timing of the force used. A jury will be told that if a given set of circumstances exists (*e.g.*, a forcible felony is occurring such as when the person is the victim of a sexual assault), the law will presume reasonable a person's belief in the necessity of using force or deadly force, and that use of force or deadly force would, therefore, be legally justified.

EXAMPLE:

Harry Homeowner is asleep in his house when he hears a noise in his kitchen. Harry enters his kitchen with his .45 drawn and confronts an armed burglar. Harry fires his weapon and the burglar will burgle no more!

In this situation, was Harry's use of deadly force in firing his gun necessary, or, more precisely, was Harry's belief that deadly force was necessary reasonable? Did Harry, legally, have to take additional actions before firing in order to have acted reasonably? In Harry's current situation, the fact that a forcible felony (and that the burglar is armed) is occurring will give Harry the right to use deadly force.

PRACTICAL LEGAL TIP

Note: a presumption is not an absolute ticket to victory. A prosecutor may attempt to overcome the presumption with other evidence that shows you did not act in self-defense. –Michael

D. No presumption of reasonableness: prosecutors are allowed to second-guess

As we discussed above, under certain circumstances, the law will deem reasonable a person's belief that force or deadly force is necessary (forcible felonies are one example). However, if a person uses force or deadly force under circumstances that do not qualify for this presumption, the issue of whether a belief of the necessity to use force or deadly force was or was not reasonable is left to the jury, and prosecutors are allowed to second-guess the reasonableness of the timing and/or degree of force used by a defendant.

PRACTICAL LEGAL TIP

A word about juries. Juries are not "picked" in Illinois. Rather, they are the first twelve people that are not "struck" from the pool of folks called a jury pool. Most of the time, in my opinion, juries get it "right," but after years of practice, some juries' decisions leave you scratching your head... That is why these legal presumptions can be critical. –Michael

Accordingly, when a defendant does not qualify for a legal presumption, a prosecutor has the opportunity to argue that a person's use of force or deadly force was not necessary. This allows for arguments in court like "should have retreated," "should have used lesser force," and so forth. In many circumstances (such as situations involving defense of property), no legal presumption of reasonable belief is afforded for uses of force or deadly force at all! In those cases, a jury will decide the issue of the reasonableness of a person's belief and, ultimately, whether or not a person is guilty of a crime.

VI. THE BURDEN OF PROOF IN CRIMINAL CASES

In criminal cases, the state attorneys or prosecutors have the burden of proof. This means that it is the state's responsibility to present enough evidence to prove the defendant committed a crime. This burden of proof that the prosecutor bears is a standard called "beyond a reasonable doubt." It is the highest level of proof used in the American justice system. The state's job at trial in attempting to prove the defendant's guilt includes eliminating any reasonable doubt that the defendant's conduct was justified.

We are now ready to look at the circumstances under which Illinois law allows a person to use deadly force to protect themselves and others in the next chapter.

CHAPTER FIVE

WHEN CAN I LEGALLY USE MY GUN: PART II
SELF-DEFENSE AND DEFENSE OF OTHERS
Understanding When Force And Deadly Force Can Be Legally Used Against Another Person

I. INTRODUCTION AND OVERVIEW

The question of "when can a person legally use deadly force against another person" is of critical importance if you are a legal Illinois firearms owner. Although a firearm is nothing more than a tool, it is a tool that by its very nature has the ability to deliver deadly force. Thus, all responsible firearms owners should understand when they are justified in using force and deadly force under the law. Failure to understand the law gets lots of good folks in serious trouble!

The primary Illinois statutes dealing with self-defense and defense of other people are contained in nine Illinois Criminal Code Sections:

- 5/7–1. Use of Force in Defense of Person
- 5/7–2. Use of Force in Defense of Dwelling
- 5/7–3. Use of Force in Defense of Other Property
- 5/7–4. Use of Force by Aggressor
- 5/7–5. Peace Officer's Use of Force in Making Arrest
- 5/7–5.5. Prohibited Use of Force by a Peace Officer
- 5/7–6. Private Person's Use of Force in Making Arrest
- 5/7–7. Private Person's Use of Force in Resisting Arrest
- 5/7–8. Force Likely to Cause Death or Great Bodily Harm

The law of justified self-defense is split between justification for the use of force and justification for the use of deadly force. Each of these scenarios contain legal situations involving reasonableness that are available under certain circumstances and are extremely powerful when deciding if a use of force or deadly force was legally justified. Likewise, the language of the law dealing with both scenarios contains Illinois' versions of the "Castle Doctrine" and "Stand Your Ground" laws, even though those specific terms are not mentioned in the statutes.

In the previous chapter, several legal concepts, such as reasonableness, imminent harm, and the categorization of force and deadly force were discussed. Those concepts have practical applications in this chapter. In this chapter, we will expand upon those topics to include when a person may be justified in using force or deadly force in self-defense, as well as those circumstances when the law specifically prohibits the use of force or deadly force.

II. DEFENDING PEOPLE WITH FORCE OR DEADLY FORCE

A. General self-defense justification: no presumption of reasonableness

The primary self-defense statutes in Illinois are found in Article 7 of the Illinois Criminal Code. Section 7-1 lays out the legal requirements for the justified use of force for self-defense. This section establishes that a person is legally justified in using force against another "to the extent that he reasonably believes that such conduct is necessary to defend himself... against such other's imminent use of unlawful force."

Section 7-1 also establishes the general standard for the justified use of deadly force. A person is legally justified in using deadly force for self-defense "only if he reasonably believes that such force is necessary to prevent imminent death or great bodily harm to himself ... or the commission of a forcible felony." As discussed in the previous chapter, what a person believes is necessary and whether that belief is reasonable is the difference between justification (not guilty) and conviction (guilty).

Who decides whether an actor's belief, is or is not reasonable that force or deadly force is necessary? Who decides if the degree of force used by someone was reasonable under a particular set of circumstances? The answer to both of these questions is the jury.

Therefore, if a person finds himself or herself facing a criminal charge and is claiming self-defense under the general self-defense provisions of Article 7, the jury will decide if that person's belief was or was not reasonable regarding the necessity of the use of force or deadly force by that person. As can be imagined, this leaves a lot of room for juries to interpret what actions are reasonable or not. It also leaves the door open for legal second-guessing by prosecutors as to when and how much force was used, including arguments that there was no imminent threat and as such, the force or deadly force was not really "necessary." If the prosecutor convinces a jury that a person used force or deadly force when or to a degree that was not "reasonably" believed to be necessary, a person's use of force or deadly force will not be legally justified, and that person will be guilty of using unlawful force or deadly force. However, the burden is on the State to prove beyond a reasonable doubt that self-defense was not reasonable and necessary.

B. Use of force to prevent forcible felony

Article 7 contains a provision that gives far more protection than is available under the general self-defense standard. Under this provision of the statute, a person can use deadly force to prevent the commission of a forcible felony even if there is no belief that death or great bodily harm is imminent. If a defendant meets the conditions enabling him or her to be afforded this protection, the law will deem "reasonable" a belief that the force that was used was necessary, limiting any argument that the force used by the accused was unreasonable.

C. Legal defenses for victims of certain violent crimes

If a person is a victim or would-be victim of a forcible felony, Illinois law allows for the justified use of force or deadly force. However, if a person is forced to defend himself or herself against someone who is committing or is about to commit one of the crimes listed in Section 720 ILL. COMP. STAT. 5/2-8 and satisfies the other requirements of the statutes, the law will provide a legal defense that a victim's belief in the necessity of force or deadly force was "reasonable." The listed crimes are: treason, first degree murder, second degree murder, predatory criminal sexual assault of a child, aggravated criminal sexual assault, criminal sexual assault, robbery, burglary, residential burglary, aggravated arson, arson, aggravated kidnapping, kidnapping, aggravated battery resulting in great bodily harm or permanent disability or disfigurement, and any other felony which involves the use or threat of physical force or violence against an individual.

1. Aggravated kidnapping

If a person is a victim or a would-be victim of an aggravated kidnapping, a Class X felony, then the law will presume reasonable his or her belief that the use of force or deadly force (Section 7-1) was necessary to defend against an attacker, and therefore, force or deadly force will be legally justified.

What is aggravated kidnapping? Generally, aggravated kidnapping occurs anytime a person abducts another person and uses or exhibits a deadly weapon during the commission of the offense. This is the definition found in Illinois Criminal Code 720 ILL. COMP. STAT. 5/10-2.

However, under Illinois law, the crime of aggravated kidnapping can actually occur in several different circumstances. Illinois law reads as follows:

§ 10-2. Aggravated kidnapping.
(a) A person commits the offense of aggravated kidnapping when he or she commits kidnapping and:
  (1) kidnaps with the intent to obtain ransom from the person kidnapped or from any other person;

(2) takes as his or her victim a child under the age of 13 years, or a person with a severe or profound intellectual disability;

(3) inflicts great bodily harm, other than by the discharge of a firearm, or commits another felony upon his or her victim;

(4) wears a hood, robe, or mask or conceals his or her identity;

(5) commits the offense of kidnapping while armed with a dangerous weapon, other than a firearm, as defined in Section 33A-1 of this Code;

(6) commits the offense of kidnapping while armed with a firearm;

(7) during the commission of the offense of kidnapping, personally discharges a firearm; or

(8) during the commission of the offense of kidnapping, personally discharges a firearm that proximately causes great bodily harm, permanent disability, permanent disfigurement, or death to another person.

As used in this Section, "ransom" includes money, benefit, or other valuable thing or concession.

EXAMPLE 1:

Jane is out jogging one evening, when a white van pulls up next to her, and a masked man with a gun jumps out, trying to grab her and drag her into his van. Jane pulls out her pepper spray, sprays the man in the face, and runs away to call police.

Next, let us change the facts slightly and then address the legal issues in each example.

Jane is out jogging one evening, when a white van pulls up next to her, and a masked man with a gun jumps out, trying to grab her and drag her into his van. Jane pulls out her Glock 42 and fires two shots, killing her attacker.

In the first example, was Jane legally justified in her use of force against the man? What about her use of deadly force in example two? The answer to both is yes. Jane's belief that the use of force (pepper spray) was necessary will be considered reasonable under Section 7-1, because the man in the white van was attempting to commit aggravated kidnapping (which is a "forcible felony")! Likewise, in the second example, Jane's belief that deadly force was necessary will also be considered reasonable for the same reason, and also results in the conclusion that Jane's use of deadly force was justified.

In these hypotheticals, the masked man with the gun was trying to abduct Jane. Whatever his ultimate purpose for trying to grab her, if Jane reasonably believed she was about to be a victim of an aggravated kidnapping, she will be entitled to a legal defense that her belief was "reasonable" in that the use of force or deadly force was necessary to stop the aggravated kidnapping. Thus, with this defense, prosecutors will be limited in their ability to second-guess whether Jane should have used less force than she did, or that she should have retreated first. The law will deem her belief in the necessity of her use of force or deadly force reasonable. These are clear examples, however. We will discuss later how the law is applied in more ambiguous cases.

2. Victims of attempted murder

It is basic self-preservation set forth in the law that if someone is trying to end your days, you may defend yourself with force or deadly force. Thus, it is no surprise that Section 7-1 of the Illinois Criminal Code allows for the use of force or deadly force to prevent someone from murdering you. As with the other listed forcible felonies, a person who defends himself or herself against murder is justified in using force or deadly force in self-defense against the attacker.

FIRST DEGREE MURDER

So, what is first degree murder? Illinois Criminal Code Section 720 ILL. COMP. STAT. 5/9-1 states:

(a) A person who kills an individual without lawful justification commits first degree murder if, in performing the acts which cause the death:

   (1) he or she either intends to kill or do great bodily harm to that individual or another, or knows that such acts will cause death to that individual or another; or

   (2) he or she knows that such acts create a strong probability of death or great bodily harm to that individual or another; or

   (3) he or she is attempting or committing a forcible felony other than second degree murder.

How should the law under Section 7-1 be applied after a self-defense shooting?

EXAMPLE:

One busy day at his job, David is working quietly at his desk when he hears an angry voice yell out, "I hate this company, and I'm going to kill every one of you!" About that time, David spots a machete in a deranged-looking stranger's hand. The stranger turns toward David with an evil look. David draws a gun from his desk drawer. As the man continues toward David with the machete raised, David fires two shots at the attacker, killing him.

In this situation, the law allows David to use force or deadly force when and to the degree he reasonably believes it is necessary to defend himself. Here, David skipped mere force and used deadly force. Was this reasonable? Should David have first used non-deadly force? Should he have used a method of dispute resolution? If he could have retreated out of a back door, was his use of deadly force really necessary? If David does not qualify for the defenses under Section 7-1, these are the types of questions and issues that will be presented to the jury to determine.

However, in this example, because David is about to be a victim of first degree murder (a "forcible felony"), the law will deem "reasonable" his belief that deadly force was necessary! This is a powerful legal defense and limits prosecutorial arguments regarding the reasonableness of when the force was used or the degree of force used, because it is legally deemed "reasonable." How do we know David acted in self-defense? In this example, the attacker makes it easy, because he cleared up any ambiguity of his intentions when he declared, "I am going to kill every one of you," while wielding a machete. Thus, under Illinois law, David, as a would-be victim of murder, is entitled to a legal defense that he had a reasonable belief that it was necessary to use force or deadly force against the attacker to prevent his own murder. Therefore, David is legally justified in using deadly force. (*See also* the discussion on "Stand Your Ground" under Section E later in this chapter).

If, for some reason, David was ever charged with a crime for killing the would-be murderer, and David puts forth "some evidence" in trial that he was about to be the victim of murder, the jury would then get to decide whether David acted in self-defense under Section 7-1. For a discussion of the legal concept of "some evidence," (*see* Section D). The jury will be told that if David reasonably believed he was about to be murdered, it is a complete defense and deadly force was legally justified. The prosecution would then have the burden of establishing beyond a reasonable doubt that David did not act in self-defense (*i.e.*, David did not know or have reason to believe he was about to be murdered). If the jury finds that the prosecution did not meet this burden of proof, it will decide his use of deadly force was legally justified.

But, how does the self-defense statute work when the example is not so clear?

EXAMPLE:

Police respond to a two-car collision in a parking lot. When the police arrive, they discover that the collision has sparked a violent road-rage incident. At the scene, one man is dead on the ground with a tire iron beside him. The other driver, Michael, a 45-year-old man with no previous criminal record, fired two shots and is now the police's prime suspect in a murder investigation. Michael claims that the other driver became irate while exchanging information, threatened him, and aggressively came toward him swinging the tire iron. However, the position of the physical evidence made it unclear as to who was the true victim in this incident. In fact, one of the officers thinks Michael is lying. Unfortunately for Michael, there are no other witnesses.

If Michael ultimately faces criminal charges for first degree murder and claims self-defense at his trial, how does the legal defense under Section 7-1 work in practice?

In order to receive the protection of Section 7-1, Michael has the initial burden of producing some evidence in court to support that he "knew or had reason to believe" that he was about to be the victim of murder (*e.g.*, the man screamed threats at him and was about to strike him with the tire iron causing Michael to be in fear of his life, so he shot the man). If Michael puts forth some evidence that the dead man was about to murder him, the law requires the prosecution to then prove beyond a reasonable doubt that the accused (in this case, Michael) did not act in self-defense. The prosecution will have an opportunity to put forth evidence that Michael was not about to be the victim of murder based on the physical evidence found at the scene as well as the investigating officer's testimony. This defense of a "forcible felony" puts Michael in a much better legal position than he would be without it.

If the jury believes Michael acted in self-defense to an attempted first degree murder or, more precisely, that the prosecution did not prove beyond a reasonable doubt that Michael did not act in self-defense, Section 7-1 is a complete defense to the charges (*See also* the discussion of No Duty to Retreat later in this Chapter). This is a very powerful legal tool in court. Having the forcible felony defense of Section 7-1 could just be the difference between a verdict of guilty or not guilty!

3. Victims of criminal sexual assault and aggravated criminal sexual assault

Like first degree murder, if a person is the victim of a criminal sexual assault or an aggravated criminal sexual assault, Illinois law allows for the legally justified use of force or deadly force (Section 7-1) to stop the assault. This self-defense statute will also provide any victim of these crimes who resists with force or deadly force a powerful legal conclusion that his or her belief in the necessity of force or deadly force against the attacker was reasonable. How does the law define sexual assault and aggravated sexual assault?

CRIMINAL SEXUAL ASSAULT

Section 720 ILL. COMP. STAT. 5/11-1.20 of the Illinois Criminal Code defines criminal sexual assault as a Class 1 felony, or under certain circumstances, a Class X felony:

§ 11-1.20. Criminal Sexual Assault.

(a) A person commits criminal sexual assault if that person commits an act of sexual penetration and:

(1) uses force or threat of force;

(2) knows that the victim is unable to understand the nature of the act or is unable to give knowing consent;

(3) is a family member of the victim, and the victim is under 18 years of age; or

(4) is 17 years of age or over and holds a position of trust, authority, or supervision in relation to the victim, and the victim is at least 13 years of age but under 18 years of age.

AGGRAVATED CRIMINAL SEXUAL ASSAULT

The crime of aggravated criminal sexual assault under Illinois law is found in Section 720 11-1.30 Ill. Comp. Stat. 5/11-1.30 and is a Class X felony.

§ 11-1.30. Aggravated Criminal Sexual Assault.

(a) A person commits aggravated criminal sexual assault if that person commits criminal sexual assault and any of the following aggravating circumstances exist during the commission of the offense or, for purposes of paragraph (7), occur as part of the same course of conduct as the commission of the offense:

    (1) the person displays, threatens to use, or uses a dangerous weapon, other than a firearm, or any other object fashioned or used in a manner that leads the victim, under the circumstances, reasonably to believe that the object is a dangerous weapon;

    (2) the person causes bodily harm to the victim, except as provided in paragraph (10);

    (3) the person acts in a manner that threatens or endangers the life of the victim or any other person;

    (4) the person commits the criminal sexual assault during the course of committing or attempting to commit any other felony;

    (5) the victim is 60 years of age or older;

    (6) the victim is a person with a physical disability;

    (7) the person delivers (by injection, inhalation, ingestion, transfer of possession, or any other means) any controlled substance to the victim without the victim's consent or by threat or deception for other than medical purposes;

    (8) the person is armed with a firearm;

    (9) the person personally discharges a firearm during the commission of the offense; or

    (10) the person personally discharges a firearm during the commission of the offense, and that discharge proximately causes great bodily harm, permanent disability, permanent disfigurement, or death to another person.

(b) A person commits aggravated criminal sexual assault if that person is under 17 years of age and: (i) commits an act of sexual penetration with a victim who is under 9 years of age; or (ii) commits an act of sexual penetration with a victim who is at least 9 years of age but under 13 years of age and the person uses force or threat of force to commit the act.

(c) A person commits aggravated criminal sexual assault if that person commits an act of sexual penetration with a victim who is a person with a severe or profound intellectual disability.

4. Victims of robbery, aggravated robbery, and armed robbery

Like the other forcible felonies, if a person is a victim or would-be victim of a robbery, aggravated robbery, or armed robbery, Illinois law allows the victim to protect himself or herself against the robber with legally justified force or deadly force. Further, like the other crimes listed in these two sections, the statutory defense of justification is met. How does Illinois law define robbery, aggravated robbery, and armed robbery?

ROBBERY

Under Illinois law Section 720 ILL. COMP. STAT. 5/18-1, robbery is a Class 2 felony. It is defined as follows:

(a) Robbery. A person commits robbery when he or she knowingly takes property, except a motor vehicle covered by Section 18-3 or 18-4, from the person or presence of another by the use of force or by threatening the imminent use of force.

AGGRAVATED ROBBERY

Aggravated robbery is found in Section 720 ILL. COMP. STAT. 5/18-1 and is a Class 1 felony. It is defined as follows:

(b) Aggravated robbery.

(1) A person commits aggravated robbery when he or she violates subsection (a) while indicating verbally or by his or her actions to the victim that he or she is presently armed

with a firearm or other dangerous weapon, including a knife, club, ax, or bludgeon. This offense shall be applicable even though it is later determined that he or she had no firearm or other dangerous weapon, including a knife, club, ax, or bludgeon, in his or her possession when he or she committed the robbery.

(2) A person commits aggravated robbery when he or she knowingly takes property from the person or presence of another by delivering (by injection, inhalation, ingestion, transfer of possession, or any other means) to the victim without his or her consent, or by threat or deception, and for other than medical purposes, any controlled substance.

ARMED ROBBERY

Armed robbery, found in Section 720 ILL. COMP. STAT. 5/18-2., is a Class X felony:

§ 18-2. Armed robbery.

(a) A person commits armed robbery when he or she violates Section 18-1; and

(1) he or she carries on or about his or her person or is otherwise armed with a dangerous weapon other than a firearm; or

(2) he or she carries on or about his or her person or is otherwise armed with a firearm; or

(3) he or she, during the commission of the offense, personally discharges a firearm; or

(4) he or she, during the commission of the offense, personally discharges a firearm that proximately causes great bodily harm, permanent disability, permanent disfigurement, or death to another person.

Tina is on her way home from work. She stops by a local convenience store for some bread and milk. As she enters the store, a masked man suddenly approaches her with a knife, grabs her by the arm, and demands her money. Tina, scared and shaken, remembers her training, opens her purse and pulls a .357 revolver and fires, killing the masked robber.

In this example, because an aggravated robbery was happening, Section 7-1 allows for the justified, legal use of force or deadly force when and to the degree Tina reasonably believes it is necessary to stop the aggravated robbery. Thus, her use of deadly force is legally justified.

What if the example is less clear?

Hank, a sixty-six-year-old disabled man, works downtown. He has to park four blocks from his company's office buildings and has to walk through some rough parts of town in order to get to his car. A man suddenly appears in front of him and says, "Hey man—give me some money!" Hank, feeling very frightened and intimidated, walks on with the now more loud and aggressive panhandler demanding, "Hey! Man! I said give me some money!" Hank now becomes extremely concerned for his safety. About that time, Hank makes a wrong turn into an alley where he is cornered. He again hears, "HEY! MAN! I SAID GIVE ME SOME MONEY!" When Hank turns around, he sees the same man, now very aggressive, with something in his hand.

Is the panhandler just being annoying, or is Hank about to be the victim of robbery, aggravated robbery, or armed robbery? This is the ultimate issue Hank may face if he decides to use force or even deadly force against the alleged aggressor. How will the law evaluate a use of deadly force under Section 7-1?

This is an example with a lot of gray area. The man never verbally threatened Hank, nor did he ever physically touch him. All the man said was "give me some money;" he didn't even demand all of Hank's money—just some. Do robbers ever demand just some money? If Hank is in genuine fear of an aggravated robbery, does he have a duty to retreat? What about the fact that Hank was cornered in an alley? If Hank takes out his legally concealed carry pistol and fires it to defend himself, what happens? Was Hank really about to be robbed, or is he a paranoid trigger-happy fellow as the prosecutor may try to portray him? Beyond that, who decides what the facts really were? This goes to show that there are lots of questions and gray area.

If Hank finds himself charged with unlawfully using force or deadly force against his alleged attacker, he can assert a legal justification based on self-defense under Section 7-1 of the Illinois Criminal Code. Again, the law will allow Hank to use force or deadly force for self-defense when and to the degree he reasonably believes it is necessary to stop unlawful force against him. In this example, before a jury will be allowed to decide if Hank acted in self-defense, Hank must present "some evidence" at trial that he reasonably believed he was about to be robbed (*see* our discussion of what constitutes "some evidence" in the next section).

Hank may attempt to satisfy the "some evidence" requirement by testifying that he was in fear for his safety and had seen the panhandler acting violently on the same street many times in the past. Hank may also say the man raised a weapon in his hand and was moving aggressively toward him, and that the assailant outweighed Hank by 75 pounds and was about a foot taller. Hank will absolutely testify he felt he was being robbed. If Hank puts forth some evidence in court that he was the victim of an attempted aggravated robbery, the jury will get to decide if Hank is credible and if his belief was reasonable, and the law then requires the prosecution to prove beyond a reasonable doubt that Hank did not act in self-defense. However, if Hank fails to put forth some evidence that he acted in self-defense, he will not be entitled to a self-defense jury instruction concerning Section 7-1, and the jury will not get to decide the issue.

D. What is "some evidence?"

So, how much evidence does a person have to offer in a trial to constitute "some evidence" in order to be entitled to a jury charge regarding self-defense? In Illinois, a defendant who raises a claim of self-defense must offer some evidence to the trial court that each of the following elements existed at the time he or she acted: (1) force had been threatened against defendant; (2) defendant was not the aggressor; (3) the danger of harm was imminent; (4) the force threatened against defendant was unlawful; (5) defendant had an actual belief: (a) that a danger existed; (b) that force was necessary to avert the danger; and (c) that the amount of force used was necessary; and (6) that defendant's beliefs were reasonable. *People v. Huddleston,* 614 N.E.2d 86 (Ill. App. 1993); *People v. Willis,* 577 N.E.2d 1215 (Ill. App. 1991). Once he or she does so, the burden shifts to the prosecution to disprove at least one of the elements of self-defense beyond a reasonable doubt.

The "some evidence" requirement may be satisfied where the evidence offered is as simple as the defendant's own testimony, which alone may be sufficient to raise the defensive theory requiring a charge. A defendant's testimony alone can be enough to establish self-defense. *People v. Francis,* 719 N.E.2d 335 (Ill. App. 1999). In other words, a defendant testifying in court at his own trial that he was attacked first and feared for his life as a result of the attack, would have submitted sufficient evidence to be entitled to a jury instruction on self-defense. It is important to note that in determining whether the testimony of a defendant raises an issue of self-defense, the truth or credibility of the defendant's testimony is not at issue. Rather, determining the truth or credibility of the defendant's testimony is the role the jury undertakes in its deliberations.

Of course, relying on a defendant's testimony to be the sole source of evidence in order to obtain a jury instruction on self-defense can be fraught with peril as well. All defendants have the right to not testify at their trial—which can be a sound trial tactic in that it prevents the State from examining the defendant under oath and on the witness stand. Once a defendant takes the witness stand, however, that defendant will be subject to examination by not only his attorney, but also by the State, examination which may ultimately contain evidence which sways a jury away from seriously considering acquittal on self-defense grounds.

E. The "Castle Doctrine" and "Stand Your Ground" laws
1. The "Castle Doctrine"

The term "Castle Doctrine" does not appear in Illinois statutory law, however, the legal concept comes from the philosophy that every person is a king or queen of his or her "castle." As such, no king or queen is required to retreat before using force or deadly force against an intruder in their castle. In Illinois, the "Castle Doctrine" type laws are implemented in Section 7-2 of the Illinois Criminal Code. Illinois' "Castle Doctrine" laws extend to a person's own dwelling as well as any dwelling in which they are a guest.

As we discussed earlier, the general rule is that a person is legally justified in using force or deadly force:

> When and to the degree a person reasonably believes the force or deadly force is necessary to to prevent imminent death or great bodily harm, or the commission of a forcible felony.

If you are in your dwelling, the law will provide you protection beyond the general rule. The law reads as follows:

§ 720 ILL. COMP. STAT. 5/7-2, Use of force in defense of dwelling.

(a) A person is justified in the use of force against another when and to the extent that he reasonably believes that such conduct is necessary to prevent or terminate such other's unlawful entry into or attack upon a dwelling.

However, he is justified in the use of force which is intended or likely to cause death or great bodily harm only if:

(1) The entry is made or attempted in a violent, riotous, or tumultuous manner, and he reasonably believes that such force is necessary to prevent an assault upon, or offer of personal violence to, him or another then in the dwelling, or

(2) He reasonably believes that such force is necessary to prevent the commission of a felony in the dwelling.

2. What is a dwelling under the "Castle Doctrine?"

Illinois law, in defining "Castle Doctrine" rights, does not use the terms home, house, or property; it uses the term "dwelling." The protections under Section 7-2 are specific, limited, and do not cover an entire piece of real property—just a dwelling.

This means that structures which are detached from the building where you sleep at night are not considered to be your dwelling. Therefore, any justified use of force or deadly force would not qualify for protections under this particular part of the law. However, if your garage, or front or back porch is connected to the structure containing your sleeping quarters (as exists in many suburban communities), it is likely considered part of your dwelling under the Illinois Criminal Code.

3. Are there defenses for protection involving other properties besides a dwelling?

Yes. Illinois law provides that force can also be used to protect other properties. The law, Section 720 Ill. Comp. Stat. 5/7-3, reads as follows:

> § 7-3. Use of force in defense of other property.
> (a) A person is justified in the use of force against another when and to the extent that he reasonably believes that such conduct is necessary to prevent or terminate such other's trespass on or other tortious or criminal interference with either real property (other than a dwelling) or personal property, lawfully in his possession or in the possession of another who is a member of his immediate family or household or of a person whose property he has a legal duty to protect. However, he is justified in the use of force which is intended or likely to cause death or great bodily harm only if he reasonably believes that such force is necessary to prevent the commission of a forcible felony.

4. In Illinois, "Stand Your Ground" means no duty to retreat

"Stand Your Ground" is a common term for laws that provide that a person has no legal duty to retreat before using force or deadly force against a person that is a threat. In Illinois, a person who is not initially an aggressor has no duty to retreat. *People v. White,* 649 N.E.2d 424 (Ill. App. 1994). The words "stand your ground" are not used in the Illinois Criminal Code but do appear in Illinois court decisions. *See e.g., People v. Bailey,* 304 N.E.2d 668 (Ill. App. 1973).

Numerous jurisdictions like Illinois have "no duty to retreat" laws that do not require fleeing before the legal use of deadly force. However, several states impose a duty on a person to retreat if reasonably available as a prerequisite to using deadly force. So when traveling, make sure you know the law of the state you are visiting. –Michael

It was said that, "A person is not required to prove that he has exhausted all reasonable means of escape other than deadly force before successfully establishing self-defense. As long as he has a legal right to be where he was at the time of the fatal confrontation, a defendant is not required to retreat, but may stand his ground." *People v. Bailey,* 304 N.E.2d 668, 670 (Ill. App. 1973). However, if there is a reasonable means to get to safety, the issues will be raised by the prosecutor as to whether the use of deadly force was your only option. The jury (or judge if you waive the jury) may decide if your belief that the use of deadly force was reasonable at the time was immediately necessary.

In order to receive the "No Duty to Retreat" protection, first, a person must satisfy all the conditions:

(1) he or she has a legal right to be at the location where force or deadly force is used, and

(2) he or she was not the aggressor against whom force or deadly force was used.

Both conditions must be satisfied in order for the "No Duty to Retreat" provisions to apply. Further, if a person does not qualify for "No Duty to Retreat" provisions, it does not mean that the person's use of force or deadly force was not legally justified. It simply means that a jury will evaluate whether the person's belief was "reasonable" that the use of force or deadly force was necessary. If a person cannot satisfy both requirements, the prosecutor will argue that because the accused could have, but did not retreat, their belief was not reasonable that the use of force or deadly force was necessary.

EXAMPLE:

One day, looking for a shortcut through the neighborhood, Tom hops a fence (a trespass) and is walking across open property to reach the street on the other side of the property. Tom is confronted by the property owner and tries to explain that he meant no harm and was just taking a shortcut. However, the property owner becomes irate and cocks his gun, aims it at Tom, and says "I'm going to kill you!"

Under this example, Tom is a trespasser. Therefore, Tom is disqualified for any legal protection under the "Stand Your Ground" theory. Thus, a prosecutor could argue that before the use of force or deadly force by Tom was necessary, Tom should have retreated. It does not mean Tom may not be ultimately legally justified in defending himself, it just makes it more difficult to convince a jury of his justification.

Now let us take the example one step further:

> Tom is scared out of his mind as he looks down the barrel of
> the property owner's shotgun. The two are about 20 feet apart.
> Tom, hearing the property owner's threat to kill him, draws his own
> firearm and fires two shots, killing the property owner.

In this example, because Tom does not have a legal right to be
there, he is not eligible for the protections of "Stand Your Ground."
Therefore, a prosecutor would be allowed to question and second-
guess when and the degree of deadly force that was used. The
prosecutor may argue that Tom did not really need to use deadly
force because a "reasonable" person would have retreated under
the circumstances. Tom does not lose his legal right to self-defense
under this example, just the protection that the "No Duty to Retreat"
provisions offer.

F. A person who provokes an attack is not entitled to a presumption of reasonableness

Article 7 of the Illinois Criminal Code contains a requirement that
in order for a person to take advantage of legal protections of self-
defense, the person must not have provoked the attack that led to
the use of force or deadly force in the first place. (*See also* Section
H discussing "Provocation" later in this Chapter).

G. When is the use of force or deadly force explicitly not legally justified under Illinois law?

1. Force not legally justified to resist arrest or search

RESISTING ARREST OR SEARCH NOT JUSTIFIED:
720 ILL. COMP. STAT. 5/7-7

The use of force against another is not justified to resist an arrest or search that the actor knows is being made by a peace officer, or by a person acting in a peace officer's presence and at his direction, even if the arrest or search is unlawful.

EXAMPLE:

Justin has been pulled over for speeding and is removed from his vehicle by a uniformed police officer. While sitting on the curb, the officer begins to search Justin's vehicle without his consent and without probable cause. Feeling violated, Justin gets up and pulls the officer out of his car and throws the officer to the ground.

Even though the officer's behavior is unusual for a mere speeding violation, and even though it appears Justin is being subjected to an illegal search and seizure, his legally justifiable recourse is to pursue the matter through the court system—not to use force against the officer!

Unfortunately, there really are instances where police officers exceed their authority and use more force than they are allowed under the law. Sometimes there are many factors leading to that excessive use of force, but officers have to follow the law, too!

This exception in the self-defense statute is crafted to protect a person in those rare scenarios where an officer is using greater force than necessary to make an arrest or search. Having said that, pay very close attention to how narrow and specific this statute is in its application—a person must meet some very specific requirements before he or she is afforded any legal protection:

1. A person must not be resisting when the officer uses greater force than necessary; and

2. That person must reasonably believe that resistance is immediately necessary to protect himself or herself from the officer's use of greater force than necessary to make the arrest or search.

The point of this section is to give fair warning: any time a person uses force against a law enforcement officer, he or she should be aware that the cards are stacked against him or her from the beginning! Ultimately, the lack of available evidence may make it so exceptionally difficult to claim this statute's protections legitimately that it loses its value except in rare instances.

PRACTICAL LEGAL TIP

The right to remain silent is a fundamental Constitutional right which is why it is so disturbing that in 2010, the US Supreme Court held that you have to say the magic words of "I invoke my right to remain silent and to counsel" in order to trigger it. Seemingly, by the Court's standard, if you don't say the magic words, police could interrogate you until the end of time. –Michael

III. DO I HAVE A LEGAL RESPONSIBILITY TO DEFEND ANOTHER PERSON?

Under Illinois law, the average person has no duty to come to the defense of another, so long as that actor was not the cause of the situation or occurrence. This is true even if a crime is in progress. Note: this lack of a legal duty does not include police officers and other professionals that may have affirmative legal duties to assist. If you see a third person that is the victim of what you believe to be the unlawful use of force or deadly force, you have no legal duty to aid that person—it is your decision. This is equally true if you are legally carrying a gun pursuant to a CCL. But what if you decide to help the third person?

A. When does Illinois law allow for the justifiable use of force or deadly force to protect someone else?

In the last sections, we addressed the law of legal justification for the use of force or deadly force for self-defense. We now turn to when the law allows the justified use of force or deadly force to protect another person or persons.

In general, if you place yourself in the "shoes" of the third person, and the law would allow the third person to use force or deadly force to protect themselves, then you are legally justified to use the same level of force to protect a third person. Illinois Criminal Code Article 7 allows a person to protect a third person from the unlawful use of force or deadly force by another in the same circumstances in which a person could justifiably use force or deadly force under Section 7-1 to protect themselves, so long as the person reasonably believes that the intervention is "necessary to prevent imminent death or great bodily harm to himself or another, or the commission of a forcible felony." 720 ILL. COMP. STAT. 5/7-1 reads as follows:

§ 7-1. Use of force in defense of person.

(a) A person is justified in the use of force against another when and to the extent that he reasonably believes that such conduct is necessary to defend himself or another against such other's imminent use of unlawful force. However, he is justified in the use of force which is intended or likely to cause death or great bodily harm only if he reasonably believes that such force is necessary to prevent imminent death or great bodily harm to himself or another, or the commission of a forcible felony.

Therefore, the same legal justifications and protections for self-defense are also available for the defense of third persons. If a person decides to aid a third person, the law of justifiable use of force will allow a person to defend a third person to the extent they may defend themselves. "Defense of others" is an affirmative defense requiring some evidence that (1) unlawful force was threatened against defendant or others, (2) defendant was not the aggressor, (3) the danger of harm was imminent, (4) the use of force was necessary, (5) defendant subjectively believed a danger existed requiring the use of force applied, and (6) defendant's belief was objectively reasonable. If a person decides to defend a third person, prudence dictates that the person defending must be sure they know what is truly happening in a situation before using force or deadly force. If a belief in the necessity of the use of force or deadly force turns out to be unreasonable, the use of force or deadly force will not be legally justified no matter how well intentioned a person may be.

B. What if the situation is not as I thought it appeared to be?

A third person and a "Good Samaritan" may not potentially see things as they really are. When a person elects to use force or deadly force to defend a third person, it can all go terribly wrong.

EXAMPLE:

Peter, a CCL holder carrying a handgun, visits his local big box store. He parks and exits his vehicle whereupon he witnesses a man struggling to get a handbag away from an elderly woman. Peter, believing the elderly woman is a victim of robbery, drops to one knee while drawing his handgun. Still seeing the man pulling the handbag away from the woman, Peter decides to protect the would-be victim of robbery and fires his gun striking the robber.

If there was in fact an armed robbery taking place, Peter's use of deadly force is likely legally justified, because if we put Peter in the shoes of the third person (the elderly woman in the example), Peter would be legally justified in using deadly force to stop the robbery. Thus, the law will deem Peter's belief that the use of deadly force was necessary and reasonable. But what if there was no robbery?

In fact, what would happen if in the instant after Peter fires his gun, the woman Peter sought to protect immediately turns to help the wounded suspected robber yelling "murderer!" at Peter while screaming in fear and grief, "why did you shoot my son?" It turns out that there was no robbery, just a son attempting to retrieve his mother's car keys because she has Alzheimer's disease and after a frantic search he had found her wandering in the store's parking lot. How does the law deal with this scenario?

In such a situation, Peter's perspective and knowledge of the situation are very different from the person he sought to defend. In this situation, if Peter's belief that a robbery was in progress was reasonable, then Peter will be legally justified. However, if a jury finds that his belief was unreasonable, Peter will not be legally justified and likely guilty of aggravated assault.

C. Do I have a duty to report a crime?

Under Illinois law, the answer for general citizens is no. Special duties to report might be in play if one is a caregiver or medical provider.

➢ CHAPTER SIX ◂

WHEN CAN I LEGALLY USE MY GUN: PART III
UNDERSTANDING WHEN DEADLY FORCE
Can Be Used Against Animals

I. CAN I LEGALLY USE DEADLY FORCE AGAINST ANIMALS?

Illinois laws and statutes fail to discuss a person's rights when using force or deadly force against an animal attack. The general rule at common law is that "[a]n individual may use force to protect himself or another human being against imminent harm from a nonhuman." 141 Am. Jur. Trials 1 (Originally published in 2015).

A. No general defense against animals statute

Illinois has no general self-defense or defense of others statute that deals with all animals. For example, if a dog is attacking you, and you have to shoot the dog, there exists no provision of the Illinois Criminal Code that specifically justifies the use of deadly force. In this situation, persons will be forced to rely on a general defense called "justification by necessity." The typical laws you would expect to find such as self-defense against an animal attacking a human being don't exist under Illinois law at all! What this means is that one may not find specific legal justification for using force or deadly force against an animal that is attacking if the animal is not a certain type of animal. Under this condition, a person may be forced to argue the general law of necessity. This chapter will examine the laws that do exist relating to the use of deadly force against an animal and how your right to self-preservation can best be accomplished.

B. The doctrine of necessity

Because there is no specific Illinois law that allows a person to use deadly force against an animal in self-defense, often the best claim for legal justification a person can make in a court is one of justification by necessity. Illinois law does recognize a very broad justification to potential criminal liability called "necessity," which is defined in Illinois Criminal Code Section 7-13 and reads as follows:

> **DEFINITION OF JUSTIFICATION BY NECESSITY:**
> **720 ILL. COMP. STAT. 5/7-13**
>
> Conduct is justified if the accused was without blame in occasioning or developing the situation and reasonably believed such conduct was necessary to avoid a public or private injury greater than the injury which might reasonably result from his own conduct.

While many of us consider our dogs to be family members, don't forget that the law considers dogs as personal property. Because dogs are personal property, the "defense of others" laws that apply to protecting other human beings do not apply to protecting our dogs. –Michael

As this law applies to animal attacks, a person may be legally justified in using force or deadly force (such as firing their gun) against an attacking animal if that person has a reasonable belief that force or deadly force is necessary to avoid injury greater than what his own conduct might cause. There exists no legal presumptions such as ones that exist when there are human-on-human attacks. So, how does this all work in practice?

Beware! Using deadly force against a dog or cat that is only digging into your flowerbed or getting into your garbage may not be justified even under the doctrine of necessity. –Michael

Jim is walking in his neighborhood when out of nowhere three large pit bulls spot him and immediately begin running toward him barking with sharp fangs showing. Jim barely has time to draw and fire his .40 caliber Glock at the lead dog just before it lunged at him. Having dispatched one dog, the other two dogs flee.

If, for some reason, Jim finds himself charged with any form of crime for his shooting of the dog (this could be anything from cruelty to animals to discharge of a firearm in city limits, *etc.*), Jim will not be able to rely on a specific statute for self-defense because there are none. Rather, Jim will have to rely on the general legal doctrine of necessity as described above.

This means that a jury would ultimately decide whether Jim's conduct met the requirements of Section 7-13. First, did Jim "reasonably" believe his conduct (in this case, drawing and firing his gun) was necessary to avoid imminent harm (being bitten, mauled, *etc.*)? So, as was covered in Chapter 4, any time a reasonable person standard is used, it will be an issue for the jury. Further, without legal presumptions available under either of the Illinois versions of "Castle Doctrine" or "Stand Your Ground" type laws, a prosecutor will fully be able to argue that Jim should have retreated, that he used too much force, or that the threat really was not reasonable.

Second, if a defendant satisfies the first part, he or she must still pass a desirability test according to the standards of reasonableness. In the case of Jim, he would argue that the desirability of a human (in this case, himself) not being bit by a dog when walking in his neighborhood outweighs the law against either discharging a firearm in the city limits, or a charge of cruelty to animals, *etc.* However, a prosecutor would be free to question all aspects of his conduct and second-guess him in court. In this case, it will be for the jury to decide if Jim, or any person in a similar situation, acted reasonably.

Illinois law states that:

> Any owner seeing his or her livestock, or poultry being injured, wounded, or killed by a dog, not accompanied by or not under the supervision of its owner, may kill such dog. 510 Ill. Comp. Stat. 5/18.

To justify killing of a dog under prior similar law, there must have existed an apparent necessity, and the killing must have been reasonably necessary under all circumstances of the case for the protection of the animal. *Anderson v. Smith*, 7 Ill.App. 354 (1880) .

It is notable that this section is specifically limited to dog attacks on animals, not people. This statute does not address the issue of defending people against animal attacks; you must look elsewhere for your legal justification there.

C. Federal law defenses

The federal law, in a comprehensive fashion, has actually had the foresight to specifically provide that a person may kill an animal protected by federal law in self-defense, such as the regulations concerning the Mexican gray wolf in 50 CFR § 17.84(k)(3)(xii), or the grizzly bear in 50 CFR § 17.40(b)(i)(B). Unlike the Illinois statutes, this makes the Federal law clear and comprehendible. Therefore, if you are carrying a firearm in a National Park (*See* Chapters 9 and 10), and you find yourself face to face with a grizzly bear, you will have a legal defense for protecting yourself.

> CHAPTER SEVEN ◄

WHEN CAN I LEGALLY USE MY GUN: PART IV
UNDERSTANDING
WHEN DEADLY FORCE
Can Be Used To Protect Property

I. OVERVIEW AND LOCATION OF THE LAW TO PROTECT PROPERTY

Illinois law allows a person to protect, with force, their property from another's unlawful interference or trespass on their property or the property of another. Further, Illinois law, under certain circumstances, will also allow a person to use legally justified deadly force to protect property. The statute in the Illinois Criminal Code dealing with legally justified force or deadly force to defend property is as follows:

720 Ill. Comp. Stat. 5/7-3. Use of force in defense of other property.

(a) A person is justified in the use of force against another when and to the extent that he reasonably believes that such conduct is necessary to prevent or terminate such other's trespass on or other tortious or criminal interference with either real property (other than a dwelling) or personal property, lawfully in his possession or in the possession of another who is a member of his immediate family or household or of a person whose property he has a legal duty to protect. However, he is justified in the use of force which is intended or likely to cause death or great bodily harm only if he reasonably believes that such force is necessary to prevent the commission of a forcible felony.

Protection of property will be analyzed under the same "reasonable person" standard discussed in Chapters 4 and 5 and will have the same requirements for a person reasonably believing that the force or deadly force used was "necessary."

II. WHEN IS SOMEONE LEGALLY JUSTIFIED TO USE "FORCE" BUT NOT "DEADLY FORCE" TO PROTECT THEIR OWN PROPERTY?

A. Prevent or terminate interference with property

Illinois law answers this question with the statutory law of the justified use of force to protect property contained in Section 7-3 of the Illinois Criminal Code. This Section discusses when a person is justified in using force to prevent or terminate another person's unlawful trespass or interference with their property, *e.g.*, stealing property, vandalizing property, *etc.*

If you catch someone in the act

In plain terms, if someone is unlawfully taking your personal property, you are justified in using force to stop them. Of course, just like instances of self-defense, you must also meet the standard of reasonable belief in the necessity of the use of force.

Fresh pursuit after property is taken

In the event a person's property has already been stolen, a person is only legally justified to use force to recover it if the crime is still ongoing. A person is not allowed to use force that is not immediate, or in "fresh pursuit," to go and recover the property days, weeks, or months later if he or she beats up the thief in the process of recovery. What does it mean to terminate property interference while the crime is ongoing or in "fresh pursuit?"

Under the Illinois statute permitting the use of force reasonably believed necessary to prevent or terminate interference with property, "prevent" refers to stopping crime before it actually happens, while "terminate" refers to stopping crime while it is happening. *People v. Hicks,* 693 N.E.2d 373 (Ill. 1998).

Ultimately, it appears that courts view "fresh pursuit" to mean "immediate without delay," as even taking a few minutes to arm oneself is sufficient to lose legal justification in using force to recover property.

In addition to attempting recovery while the crime is ongoing or in fresh pursuit after dispossession of property, a person must have a reasonable belief that the other person wasn't entitled to take it in the first place. In other words, if an ordinary, reasonable person would take the item back believing the thief had no right to it, then a person may be justified in doing the same thing. Keep in mind, though, this section only justifies the use of force. If the thief used force, a threat, or fraud to take it from you, you might also be justified.

B. No legal presumption of reasonableness when defending property

Illinois law provides no legal presumptions of reasonableness for uses of force to protect property, whether it is preventing or terminating a trespass or interference or the recovery of property. Thus, the jury will be the ultimate arbiter of the reasonableness of conduct.

The analysis so far leads us to the question: if force may legally be used to prevent or terminate trespass or interference with property, what constitutes a trespass or interference with property?

C. What is trespassing?

The commonly understood meaning of trespass is "an unlawful interference with one's person, property, or rights." This definition has been expanded to refer typically to "any unauthorized intrusion or invasion of private premises or land of another." Black's Law Dictionary, 6th ed. This commonly understood definition of trespass is different and more expansive than the offense of criminal trespass found in Section 21-3 of the Illinois Criminal Code. The Illinois Criminal Code defines a criminal trespass as:

21-3. Criminal trespass to real property.
(a) A person commits criminal trespass to real property when he or she:
  (1) knowingly and without lawful authority enters or remains within or on a building;
  (2) enters upon the land of another, after receiving, prior to the

entry, notice from the owner or occupant that the entry is forbidden;

(3) remains upon the land of another, after receiving notice from the owner or occupant to depart;

(3.5) presents false documents or falsely represents his or her identity orally to the owner or occupant of a building or land in order to obtain permission from the owner or occupant to enter or remain in the building or on the land;

(3.7) intentionally removes a notice posted on residential real estate as required by subsection (l) of Section 15-1505.8 of Article XV of the Code of Civil Procedure before the date and time set forth in the notice; or

(4) enters a field used or capable of being used for growing crops, an enclosed area containing livestock, an agricultural building containing livestock, or an orchard, in or on a motor vehicle (including an off-road vehicle, motorcycle, moped, or any other powered two-wheel vehicle) after receiving, prior to the entry, notice from the owner or occupant that the entry is forbidden or remains upon or in the area after receiving notice from the owner or occupant to depart.

For purposes of item (1) of this subsection, this Section shall not apply to being in a building which is open to the public while the building is open to the public during its normal hours of operation; nor shall this Section apply to a person who enters a public building under the reasonable belief that the building is still open to the public.

(b) A person has received notice from the owner or occupant within the meaning of Subsection (a) if he or she has been notified personally, either orally or in writing, including a valid court order as defined by subsection (7) of Section 112A-3 of the Code of Criminal Procedure of 1963 granting remedy (2) of subsection (b) of Section 112A-14 of that Code, or if a printed or written notice forbidding such entry has been conspicuously posted or exhibited at the main entrance to the land or the forbidden part thereof.

(b-5) Subject to the provisions of subsection (b-10), as an alternative to the posting of real property as set forth in subsection (b), the owner or lessee of any real property may post the property by placing identifying purple marks on trees or posts around the area to be posted. Each purple mark shall be:

(1) A vertical line of at least 8 inches in length and the bottom of the mark shall be no less than 3 feet nor more than 5 feet high. Such marks shall be placed no more than 100 feet apart and shall be readily visible to any person approaching the property; or

(2) A post capped or otherwise marked on at least its top 2 inches. The bottom of the cap or mark shall be not less than 3 feet but not more than 5 feet 6 inches high. Posts so marked shall be placed not more than 36 feet apart and shall be readily visible to any person approaching the property. Prior to applying a cap or mark which is visible from both sides of a fence shared by different property owners or lessees, all such owners or lessees shall concur in the decision to post their own property.

Nothing in this subsection (b-5) shall be construed to authorize the owner or lessee of any real property to place any purple marks on any tree or post or to install any post or fence if doing so would

> violate any applicable law, rule, ordinance, order, covenant, bylaw, declaration, regulation, restriction, contract, or instrument.

In other words, unlike the common definition of trespass where a person becomes a trespasser whether they realized it or not (unwittingly walking across the King's hunting grounds, for instance), under the Illinois Criminal Code prior to committing a criminal offense a person must have knowledge that they are in a place they do not belong or are not welcome. In addition, the crime of criminal trespass is strictly limited to when a person is found in or on a piece of property without permission—the offense does not cover situations involving personal property.

D. Trespass, for legal justification, is not just "criminal trespass"

How, then, is "trespasser" defined in Section 7-3 for purposes of defending property? Because the plain language of Section 7-3 refers only to terminating "the other's trespass" and does not reference a "criminal trespass," it is clear that the statute intends to follow a broader definition of trespass than just the offense of criminal trespass found in 720 ILL. COMP. STAT. 5/21-3. In other words, a person may be potentially legally justified in using force against a person found trespassing on their land—even if that person has not committed the crime of criminal trespass, but only so long as the use of force is accompanied with a reasonable belief that it is necessary to terminate the trespass. Without a specific definition of what "trespass" means as found in Section 7-3, in the vast majority of cases, a jury will be the ultimate arbiter of whether or not a person had a reasonable belief that it was necessary to terminate another person's trespass on the land.

E. What is unlawful interference with property?

You have a legal right to prevent or terminate "interference with property," but what does this mean? It can be a theft, destruction, vandalism, or anything else that diminishes a person's right to their property. Whether particular conduct rises to "interference with property" is an issue that a jury decides.

F. Is there a statutory minimum value of property before force may be legally used to protect it?

No. There exists no statutory minimum value for property before force may be used to protect it. Section 7-3 does not specify that property a person seeks to protect must be of a certain, minimum dollar value in order for a person to protect it.

Realistically, even though a person may be in the process of taking tangible, movable property, some property may be of so little value that the use of force to protect or recover it would not be deemed reasonable by a reasonable person (people on a jury).

EXAMPLE:

One day at work, Fred walks into Ricky's office and takes his red stapler off of Ricky's desk and walks away. Ricky, upset at having his favorite stapler pilfered from his desk, jumps up, chases Fred down, shoves him to the ground, and starts beating on Fred to recover his property. On his way to chase Fred, Ricky also passes the office supply closet where black staplers are available for anyone to take and use.

Was Ricky's use of force against Fred legally justified? Maybe, but very likely, maybe not. It will be a very hard sell to a jury that a person was beat up over a red stapler. However, some members of a jury may value a red stapler much differently than a black stapler. What if a thief is stealing irreplaceable family photos? There's no monetary value to be placed there—only personal sentiment. Again, the law is silent on the subject of any monetary value of property to be defended.

The point to be made here is that some items simply may not have enough value (financial, sentimental, or otherwise) to provide a person with a reasonable belief that the use of force or deadly force is necessary to protect or recover the item. In this example, not only does the stapler have little monetary value, but there are others readily available for replacement from the supply closet. It would be hard to imagine a jury finding a person to be justified in even using force, let alone deadly force, for such a petty larceny! Remember, your conduct will always be evaluated under a reasonable person standard and there are no legal presumptions available for defending property under Section 7-3.

III. WHEN IS SOMEONE LEGALLY JUSTIFIED IN USING DEADLY FORCE TO PROTECT OR RECOVER THEIR OWN PROPERTY?

The use of deadly force is only allowed to prevent the commission of a forcible felony (*see* previous sections on forcible felonies). A person is not justified in taking human life to prevent mere trespass to his property, except in the case of his dwelling house, which he may defend, even to the extent of taking of life, if necessary or apparently necessary to prevent persons from forcibly entering it against his will. *People v. Smith,* 88 N.E.2d 444 (Ill. 1949).

EXAMPLE:

After a long day at work, Gordon finally pulls into his driveway just in time to see two masked men running out of his front door with his favorite television and his grandfather's expensive watch on one of the man's wrists. Gordon gets out of his car and demands that the men stop where they are, but they ignore him and run away. Gordon pulls his Glock 17 and fires at the fleeing men, killing one and injuring the other.

Was Gordon justified under Section 7-3 to use deadly force? To answer this question, start by asking whether the men were engaged in a "forcible felony." Gordon has to show a jury that he had a reasonable belief that it was necessary to use force intended or likely to cause death or great bodily harm to stop the ongoing commission of a forcible felony involving his property or a trespass. It seems pretty clear that with his TV and watch being stolen, there is both interference with property and a trespass. The acts probably constituted a residential burglary, a forcible felony.

IV. CAN I PROTECT ANOTHER PERSON'S PROPERTY?

Illinois law allows a person to use force to protect property that was originally lawfully in his possession or in the possession of another who is a member of his immediate family or household or of a person whose property he has a legal duty to protect.

If a person satisfies one of these requirements, then both prongs of the test are met and the person may be justified.

Let's return to our earlier example with Gordon and see how things would play out if another person's property was involved.

After a long day at work, Gordon pulls into his own driveway one night and witnesses two men climbing out of his neighbor's window which appears to be broken and with what looks to be his neighbor's television. Gordon exits his vehicle gun drawn and demands the two men stop. When the men ignore his command, Gordon shoots and wounds both men.

USE OF FORCE IN DEFENSE OF OTHER PROPERTY:
720 Ill. Comp. Stat. 5/7-3

(a) A person is justified in the use of force against another when and to the extent that he reasonably believes that such conduct is necessary to prevent or terminate such other's trespass on or other tortious or criminal interference with either real property (other than a dwelling) or personal property, lawfully in his possession or in the possession of another who is a member of his immediate family or household or of a person whose property he has a legal duty to protect. However, he is justified in the use of force which is intended or likely to cause death or great bodily harm only if he reasonably believes that such force is necessary to prevent the commission of a forcible felony.

Is Gordon legally justified in using deadly force under this scenario? It is not very likely. We evaluate legal justification by determining first, would Gordon have been justified in using deadly force if the property he was protecting was his own? The answer seems clear that he would have been (*e.g.*, burglary or theft during the nighttime, *etc.*). However, since Gordon was not under a legal duty to protect his neighbor's property, he would not be legally justified in using force or deadly force.

V. HOW ARE THE CRIMES ASSOCIATED WITH DEFENDING PROPERTY DEFINED UNDER ILLINOIS LAW?

In the previous sections, we discussed circumstances where if certain crimes are being or have been committed, a person may have a legal justification in using force or deadly force to defend their property. How does Illinois law define those crimes?

1. Arson: A person commits arson when, by means of fire or explosives, he knowingly damages any real property, or any personal property having a value of $150 or more, of another without his consent. *See* 720 ILL. COMP. STAT. 5/20-1.

2. Burglary: A person commits burglary when without authority he knowingly enters or without authority remains within a building, house trailer, watercraft, aircraft, motor vehicle, railroad car, or any part thereof with intent to commit a felony or theft. *See* 720 ILL. COMP. STAT. 5/19-1.

3. Robbery: A person commits robbery when he or she takes property from the person or presence of another by the use of force or by threatening the imminent use of force. *See* 720 ILL. COMP. STAT. 5/18-1.

4. Armed Robbery: A person commits armed robbery when he or she violates Section 18-1 and he or she carries on or about his or her person, or is otherwise armed with a firearm. *See* 720 ILL. COMP. STAT. 5/18-2.

5. Theft: A person commits theft when he or she knowingly obtains or exerts unauthorized control over property of the owner. *See* 720 ILL. COMP. STAT. 5/16-1.

VI. HOW CAN I ASSIST LAW ENFORCEMENT?

A. Basic Illinois Law

> **PRIVATE PERSON'S USE OF FORCE IN MAKING ARREST:**
> **720 ILL. COMP. STAT. 5/7-6**
>
> a) A private person who makes, or assists another private person in making a lawful arrest is justified in the use of any force which he would be justified in using if he were summoned or directed by a peace officer to make such arrest, except that he is justified in the use of force likely to cause death or great bodily harm only when he reasonably believes that such force is necessary to prevent death or great bodily harm to himself or another.
>
> b) A private person who is summoned or directed by a peace officer to assist in making an arrest which is unlawful, is justified in the use of any force which he would be justified in using if the arrest were lawful, unless he knows that the arrest is unlawful.

B. Acting under a police officer's direction

Almost without fail, as attorneys we are regularly asked about whether you can make a citizen's arrest, and how you can best assist law enforcement in dicey situations. Since every legal situation is unique, here we'll just provide a brief summary of the general law, as well as reference some of the statutes governing the use of a citizen's arrest and how to assist authorities.

Illinois law states that you may detain and arrest an individual who is committing a crime in your presence.

Section 7-5 operates as the statute under which law enforcement is able to use force against a suspect. In order to enable officers to use all available resources at their disposal (such as an ordinary citizen), the statute is expanded to include individuals acting at an officer's direction.

C. Not acting under a police officer's direction

More in the area of authorizing a "citizen's arrest" is the language found in Section 5/107-3. Unlike, Section 5/7-6(b), this section does not require being in an officer's presence.

This statute allows an ordinary person to use force when making or assisting in making an arrest, since it does not require the person to be in a peace officer's presence! Once again, you must meet the same "reasonable belief" and "necessity" standards we've outlined throughout this chapter before you may use force. Where possible, you also need to identify yourself and the reason you're making the arrest, unless you believe such is already known or can't be made known. Take notice, however, this statute does not authorize the use of deadly force.

In addition, the Illinois Code of Criminal Procedure authorizes the warrantless citizen's arrest of an individual in the event he has reasonable grounds (*i.e.,* probable cause) to believe an offense has been committed. The statute reads:

> 725 ILL. COMP. STAT. 5/107-3. Arrest by Private Person. Any person may arrest another when he has reasonable grounds to believe that an offense other than an ordinance violation is being committed.

A citizen can even make an arrest for simple violations of the vehicle code such as speeding. *See, e.g., People v. Gutt*, 267 Ill. App. 3d 95, 640 N.E.2d 1013 (2d Dist. 1994).

If you use your firearm for defensive purposes, the first number you should call is 911. But keep your call brief: you only need to tell the operator that you have been the victim of a crime, where you are located, and some identifying information. After that, hang up! You are not required to remain on the line and doing so could cause you problems later. Remember, all 911 calls are recorded and operators are trained to gather as much information as possible. No matter how justified you are in your use of a firearm, something you say on a 911 call may become a real headache later at trial. –Michael

D. When can a person use deadly force in assisting law enforcement?

In order to be legally justified in using deadly force to help law enforcement, a person must comply with the requirements of Section 7-6.

Like nearly every law authorizing the use of deadly force, this statute also only justifies using deadly force as a private citizen if you would first be justified in using mere force. However, deadly force may only legally be used under the same circumstances that would apply for self-defense.

In other words, there is not a circumstance under Sections 7-5 or 7-6 where you, as an ordinary citizen, are legally justified in using deadly force simply to execute an arrest unless a police officer is present and has so directed. Then, two requirements must be met:

(1) Such force is necessary to prevent the arrest from being defeated by resistance or escape; and

(2) The person to be arrested has committed or attempted a forcible felony which involves the infliction or threatened infliction of great bodily harm or is attempting to escape by use of a deadly weapon, or otherwise indicates that he will endanger human life or inflict great bodily harm unless arrested without delay.

E. Detaining potential thieves: "retailer's privilege"

Illinois law provides an affirmative defense to unlawful restraint to merchants under the statute below:

> 720 ILL. COMP. STAT. 5/16-26. Detention; affirmative defense.
>
> (a) Detention. Any merchant who has reasonable grounds to believe that a person has committed retail theft may detain the person, on or off the premises of a retail mercantile establishment, in a reasonable manner and for a reasonable length of time for all or any of the following purposes:
>
> (1) To request identification;
>
> (2) To verify such identification;
>
> (3) To make reasonable inquiry as to whether such person has in his possession unpurchased merchandise and to make reasonable investigation of the ownership of such merchandise;
>
> (4) To inform a peace officer of the detention of the person and surrender that person to the custody of a peace officer; or

(5) In the case of a minor, to immediately make a reasonable attempt to inform the parents, guardian or other private person interested in the welfare of that minor and, at the merchant's discretion, a peace officer, of this detention and to surrender custody of such minor to such person.

A merchant may make a detention as permitted in this section off the premises of a retail mercantile establishment only if such detention is pursuant to an immediate pursuit of such person.

A merchant shall be deemed to have reasonable grounds to make a detention for the purposes of this section if the merchant detains a person because such person has in his or her possession either a theft detection shielding device or a theft detection device remover.

(b) Affirmative defense. A detention as permitted in this Section does not constitute an arrest or an unlawful restraint, as defined in Section 10-3 of this Code, nor shall it render the merchant liable to the person so detained.

(c) For the purposes of this Section, "minor" means a person who is less than 19 years of age, is unemancipated, and resides with his or her parent or parents or legal guardian.

720 Ill. Comp. Stat. 5/16-26.

The most common application of this particular statute is in the retail-store setting. Thus, it is often called "retailer's" or "shop-keeper's privilege" or right. Common scenarios include when a loss prevention officer for the store will take a person into some type of custody while they investigate whether an item was stolen from their business.

VII. WHAT CRIMES CAN I BE CHARGED WITH WHEN MY USE OF DEADLY FORCE IS NOT JUSTIFIED?

We've reached the end of our discussion on when you may be justified to use a weapon in defense of your person or property.

If you are not justified in your use of deadly force you may be charged with one of the following crimes.

CRIMES INVOLVING USE OF DEADLY FORCE, NOT JUSTIFIED.

1. **Murder**: *See* 720 ILL. COMP. STAT. 5/9
2. **Attempted Murder**: *See* 720 ILL. COMP. STAT. 5/8-4
3. **Aggravated Battery**: *See* 720 ILL. COMP. STAT. 5/12-4
4. **Aggravated Discharge of a Firearm**: *See* 720 Ill. Comp. Stat. 5/24-1.2
5. **Aggravated Assault**: *See* 720 ILL. COMP. STAT. 12-2

> CHAPTER EIGHT ◄

LAW OF HANDGUN CARRY: PART I
THE LICENSE
Qualifications, Requirements, Appeals, And Regulations

In 2013, the Illinois Legislature passed a law allowing for the issuance of Concealed Carry Licenses ("CCL"). It was a great change in the laws that existed prior to 2013, but carrying a visible handgun is still strictly prohibited. It took a great deal of political wrangling, but Illinois became the 49th state in the Union to recognize some form of allowing the carrying of handguns in public places.

In Illinois, qualified individuals may obtain a CCL, which allows the carrying of a concealed handgun on or about their person for any lawful purpose.

To obtain a CCL, a person must meet certain requirements and submit an application to the Illinois State Police. This chapter deals exclusively with the licensed carrying of a handgun in Illinois.

I. THE EVOLUTION OF THE ILLINOIS HANDGUN CARRY LAWS

On July 9, 2013, after lengthy litigation and political fighting, Illinois finally allowed the carrying of firearms in public. Illinois was one of the last states in the country to enact such laws. Prior to 2013, both parties had attempted to pass concealed carry laws, but were unsuccessful. Illinois remained the only state to completely ban carrying a firearm in public in any form. In late 2012, the U.S. Court of Appeals for the Seventh Circuit in *Moore v. Madigan*, 702 F.3rd 933 (7th Cir. 2012) held the current Illinois statutes prohibiting concealed carry unconstitutional. The court gave the legislators 180 days to write a bill allowing individuals to carry firearms outside the home for the purpose of self-defense. During the early part of 2013, the legislators continuously negotiated over the concealed carry bill. Several versions were filed by both parties and vigorous negotiations lasted until almost the last day of the spring session. The bill was sent to the Governor after the General Assembly submitted the bill on the final day of the spring session. The Governor vetoed the bill, and the legislators were forced to call a special summer session to override the Governor's amendatory veto. The Firearm Concealed Carry Act finally became effective on July 9, 2013, just ahead of the deadline imposed by the Seventh Circuit. 430 ILL. COMP. STAT. 66/1.

II. QUALIFICATIONS FOR AND STEPS TO GET A CCL
A. Persons who are legally qualified to obtain a CCL

In this section, we will discuss the requirements to apply for an Illinois CCL, as well as potential disqualifications. In addition to the requirements listed below, applicants must also complete state mandated education with a CCL instructor certified by the Illinois State Police. Pursuant to the Firearm Concealed Carry Act, 430 Ill. Comp. Stat 65/1 *et seq.*, first and foremost the applicant must have a valid Firearm Owner's Identification ("FOID") card. A person is NOT eligible for a FOID card and therefore, NOT eligible for a CCL, if he or she:

(1) is prohibited from possessing firearms or ammunition by any state or federal law;

(2) has been convicted of a felony;

(3) is addicted to narcotics;

(4) has been a patient in a mental health facility in the past five years;

(5) is intellectually disabled;

(6) is admitted to the United States under a non-immigrant visa;

(7) is an undocumented immigrant;

(8) is subject to an order of protection prohibiting him or her from possessing firearms;

(9) has been convicted of battery, assault, aggravated assault, or a violation of an order of protection in which a firearm was used or possessed;

(10) has been convicted of domestic battery or aggravated domestic battery;

(11) has been adjudicated a delinquent minor for an offense that would be a felony;

(12) has been adjudicated as a mentally disabled person;

(13) has been involuntarily admitted into a mental health facility;

(14) is developmentally disabled; or

(15) has a mental condition that poses a clear and present danger to the applicant, any other person, or persons of the community.

430 Ill. Comp. Stat 65/8

Additional Requirements

A CCL applicant must:

(1) be at least 21 years of age;

(2) must not have been convicted of a misdemeanor involving the use or threat of physical force or violence or two or more D.U.I. violations within five years of the application;

(3) must not be the subject of a pending arrest warrant, prosecution, or proceeding for an offense or action that could lead to disqualification to own or possess a firearm;

(4) must not have been in residential or court ordered treatment for alcohol detoxification, or drug treatment within five years prior to application; and

(5) must have successfully completed the required firearms training. 430 ILL. COMP. STAT 66/25

B. What does it mean to be "addicted to narcotics" so as to be disqualified from receiving a FOID and CCL?

A person is legally disqualified from receiving a FOID and therefore cannot receive a CCL if he or she is "addicted to narcotics."

A person is legally addicted to narcotics if that person has been:

(1) convicted of an offense involving the use or possession of cannabis, a controlled substance, or methamphetamine within the past year; or

(2) determined by the Department of State Police to be addicted to narcotics based upon federal law or federal guidelines.

"Addicted to narcotics" does not include possession or use of a prescribed controlled substance under the direction and authority of a physician or other person authorized to prescribe the controlled substance when the controlled substance is used in the prescribed manner. 430 Ill. Comp. Stat. 65/1.1.

Note: at the time of the preparation of this book, possession of marijuana was still illegal in Illinois. Beginning January 1, 2020, recreational marijuana is legal in Illinois.

C. What does it mean to be "adjudicated as a person with a mental disability" so as to be disqualified from receiving a FOID and CCL?

"Adjudicated as a person with a mental disability," means the person is the subject of a determination by a court, board, commission or other lawful authority that the person, as a result of marked subnormal intelligence, or mental illness, mental impairment, incompetency, condition, or disease:

(1) presents a clear and present danger to himself, herself, or to others;

(2) lacks the mental capacity to manage his or her own affairs or is adjudicated a person with a disability as defined in Section lla-2 of the Probate Act of 1975;

(3) is not guilty in a criminal case by reason of insanity, mental disease or defect;

(3.5) is guilty but mentally ill, as provided in Section 5-2-6 of the Unified Code of Corrections;

(4) is incompetent to stand trial in a criminal case;

(5) is not guilty by reason of lack of mental responsibility under Articles 50a and 72b of the Uniform Code of Military Justice, 10 U.S.C. 850a, 876b;

(6) is a sexually violent person under subsection (t) of Section 5 of the Sexually Violent Persons Commitment Act;

(7) is a sexually dangerous person under the Sexually Dangerous Persons Act;

(8) is unfit to stand trial under the Juvenile Court Act of 1987;

(9) is not guilty by reason of insanity under the Juvenile Court Act of 1987;

(10) is subject to involuntary admission as an inpatient as defined in Section 1-119 of the Mental Health and Developmental Disabilities Code;

(11) is subject to involuntary admission as an outpatient as defined in Section 1-119.1 of the Mental Health and Developmental Disabilities Code;

(12) is subject to judicial admission as set forth in Section 4-500 of the Mental Health and Developmental Disabilities Code; or

(13) is subject to the provisions of the Interstate Agreements on Sexually Dangerous Persons Act.

430 ILL. COMP. STAT 65/1.1

"Clear and present danger" means a person who:

(1) communicates a serious threat of physical violence against a reasonably identifiable victim or poses a clear and imminent risk of serious physical injury to himself, herself, or another person as determined by a physician, clinical psychologist, or qualified examiner; or

(2) demonstrates threatening physical or verbal behavior, such as violent, suicidal, or assaultive threats, actions, or other behavior, as determined by a physician, clinical psychologist, qualified examiner, school administrator, or law enforcement official.

D. If you don't disclose or you attempt to deceive in your application for a FOID or CCL you can be denied and charged with a crime

At the time of the writing of this book there is no requirement to be fingerprinted to obtain either a FOID or CCL. Remember you cannot obtain a CCL without first getting a FOID card. The application requires you to swear that the information in the application is true.

> "Any person who knowingly enters false information on an application for a Firearm Owner's Identification Card, who knowingly gives a false answer to any question on the application, or who knowingly submits false evidence in connection with an application is guilty of a Class 2 felony."

430 ILL. COMP. STAT 65/14(d-5)

The application for a Concealed Carry License states as follows:

> "The license application shall be in writing, under penalty of perjury, on a standard form... Each application form shall include the following statement printed in bold type WARNING: ENTERING FALSE INFORMATION ON THIS FORM IS PUNISHABLE AS PERJURY UNDER SECTION 32-2 OF THE CRIMINAL CODE OF 2012."

It should be noted that to expedite the application for a CCL, you must be fingerprinted. The Illinois State police will check each applicant's criminal background, therefore, your failure to disclose will most likely be grounds to deny the application and could possibly lead to criminal charges.

Many applicants forget about things that may have happened many years ago, but which require disclosure in the application. The best practice is: when in doubt, disclose! Otherwise, a person may face unwanted delays or even a denial of their application. Note: be very careful in the wording of your disclosures. We have seen many applicants encounter difficulties in not using precise descriptions of their legal history, medical condition, *etc.* Be careful with your words!

E. What if I received court supervision or deferred prosecution? Can I get a FOID or CCL?

The laws regarding the issuance of a FOID card are clearly stated in the statute 430 ILL. COMP. STAT. 65, *et al*. The statute provides that a card SHALL be issued to an individual if that person is not otherwise prohibited from having a card. The list of prohibitions includes:

- he or she has not been convicted of a felony under the laws of this or any other jurisdiction;
- he or she has not been convicted within the past five years of battery, assault, aggravated assault, violation of an order of protection, or a substantially similar offense in another jurisdiction, in which a firearm was used or possessed; and
- he or she has not been convicted of domestic battery, aggravated domestic battery, or a substantially similar offense in another jurisdiction...

430 ILL. COMP. STAT. 65/4(2).

In Illinois, court supervision or deferred prosecution are not technically convictions and are eligible for expungement. However, as previously stated, you should list this criminal history in your FOID application.

The Illinois State Police has great discretion when deciding to issue or deny an application. An arrest, without a conviction of any kind can be used to deny an application.

If an applicant has five or more arrests for any reason, that have been entered into the Criminal History Records Information ("CHRI") System, within the past seven years preceding the date of application for a license, or has three or more arrests within the seven years preceding the date or application for a license for any combination of gang-related offenses, the Department shall object and submit the applicant's arrest record to the extent the board is allowed to receive that information under state and federal law.

Therefore, even an arrest that results in a finding of "not guilty" can be used to deny the applicant his CCL.

F. Suspension and revocation of a FOID or CCL

1. What is the difference between suspension and revocation?

To begin, it is important to know that there is a difference between a suspension and a revocation of a person's FOID or CCL. Section 430 ILL. COMP. STAT. 65/8 lays out the grounds for revocation or denial. The grounds are the same as stated earlier under 430 ILL. COMP. STAT. 65, pertaining to the qualifications to receive a FOID card. Pursuant to 430 ILL. COMP. STAT. 65/9.5, a person who receives a revocation notice under this Act shall, within 48 hours of receiving notice of the revocation:

(1) surrender his or her FOID card to the local law enforcement agency where the person resides; and

(2) complete a Firearm Disposition Record on a form prescribed by the Department of State Police and place his or her firearms in the location or with the person reported in the Firearm Disposition Record.

Revocations are appealable to the Illinois State Police Board.

Section 430 ILL. COMP. STAT. 65/8.3 describes suspension of a FOID card.

"The Department of State Police may, by rule in a manner consistent with the Department's rules concerning revocation, provide for the suspension of the Firearm Owner's Identification Card of a person whose FOID card is subject to revocation and seizure under this Act for the duration of the disqualification if the disqualification is not a permanent grounds for revocation of a Firearm Owner's Identification Card under this Act."

Suspension or revocation of a CCL is governed by 430 ILL. COMP. STAT. 66/70.

(a) A license issued or renewed under this Act shall be revoked if, at any time the licensee is found to be ineligible for a license under this Act, or the licensee no longer meets the eligibility requirements of the Firearm Owners Identification Card Act.

(b) A license shall be suspended if an order of protection, including an emergency order of protection, plenary order of protection, or interim order of protection under Article 112A of the Code of Criminal Procedure of 1963 or under the Illinois Domestic Violence Act of 1986, or if a firearms restraining order, including an emergency firearms restraining order, is issued against a licensee for the duration of the order, or if the Department is made aware of a similar order issued against the licensee in any other jurisdiction. If an order of protection is issued against a licensee, the licensee shall surrender the license, as applicable, to the court at the time the order is entered or to the law enforcement agency or entity serving the process at the time the licensee is served the order.

(c) A license is invalid upon expiration of the license, unless the licensee has submitted an application to renew the license, and the applicant is otherwise eligible to possess a license under this Act.

(d) A licensee shall not carry a concealed firearm while under the influence of alcohol, or other drug or drugs, intoxicating compound or combination of compounds, or any combination thereof, under the standards set forth in subsection (a) of Section 11-501 of the Illinois Vehicle Code. A licensee in violation of this subsection (d) shall be guilty of a Class A misdemeanor for a first or second violation and a Class 4 felony for a third violation. The Department may suspend a license for up to 6 months for a second violation and shall permanently revoke a license for a third violation.

(e) Except as otherwise provided, a licensee in violation of this Act shall be guilty of a Class B misdemeanor. A second or subsequent violation is a Class A misdemeanor. The Department may suspend a license for up to 6 months for a second violation and shall permanently revoke a license for 3 or more violations of Section 65 of this Act. Any person convicted of a violation under this Section shall pay a $150 fee to be deposited into the Mental Health Reporting Fund, plus any applicable court costs or fees.

(f) A licensee convicted or found guilty of a violation of this Act who has a valid license and is otherwise eligible to carry a concealed firearm shall only be subject to the penalties under this Section and not be subject to the penalties under Section 21-6, paragraph (4), (8), or (10) of subsection (a) of Section 24-1, or subparagraph, (A-5) or (B-5) of paragraph (3) of subsection (a) of Section 24-1.6 of the Criminal Code of 2012. Except as otherwise provided in this subsection, nothing in this subsection prohibits the licensee from being subjected to penalties for violations other than those specified in this Act.

(g) A licensee whose license is revoked, suspended, or denied shall within 48 hours of receiving notice of the revocation, suspension, or denial, surrender his or her concealed carry license to the local law enforcement agency where the person resides. The local law enforcement agency shall provide the licensee a receipt and transmit the concealed carry license to the Department of State Police. If the licensee whose concealed carry license has been revoked, suspended, or denied fails to comply with the requirements of this subsection, the law enforcement agency where the person resides may petition the circuit court to issue a warrant to search for and seize the concealed carry license in the possession and under the custody or control of the licensee whose concealed carry license has been suspended, revoked, or denied. The observation of a concealed carry license in the possession of a person whose license has been revoked, suspended, or denied constitutes a sufficient basis for the arrest of that person for a violation of this subsection. A violation of this subsection is a Class A misdemeanor.

(h) A license issued or renewed under this Act shall be revoked if, at any time, the licensee is found ineligible for a Firearm Owner's Identification Card, or a licensee no longer possesses a valid Firearm Owner's Identification Card. A licensee whose license is revoked under this subsection (h) shall surrender his or her concealed carry license as provided for in subsection (g) of this Section. This subsection shall not apply to a person who has filed an application with the State Police for renewal of a Firearm Owner's Identification Card and who is not otherwise ineligible to obtain a Firearm Owner's Identification Card.

We will discuss the process a person must follow if their FOID or CCL is suspended, denied, or revoked later in this chapter.

2. Under what circumstances can the Illinois CCL be revoked or suspended?

The previous section of this chapter discusses some of the circumstances under which the CCL can be revoked or suspended, however, it does not cover other areas which are discretionary.

Local law enforcement is given wide latitude to make objections to CCL applications.

430 ILL. COMP. STAT. 66/15 contains the possible objections by law enforcement agencies.

(a) Any law enforcement agency may submit an objection to a license application based upon a reasonable suspicion that the applicant is a danger to himself or herself or others, or a threat to public safety. The objection shall be made by the chief law enforcement officer of the law enforcement agency, or his or her designee, and must include any information relevant to the objection. If a law enforcement agency submits an objection within 30 days after the entry of an applicant into the database, the Department shall submit the objection and all information available to the Board under state and federal law related to the application to the Board within 10 days of completing all necessary background checks.

(b) If an applicant has 5 or more arrests for any reason, that have been entered into the Criminal History Records Information ("CHRI") System, within 7 years preceding the date of application for a license, or has 3 or more arrests within 7 years preceding the date of application for a license for any combination of gang-related offenses, the Department shall object and submit the applicant's arrest record to the extent the Board is allowed to receive that information under state and federal law, the application materials, and any additional information submitted by a law enforcement agency to the Board. For purposes of this subsection, "gang-related offense" is an offense described in Section 12-6.4, Section 24-1.8, Section 25-5, Section 33-4, or Section 330-4, or in paragraph (1) of (b) of Section 16-30, paragraph (2) of subsection 31-4, or item (iii) of paragraph (1.5) of subsection (i) of Section 48-1 of the Criminal Code of 2012.

(c) The referral of an objection under this Section to the Board shall toll the 90-day period for the Department to issue or deny the applicant a license under subsection (i) of Section 10 of this Act, during the period of review and until the Board issues its decision.

(d) If no objection is made by a law enforcement agency or the Department under this Section, the Department shall process the application in accordance with this Act.

The Illinois version of the "Red Flag" statute became effective on January 1, 2019. The statute establishes the provisions of Illinois' Firearms Restraining Orders. These orders can result in revocation of a CCL in addition to forfeiture of firearms. It provides that a petitioner may request an emergency firearms restraining order by filing an affidavit or verified pleading alleging that the respondent poses an immediate and present danger of causing personal injury to himself, herself, or another by having in his or her custody or control, purchasing, or possessing a firearm, or firearms presently believed by the petitioner to be possessed or controlled by the respondent. The petitioner may be a family member of the respondent or law enforcement officer, who files a petition alleging that the respondent poses a danger of causing personal injury to himself, herself, or another. The Red Flag law establishes factors that the court must consider before issuing a firearms restraining order. If the court issues the order, the respondent must: (1) refrain from having in his or her custody or control, purchasing, possessing, or receiving additional firearms for the duration of the order; and (2) turn over to the local law enforcement agency any firearm, Firearm Owner's Identification Card, or concealed carry license in his or her possession. The respondent may petition the court to transfer the firearm to a person who is lawfully able to possess the firearm if the person does not reside at the same address as the respondent.

This law is relatively new and has not been challenged in court as of the Summer of 2019.

3. If my FOID or CCL is denied, revoked, or suspended, can I appeal?

If your FOID or CCL is denied, revoked, or suspended you can appeal. Because you cannot have a valid CCL without a FOID, we will first discuss the procedure for appealing the denial, revocation, or suspension of a FOID and then the appeal process for the CCL.

FOID

Pursuant to 430 ILL. COMP. STAT. 65/10:

(a) whenever an application for a Firearm Owner's Identification Card is denied, whenever the Department fails to act on an application within 30 days of its receipt, or whenever such a card is revoked or seized as provided for in Section 8 of this Act, the aggrieved party may appeal to the Director of State Police for a hearing upon such denial, revocation or seizure, unless the denial, revocation, or seizure was based upon a forcible felony, stalking, aggravated stalking, domestic battery, any violation of the Illinois Controlled Substances Act, the Methamphetamine Control and Community Protection Act, or the Cannabis

Control Act that is classified as a Class 2 or greater felony, any felony violation of Article 24 of the Criminal Code of 1961 or the Criminal Code of 2012, or any adjudication as a delinquent minor for commission of an offense that if committed by an adult would be a felony, in which case the aggrieved party may petition the circuit court in writing in the county of his or her residence for a hearing upon such denial, revocation, or seizure...

Further, Section 430 ILL. COMP. STAT. 65/11, states the law in relation to judicial review of final administrative decisions:

(a) all final administrative decisions of the Department under this Act, except final administrative decisions of the Director of the State Police to deny a person's application for relief under subsection (f) of Section 10 of this Act, shall be subject to judicial review under the provisions of the Administrative Review Law, and all amendments and modifications thereof, and the rules adopted pursuant thereto. The term "administrative decision" is defined in Section 3-101 of the Code of Civil Procedure;

(b) any final administrative decision by the Director of State Police to deny a person's application for relief under subsection (f) of Section 10 of this Act is subject to de novo judicial review by the circuit court, and any party may offer evidence that is otherwise proper and admissible without regard to whether that evidence is part of the administrative record.

It must be remembered that without a valid FOID card, you cannot have a valid CCL. Therefore, if your FOID card is denied, revoked, or seized, your CCL becomes invalid. We will now discuss the appeal process if your CCL is denied, suspended, or revoked.

CCL appeal

CCL appeals are covered under 430 ILL. COMP. STAT. 66/87, Administrative and Judicial Review.

(a) Whenever an application for a concealed carry license is denied, whenever the Department fails to act on an application within 90 days of its receipt, or whenever a license is revoked or suspended as provided in this Act, the aggrieved party may appeal to the Director for a hearing upon the denial, revocation, suspension, or failure to act on the application, unless the denial was made by the Concealed Carry Licensing Review Board, in which case the aggrieved party may petition the circuit court in writing in the county of his or her residence for a hearing upon the denial.

(b) All final administrative decisions of the Department or the Concealed Carry Licensing Review Board under this Act shall be subject to judicial review under the provisions of the Administrative Review Law. The term "administrative decision" is defined in Section 3-101 of the Code of Civil Procedure.

In Illinois, it does not take much to lose your FOID or CCL; the laws are strict and the appeal process is limited. If you lose your FOID or CCL for any reason you should contact an attorney quickly, because the appeal process gives the aggrieved party a very short time to move on their appeal.

III. THE CCL APPLICATION AND PROCESS

The CCL application can be found on the Illinois State Police website. The application itself is in accordance with Section 430 ILL. COMP. STAT. 66/30, which lists the contents of a license application.

(a) The license application shall be in writing, under penalty of perjury, on a standard form adopted by the Department and shall be accompanied by the documentation required in this Section and the applicable fee. Each application form shall include the following statement printed in bold type: "WARNING: ENTERING FALSE INFORMATION ON THIS FORM IS PUNISHABLE AS PERJURY UNDER SECTION 32-2 OF THE CRIMINAL CODE OF 2012."

(b)The application shall contain the following:

(1) the applicant's name, current address, date and year of birth, height, weight, hair color, eye color, maiden name or any other name the applicant has used or identified with, and any address where the applicant resided for more than 30 days within the 10 years preceding the date of the license application;

(2) the applicant's valid driver's license number or valid state identification card number;

(3) a waiver of the applicant's privacy and confidentially rights and privileges under all federal and state laws...;

(4) an affirmation that the applicant possesses a currently valid Firearm Owner's Identification Card and card number if possessed or notice the applicant is applying for a Firearm Owner's Identification Card in conjuction with the license application;

(5) an affirmation that the applicant has not been convicted or found guilty of:

(A) a felony;

(B) a misdemeanor involving the use or threat of physical force or violence to any person within the 5 years preceding the date of the application; or

(C) 2 or more violations related to the driving while under the influence of alcohol, other drug or drugs, intoxicating compound or compounds, or any combination thereof, within the 5 years preceding the date of the license application; and

(6) whether the applicant has failed a drug test for a drug for which the applicant did not have a prescription, within the previous year, and if so, the provider of the test, the specific substance involved, and the date of the test;

(7) written consent for the Department to review and use the applicant's Illinois digital driver's license or Illinois identification card photograph and signature;

(8) a full set of fingerprints submitted to the Department in electronic format, provided the Department may accept an application submitted without a set of fingerprints in which case the Department shall be granted 30 days in addition to the 90 days provided under Section (e) of Section 10 of this Act to issue or deny a license;

(9) a head and shoulder color photograph in a size specified by the Department taken within the 30 days preceding the date of the license application; and

(10) a photocopy or any certificates or other evidence of compliance with the training requirements under this Act.

It should be noted that Illinois, at the time of this writing, does not require fingerprints (subsection 8). Legislation has been introduced to require fingerprints to obtain a CCL.

An applicant is also required to take and pass firearm training to obtain a CCL. The requirements are clearly stated in the statutes.

430 ILL. COMP. STAT. 66/75 contains applicant firearm training requirements:

(a) within 60 days of the effective date of this Act, the Department shall begin approval of firearm training courses and shall make a list of approved courses available on the Department's website;

(b) an applicant for a new license shall provide proof of completion of a firearms training course or combination of courses approved by the Department of at least 16 hours, which include range qualification time under subsection (c) of this Section, that covers the following:

(1) firearm safety;

(2) the basic principles of marksmanship;

(3) care, cleaning, loading, and unloading of a concealable firearm;

(4) all applicable state and federal laws relating to the ownership, storage, carry, and transportation of a firearm; and

(5) instruction on the appropriate and lawful interaction with law enforcement while transporting or carrying a concealed firearm;

(c) an applicant for a new license shall provide proof of certification by an instructor that the applicant passed a live fire exercise with a concealable firearm consisting of:

(1) a minimum of 30 rounds; and

(2) 10 rounds from a distance of 5 yards; 10 rounds from a distance of 7 yards; and 10 rounds from a distance of 10 yards at a B-27 silhouette target approved by the Department;

(d) an applicant for renewal of a license shall provide proof of completion of a firearms training course or combination of

courses approved by the Department of at least 3 hours; and
(e) a certificate of completion for the applicant's firearm training
course shall not be issued to a student who:
(1) does not follow the orders of the certified firearms instructor;
(2) in the judgment of the certified instructor, handles a firearm
in a manner that poses a danger to the student or to others; or
(3) during the range firing portion of testing fails to hit the target
with 70% of the rounds fired.

It is important to locate a certified trainer that has an excellent reputation and that the applicant feels comfortable with.

The next chapter will discuss the laws regarding where it is legal in Illinois to carry a firearm.

CHAPTER NINE

LAW OF HANDGUN CARRY: PART II
WHAT, HOW, AND WHERE
You Can Legally Carry With A CCL

The law as it pertains to what, how, and where you can carry in Illinois is all clearly stated in the Illinois Combined Statutes under Section 430 ILL. COMP. STAT. 66. It must always be remembered that Illinois is NOT an open carry state.

I. HOW TO CARRY

"Concealed firearm" means a loaded or unloaded handgun carried on or about a person completely or mostly concealed from view of the public or on or about a person within a vehicle. 430 ILL. COMP. STAT. 66/5.

It is required that the licensee always possesses his or her license at all times when carrying a concealed firearm. There is an exception for when the licensee is carrying or possessing a concealed firearm on his or her land or in his or her abode, legal dwelling, or fixed place of business, or on the land or in the legal dwelling of another person as an invitee with that person's permission. 430 ILL. COMP. STAT. 66/10(g)(1). Therefore, it is extremely important to inform the person whose home you are visiting that you are carrying and make sure they have no objection. If the owner of the premises does not permit you to have the handgun in their home, you must either leave or remove the gun.

The other exception to possessing your handgun without having your license with you is when the handgun is broken down in a non-functioning state, is not immediately accessible, or is unloaded and enclosed in a case. 430 ILL. COMP. STAT. 66/10(g)(3).

The question often arises as to what you should do if you are stopped in your vehicle by an officer and you are carrying your handgun in your vehicle.

"If an officer of a law enforcement agency initiates an investigative stop, including, but not limited to a traffic stop, of a licensee or of a non-resident carrying a concealed firearm under subsection (e) of Section 40 of this Act, upon request of the officer the licensee or non-resident shall disclose to the officer that he or she is in possession of a concealed firearm under this Act, or present the license upon the request of the officer." 430 ILL. COMP. STAT. 66/10(h).

It is important to note the language in the statute clearly states, "upon request of the officer," which means that unless the officer specifically asks, you are not required to tell him. HOWEVER, it is strongly suggested that if you are pulled over for a traffic stop in Illinois you do the following:

1. put both hands on the steering wheel and keep them there;
2. tell the officer when he approaches that you have a CCL and have your firearm in your vehicle;
3. tell him where the firearm is but do not reach for it or touch it;
4. ask the officer what he wants you to do;
5. never reach for the gun to show it to him; and
6. listen to what the officer tells you to do.

If you are driving your vehicle and the officer runs your license plates before he approaches, chances are he will know you have a FOID card and possibly a CCL. Volunteering the fact that you are carrying before the officer asks will limit the chances that you end up face down on the pavement with the officer's knee in your back. Secondly, if it is a minor traffic offense and you "front" the fact that you are carrying, there is a good chance the officer will give you a pass and not write the citation.

II. WHERE YOU CANNOT CARRY

The list of prohibited areas in Illinois where it is strictly illegal to carry is contained in the Illinois Combined Statutes under Section 66/65.

A licensee under this Act shall not knowingly carry a firearm on or into:
   (1) any building, real property, and parking area under the control

of a public or private elementary or secondary school;

(2) any building, real property, and parking area under the control of a pre-school or child care facility, including any room or portion of a building under the control of a pre-school or child care facility. Nothing in this paragraph shall prevent the operator of a child care facility in a family home from owning or possessing a firearm in the home or license under this Act, if no child under child care is present in the home or the firearm in the home is stored in a locked container when a child under child care is present in the home;

(3) any building, parking area, or portion of a building under the control of an officer of the executive or legislative branch of government, provided that nothing in this paragraph shall prohibit a licensee from carrying a concealed firearm onto the real property, bikeway, or trail in a park regulated by the Department of Natural Resources or any other designated public hunting area or building where firearm possession is permitted as established by the Department of Natural Resources under Section 1.8 of the Wildlife Code;

(4) any building designated for matters before a circuit court, appellate court, or the Supreme Court, or any building or portion of a building under the control of the Supreme Court;

(5) any building or portion of a building under the control of a unit of local government;

(6) any building, real property, and parking area under the control of an adult or juvenile detention or correctional institution, prison, or jail;

(7) any building, real property, and parking area under the control of a public or private hospital or hospital affiliate, mental health facility, or nursing home;

(8) any bus, train, or form of transportation paid for in whole or part with public funds, and any building, real property,

and parking area under the control of a public transportation facility paid for in whole or part with public funds;

(9) any building, real property, and parking area under the control of an establishment that serves alcohol on its premises, if more than 50% of the establishment's gross receipts within the prior 3 months is from the sale of alcohol. The owner of establishment who knowingly fails to prohibit concealed firearms on its premises as provided in this paragraph or who knowingly makes a false statement or record to avoid the prohibition on concealed firearms under this paragraph is subject to the penalty under subsection (c-5) of Section 10-1 of the Liquor Control Act of 1934;

(10) any public gathering or special event conducted on property open to the public that requires the issuance of a permit from the unit of local government, provided this prohibition shall not apply to a licensee who must walk through a public gathering in order to access his or her residence, place of business, or vehicle;

(11) any building or real property that has been issued a Special Event Retailer's license as defined in Section 1-3.17.1 of the Liquor Control Act during the time designated for the sale of alcohol by the Special Event Retailer's license, or a Special use permit license as defined in subsection (q) of Section 5-1 of the Liquor Control Act during the time designated for the sale of alcohol by the Special use permit license;

(12) any public playground;

(13) any public park, athletic area, or athletic facility under the control of a municipality or park district, provided nothing in this Section shall prohibit a licensee from carrying a concealed firearm while on a bike trail or bikeway if only a portion of the trail or bikeway includes a public park;

(14) any real property under the control of the Cook County Forest Preserve District;

(15) any building, classroom, laboratory, medical clinic, hospital, artistic venue, athletic venue, entertainment venue, officially recognized university related organization property, whether owned or leased, and any real property, including parking areas, sidewalks, and common areas under the control of a public or private community college, college, or university;

(16) any building, real property, or parking area under the control of a gaming facility licensed under the Riverboat Gambling Act of 1975, including any inter-track wagering location licensee;

(17) any stadium, arena, or the real property or parking area under the control of a stadium, arena, or any collegiate or professional sporting event;

(18) any building, real property, or parking area under the control of a public library;

(19) any building, real property, or parking area under the control of an airport;

(20) any building, real property, or parking area under the control of an amusement park;

(21) any building, real property, or parking area under the control of a zoo or museum;

(22) any street, driveway, parking area, property, building, or facility, owned, leased, controlled, or used by a nuclear energy, storage, weapons, or development site or facility regulated by the federal Nuclear Regulatory Commission. The licensee shall not under any circumstances store a firearm or ammunition in his or her vehicle or in a compartment or container within a vehicle located anywhere in or on the

street, driveway, parking area, property, building, or facility described in this paragraph; and

(23) any area where firearms are prohibited under federal law.

(24) When carried upon one's person, any public street, alley, or other public lands within the corporate limits of a city, village or incorporated town, except when an invitee thereon or therein, for the purpose of the display of such weapon or the lawful commerce in weapons, or except when on his land or in his own abode, legal dwelling, or fixed place of business, or on the land or in the legal dwelling of another person as an invitee with that person's permission, any pistol, revolver, stun gun or taser or other firearm.

(25) Any place, when one carries or possesses any firearm, stun gun or taser or other deadly weapon, which is licensed to sell intoxicating beverages, or at any public gathering held pursuant to a license issued by any governmental body or any public gathering at which an admission is charged, excluding a place where a showing, demonstration or lecture involving the exhibition of unloaded firearms is conducted.

(a-5) Nothing in this Act shall prohibit a public or private community college, college, or university from:

(1) prohibiting persons from carrying a firearm within a vehicle owned, leased, or controlled by the college or university;

(2) developing resolutions, regulations, or policies regarding student, employee, or visitor misconduct and discipline, including suspensions and expulsions;

(3) developing resolutions, regulations, or policies regarding the storage or maintenance of firearms, which must include designated areas where persons can park vehicles that carry firearms; and

(4) permitting the carrying or use of firearms for the purpose of instruction and curriculum of officially recognized programs, including but not limited to military science and law enforcement training programs, or in any designated area used for hunting purposes or target shooting.

(a-10) The owner of private real property of any type may prohibit the carrying of concealed firearms on the property under his or her control. The owner must post a sign in accordance with subsection (d) of this Section indicating that firearms are prohibited on the property, unless the property is a private residence.

(b) Notwithstanding subsection (a), (a-5), and (a-10) of this Section except under paragraph (22) or (23) of subsection (a), any licensee prohibited from carrying a concealed firearm into the parking area of a prohibited location specified in subsection (a), (a-5), or (a-10) of this Section shall be permitted to carry a concealed firearm on or about his or her person within a vehicle into the parking area and may store a firearm or ammunition concealed in a case within a locked vehicle or locked container out of plain view within the vehicle in the parking area. A licensee may carry a concealed firearm in the immediate area surrounding his or her vehicle within a prohibited parking lot area only for the limited purpose of storing or retrieving the firearm within the vehicle's trunk. For purposes of this subsection, "case" includes a glove compartment or console that completely encloses the concealed firearm or ammunition, the trunk of the vehicle, or a firearm carrying box, shipping box, or other container.

(c) A licensee shall not be in violation of this Section while he or she is traveling along a public right of way that touches or crosses any of the premises under subsection (a), (a-5), or (a-10) of this Section if the concealed firearm is carried on his or her person in accordance with the provisions of this Act or is being transported in a vehicle by the licensee in accordance with all other applicable provisions of law.

(d) Signs stating that the carrying of firearms is prohibited shall be clearly and conspicuously posted at the entrance of a building, premises, or real property specified in this Section as a prohibited area, unless the building or premises is a private residence. Signs shall be of a uniform design as established by the Department and shall be 4 inches by 6 inches in size. The Department shall adopt rules for standardized signs to be used under this subsection.

Section 430 ILL. COMP. STAT. 66/65.
These restrictions appear to be, for all intents and purposes, extremely thorough limits on the places that you can legally carry in Illinois. We must continue to remind you that concealed carry is in its infancy here in Illinois. The prohibited areas could change with very little notice, if any to the licensee. The licensee has to remain vigilant and educated when it comes to prohibited areas. Ignorance of the law is not a defense to violating the concealed carry laws in Illinois. The Illinois State Police website (isp.state.il.us) is the best and most current source.

III. PENALTIES

The penalties for violating any of the previous statutes pertaining to carrying in a prohibited area are stated in the Illinois Statutes Section 430 ILL. COMP. STAT. 66/70 Violations:

(e) except as otherwise provided, a licensee in violation of this Act shall be guilty of a Class B misdemeanor. A second or subsequent violation is a Class A misdemeanor. The Department may suspend a license for up to 6 months for a second violation and shall permanently revoke a license for 3 or more violations of Section 65 of this Act. Any person convicted of a violation under this Section shall pay a $150 fee to be deposited into the Mental Health Reporting Fund, plus any applicable court costs or fee; and

(g) a licensee whose license is revoked, suspended, or denied shall within 48 hours of receiving notice of the revocation, suspension, or denial, surrender his or her concealed carry license to the local law enforcement agency where he or she resides.

In Illinois, we are not only subjected to possible penalties through the court system, we can also face the loss of the right to possess or carry a weapon administratively through the Illinois State Police. The Illinois State Police have been granted a great deal of latitude in revoking, suspending, and denying an individual a FOID card or CCL. If a licensee is charged with a crime, which, if convicted, could cause the licensee to become ineligible for a FOID or CCL, he could still lose his rights to own or carry a firearm, even if the charges are dismissed or he is found not guilty. The Illinois State Police Review Board can revoke, suspend, or deny a FOID or CCL based on the allegations alone. It is strongly suggested that if you find yourself in a situation where you are not only facing a possible jail sentence, but also losing your right to own or carry a firearm, you should consult with an attorney experienced in criminal defense as well as gun owner rights.

CHAPTER TEN

POSSESSING, CARRYING, AND TRANSPORTING FIREARMS WITHOUT A CCL

T his chapter deals with when and where a person may possess, carry, or transport a firearm if they do not have an Illinois Concealed Carry License ("CCL").

The laws discussed in this chapter are found primarily in Illinois Compiled Statutes Chapter 430 Article 65 entitled "Firearm Owners Identification Card Act," Chapter 430 Article 66 entitled "Firearms Concealed Carry Act" and Illinois Criminal Code 5/24-1 entitled "Unlawful Use of Weapons." These Chapters govern where and when firearms can be possessed and carried in Illinois, and they also contain various exceptions to any such rules.

There are four general laws that apply to firearm ownership and possession in Illinois. First, unless specifically exempted by statute, any Illinois resident who acquires or possesses firearms, firearm ammunition, tasers, or stun guns within the state must have in their possession a valid Firearm Owner's Identification Card ("FOID") issued in his or her name. Nonresidents are not required to have a FOID.

Second, persons with a FOID but without a CCL are only allowed to possess a concealed firearm when they are on their land or in their own abode, legal dwelling, or fixed place of business, or on the land or in the legal dwelling of another person as an invitee with that person's permission. *See* 720 ILL. COMP. STAT. 5/24-1(a) (4). There are exceptions and defenses to this that are discussed later in this chapter.

Third, Illinois does not generally allow a person who has a FOID but not a CCL to possess or carry a firearm in any manner upon any public street, alley, or other public lands within the corporate limits of a city, village, or incorporated town. There are exceptions and defenses to this that are discussed later in this chapter. *See* 720 ILL. COMP. STAT. 5/24-1(a)(10).

Fourth, Illinois allows certain towns and municipalities (*i.e.* those with power under the Illinois "home rule" authority) to pass laws or ordinances that can further restrict the right to carry or possess firearms. So, all firearms owners are advised to check with their local police regarding any local laws that could modify the rules discussed here.

The FOID is NOT a "concealed carry" card. It is required to possess firearms, firearm ammunition, stun guns, and tasers in the state of Illinois. The FOID card does not confer any privileges to "carry" a gun. Certain persons are exempt from the requirement to have a FOID. The FOID Act, 430 ILL. COMP. STAT. 65/2(b) outlines the following exemptions:

EXEMPTIONS TO THE REQUIREMENT OF A FOID:
430 ILL. COMP. STAT. 65/2(b)

- United States Marshals, while engaged in the operation of their official duties.
- Members of the Armed Forces of the United States or the National Guard, while engaged in the operation of their official duties.
- Federal officials required to carry firearms, while engaged in the operation of their official duties.
- Members of bona fide veteran's organizations which receive firearms directly from the Armed Forces of the United States, while using the firearms for ceremonial purposes with blank ammunition.
- Nonresident hunters during hunting season, with valid nonresident hunting licenses and while in an area where hunting is permitted; however, at all other times and in all other places these persons must have their firearms unloaded and enclosed in a case.
- Nonresidents while on a firing or shooting range recognized by the Department of State Police.

- Nonresidents while at a firearm showing or display recognized by the Department of State Police.
- Nonresidents whose firearms are unloaded and enclosed in a case.
- Nonresidents who are currently licensed or registered to possess a firearm in their resident state.
- Unemancipated minors while in the custody and immediate control of their parent or legal guardian and the parent or legal guardian currently has a valid FOID.
- Color guards of bona fide veteran's organizations or members of bona fide American Legion bands while using firearms for ceremonial purposes with blank ammunition.
- Nonresident hunters whose state of residence does not require them to be licensed or registered to possess a firearm and only during hunting season. The nonresident must have a valid hunting license and be accompanied by and be using a firearm owned by a person who possesses a valid FOID. This is allowed only while in an area within a commercial club licensed under the Wildlife Code where hunting is permitted and controlled, but in no instance upon sites owned or managed by the Department of Natural Resources.
- Resident hunters who are properly authorized to hunt and, while accompanied by a person who possesses a valid FOID, hunt in an area within a commercial club licensed under the Wildlife Code where hunting is permitted and controlled.
- A person who is otherwise eligible to obtain a FOID under this Act and is under the direct supervision of a FOID holder who is 21 years of age or older while the person is on a firing

or shooting range or is a participant in a firearms safety and training course recognized by a law enforcement agency or a national, statewide shooting sports organization.

- Competitive shooting athletes whose competition firearms are sanctioned by the International Olympic Committee, the International Paralympic Committee, the International Shooting Sport Federation, or USA Shooting. The use must be in connection with such athletes' training for and participation in shooting competitions at the 2016 Olympic and Paralympic Games and sanctioned test events leading up to the 2016 Olympic and Paralympic Games.

- Law enforcement officials of this or any other jurisdiction, while engaged in the operation of their official duties.

I. WHERE ARE FIREARMS (LONG GUNS OR HANDGUNS) PROHIBITED UNDER ILLINOIS LAW?

Under Illinois law, there are certain places where all firearms, including long guns and handguns, are forbidden. Illinois statute 430 ILL. COMP. STAT. 66/65 lists at least 23 areas where a person is prohibited from possessing or carrying firearms regardless of whether the person is a CCL holder.

A. Prohibited places for all weapons

Illinois law states that a person cannot knowingly carry or possess a firearm of any kind in the following areas:

(1) Any building, real property, and parking area under the control of a public or private elementary or secondary school.

(2) Any building, real property, and parking area under the control of a pre-school or child care facility, including any

room or portion of a building under the control of a pre-school or child care facility. Nothing in this paragraph shall prevent the operator of a child care facility in a family home from owning or possessing a firearm in the home or license under this Act, if no child under child care at the home is present in the home or the firearm in the home is stored in a locked container when a child under child care at the home is present in the home.

(3) Any building, parking area, or portion of a building under the control of an officer of the executive or legislative branch of government, provided that nothing in this paragraph shall prohibit a licensee from carrying a concealed firearm onto the real property, bikeway, or trail in a park regulated by the Department of Natural Resources or any other designated public hunting area or building where firearm possession is permitted as established by the Department of Natural Resources under Section 1.8 of the Wildlife Code.

(4) Any building designated for matters before a circuit court, appellate court, or the Supreme Court, or any building or portion of a building under the control of the Supreme Court.

(5) Any building or portion of a building under the control of a unit of local government.

(6) Any building, real property, and parking area under the control of an adult or juvenile detention or correctional institution, prison, or jail.

(7) Any building, real property, and parking area under the control of a public or private hospital or hospital affiliate, mental health facility, or nursing home.

(8) Any bus, train, or form of transportation paid for in whole or in part with public funds, and any building, real property, and parking area under the control of a public transportation

facility paid for in whole or in part with public funds.

(9) Any building, real property, and parking area under the control of an establishment that serves alcohol on its premises, if more than 50% of the establishment's gross receipts within the prior 3 months is from the sale of alcohol. The owner of an establishment who knowingly fails to prohibit concealed firearms on its premises as provided in this paragraph or who knowingly makes a false statement or record to avoid the prohibition on concealed firearms under this paragraph is subject to the penalty under subsection (c-5) of Section 10-1 of the Liquor Control Act of 1934.

(10) Any public gathering or special event conducted on property open to the public that requires the issuance of a permit from the unit of local government, provided this prohibition shall not apply to a licensee who must walk through a public gathering in order to access his or her residence, place of business, or vehicle.

(11) Any building or real property that has been issued a Special Event Retailer's license as defined in Section 1-3.17.1 of the Liquor Control Act during the time designated for the sale of alcohol by the Special Event Retailer's license, or a Special use permit license as defined in subsection (q) of Section 5-1 of the Liquor Control Act during the time designated for the sale of alcohol by the Special use permit license.

(12) Any public playground.

(13) Any public park, athletic area, or athletic facility under the control of a municipality or park district, provided nothing in this Section shall prohibit a licensee from carrying a concealed firearm while on a trail or bikeway if only a portion of the trail or bikeway includes a public park.

(14) Any real property under the control of the Cook County

Forest Preserve District.

(15) Any building, classroom, laboratory, medical clinic, hospital, artistic venue, athletic venue, entertainment venue, officially recognized university-related organization property, whether owned or leased, and any real property, including parking areas, sidewalks, and common areas under the control of a public or private community college, college, or university.

(16) Any building, real property, or parking area under the control of a gaming facility licensed under the Riverboat Gambling Act or the Illinois Horse Racing Act of 1975, including an inter-track wagering location licensee.

(17) Any stadium, arena, or the real property or parking area under the control of a stadium, arena, or any collegiate or professional sporting event.

(18) Any building, real property, or parking area under the control of a public library.

(19) Any building, real property, or parking area under the control of an airport.

(20) Any building, real property, or parking area under the control of an amusement park.

(21) Any building, real property, or parking area under the control of a zoo or museum.

(22) Any street, driveway, parking area, property, building, or facility, owned, leased, controlled, or used by a nuclear energy, storage, weapons, or development site or facility regulated by the federal Nuclear Regulatory Commission. The licensee shall not under any circumstance store a firearm or ammunition in his or her vehicle or in a compartment or container within a vehicle located anywhere in or on the street, driveway, parking area, property, building, or facility

described in this paragraph.

(23) Any area where firearms are prohibited under federal law.

(24) When carried upon one's person, any public street, alley, or other public lands within the corporate limits of a city, village or incorporated town, except when an invitee thereon or therein, for the purpose of the display of such weapon or the lawful commerce in weapons, or except when on his land or in his own abode, legal dwelling, or fixed place of business, or on the land or in the legal dwelling of another person as an invitee with that person's permission, any pistol, revolver, stun gun or taser or other firearm.

(25) Any place, when one carries or possesses any firearm, stun gun or taser or other deadly weapon, which is licensed to sell intoxicating beverages, or at any public gathering held pursuant to a license issued by any governmental body or any public gathering at which an admission is charged, excluding a place where a showing, demonstration or lecture involving the exhibition of unloaded firearms is conducted.

In addition, community colleges, colleges, and universities (whether public or private) can regulate the manner in which persons store their firearms in their vehicles, regardless of the issuance of a CCL.

Finally, the owner of private real property of any type may prohibit the carrying of concealed firearms on the property under his or her control. The owner must post a sign in accordance with the law indicating that firearms are prohibited on the property, unless the property is a private residence.

B. Defenses and exceptions to prohibited places

There are, of course, certain exceptions to possessing firearms in the places listed above. Except under paragraphs (22) or (23) of the above (Nuclear Regulatory Facility or "where federal law prohibits"), any person prohibited from carrying a concealed firearm into the parking area of a prohibited location specified in the above areas shall be permitted to carry a concealed firearm on or about his or her person within a vehicle into the parking area and may store a firearm or ammunition concealed in a case within a locked vehicle or locked container out of plain view within the vehicle in the parking area, provided they are a CCL holder.

A person may also carry a concealed firearm in the immediate area surrounding his or her vehicle within a prohibited parking lot area only for the limited purpose of storing or retrieving a firearm within the vehicle's trunk, if they are a CCL holder. For purposes of this scenario, "case" includes a glove compartment or console that completely encloses the concealed firearm or ammunition, the trunk of the vehicle, or a firearm carrying box, shipping box, or other container.

A CCL holder is not in violation of the law while he or she is traveling along a public right of way that touches or crosses any of the premises listed above, if the concealed firearm is carried on his or her person in accordance with the provisions of the Concealed Carry Act or is being transported in a vehicle by the licensee in accordance with all other applicable provisions of law.

It should be noted that the law says signs stating that the carrying of firearms is prohibited shall be clearly and conspicuously posted at the entrance of a building, premises, or real property listed above as a prohibited area, unless the building or premises is a private residence. Signs shall be of a uniform design as established and shall be 4 inches by 6 inches in size. The Department of State Police shall adopt rules for standardized signs to be used under this subsection.

What is the parking lot exemption for CCL holders in prohibited places?
Any licensee prohibited from carrying a concealed firearm into the parking area because it is a prohibited location shall be permitted to carry a concealed firearm on or about his or her person when in a vehicle into the parking area and may store the firearm or ammunition concealed in a case within the locked vehicle or locked container out of plain view within the vehicle in the parking area. A licensee may carry a concealed firearm in the immediate area surrounding the vehicle while storing or retrieving a firearm from the vehicle's trunk. This exception does not apply to any area where firearms are prohibited under federal law or to property regulated by the federal Nuclear Regulatory Commission.

1. Defenses to possessing a firearm at schools
The prohibition against the possession of firearms in or near schools does not generally apply to law enforcement officers or security officers of such school, college, or university or to students carrying or possessing firearms for use in training courses, parades, hunting, target shooting on school ranges, or otherwise with the consent of school authorities and when the firearms are transported unloaded and enclosed in a suitable case, box, or transportation package. *See* 720 ILL. COMP. STAT. 5/24-1(c)(3).

2. Defenses to possessing a firearm in a public place
The possession or carrying of a firearm on public property as

described in subsection (24) has an exception. The prohibition does not apply to or affect transportation of weapons that meet one of the following conditions:

(i)   are broken down in a non-functioning state;

(ii) are not immediately accessible;

(iii) are unloaded and enclosed in a case, firearm carrying box, shipping box, or other container by a person who has been issued a currently valid Firearm Owner's Identification Card; or

(iv) are carried or possessed in accordance with the Firearm Concealed Carry Act by a person who has been issued a currently valid license under the Firearm Concealed Carry Act.

3. Defenses to possessing a firearm at bars or licensed public gatherings

Under Illinois law, subsection (25) does not apply to any auction or raffle of a firearm held pursuant to a license or permit issued by a governmental body, nor does it apply to persons engaged in firearm safety training courses.

C. Defenses to possession of concealed weapons outside of the home or business by non-CCL holders

Section 720 ILL. COMP. STAT. 5/24-1(a)(4), which prohibits those who only have a FOID from carrying concealed weapons outside of the home or business, does not apply to or affect transportation of weapons that meet one of the following conditions:

(i)   the weapons are broken down in a non-functioning state;

(ii) the weapons are not immediately accessible;

(iii) the weapons are unloaded and enclosed in a case, firearm carrying box, shipping box, or other container by a person who has been issued a currently valid Firearm Owner's

Identification Card; or

(iv) the weapons are carried or possessed in accordance with the Firearm Concealed Carry Act by a person who has been issued a currently valid license under the Firearm Concealed Carry Act.

D. Defenses to the carrying of firearms (and other weapons) on public lands or streets within cities, villages, or incorporated towns

Section 720 ILL. COMP. STAT. 5/24-1(a)(10) generally forbids the open carrying of firearms by FOID cardholders (without a CCL). Exceptions apply when the possessor is an invitee thereon or therein, for the purpose of the display of such weapon or the lawful commerce in weapons, or except when the person is on his land or in his own abode, legal dwelling, or fixed place of business, or on the land or in the legal dwelling of another person as an invitee with that person's permission.

A further exception to Section 720 ILL. COMP. STAT. 5/24-1(a)(10) applies when the person is engaged in the transportation of the weapons and the weapons meet one of the following conditions:

(i) they are broken down in a non-functioning state;

(ii) they are not immediately accessible;

(iii) they are unloaded and enclosed in a case, firearm carrying box, shipping box, or other container by a person who has been issued a currently valid Firearm Owner's Identification Card; or

(iv) they are carried or possessed in accordance with the Firearm Concealed Carry Act by a person who has been issued a currently valid license under the Firearm Concealed Carry Act.

II. LAW CONCERNING HANDGUNS

In Illinois, the possession of handguns is prohibited in the same manner as are all other firearms.

AGGRAVATED UNLAWFUL USE OF A WEAPON:

720 ILL. COMP. STAT. 5/24-1.6

(a) A person commits the offense of aggravated unlawful use of a weapon when he or she knowingly:

(1) Carries on or about his or her person or in any vehicle or concealed on or about his or her person except when on his or her land or in his or her abode, legal dwelling, or fixed place of business, or on the land or in the legal dwelling of another person as an invitee with that person's permission, any pistol, revolver, stun gun or taser or other firearm; or

(2) Carries or possesses on or about his or her person, upon any public street, alley, or other public lands within the corporate limits of a city, village or incorporated town, except when an invitee thereon or therein, for the purpose of the display of such weapon or the lawful commerce in weapons, or except when on his or her own land or in his or her own abode, legal dwelling, or fixed place of business, or on the land or in the legal dwelling of another person as an invitee with that person's permission, any pistol, revolver, stun gun or taser or other firearm; and

(3) One of the following factors is present:

(A) the firearm, other than a pistol, revolver, or handgun, possessed was uncased, loaded, and immediately accessible at the time of the offense;

AGGRAVATED UNLAWFUL USE OF A WEAPON:
720 Ill. Comp. Stat. 5/24-1.6

(A-5) the pistol, revolver, or handgun possessed was uncased, loaded, and immediately accessible at the time of the offense and the person possessing the pistol, revolver, or handgun has not been issued a currently valid license under the Firearm Concealed Carry Act;

(B) the firearm, other than a pistol, revolver, or handgun, possessed was uncased, unloaded, and the ammunition for the weapon was immediately accessible at the time of the offense;

(B-5) the pistol, revolver, or handgun possessed was uncased, unloaded, and the ammunition for the weapon was immediately accessible at the time of the offense and the person possessing the pistol, revolver, or handgun has not been issued a currently valid license under the Firearm Concealed Carry Act;

(C) the person possessing the firearm has not been issued a currently valid Firearm Owner's Identification Card;

(D) the person possessing the weapon was previously adjudicated a delinquent minor under the Juvenile Court Act of 1987 for an act that if committed by an adult would be a felony;

(E) the person possessing the weapon was engaged in a misdemeanor violation of the Cannabis Control Act, in a misdemeanor violation of the Illinois Controlled Substances Act, or in a misdemeanor violation of the Methamphetamine Control and Community Protection Act;

(F) (blank);

(G) the person possessing the weapon had an order of protection issued against him or her within the previous 2 years;

(H) the person possessing the weapon was engaged in the commission or attempted commission of a misdemeanor involving the use or threat of violence against the person or property of another; or

(I) the person possessing the weapon was under 21 years of age and in possession of a handgun, unless the person under 21 is engaged in lawful activities under the Wildlife Code or described in subsection 24-2(b)(1) and (b)(3).

720 Ill. Comp. Stat. 5/24-(b)(1): Members of any club or organization organized for the purpose of practicing shooting at targets upon established target ranges, whether public or private, and the patrons of such ranges, while such members or patrons are using their firearms on those target ranges.

(b)(3) Hunters, trappers or fishermen with a license or permit while engaged in hunting, trapping or fishing.

A. What is an "abode"?

Under Illinois law, a person may possess and conceal a firearm when they are on their land or in their own abode, legal dwelling, or fixed place of business, or on the land or in the legal dwelling of another person as an invitee with that person's permission. *See* Section 720

ILL. COMP. STAT. 5/24-1(a)(4). The term "abode," as used in Section (a)(4) prohibiting the carrying of a concealed weapon except in one's abode, refers to an individual's overnight living quarters and is not limited to a person's dwelling or residence. *See People v. Taylor,* 328 N.E.2d 325 (Ill. App. 1975). In *Taylor,* the defendant presented evidence that he lived, on occasion, in the apartment in which he was arrested for carrying a concealed weapon and he had no other place where he had any other possessions. Evidence was also provided that, upon being arrested and asked where he lived, he had given to the police an address other than the one in which he was arrested. However, the appellate court held that the defendant's statement regarding where he lived was insufficient to prove beyond a reasonable doubt that he was not carrying the weapon in his "abode," and, therefore, he was entitled to the exemption from prohibition against carrying concealed weapons, thus reversing his conviction.

Significantly, an apartment building's public areas to which tenants and invitees have access are not the "abode" of any tenant for purposes of this exception. *People v. Wilson,* 332 N.E.2d 6 (Ill. App. 1975).

Finally, the sidewalk in front of one's house is not protected. It has been held that a sidewalk, which is subject to regulation use by a municipality, does not come within the language "except when on his own land or in his own abode or fixed place of business." Therefore, a sidewalk does not fall under the exemption to this paragraph prohibiting possession of a handgun; that is true even if the sidewalk is in front of the defendant's place of residence. *People v. Carter,* 444 N.E.2d 840 (Ill. App. 1983).

B. What is a "fixed place of business"?

Illinois law allows a person to carry a concealed weapon at their fixed place of business with only a FOID card (no CCL is needed). An employee of a business cannot use this exception. It was held in one case that a person had no proprietary interest in a restaurant at which he was employed as a dishwasher, so he was not in his "fixed place of business" within the exception to this paragraph proscribing unlawful use of weapons. Thus, the fact that he carried the pistol into the restaurant and its adjacent parking lot without a CCL was sufficient to prove his guilt. *People v. Free,* 445 N.E.2d 529 (Ill. App. 1983).

In yet another case, a concealed weapon in a jacket on the seat of a taxicab being driven by a defendant was not within his "fixed place of business" within the statutory exception pertaining to carrying of a concealed weapon when a person is at his fixed place of business. *People v. Cosby*, 255 N.E.2d 54 (Ill. App. 1969). There the court stated that the phrase "fixed place of business" as used in the section permitting the carrying of concealed weapons by a person when on or in his fixed place of business meant a place that was stationary or permanent and did not include a moving vehicle such as a taxicab.

1. When is an RV considered an "abode"?

This question is unanswered in Illinois, but if the RV is parked and at that time being used for overnight living, it may fit the definition of abode as described above.

2. Open carrying of handguns on one's own premises

Illinois law does not make it a crime to openly carry a handgun on your own abode, legal dwelling, or fixed place of business;

therefore, it is legal. However, as a practical legal matter, a person may not carry a firearm which disturbs another and "provokes or threatens to provoke a breach of the peace." If a person carries it in this manner, the person could be charged with the crime of disorderly conduct under Illinois law. *See* 720 ILL. COMP. STAT. 5/26-1.

3. Can a person legally conceal a handgun with their body while in a vehicle?

Yes, but only if the firearm is being transported, it is broken down, and in a non-functioning state; or in a container, case or box, or if the person is in compliance with the CCL laws.

C. Disqualified persons

1. May I keep a handgun in my vehicle if there are children in the car?

Having children in the car does not change the law on whether a person is able (or not able) to possess a handgun in the vehicle legally. A firearm may only be kept in a vehicle if it is being transported and one of the following conditions is met:

(i)   the handgun is broken down in a non-functioning state;

(ii)   it is not immediately accessible;

(iii)   it is unloaded and enclosed in a case, firearm carrying box, shipping box, or other container by a person who has been issued a currently valid Firearm Owner's Identification Card; or

(iv)   it is carried or possessed in accordance with the Firearm Concealed Carry Act by a person who has been issued a currently valid license under the Firearm Concealed Carry Act.

2. Is it illegal for an owner of a vehicle to possess a handgun when a passenger in the vehicle is a felon or is otherwise disqualified from possessing firearms?

The fact that there is a felon in the car does not change the law, so long as the felon (or person disqualified) never possesses the firearm. If the possessor of the handgun has complied with the law, then the mere presence of a felon is irrelevant.

3. A person cannot "give" a handgun to someone who intends to break the law

This one is simple. If someone asks you for your gun in order to rob a bank or knock-off a liquor store, it is a crime for you to give them the gun.

D. What is "concealment"?

A weapon is "concealed," within meaning of the Concealed Weapons Statute, when it is concealed from ordinary observation. *People v. Williams*, 350 N.E.2d 81 (Ill. App. 1976).

In one case, evidence that the defendant was in possession of a weapon and was wearing a shoulder holster, without showing that he had worn a garment over the holster, required too much speculation to sustain conviction for unlawful use of weapons. *People v. Guthrie*, 376 N.E.2d 425 (Ill. 1978).

In another case, evidence that a pistol found at the scene of a probationer's arrest was not concealed but was lying in plain sight on the ground two feet away from probationer, just under the door to the driver's seat of the car probationer had been driving, did not establish that probationer had committed the offense of unlawful use of weapons by being in possession of pistol, revolver, or other firearm concealed on or about his person or in his vehicle. *People v. White*, 338 N.E.2d 81 (Ill. 1975).

Another case held that a gun which was in the defendant's coat pocket, with the butt covered by defendant's hand, was "concealed" and the conviction was upheld. *People v. Taylor*, 332 N.E.2d 735 (Ill. App. 1975).

The court in *People v. Williams* held that the evidence proved beyond a reasonable doubt that defendant who was standing in a hallway carrying a brown paper bag from which protruded four or five inches of a rifle was guilty of carrying a concealed weapon. *People v. Williams*, 305 N.E.2d 186 (Ill. App. 1973).

A conviction was also upheld for carrying a concealed weapon of a defendant who was first observed without a shotgun and then observed removing the shotgun from inside his pants and beneath his jacket. *People v. Moore*, 302 N.E.2d 658 (Ill. App. 1973).

D. Can a person possess or transport a "machine gun" or a "sawed-off shotgun"?

In Illinois it is illegal to possess either a machine gun or a sawed-off shotgun. Illinois law, Section 720 ILL. COMP. STAT. 5/24-1(a)(7), states that it is illegal for a person to sell, manufacture, purchase, possess, or carry:

(i) a machine gun, which shall be defined for the purposes of this subsection as any weapon, which shoots, is designed to shoot, or can be readily restored to shoot, automatically more than one shot without manually reloading by a single function of the trigger, including the frame or receiver of any such weapon, or sell, manufacture, purchase, possess, or carry any combination of parts designed or intended for use in converting any weapon into a machine gun, or any combination or parts from which a machine gun can be assembled if such parts are in the possession or under the control of a person; or

(ii) any rifle having one or more barrels less than 16 inches in length or a shotgun having one or more barrels less than 18 inches in length or any weapon made from a rifle or shotgun, whether by alteration, modification, or otherwise, if such a weapon as modified has an overall length of less than 26 inches.

E. What is a "non-functioning state?"

A person is not guilty of Unlawful Use of a Weapon ("UUW") if the firearm is in a "non-functioning state." Several cases illustrate what is (or is not) a non-functioning state.

In one case, it was recognized that a weapon could be in such a state of disrepair (or its design so completely altered) that it could no longer be said to be "designed" for that purpose and, therefore, no longer a threat to public health, safety, and decency. *People v. Williams,* 915 N.E.2d. 815 (Ill. App. 2009).

In another case, it was held that a police officers' testimony that the gun was not in a broken-down state was sufficient to support a conviction for unlawful use of weapons, despite the defendant's contrary testimony and minor discrepancies between testimony of officers; the question as to the state of the gun was not a matter about which there was any equivocation by officers. *People v. Freeman,* 579 N.E.2d. 576 (Ill. App. 1991).

A conviction was reversed where the appellate court found that the evidence was insufficient, since the weapon in question was a broken and rusted gun and was not a deadly 'weapon' within the purview of this paragraph. *People v. Worlds*, 400 N.E.2d. 85 (Ill. App. 1980).

Being merely inoperable is not the same as being in a "non-functioning" state. More is required. In one case the court ruled that the fact that the pistol was inoperable and unloaded, did not exempt it from the UUW statute. *People v. White*, 338 N.E.2d 81 (Ill. App. 1975).

a. What is "transporting?"

Unfortunately, there is no statutory definition of the term "transporting." Ultimately, any time a person is in a moving car with a gun, it has been assumed by the courts that the gun was being "transported." Who, then, determines whether a person was transporting or not? Ultimately, a jury will make the determination.

III. LAW CONCERNING LONG GUNS
A. May be carried openly in public

Illinois law does require a person to have a permit to carry a long gun (called FOID, *see* above), and the law requires that a long gun not be concealed when in public. In other words, Illinois law treats handguns and long guns the same (unless the person holds a CCL). There is no statute that addresses the manner in which a long gun may be carried other than that it may not be concealed and it may not be displayed in a public place in a manner calculated to alarm (the crimes of disorderly conduct or assault might apply).

B. Manner in which long guns may not be displayed in public

A person may legally display a long gun in public under the same restrictions that apply to a handgun. (*See* previous sections).

DISORDERLY CONDUCT:
720 Ill. Comp. Stat. 5/26-1

(a)(1), a person is criminally liable for disorderly conduct "when he or she knowingly does any act in such unreasonable manner as to alarm or disturb another and to provoke a breach of the peace."

C. May I keep a long gun in my vehicle under Illinois law?

Like handguns, a person with a FOID card may transport a long gun in a vehicle when it meets one of the following conditions:

(i)   it is broken down in a non-functioning state;

(ii) it is not immediately accessible;

(iii) it is unloaded and enclosed in a case, firearm carrying box, shipping box, or other container by a person who has been issued a currently valid Firearm Owner's Identification Card; or

(iv) it is carried or possessed in accordance with the Firearm Concealed Carry Act by a person who has been issued a currently valid license under the Firearm Concealed Carry Act.

D. May I possess a long gun while riding in another person's vehicle?

Yes, under the same conditions as the driver (listed above).

E. May I have a long gun on a boat or other watercraft?

Yes, a person may transport a firearm in boats and other watercraft under the same rules which allow the possession and carrying of a long gun in a vehicle.

IV. POSSESSING AND CARRYING HANDGUNS IN PLACES OTHER THAN A PERSON'S PREMISES OR VEHICLE WITHOUT A CCL

In this section, we will answer some of the common questions about places that are not a person's own premises or their vehicle, and whether or not a person can possess and carry a handgun.

A. May a person keep a firearm in their hotel room?

Probably yes, but this area has not yet been clarified by Illinois courts. A hotel room is considered an "abode," just like other overnight living quarters, which would allow for unfettered possession. However, a hotel, or any private business has the right and ability to prohibit the possession of firearms in or on their property by not just CCL holders, but also by persons who do not possess a CCL. For individuals who do not possess a CCL, a business is required to provide signage that the possession of firearms is prohibited. Additionally, Illinois law prohibits the possession or carrying of firearms on any premises where alcohol is served, so this may also have an impact on the right to bring a weapon into a hotel room.

B. Signs where alcohol is sold

In places where alcohol is sold, individuals may often see a sign at the entrance prohibiting firearms which states that the unlicensed possession of a weapon is a felony under state law. Moreover, Illinois prohibits the possession of firearms of any kind on the premises of places that sell alcohol. This sign applies to all individuals whether or not they possess a CCL.

V. TRAVELING ACROSS STATE LINES WITH FIREARMS

Many people vacation and travel outside of Illinois. How then does a person pass through states that have restrictive firearms laws or those different from Illinois? For example, how does a person legally pass through a state that prohibits the possession of a handgun without a license from that state? The answer: safe-passage legislation.

A. Federal law: qualifying for firearms "Safe Passage"

Traveling across state lines with a firearm means that a person may need to use the provisions of the federal law known as the "Safe Passage" provision. Federal law allows individuals who are legally in possession of firearms in their state (the starting point of traveling) to travel through states that are not as friendly. This protection is only available under federal law to transport such firearms across state lines for lawful purposes, as long as they comply with the requirements of the Firearm Owners' Protection Act, 18 U.S.C. § 926A, nicknamed the "Safe Passage" provision. The first requirement to qualify for the Federal Safe Passage provision is that throughout the duration of the trip through the anti-firearm state, the firearm must be unloaded and locked in the trunk, or locked in a container that is out of reach or not readily accessible from the passenger compartment. The ammunition also must be locked in the trunk or a container. Note that for the storage of both firearms and ammunition, the glove box and center console compartment are specifically not allowed under the statute.

B. Safe Passage requires legal start to legal finish

To get protection under federal law, a gun owner's journey must start and end in states where the traveler's possession of the firearm is legal; for instance, a person traveling with their Glock 17 starting in Illinois and ending in Vermont. Even though a person must drive through New York or Massachusetts to get to Vermont, as long as the person qualifies under the Safe Passage provision then they may legally pass through. However, if the start point was Illinois and the end point was New York (a place where the handgun would be illegal), there is no protection under the federal law. Safe passage requires legal start and legal finish.

Although traveling across state lines naturally invokes federal law, it is important to remember that whenever a person finally completes their journey and reaches their destination state, the laws of that state control the possession, carrying, and use of the firearm. Federal law does not make it legal or provide any protection for possession of a firearm that is illegal under the laws of the destination state (*i.e.*, the end state of your travels).

C. What is the definition of "traveling" for Safe Passage provisions?

The final requirement for protection under the federal law is that individuals MUST be "traveling" while in the firearm hostile state. The legal definition of "traveling" is both murky and narrow. The Safe Passage provision protection has been held in courts to be limited to situations that strictly relate to traveling and nothing more. Traveling is a term that is not defined in the federal statute; however, it has received treatment in the courts that is indicative of what one can expect. Generally speaking, if a person stops somewhere for too long they cease to be traveling and, therefore, lose their protection under the Safe Passage provision. How long this time limit is has not been determined either statutorily or by case law with any definitiveness.

While stopping for gas or restroom breaks may not disqualify a person from the traveling protection, any stop for an activity not directly related to traveling could be considered a destination and thus you would lose the legal protection. For example, in Chicago anyone in the city for more than 24 hours is not considered to be traveling under local policy. In an actual case, stopping for a brief nap in a bank parking lot in New Jersey caused a Texan driving back home from Maine to lose the traveling protection. *See Reininger v. New Jersey*, No. 14-5486-BRM, 2018 WL 3617962 (D.N.J. July 30, 2018). He received 5 years in prison for possession of weapons that are illegal under New Jersey law. Of course, if the driver would have made it to Allentown, Pennsylvania, he would have been safe. The moral of the story is to travel through these gun-unfriendly States as fast as you can without breaking the speed limit, of course!

D. Protection under federal law does not mean protection from prosecution in unfriendly states

To make matters even worse for firearms travelers, even if a person qualifies for protection under the federal Safe Passage provision, New Jersey and New York seem quite proud to treat this protection as an affirmative defense. This means that someone can be arrested even though he or she met all of the requirements of the federal statute. Then, they would have to go to court to assert this defense. In other words, while a person could beat the rap, they will not beat the ride! This becomes even more troublesome in the instance of someone who is legally flying with their firearm, and then due to flight complications, must land in New Jersey or New York, as travelers in this position have been arrested or threatened with arrest. Once again, the Safe Passage provision only applies while a person is traveling; as soon as they arrive at their destination and cease their travels, the laws of that state control a person's actions. Remember:

check all applicable state and local firearms laws before you leave for your destination!

VI. AIR TRAVEL WITH A FIREARM

A. How do I legally travel with a firearm as a passenger on a commercial airline?

It is legal to travel with firearms on commercial airlines so long as the firearms transported are unloaded and in a locked, hard-sided container as checked baggage. Under federal law, the container must be completely inaccessible to passengers. Further, under U.S. Homeland Security rules, firearms, ammunition, and firearm parts, including firearm frames, receivers, clips, and magazines, are prohibited in carry-on baggage. Finally, "Realistic replicas of firearms are also prohibited in carry-on bags and must be packed in checked baggage. Rifle scopes are permitted in carry-on and checked bags."

1. Firearms must be inaccessible

Federal law makes it a crime subject to fine, imprisonment for up to 10 years, or both, if a person "when on, or attempting to get on, an aircraft in, or intended for operation in, air transportation or intrastate air transportation, has on or about the individual or the property of the individual a concealed dangerous weapon that is or would be accessible to the individual in flight." 49 U.S.C. § 46505(b). Additionally, under 49 U.S.C. § 46303(a) "[a]n individual who, when on, or attempting to board, an aircraft in, or intended for operation in, air transportation or intrastate air transportation, has on or about the individual or the property of the individual a concealed dangerous weapon that is or would be accessible to the individual in flight is liable to the United States Government for a civil penalty of not more than $10,000 for each violation."

2. Firearms must be checked in baggage

The following guidelines are provided by the TSA for traveling with firearms on airlines: You may transport unloaded firearms in a locked hard-sided container as checked baggage only. Declare the firearm and/or ammunition to the airline when checking your bag at the ticket counter. The container must completely secure the firearm from being accessed. Locked cases that can be easily opened are not permitted. Be aware that the container the firearm was in when purchased may not adequately secure the firearm when it is transported in checked baggage.

Firearms

- When traveling, comply with the laws concerning possession of firearms as they vary by local, state and international governments.
- If you are traveling internationally with a firearm in checked baggage, please check the U.S. Customs and Border Protection website for information and requirements prior to travel.
- Declare each firearm each time you present it for transport as checked baggage. Ask your airline about limitations or fees that may apply.
- Firearms must be unloaded and locked in a hard-sided container and transported as checked baggage only. As defined by 49 CFR 1540.5 a loaded firearm has a live round of ammunition, or any component thereof, in the chamber or cylinder or in a magazine inserted in the firearm. Only the passenger should retain the key or combination to the lock unless TSA personnel request the key to open the firearm container to ensure compliance with TSA regulations. You may use any brand or type of lock to secure your firearm case, including TSA-recognized locks.

- Firearm parts, including magazines, clips, bolts and firing pins, are prohibited in carry-on baggage, but may be transported in checked baggage.
- Replica firearms, including firearm replicas that are toys, may be transported in checked baggage only.
- Rifle scopes are permitted in carry-on and checked baggage.

[WARNING] United States Code, Title 18, Part 1, Chapter 44, firearm definitions includes: any weapon (including a starter gun) which will, or is designed to, or may readily be converted to expel a projectile by the action of an explosive; the frame or receiver of any such weapon; any firearm muffler or firearm silencer; and any destructive device. As defined by 49 CFR 1540.5 a loaded firearm has a live round of ammunition, or any component thereof, in the chamber or cylinder or in a magazine inserted in the firearm.

Ammunition
- Ammunition is prohibited in carry-on baggage, but may be transported in checked baggage.
- Firearm magazines and ammunition clips, whether loaded or empty, must be securely boxed or included within a hard-sided case containing an unloaded firearm. Read the requirements governing the transport of ammunition in checked baggage as defined by 49 CFR 175.10 (a)(8).
- Small arms ammunition, including ammunition not exceeding .75 caliber and shotgun shells of any gauge, may be carried in the same hard-sided case as the firearm.

Transportation Security Administration. (2019). Transporting Firearms and Ammunition. [online] Available at: https://www.tsa.gov/travel/transporting-firearms-and-ammunition [Accessed 10 JULY 2019].

B. May I have a firearm while operating or as a passenger in a private aircraft flying just in Illinois?

Generally, yes. For purposes of Illinois state law, a private aircraft is treated like any other motorized vehicle. For more information concerning how to transport firearms in vehicles (or private local aircraft), *see* our earlier discussion in this chapter under Sections II and III.

C. May I have a firearm in a private aircraft that takes off from Illinois and lands in another state?

In situations where a private aircraft is taking off from one state and landing in another, the law will simply view this as traveling interstate with firearms. Where no other statutes apply to the person's flight, the person will be subject to the provisions of 18 U.S.C. § 926A regarding the interstate transportation of a firearm: "any person who is not otherwise prohibited by this chapter from transporting, shipping, or receiving a firearm shall be entitled to transport a firearm for any lawful purpose from any place where he may lawfully possess and carry such firearm to any other place where he may lawfully possess and carry such firearm if, during such transportation the firearm is unloaded, and neither the firearm nor any ammunition being transported is readily accessible or is directly accessible from the passenger compartment of such transporting vehicle."

This statute allows a person to transport firearms between states subject to the following conditions: that the person can lawfully possess the firearm at his or her points of departure and arrival, and the firearm remains unloaded and inaccessible during the trip. However, what if the person is a CCL holder and wants to carry concealed between states? Fortunately, 18 U.S.C. § 927 states that

Section 926A does not preempt applicable state law. Thus, if a person can lawfully carry a weapon in the state in which he or she boards the aircraft and in the state in which he or she lands, the CCL holder is not subject to the unloaded and inaccessible restrictions of Section 926A, unless, of course, there are stops in more restrictive states.

For operations of private aircraft within one state, a person will only be subject to the laws of the state within which he or she is operating. The person will need to review their state's statutes to determine whether they impose any restrictions on possession of firearms within non-secure areas of airports. The person will also need to be familiar with the airports he or she will be visiting to determine whether each airport has any restrictions (*e.g.*, posting to prohibit concealed carry, *etc.*).

VII. UNDERSTANDING GUN-FREE SCHOOL ZONE LAWS

The discussion of gun-free school zones is one that covers many different areas of the law and affects both persons who hold a CCL and FOID card, as well as persons who do not. That is because the "Gun Free School Zone" law and its meaning cause a lot of confusion. Signs warning about being in a "gun free school zone" are common around schools, but what does this mean to people lawfully in possession of firearms? There are actually both Illinois and federal "gun free school zone" laws, each with very different meanings and consequences. For this reason, we will explain the applicable rules to individuals who possess and do not possess a CCL in this Chapter, although it has been dedicated to possessing or carrying a firearm with only a FOID card.

A. Illinois "School Zone" law: enhancement statute

The Illinois "School Zone" law is part of the Illinois Criminal Code at Sections 720 ILL. COMP. STAT. 5/24-1(c)(1), (1.5) and (2). These portions of the statute do not create any new crimes or make any rights under other statutes inapplicable, but they are what is legally known as enhancement penalties. This means that if a person is already committing a weapons crime in violation of Illinois law, and if it is shown at the trial of the defendant that the crime occurred within 1,000 feet of a school or a school function, then the range of punishment for that crime is increased.

Since CCL holders as well as other lawful individuals are allowed to carry concealed handguns in their motor vehicles under Illinois Concealed Carry Law in and near some of these locations, this law does not prohibit them from carrying a concealed weapon within 1,000 feet of the premises of a school while transporting the weapons. The state law only applies to people who are committing, or who have committed, a weapons crime near a school.

B. Federal "Gun Free School Zone" law: 18 U.S.C. § 922(q)

The text of the federal "Gun Free School Zone" law is found in 18 U.S.C. § 922(q), and, in contrast to Illinois law, creates its own independent criminal offense. This law states that it is a federal crime for a person to possess a firearm that has moved through interstate commerce (this includes virtually all firearms), on the grounds of or within 1,000 feet of a public, parochial, or private school. As surprising as it may seem, under this federal law, the mere possession of a firearm by the occupant of a motor vehicle while driving past a school or dropping off a child, is a federal crime.

However, federal law provides seven exceptions:

1. *Exception one*: if the possession is on private property which is not part of the school grounds. This means that a person living within 1,000 feet of a school can keep a firearm in their house.

2. *Exception two*: if the individual possessing the firearm is licensed to do so by the state in which the school zone is located or a political subdivision of the state, and the law of the state or political subdivision requires that, before an individual obtains such a license, the law enforcement authorities of the state or political subdivision verify that the individual is qualified under law to receive the license. This means that a CCL holder may transport a concealed firearm into a gun free school zone and keep it in the vehicle. However, there is one important note about the statute: a person can only lawfully carry in a school zone located in the state that issued the firearms license. Therefore, if a person has an Illinois CCL they can only carry through Illinois school zones. If that Illinois CCL holder is traveling through another state, the exception under federal law does not apply to them, and they are in violation of this law. It also means that an Illinois resident, who holds a non-resident non-Illinois concealed carry license or permit, does not benefit from this exception and is in violation of the law if they take a firearm into a school zone.

3. *Exception three*: if the firearm is not loaded, and is in a locked container, or a locked firearms rack that is on a motor vehicle. This means that if a firearm is unloaded and carried in a locked case, or other type of locked container, such as a glove box or trunk, there is no violation of the federal law.

4. *Exception four*: if the firearm is carried by an individual for use in a program approved by a school in the school zone. This exception covers school-sponsored shooting activities, such as an ROTC program.

5. *Exception five*: if the firearm is carried by an individual in accordance with a contract entered into between a school in the school zone and the individual or an employer of the individual. This means that school security guards can carry firearms while on the job.
6. *Exception six*: if the firearm is carried by a law enforcement officer acting in his or her official capacity. This exception covers police officers while on-duty only. It does not appear to cover them while they are off-duty, even if they are required by state law to carry while off-duty.
7. *Exception seven*: if the firearm is unloaded and is in the possession of an individual while traversing school property for the purpose of gaining access to public or private lands open to hunting, if the entry on school premises is authorized by school authorities. This means that if a hunter must cross school property to get to a lawful hunting ground, they must have the permission of the school, and the firearm must be unloaded.

Keep in mind that Illinois law prohibits the possession of a firearm in "[a]ny area where firearms are prohibited under federal law." 430 ILL. COMP. STAT. 66/65(a)(23).

C. Reconciling Illinois and federal laws on gun-free school zones

The law puts a vast number of unknowing and unsuspecting people in conflict with federal law while perhaps being in full compliance with state law. As a result, it is likely that this law is violated thousands of times a day. However, while this has been federal law since 1996 and its predecessor was the law since 1990, there does not appear to be a wave of federal prosecutions for the mere possession of a firearm by a person who is only driving through a school zone or picking up or dropping off their child. Nevertheless, even though it appears that the Feds are not inclined to enforce some of the provisions of this statute today, the law is on the books right now.

D. "School Marshals:" teachers with guns

A teacher or administrator is not permitted to possess a handgun inside a school building or school.

E. Is a person legally permitted to possess a firearm in their vehicle in the parking lot of a college or university?

Yes, all individuals with a CCL may possess a firearm in a vehicle the person owns or is under their control in a college or university parking lot provided they comply with any rules or regulations that may have been created by that college or university. Under Illinois law, colleges and universities may also pass their own rules and regulations to prevent employees, visitors, and students from having firearms in their cars. The CCL statute in pertinent part reads as follows:

(a-5) Nothing in this Act shall prohibit a public or private community college, college, or university from:

(1) prohibiting persons from carrying a firearm within a vehicle owned, leased, or controlled by the college or university;

(2) developing resolutions, regulations, or policies regarding student, employee, or visitor misconduct and discipline, including suspension and expulsion;

(3) developing resolutions, regulations, or policies regarding the storage or maintenance of firearms, which must include designated areas where persons can park vehicles that carry firearms; and

(4) permitting the carrying or use of firearms for the purpose of instruction and curriculum of officially recognized programs, including but not limited to military science and law enforcement training programs, or in any designated area used for hunting purposes or target shooting.

430 ILL. COMP. STAT. 66/65.

CHAPTER ELEVEN

RESTORATION OF FIREARMS RIGHTS: THE LAW OF PARDONS AND EXPUNGEMENTS

I. IS IT POSSIBLE TO RESTORE A PERSON'S RIGHT TO BEAR ARMS?

What happens after a person has been convicted of a crime, is it possible to later clear their name and/or criminal record? If possible, then what is the process for removing a conviction and restoring a person's right to purchase and possess firearms? This chapter will explain how a person under very limited circumstances can have arrest records, criminal charges, and even criminal convictions removed or nullified. But a word of caution, success in this arena may be rare. Further, each state has different rules concerning these issues, as well as a completely different set of rules under federal law. Before we begin a meaningful discussion, it is important to explain two terms and concepts: clemency and expungement.

A. What is clemency?

Clemency is the action the government, usually the chief executive (*e.g.*, the President on the federal level or a governor on the state level), takes in forgiving or pardoning a crime or canceling the penalty of a crime, either wholly, or in part. Clemency can include: full pardons after a conviction; full pardons after completion of deferred adjudication community supervision; conditional pardons; pardons based on innocence; commutations of a sentence; emergency medical reprieves; and family medical reprieves. Clemency can be granted for federal crimes at the federal level; and state crimes at the state level.

B. What is an expungement?

An expungement is the physical act of destroying or purging government criminal records, unlike sealing which is simply hiding the records from the public. Under certain circumstances, a person may have their criminal record either expunged or sealed.

PRACTICAL LEGAL TIP

While our intention is to provide you with as much information as possible as to how you can have your firearms rights restored if you are convicted of a crime, it's also important to make sure you are aware of how rarely pardons, expungements, and restorations of firearms rights are granted. While it's certainly worth the effort to apply for a pardon (in the event you receive one), be careful not to get your hopes up, because they are seldom granted. –Michael

II. FEDERAL LAW

A. Presidential pardon

Under Article II, Section 2 of the United States Constitution, the President of the United States has the power "to grant reprieves and pardons for offenses against the United States, except in cases of impeachment." The President's power to pardon offenses has also been interpreted to include the power to grant conditional pardons, commutations of sentence, conditional commutations of sentence, remission of fines and forfeitures, respites, and amnesties. However, the President's clemency authority only extends to federal offenses; the President cannot grant clemency for a state crime.

1. How does a person petition for federal clemency or a pardon?

Under federal law, a person requesting executive clemency must petition the President of the United States and submit the petition to the Office of the Pardon Attorney in the Department of Justice. The Office of the Pardon Attorney can provide petitions and other required forms necessary to complete the application for clemency. *See* 28 CFR § 1.1. Petition forms for commutation of sentence may also be obtained from the wardens of federal penal institutions. In addition, a petitioner applying for executive clemency with respect to military offenses should submit his or her petition directly to the Secretary of the military branch that had original jurisdiction over the court-martial trial and conviction of the petitioner.

The Code of Federal Regulations requires an applicant to wait five years after the date of the release of the petitioner from confinement, or in a case where no prison sentence was imposed, an applicant is required to wait five years after the date of conviction prior to submitting a petition for clemency. The regulation further states that "generally, no petition should be submitted by a person who is on probation, parole, or supervised release." 28 CFR § 1.2. With that in mind, the President can grant clemency at any time, whether an individual has made a formal petition or not. For example, President Gerald Ford granted a full and unconditional pardon to former President Richard Nixon prior to any indictment or charges being filed related to his involvement in Watergate.

2. What should a petition for clemency include?

Petitions for executive clemency should include the information required in the form prescribed by the United States Attorney General. This includes information:

(1) that the person requesting clemency must state specifically the purpose for which clemency is sought, as well as attach any and all relevant documentary evidence that will support how clemency will support that purpose;

(2) that discloses any arrests or convictions subsequent to the federal crime for which clemency is sought;

(3) that discloses all delinquent credit obligations (whether disputed or not), all civil lawsuits to which the applicant is a party (whether plaintiff or defendant), and all unpaid tax obligations (whether local, state, or federal); and

(4) that includes three character affidavits from persons not related to the applicant by blood or marriage.

In addition, acceptance of a Presidential pardon generally carries with it an admission of guilt. For that reason, a petitioner should include in his or her petition a statement of the petitioner's acceptance of responsibility, an expression of remorse, and atonement for the offense. All of the requirements are contained in 28 CFR §§ 1.1-1.11.

3. What happens after a petition for executive clemency is submitted?

All petitions for federal clemency are reviewed by the Office of the Pardon Attorney in the Department of Justice. A non-binding recommendation on an application is made to the President. Federal regulations also provide for guidelines and requirements to notify victims of the crimes, if any, for which clemency is sought. The President will either grant or deny a pardon. There are no hearings held on the petition, and there is no appeal of the President's decision.

4. What is the effect of a Presidential pardon?

A pardon is the forgiveness of a crime and the cancellation of the penalty associated with that crime. While a Presidential pardon will restore various rights lost as a result of the pardoned offense, it will not expunge the record of your conviction. This means that even if a person is granted a pardon, the person must still disclose their conviction on any form where such information is required, although the person may also disclose the fact that the offense for which they were convicted was pardoned.

B. Expungement of federal convictions

1. No law exists for general federal expungement

Congress has not provided federal legislation that offers any comprehensive authority or procedure for expunging criminal offenses. There exist only statutes that allow expungement in certain cases for possession of small amounts of controlled substances and, interestingly, a procedure to expunge DNA samples of certain members of the military who were wrongfully convicted. Because there is no statutory guidance, federal courts have literally made up the rules and procedures themselves, often coming to different conclusions. Some federal court circuits have stated they have no power to expunge records. However, other federal courts have indicated that they do have the power to expunge. The Supreme Court has passed on hearing cases that would have resolved the split between the circuits. This issue remains legally murky.

2. Possible procedure for federal expungement

There are no statutory guidelines for how to seek an expungement under federal law, however, the place to start would be to file a motion with the federal court that issued the conviction, which a person wants to have expunged. However, federal judges very rarely grant these types of motions. The court weighs the interests of the government in keeping open, unredacted records, against the injury to the individual of maintaining a criminal record. Some of the areas where expungement has worked are in incidents of extreme police misconduct, or where the conviction is being misused against the person. Unless there exist compelling reasons, a federal judge is highly unlikely to grant expungement.

3. Expungement for drug possession: statutory authority

Under a federal law entitled "Special probation and expungement procedures for drug possessors," certain persons are allowed to request a federal court to issue an expungement order from all public records. 18 U.S.C. § 3607. Congress intended this order to restore the person to the status he or she "occupied before such arrest or institution of criminal proceedings." 18 U.S.C. § 3607(c).

In order to qualify for the expungement, you must have been under the age of 21 when you were convicted, you must have no prior drug offenses, and your conviction must have been for simple possession of a small amount of a controlled substance.

4. How does a person have firearms rights restored under federal law?

Under the Gun Control Act of 1968, a person who has received a Presidential pardon is not considered convicted of a crime preventing the purchase and possession of firearms subject to all other federal laws. *See* 18 U.S.C. §§ 921(a)(20)(B) and (a)(33)(B)(ii). In addition, persons who had a conviction expunged or set aside, or who have had their civil rights restored are not considered to have been convicted for purposes of the GCA "unless the pardon, expungement, or restoration of civil rights expressly provides the person may not ship, transport, possess, or receive firearms." 18 U.S.C. §§ 921(a)(20)(B) and (a)(33)(B)(ii).

The GCA also provides the United States Attorney General with the authority to grant relief from firearms disabilities where the Attorney General determines that the person is not likely to act in a manner dangerous to the public safety and where granting relief would not be contrary to the public interest. 18 U.S.C. § 925(c). The Attorney General has delegated this authority to the ATF. Unfortunately, the ATF reports that it has been prohibited from spending any funds in order to investigate or act upon applications from individuals seeking relief from federal firearms disabilities. This means that until the ATF's prohibition has been lifted, a person's best—and most likely—option to have their firearms rights restored is through a Presidential pardon. *See* www.atf.gov.

III. ILLINOIS LAW

A. Clemency by Governor and Prisoner Review Board

The Governor of Illinois possesses the authority to grant executive clemency; the Illinois Constitution provides that, "The Governor may grant reprieves, commutations and pardons, after conviction, for all offenses on such terms as he thinks proper. The manner of applying therefore may be regulated by law." Pursuant to Section 730 ILL. COMP. STAT. 5/3-3-13, the specifics are articulated as to the procedure for executive clemency.

(a) Petitions seeking pardon, commutation, or reprieve shall be addressed to the Governor and filed with the Prison Review Board. The petition shall be in writing and signed by the person under conviction or by a person on his behalf. It shall contain a brief history of the case, the reason for seeking executive clemency, and other relevant information the Board may require.

(a-5) After a petition has been denied by the Governor, the Board may not accept a repeat petition for executive clemency for the same person until one full year has elapsed from the date of the denial. The Chairman of the Board may waive the one year requirement if the petitioner offers, in writing, new information that was unavailable to the petitioner at the time of the filing of the prior petition and which the Chairman determines to be significant. The Chairman also may waive the one-year waiting period if the petitioner can show that a change in circumstances of a compelling humanitarian nature has arisen since the denial of the prior petition.

(b) Notice of the proposed application shall be given by the Board to the committing court and state's attorney of the county where the conviction was had.

(b-5) Victims registered with the Board shall receive reasonable written notice not less than 30 days prior to the executive clemency hearing date. The victim has the right to submit a victim statement to the Prison Review Board for consideration at an executive clemency hearing as provided in subsection (c) of this Section. Victim statements provided to the Board shall be confidential and privileged, including any statements received prior to the effective date of this amendatory Act of the 101st General Assembly, except if the statement was an oral statement made by the victim at a hearing open to the public.

(c) The Board shall, upon due notice, give a hearing to each application, allowing representation by counsel, if desired, after which it shall confidentially advise the Governor by a written report of its recommendations, which shall be determined by majority vote. The written report to the Governor shall be confidential and privileged, including any reports made prior to the effect of this amendatory Act of the 101st General Assembly. The Board shall meet to consider such petitions no less than 4 times each year. Application for executive clemency under this section may not be commenced on behalf of a person who has been sentenced to death without the written consent of the defendant, unless the defendant, because of a mental or physical condition, is incapable of asserting his or her own claim.

(d) The Governor shall decide each application and communicate his decision to the Board, which shall notify the petitioner. In the event a petitioner who has been convicted of a Class X felony is granted a release, after the Governor has communicated such decision to the Board, the Board shall give written notice to the sheriff of the county from which the offender was sentenced if such sheriff has requested that such notice be given on a continuing basis. In cases where arrest of the offender or commission of the offense took place in any municipality with a population of more than 10,000 persons, the Board shall also give written notice to the proper law enforcement agency for said municipality which has requested notice on a continuing basis.

(e) Nothing in this Section shall be construed to limit the power of the Governor under the constitution to grant a reprieve, commutation of sentence, or pardon.

The difference between a pardon, reprieve, and commutation in Illinois should be understood. A pardon is an "act of grace" by the Governor that nullifies the legal consequence of a criminal conviction. There are two types of pardons, conditional and unconditional. An unconditional pardon immediately restores all the rights and privileges lost because of the conviction, while a conditional pardon imposes one or more terms (conditions) that must occur before the pardon is effective. A commutation occurs when the Governor only reduces the judicially imposed sentence of a person convicted of a crime. Reprieves are a temporary relief from, or a postponement of, a judicially imposed punishment. They usually occur in the context of the death penalty and are typically granted in such cases to give the Governor more time to review a case and decide whether to grant a pardon or commutation.

The Governor's executive clemency powers are virtually unlimited. The phrase "on such terms as he deems proper" gives the Governor broad discretion. Illinois courts have consistently held that the Governor's power is absolute and not subject to limitation by courts or the General Assembly. The only limitation imposed by the Illinois Constitution is the requirement that the General Assembly may establish (or modify) a procedure for applying.

B. Expunging and sealing in Illinois

In Illinois, certain arrests and convictions can be expunged from your record as though they never existed. In some instances, although you cannot expunge the arrest or conviction, you can request they be sealed, which would limit the availability of these records to the general public.

We will first discuss the expungement process and which cases are eligible, as well as waiting times to get an expungement order.

You can immediately apply for expungement of the cases on your record that meet the following criteria:

(a) you were released without charging (including for a minor traffic offense), you were acquitted, and/or your case(s) were dismissed. Some examples: finding of not guilty, or a "SOL" (stricken off with leave to reinstate), finding of no probable cause, or *nolle prosequi*;

(b) your conviction(s) were vacated or reversed; or

(c) you were granted an executive pardon from the Governor.

Certain cases require a waiting period before the expungement can be granted. The following are the rules regarding these cases.

You can apply for expungement of your cases on your criminal record five years after completion of supervision if:

(a) there are no supervisions on your record for a sexual offense against a child, driving under the influence or reckless driving; and

(b) your record consists of supervision for one of the following:
   (1) domestic battery;
   (2) criminal sexual abuse supervision;
   (3) retail theft (if committed before 12/3/2011);

(4) operation of uninsured motor vehicle supervision;

(5) operation of motor vehicle when registration suspended for non-insurance;

(6) display of false insurance card; or

(7) scrap processors to keep records. *See* 20 ILL. COMP. STAT. 2630/5.2(b)(2)(B).

There is a two-year waiting period for successful completion of supervision for offenses that are not listed above. *See* 20 ILL. COMP. STAT. 2630/5.2(b)(2)(B).

You can apply for expungement of cases on your criminal record five years after successful completion of probation for the following if:

(1) there are no supervisions on your record for a sexual offense against a child, driving under the influence or reckless driving; and

(2) your record consists of:

    (a) Section 10, Cannabis Control Act probation;

    (b) Section 410, Illinois Controlled Substance Act probation;

    (c) Section 70, Methamphetamine Control and Community Protection Act probation;

    (d) Section 40-10, Alcoholism and Other Drug Use Dependency Act probation;

    (e) Section 10 Steroid Control Act probation; and

    (f) Section 5-6-3.4 of the Unified Code of Corrections, Second Chance probation.

We will now review the procedures to have your arrest or conviction sealed in Illinois. There is no waiting period to apply for sealing of your cases if the following criteria are met:

(1) you were released without charging, you were acquitted, or your case(s) were dismissed; or

(2) your conviction(s) were vacated or reversed.

There would be a two-year waiting period for the following, unless sealed upon termination of the last sentence imposed:

(1) a sexual offense committed against a minor;

(2) an offense under Section 11-501 of the Illinois Vehicle Code;

(3) an offense under Section 11-503 of the Illinois Vehicle Code;

(4) an offense included in Article 11 of the Criminal Code of 2012;

(5) an offense under Section 11-1.50 (criminal sexual abuse);

(6) an offense under Section 125 of the Stalking No Contact Order Act;

(7) an offense which is a Class A misdemeanor under the Humane Care for Animals Act; or

(8) any offense or attempted offense that would subject the person to registration under the Sex Offender Registration Act.

If you have misdemeanor supervisions for cases that are not in the above list, then those cases qualify for sealing when two years have elapsed since the termination of the last sentence on your record, unless the court finds that you qualify for sealing upon the termination of the last sentence. The cases that qualify for sealing may be sealed upon termination of the last sentence if you earned a high school diploma, associate's degree, career certificate, vocational technical certification, bachelor's degree, or passed the high school level test of General Educational Development, during the period of sentence, after release, or mandatory supervised release. If the petition for sealing upon termination of the last sentence is denied by the court, the two-year waiting period should apply to any subsequent petitions for sealing.

If you received a conviction (not supervision) the following rules apply regarding sealing of the records.

There is a three year waiting period if you received a misdemeanor conviction for any of the following offenses:

(1) a sexual offense committed against a minor;

(2) an offense under 11-501 of the Illinois Vehicle Code (driving under the influence of alcohol, other drug, or drugs) or a similar provision of a local ordinance;

(3) an offense under Section 11-503 of the Illinois Vehicle Code (reckless driving; aggravated reckless driving) or a similar provision of a local ordinance;

(4) an offense included in Article 11 of the Criminal Code of 2012 (sexual offenses) or a similar provision of a local ordinance;

(5) an offense under Sections 11-1.50 (criminal sexual abuse), 12-3.1 (battery of an unborn child/aggravated battery of an unborn child), 12-3.2 (domestic battery), 12-3.4 (violation of an order of protection), or 48-1 (dog fighting) of the Criminal Code of 2012 or a similar provision of a local ordinance;

(6) an offense under Section 125 of the Stalking No Contact Order Act, or Section 219 of the Civil No Contact Order Act, or a similar provision of a local ordinance;

(7) an offense which is a Class A misdemeanor under the Humane Care for Animals Act; or

(8) any offense attempted that would subject the person to registration under the Sex Offender Registration Act.

If the answer is "yes" to any of the above-listed, those cases do not qualify for sealing even after the three-year waiting period has elapsed.

If you received probation for any of the following, there is a three-year waiting period to apply for the case to be sealed:

(1) Section 10, of the Cannabis Control Act;
(2) Section 410, Illinois Controlled Substances Act;
(3) Section 70, Methamphetamine Control and Community Protection Act; or
(4) Section 5-6-3.3 of the Unified Code of Corrections.

If you received probation for any of the above, you qualify for sealing when three years have elapsed since the termination of the last sentence on your record, unless the court finds you qualify for sealing upon termination of the last sentence.

In Illinois, certain felony convictions can also be sealed. After a three-year waiting period, the following Class 4 convictions can be sealed:

(1) Section 11-14 of the Criminal Code of 2012 (prostitution);
(2) Section 4 of the Cannabis Control Act of 2012 (possession prohibited). Note: with the legalization of recreational marijuana, beginning January 1, 2020, all of these convictions will be automatically expunged from your record;
(3) Section 402 of the Illinois Controlled Substances Act (possession of a controlled or counterfeit substance);
(4) the Methamphetamine Precursor Control Act;
(5) the Steroid Control Act;

(6) theft under Section 16-1 of the Criminal Code of 2012;

(7) retail theft under paragraph (a) of Section 16-25 of the Criminal Code of 2012;

(8) deceptive practices under Section 17-1 of the Criminal Code of 2012;

(9) forgery under Section 17-3 of the Criminal Code of 2012; and

(10) possession of burglary tools under Section 19-2 of the Criminal Code of 2012.

If your conviction is listed above, it qualifies for sealing when three years have elapsed since the termination of the last sentence on your record.

The following is a list of the more serious Class 3 felony convictions that can be sealed:

(1) theft under Section 16-1 of the Criminal Code of 2012;

(2) retail theft under Section 16A-3 or paragraph (a) of Section 16-25 of the Criminal Code of 1961 or 2012;

(3) deceptive practices under Section 17-1 of the Criminal Code of 2012;

(4) forgery under Section 17-3 of the Criminal Code of 1961 or 2012; and

(5) possession with intent to manufacture or deliver a controlled Substance under Section 401 of the Illinois Controlled Substances Act.

If your conviction is listed above, then you can qualify to have the conviction sealed after the three years have elapsed since the termination of the last sentence.

Finally, it must be understood that in any petitions to expunge or seal, an objection can be made by the prosecutor, arresting agency, chief legal officer of the unit of local government that arrested you, or Illinois State Police. The objection must be filed by the above-listed entities within 60 days after they receive a copy of your petition. Objections must be in writing and must state with specificity the nature of the objection. An objection is not the same as a denial; only a judge can deny the petition. If an objection is filed, the petitioner would receive notice in the mail from the clerk's office containing the court hearing date. At this hearing, the parties would be in the courtroom with the judge, who would hear the evidence from both the petitioner and any objector and decide whether the petition should be granted or denied.

➢ CHAPTER TWELVE ◄

I'M BEING SUED FOR WHAT?
CIVIL LIABILITY
If You Have Used Your Gun

I. WHAT DOES IT MEAN TO BE SUED?

The term "lawsuit" refers to one party's assertion in a written filing with a court that another party has violated the law. In the context of firearms, typically the party suing has been injured and wants a ruling or judgment from the court stating that the party was injured and entitling the party to money.

A. What is a civil claim or lawsuit?

A civil "lawsuit" or "suit" refers to the actual filing of written paperwork with a court (1) asserting that another party violated the law, and (2) seeking some type of redress. A "claim" can exist without the filing of a lawsuit. A claim is simply the belief or assertion that another party has violated the law. Many parties have claims they never assert, or sometimes parties informally assert the claim in hopes of resolving the disputes without the filing of a lawsuit. Also, another term commonly used is "tort" or "tort claim." A tort is a civil claim arising out of a wrongful act, not including a breach of contract or trust that results in injury to another's person, property, reputation, or the like. The claims described below are all tort claims.

B. Difference between "civil claims" and "criminal charges"

To start with the basics, there are two different aspects of the legal system that gun owners may face after the use of a firearm: criminal and civil. There are several names and descriptive terms used for each (*e.g.*, civil lawsuit, criminal actions, civil claims, criminal proceedings, *etc.*), but regardless of the terms, the same breakdown applies; most cases are either criminal or civil. There is another subgroup of proceedings called administrative actions. Those actions are not covered by this chapter but can sometimes impact CCL holders. For example, appealing the denial, supervision, or revocation of a CCL is an administrative act. (*See* Chapters 8 and 9 for more information).

With that said, the three primary differences between a criminal action and a civil proceeding are:
1) who or what is bringing the action or lawsuit;
2) what are they seeking; and
3) what is the burden of proof?

These differences are fairly straightforward.

1. State versus individual bringing claims

In a criminal case, the party bringing the action is the "sovereign," meaning the United States, state, municipality, county, *etc.*, that believes a person violated their laws. Even if an individual calls the police, fills out a criminal complaint, or even asks the district attorney to file charges, the party that actually brings a criminal action is the state, county, *etc.*, not the individual.

However, a civil action may be filed by any individual, business, or other entity (partnership, LLC, trust, *etc.*). The entity bringing the claim is called the "plaintiff." Even governmental entities can bring civil claims; *i.e.*, if you negligently shoot a county propane tank causing a fire, the county can sue you civilly for those damages. The typical gun case, though, will involve an individual filing a lawsuit against another individual for damages caused by the firearm. If the incident occurs at a place of business, the plaintiff may also sue the business claiming that it is in some way at fault for the incident. The party being sued is typically called the "defendant."

2. Relief sought/awarded

In a criminal case, the entity prosecuting the case is usually seeking to imprison or fine you. Most crimes are punishable by "X" number of days/months/years in prison or jail, and a fine not to exceed "X" amount of dollars.

By contrast, the plaintiff in the civil case is almost always seeking a monetary award. Several other types of relief are available (declaratory, injunctive, specific performance), but for the most part, gun cases will involve the plaintiff seeking monetary damages.

3. Burden of proof

In a criminal case, the amount of evidence to convict is "beyond a reasonable doubt." In civil cases, however, a plaintiff must prove a person is liable for damages by a "preponderance of the evidence" standard. A preponderance of the evidence is a much lower standard than the criminal standard of beyond a reasonable doubt. It generally means that the party with the greater weight of credible evidence wins that issue. The preponderance of the evidence has been described as more than half, that is, if the evidence demonstrates that something more likely occurred than not, this meets the burden of proof. Whereas in a criminal case, if there exists any "reasonable doubt," the burden of proof is not met. It does not mean the party with the most exhibits or greater number of witnesses will prevail. One highly credible witness can prevail over the testimony of a dozen biased, shady witnesses.

EXAMPLE:

John mistakes a utility meter reader for a burglar due to his disheveled appearance, tool bag, and because he looks to be snooping around John's house. John fires a shot without warning and injures the meter reader.

Possible criminal liability: the State of Illinois could bring criminal charges against John for a number of crimes (aggravated assault, attempted murder, reckless discharge of a firearm, and so forth). The State would be seeking to imprison and/or fine John for his conduct, and it would be required to prove that John committed the crime at issue "beyond a reasonable doubt."

Possible civil liability: the meter reader could also file a civil lawsuit against John alleging that John was negligent or committed the tort of assault. The meter reader would seek monetary damages and be required to prove his claims by a "preponderance of the evidence."

C. Impact of result in one court upon the other
1. Can a result in a criminal trial be used in a civil trial?

Yes, because of the legal doctrines of *res judicata* and collateral estoppel. These two legal doctrines govern the impact of a ruling or judgment in one case, upon a separate case involving the same set of facts and circumstances. For the present discussion, if a person is found guilty of a crime in a criminal proceeding, because that court uses a higher standard of "beyond a reasonable doubt" than the civil requirement of "preponderance of the evidence," the finding of the criminal court may be used for purposes of establishing civil liability. Entire chapters in law books have been written on these topics, so, suffice to say, this section is a brief overview of these laws.

The criminal concept of *nolo contendere* or "no contest" often generates confusion in this area. In a criminal case, a plea of *nolo contendere* or no contest means that the defendant does not admit guilt. The plea, however, still results in a judgment that the defendant is guilty of the crime and that judgment can be used to help establish the defendant's liability in a separate civil case.

EXAMPLE:

Patrick and Joseph are at a BBQ, when they start arguing about which team is better, the Bears or the Packers. Patrick shoots Joseph for supporting the wrong team. Not only is Patrick charged and convicted of aggravated assault, Joseph sues him because of his injuries.

Joseph's lawsuit against Patrick, for medical bills, physical impairment, pain, and suffering is a civil action. Joseph will very likely be allowed to use the finding of Patrick's guilt in the criminal case (because it used the higher standard of beyond a reasonable doubt) to help establish his burden in the civil case (the lower preponderance of the evidence standard) that Patrick owes him monetary damages. This is an example of collateral estoppel; Patrick will not be permitted to re-litigate his guilt in the civil case.

Both doctrines are based on the concept that a party to a legal proceeding should not be able to endlessly litigate issues that have already been decided by the legal system. At its most basic level, it means that a party to a legal proceeding who receives a final ruling on a particular issue, win or lose, cannot attempt to have another trial court or even the same court decide the same issue.

Note about appeals: this is a different concept than an appeal, or asking the court in the first proceeding to reconsider its ruling, or grant a new trial. An appeal is a request to a higher court to review the decision of a lower court. Likewise, in any given case, the parties will have numerous opportunities to ask the current court to reconsider its rulings, or even ask for a new trial after a trial is completed. Collateral estoppel and *res judicata* come into play after a final judgment that is no longer subject to appeal or revision by the trial court.

EXAMPLE:

Emily is sued for accidentally shooting Nancy. Nancy wins a judgment of $350 against Emily, much less than Nancy believed she was damaged.

In that case, Nancy can appeal the decision, or even ask the trial court for a new trial. However, Nancy cannot file another, or new, lawsuit regarding the same incident and attempt to recover more in the second case because of the doctrine of *res judicata*. In order for the doctrine to apply, the parties, facts, circumstances, and issues must be the same.

EXAMPLE:

Enrique fires his hunting rifle from his deer blind, hitting Phillip with one round. Phillip files a civil suit against Enrique and loses at trial. The court awards Phillip no damages. Phillip appeals and loses the appeal also.

Phillip is legally barred from recovering in another lawsuit against Enrique involving the same incident. However, Phillip is not barred from filing suit against Enrique for damages arising out of another set of facts and circumstances, for example, if the two are involved in a car wreck on a different day.

2. Civil case result impact on criminal case

Suppose you lose a civil suit and a judgment is entered against you arising out of a shooting incident. Can that judgment be used to establish that you committed a crime? No. The burden of proof is much higher in the criminal context than the civil case. The plaintiff proved his civil case by a "preponderance of the evidence." This does not mean that he proved his case "beyond a reasonable doubt," meaning a separate criminal trial is required to make that determination.

The one area where a civil case can impact a criminal case is the potential overlapping use of evidence and testimony. Your admission in one case can almost always be used against you in another case. Meaning, your sworn testimony in the civil case ("yes, I shot the guy") can almost always be used against you in the criminal case, and vice versa.

II. WHAT MIGHT YOU BE SUED FOR? GUN-RELATED CLAIMS IN CIVIL COURTS

A. Liability for unintentional discharge

This section deals with accidental or unintentional discharges of your firearm. Common unintentional discharges are associated with hunting and cleaning accidents or the mishandling of a weapon. Intentional shootings are addressed in the following section.

With that said, the following are the types of civil claims that may be asserted in connection with an unintentional discharge.

1. Negligence/gross negligence

Most civil cases for damages resulting from an accidental discharge will include a negligence or gross negligence claim. What does this mean and what does a plaintiff have to prove before they can win? Under Illinois law, negligence is defined as the failure to do something which a reasonably careful person would do, or the doing of something which a reasonably careful person would not do, under similar circumstances. This is an "objective standard," meaning, the test is not whether you believed you acted carefully, but whether the judge or jury believes you acted as a reasonably careful person would have acted. Of course, this is the definition of negligence in the civil context. There is actually a different definition of criminal negligence, which is beyond the scope of this book's discussion.

What is "gross negligence" and how is it different than "regular" negligence? Many gun cases will include a claim for gross negligence by the plaintiff. The primary reason for this is that if a plaintiff establishes gross negligence by a defendant, the plaintiff may be entitled to additional types of damages or amounts of money that are legally not available if mere negligence is established. In Illinois gross negligence means recklessness or "a course of action which shows an utter indifference to or a conscious disregard for a person's own safety and the safety of others." *Resolution Trust Corp. v. Franz,* 909 F. Supp 1128 (N.D. Ill. 1995).

The defendant's state of mind is also a key difference between negligence and gross negligence. Negligence involves an objective standard—how would a reasonable person have acted? Gross negligence applies a subjective component—was this particular person actually aware of the risk involved?

EXAMPLE:

Caitlyn has practiced her shooting at a private range on her country property for 20 years, without incident. She shoots towards an area where she has never seen another person, and she believes the range of her guns cannot reach her property line. One day, a neighbor is hit by a shot as he is strolling through the woods just off of Caitlyn's property.

Caitlyn might be liable for negligence if a jury determines, for example, that a reasonably careful person would have acted differently, tested the range of her guns, or built a different type of backstop or berm, *etc.* However, Caitlyn did not subjectively show an utter indifference to or a conscious disregard for her own safety or the safety of others, so there would be no evidence of gross negligence. However, change Caitlyn's awareness and it changes the result.

> **EXAMPLE:**
>
> Caitlyn has received several complaints over the years about bullets leaving her property and hitting her neighbor's property. Nevertheless, she ignores the complaints and continues practicing in the direction that she typically shoots. One day while practicing, her bullet leaves her property and hits her neighbor. Caitlyn is later sued by the neighbor for gross negligence.

In this example, Caitlyn may very well be liable for gross negligence because she subjectively showed an utter indifference to or conscious disregard to the safety of others by allowing her shots to reach the neighbor's property when there were people in the same area (*i.e.*, the folks who reported the shots), and she continued to shoot without changing direction or building a backstop or berm and someone was injured as a result.

2. Negligent entrustment of a firearm

Illinos recognizes a claim for negligent entrustment of a firearm. "The action consists of entrusting a dangerous article to another whom the lender knows, or should know, is likely to use it in a manner involving an unreasonable risk of harm to others. It is negligent to permit a third person to use a thing or to engage in an activity which is under the control of the actor, if the actor knows or should know that such person intends or is likely to use the thing or to conduct himself in the activity in such a manner as to create an unreasonable risk of harm to others." *Teter v. Clemens*, 492 N.E.2d 1340 (Ill. 1986).

Stephen lets his adult grandson Gene borrow a shotgun to take on a fishing trip because he knows there are water moccasins in the spot where they plan to fish. Gene has never been in trouble with the law, has repeatedly been trained in firearms safety, and has never had an incident with a gun. However, while on the trip, Gene accidentally shoots a fellow fishing buddy with Stephen's shotgun. The fishing buddy, now turned plaintiff, sues Gene for negligence and Stephen for negligent entrustment of a firearm.

Can the plaintiff win his claim for negligent entrustment? Probably not. Stephen might get sued for giving the shotgun to his grandson, but the facts described do not establish negligent entrustment under Illinois law. Stephen should prevail in any lawsuit. There are no facts showing Stephen's knowledge that Gene was likely to use the shotgun in a manner involving an unreasonable risk of harm to others. Thus, the negligent entrustment claim would legally fail.

3. Is negligent storage of a firearm recognized in Illinois?

Illinois prohibits any person from storing or leaving his or her firearm unlocked and accessible to a minor under the age of 14 if that person knows or has reason to believe that the minor under the age of 14 who does not have a Firearm Owner's Identification Card ("FOID") is likely to gain access to the firearm and the minor causes death or great bodily harm with that firearm. 720 ILL. COMP. STAT. 5/24-9(a).

This provision does not apply if the firearm is: 1) secured by a device, other than the firearm safety, designed to render the firearm temporarily inoperable; 2) placed in a securely locked box or container; and 3) placed in some other location that a reasonable person would believe to be secured from the minor under the age of 14. The prohibition also is inapplicable to any firearm obtained by the minor because of an unlawful entry of the premises by the minor or another person, or if the minor gains access to a firearm and uses it in a lawful act of self-defense or defense of another. 720 ILL. COMP. STAT. 5/24-9(c).

B. Intentional discharge: a person intended to shoot

1. Negligence/gross negligence

Just because you intend to shoot someone, or otherwise "use" your gun, does not necessarily mean that the plaintiff will not assert negligence or gross negligence claims. In other words, you may have fully intended to pull the trigger, but the plaintiff may claim you were negligent for any number of reasons; for example, you mistook the mailman for a burglar, or you were negligent in shooting at a criminal. The negligence and gross negligence claims, as defined above, can be brought even if you intended to pull the trigger.

2. Assault and battery

If a person has shot at or shot someone, if they are sued, it may include a claim for assault and battery. This is an intentional act, not an accident or a claim based on a deviation from a standard of care. An assault occurs when someone engages in conduct that places another person in reasonable apprehension of receiving a battery. A battery occurs when a person causes bodily harm to another or makes insulting or provoking physical contact with another.

Bernice is startled while driving. Mark is standing next to her passenger window at a light screaming that she cut him off in traffic, but taking no action to indicate he intends to harm Bernice or do anything besides verbally lodge his complaints. In response, Bernice fires a shot at Mark to make him go away, and hits him in the leg.

Bernice has committed a battery. She intended to and did cause bodily harm to Mark without a legal justification. Therefore, a civil jury would likely find Bernice liable and award damages to Mark.

Bernice is startled while driving. Mark is standing next to her passenger window at a light screaming that she cut him off in traffic, but taking no action to indicate he intends to harm Bernice or do anything besides verbally lodge his complaints. In response, Bernice points her gun at Mark and says "You're dead!" She fires her gun but misses.

Bernice has committed an assault. She knowingly engaged in conduct that placed Mark in reasonable apprehension of receiving a battery without any legal justification.

3. Unlawful restraint: being sued for detaining people

What if a gun owner detains someone at gunpoint? If the person who was detained later decides to sue, they will likely include a claim for "unlawful restraint." Illinois recognizes a civil claim for unlawful restraint. This claim can arise when someone detains a person while waiting for the police (*e.g.,* homeowners detaining burglars, *etc.*). However, it can also come up commonly in shoplifting cases. Unlawful restraint is when a person knowingly without legal authority detains another. 720 ILL. COMP. STAT. 5/10-3.

> **EXAMPLE:**
>
> Elizabeth fears she is about to be attacked in a grocery store parking lot by Richard. Richard follows her step-by-step through the parking lot and stops right next to Elizabeth's car. Elizabeth draws her .380 and tells Richard to "stay right there while I call the police." Richard complies, and Elizabeth holds him at gunpoint until the police arrive. When the police arrive, they determine that Richard was an out-of-uniform store employee tasked with rounding up the grocery carts in the parking lot and was no threat to Elizabeth.

If a jury determines that Elizabeth acted without justification (*i.e.*, she was not reasonably in fear of bodily injury or death), Elizabeth could be civilly liable for unlawfully restraining Richard and may owe him damages.

4. Wrongful death

If a person is in the unfortunate position of having shot and killed another individual and a civil suit occurs because of the shooting, it likely will include a claim for wrongful death. In Illinois, "[a] person is liable for damages arising from an injury that causes another person's death if the person dies because of another person's: 1) wrongful act; 2) neglect; or 3) default and that death precludes the victim from bringing an action for damages against the offender. 740 ILL. COMP. STAT. 180/1.

A wrongful death claim can be proven by establishing that one of the other claims described in this chapter caused the death of another person. In other words, the "wrongful act, neglect, or default" needed to establish a wrongful death claim, can be established by proving that the defendant was liable for a tort such as battery or negligence and that the tort caused the death of a person.

III. WHAT CAN THE PLAINTIFF RECOVER?

If a person is sued in civil court and the plaintiff convinces a jury that the defendant was liable for damages, what and how much can a plaintiff get? There are scores of cases discussing the details of each category of damages that a plaintiff can recover in a civil lawsuit. The following is a brief description of two very important concepts: "proximate cause," which is essential to recover damages in most circumstances; and the basic types of damages that a plaintiff may typically seek in a gun case.

A. Proximate cause

One basic concept that is important to most civil claims, and is usually required to recover damages, is "proximate cause." Virtually every tort claim will require the plaintiff to prove that their damages were proximately caused by the defendant. "Proximate cause" is defined as cause that was a substantial factor in bringing about an event and without which the event would not have occurred. This concept is often discussed and has few bright-line tests.

For a gun owner, the most obvious cases of proximate cause are pulling the trigger on a firearm and hitting the aimed at person or thing. The law will hold that your action proximately caused whatever physical damage the bullet did to persons or property.

But what about those circumstances where the use of the gun is so far removed from the damages claimed? This is where the doctrine of proximate cause will cut off liability. If the damage is too far removed from the act of firing the gun, then it cannot be a proximate cause of the damage.

EXAMPLE:

James is cleaning his AR-15 one night in his apartment and is negligent in his handling of the rifle. He has an accidental discharge and the bullet goes through the wall of his apartment and strikes his neighbor, Donny, in the leg. Donny, although in massive pain, received prompt medical care from his wife, Catherine, and made a speedy recovery.

If James is later sued by Donny and his wife Catherine, James' negligence undoubtedly "proximately caused" damages for things like Donny's medical bills, hospital stay, and perhaps even lost wages. But what if Catherine claims that because of her having to treat Donny's wounds that she missed a big job interview and lost out on a big raise in pay and that she wants James to pay that as a component of damages? The law would hold that Catherine likely could not recover damages for her lost raise in pay because the loss would not be "proximately caused" by the sued upon action. To put it another way, it is reasonably foreseeable that the negligent discharge of a firearm will cause medical bills for someone struck by a bullet. Therefore, this is recoverable. However, the law would say that the loss of a possible job opportunity for the wife who treated the person who was actually shot is not a reasonably foreseeable consequence of negligently discharging a firearm and, therefore, was not proximately caused by the act of negligence. In that case, there will be no recovery for the plaintiff, Catherine.

Proximate cause must be established in every case and may appear to be arbitrary legal-line drawing, because it is.

B. What types of damages can a plaintiff recover?

The following is merely a brief snapshot of the types of damages recoverable in a firearms case. To recover any of the damages below, the plaintiff must first prove one of the claims above by a preponderance of the evidence. For example, if the jury determines a defendant was not negligent, a plaintiff cannot recover his or her medical costs, no matter how severe the plaintiff's injuries. Some of the damages a plaintiff can try to recover include:

- lost wages;
- medical costs;
- disability;
- pain & suffering (physical, mental & emotional);
- funeral and burial costs;
- disfigurement;
- loss of companionship;
- loss of household services;
- lost future wages;
- future medical costs; and
- punitive or exemplary damages (Note: the standard of proof for punitive/exemplary damages is "clear and convincing evidence" which is higher than a "preponderance of the evidence." Punitive damages are also only available in cases of intentional or reckless conduct, or gross negligence.)

A court can find the defendant 100% at fault, but award no damages because the plaintiff failed to prove damages by a preponderance of the evidence. For example, a plaintiff who seeks reimbursement for medical expenses but has no evidence that they ever went to a doctor or hospital, will very unlikely be able to recover for medical expenses.

IV. HOW GOOD ARE ILLINOIS CIVIL IMMUNITY LAWS FOR GUN OWNERS?

A. No immunity from lawsuits

There is a common misunderstanding that there exists a law that if you are legally justified in using your gun that you can't be sued. This is just not the case. First, if a person has the filing fee, anyone can sue anyone else in the State of Illinois. There is no procedure to stop anyone else from filing a lawsuit. Winning a lawsuit is a different issue entirely. If someone files the lawsuit, no matter how frivolous, it still must be shown to the court that this or that defense bars this lawsuit. This process can take significant time, money, and legal energy even for the most frivolous of cases. In short, lawyers get paid and even if you beat the "rap," you still have to take the civil "ride." So, if there is no immunity to lawsuits for gun owners, what protection is there?

B. Immunity for certain claims

Most important for gun owners if they find themselves included in a civil suit after a justified use of force in Illinois, is 720 ILL. COMP. STAT. 5/7-1(b).

Use of force in defense of person...(b) In no case shall any act involving the use of force justified under this Section give rise to any claim or liability brought by or on behalf of any person acting within the definition of "aggressor" set forth in Section 7-4 of this Article (750 ILL. COMP. STAT. 5/7-4), or the estate, spouse, or other family member of such person, against the person or estate of the person using such justified force, unless the use of force involves willful or wanton misconduct.

This section provides that a person who uses force or deadly force that is justified under Chapter 720 ILL. COMP. STAT. 5/7-1 of the Illinois Criminal Code is immune from civil liability for personal injury or death that results from the defendant's use of force or deadly force. This statute does not prevent lawsuits; it just makes one that is filed harder to win. Immunity from liability is an affirmative defense, and, as such, this defense will be considered only after a plaintiff is well into the pain a civil suit may cause an innocent defendant.

EXAMPLE:

Brooke is the victim of a home invasion. She fires several shots at the intruder. The intruder is hit and stopped. One shot, however, misses the intruder and hits a propane tank at the house across the street. The propane tank explodes and burns down the neighbor's home.

The resulting damage is neither personal injury nor death. It is very unlikely that the immunity statute will provide Brooke with any protection from a civil suit by the neighbor for the damages to the house.

C. Justification

All of the justifications under Chapter 720 ILL. COMP. STAT. 5/7-1 (b) can also be asserted as affirmative defenses in a civil action. This means, for example, if you shoot someone in defense of yourself, others, or your property and are sued as a result, you may assert the applicable sections of the Criminal Code as a defense to the civil claims. If the judge or jury agrees that you acted in self-defense, or properly used force to defend others or property, the plaintiff will be barred from recovery.

D. Statute of limitations for civil claims

The statute of limitations is a doctrine in Illinois (and almost every other jurisdiction) that requires civil claims to be brought within a certain period of time after the incident. If the claim is not brought within the statute of limitations period, it is barred. There are a number of issues relating to when the statute of limitations starts to run in many cases, but for the most part, limitations will start to run immediately after a shooting incident. The statute of limitations can vary from claim to claim, most, however, are between one and four years. In Illinois, the limitations period most likely to apply to gun cases is going to be two years. Assault, battery, negligence, wrongful death, and unlawful restraint claims all provide two-year limitations periods.

What does this mean for gun owners? If you use your gun, the plaintiff must bring a civil suit against you within two years of the incident in almost all cases or else the claim will be barred.

E. Superseding or intervening criminal conduct

Illinois law recognizes a doctrine that absolves someone from responsibility for conduct that might otherwise be a tort (*e.g.*, negligence) if a criminal act breaks the causal connection between the tort and the injury. Generally, a third party's criminal conduct is a superseding cause which relieves the negligent actor from liability. However, the actor's negligence will not be excused where the criminal conduct is a foreseeable result of the actor's negligence. *Kramer v. Szczepaniak,* 123 N.E.3d 431 (Ill. App. 2018).

EXAMPLE:

Jonathan allows his nephew Andrew to use his handgun for protection. Jonathan knows Andrew has been in trouble with the law repeatedly and has been accused of armed robbery. While Andrew has the handgun, his apartment is burglarized, and the gun is stolen and used in a crime spree. During the crime spree, Melanie is shot and injured.

Melanie would not be able to recover from Jonathan, even though he may have been negligent in giving his gun to Andrew, because the criminal act of burglarizing Andrew's apartment and subsequent crime spree were superseding causes that broke the link between Jonathan's actions and the resulting injuries.

F. Contributory negligence

Illinois has a doctrine called contributory negligence. If this defense is applicable and properly raised, either the judge or the jury will be asked to determine the percentage of fault or responsibility of the parties involved in the incident. The damages are then apportioned based upon the percentages assigned by the judge or jury.

EXAMPLE:

> Ronny is a young adult trick-or-treater. He uses a fake gun as a part of his costume and knocks loudly on Carol's door at 11:30 p.m. on October 31. Carol, having forgotten about Halloween, is frightened by the knock, the fake gun, and the late hour of Ronny's arrival. She fires through the door, injuring Ronny.

In the civil suit that follows by Ronny against Carol, the jury will be permitted to consider whether Ronny's negligence, if any, contributed to cause the resulting injuries. The jury could determine that Ronny was 0% at fault, 100%, or anything in between. This will reduce the amount of damages that Ronny can recover. By way of example only, if the jury awarded Ronny $100,000 in damages, but found he was 30% at fault, and Carol 70%, Ronny would only be able to recover $70,000 of his damages.

In Illinois, this rule only applies where the damaged party is 50% or less at fault. In other words, if the plaintiff bringing the lawsuit is determined to be more than 50% responsible for the injuries, he or she cannot recover any damages. This can be important for the average gun owner in that a carjacker/home invader who is the overwhelming cause of an incident cannot recover just because the judge or jury finds you made a slight misstep in defending yourself or your home.

V. WHAT ABOUT THIRD PARTIES?

Illinois law provides a different standard when it comes to injuries to third parties. In this section, a third party generally means someone who is not a party to the encounter with the firearm (*e.g.*, bystanders, witnesses, folks nearby who were not the intended target, *etc.*).

Even if you defend yourself, others, or property, but you create an unreasonable risk to others in doing so, you can be liable if one of those third parties is injured.

EXAMPLE:

Heather shoots at Calvin as he unlawfully breaks into Heather's occupied home at night. She fires a single shot with her .22 that narrowly misses Calvin but hits a man washing his car down the street.

Heather is probably not liable to the man down the street, because her conduct did not unreasonably place third parties at risk.

EXAMPLE:

Rick shoots at Calvin as he unlawfully breaks into Rick's occupied home at night. Rick fires 30 shots with his fully-automatic M-16, missing with the initial burst. Calvin turns and runs. Rick continues to fire haphazardly at Calvin as he runs down the street. One shot hits a man washing his car four houses away.

Rick could very likely be liable to the man washing his car because he unreasonably placed third parties at risk by, recklessly firing a fully automatic weapon down a neighborhood street.

VI. WILL INSURANCE COVER IT IF I SHOOT SOMEONE?

A. Homeowners insurance

With few exceptions, almost every homeowner's insurance policy excludes coverage for intentional acts. The act of using your firearm in self-defense is almost always an intentional act. You intended to stop the threat. Plaintiffs' attorneys will very likely assert a negligence claim against a homeowner in an attempt to fall within the coverage and negotiate a settlement with the insurance carrier. However, at the end of the day, if the only evidence is that you intentionally shot the plaintiff because you intended to stop a threat, it is likely that any policy with an intentional act exclusion will not provide coverage for any damages awarded.

B. Auto insurance

Scores of cases around the country exist where the parties allege that a gun incident is covered by automobile insurance merely because the use of the firearm occurs in the auto or involves an auto. Almost universally, courts have held that these incidents are not covered under insurance policies merely because the discharge occurs in a car or involves a car.

EXAMPLE:

Jeff is cleaning his 9mm handgun in the car. It accidentally discharges causing his passenger Connie severe injuries.

This event will almost certainly not be covered by auto insurance.

Jeff discharges his 9mm handgun in the car at Connie during an attempted carjacking, causing Connie severe injuries and also hitting a bystander.

This event will almost certainly not be covered by auto insurance.

For an injury to fall within the "use" coverage of an automobile policy:
1) the accident must have arisen out of the inherent nature of the automobile;
2) the accident must have arisen within the natural territorial limits of an automobile;
3) the actual use must not have terminated; and
4) the automobile must not merely contribute to cause the condition which produces the injury, but must itself produce injury.

VII. WHAT CIVIL LIABILITY DOES A PERSON FACE IF THEIR CHILDREN ACCESS THEIR FIREARMS?

A. Parents are not responsible for minor children's actions merely because they are parents!

As a general rule, minors are civilly liable for their own torts (that is, their wrongful actions such as negligence, gross negligence, assault, *etc.*). The mere fact of paternity or maternity does not make a parent liable to third parties for the torts of his or her minor children. Under this general rule, parents are not responsible for their minor children's tortious actions when the minor child commits a tort and the parent had no direct relationship to the child's action, such as providing a firearm in a negligent manner, failing to supervise the child, or allowing the child to engage in behavior the parent knows is dangerous or risky.

B. Parents who fail to "parent" may become responsible for minor children's actions

While a parent who has no direct relationship to a minor child's tortious actions is generally not liable for that child's actions, if the parent negligently allows his child to act in a manner likely to harm another, if he gives his child a dangerous instrumentality, or if he does not restrain a child known to have dangerous tendencies, the parent may be liable.

Another issue related to negligent storage is whether or not the storage of a gun in violation of 720 ILL. COMP. STAT. 5/24-9(a) could result in civil liability, in addition to the severe criminal penalties in the statute.

> CHAPTER THIRTEEN <

BEYOND FIREARMS: KNIVES, CLUBS, AND TASERS

I. INTRODUCTION

In addition to Illinois' many firearms laws, there also exist state laws governing the possession and use of "other weapons." This includes any object that is not a firearm, but could be used as a weapon. This chapter will briefly discuss the laws governing these other weapons, including weapons that are absolutely illegal under the law, weapons that are illegal to carry, and exceptions to the laws prohibiting the carrying of illegal weapons.

Pursuant to statute 720 Ill. Comp. Stat. 5/24-1, "Unlawful Use of Weapons," the law prohibits certain weapons in Illinois.

(a) A person commits the offense of unlawful use of weapons when he knowingly:

(1) Sells, manufactures, purchases, possesses or carries any bludgeon, black-jack, slung-shot, sand-club, sand bag, metal knuckles or any other knuckle weapon regardless of its composition, throwing star, or any knife, commonly referred to as a switchblade knife, which has a blade that opens automatically by hand pressure applied to a button, spring or other device in the handle of the knife, or a ballistic knife, which is a device that propels a knifelike blade as a projectile by means of a coil spring, elastic material or compressed gas; or

(2) Carries or possesses with intent to use the same unlawfully against another, a dagger, dirk, billy, dangerous knife, razor, stiletto, broken bottle or other piece of glass, stun gun or taser or any other dangerous or deadly weapon or instrument of like character.

The language in paragraph (2) of the statute states "...with the intent to use the same unlawfully against another..." In addition, it contains the catchall " or instrument of like character."

Before we discuss other weapons (weapons not classified as firearms), we should clearly explain what the statutes in Illinois exclude as "firearms." "Firearm" means any device, by whatever means known, which is designed to expel a projectile or projectiles by the action of an explosion, expansion of gas or escape of gas, excluding, however:

(1) Any pneumatic gun, paint ball gun, or B-B gun which expels

a singular globular projectile not exceeding .18 inch diameter or which has a maximum muzzle velocity of less than 700 feet per second;

(1.1) Any pneumatic gun, spring gun, paint ball gun, or B-B gun which expels breakable paint balls containing washable marking colors;

(2) Any device used exclusively for signaling or safety and required or recommended by the United States Coast Guard or the Interstate Commerce Commission;

(3) Any device used exclusively for the firing of stud cartridges, explosive rivets or similar industrial ammunition; and

(4) An antique firearm (other than a machine gun) which, although designed as a weapon, the Department of State Police finds by reason of the date of its manufacture, value, design, and other characteristics is primarily a collector's item and is not likely to be used as a weapon.

A. Knives

Illinois classifies not just the nature of the knife in relation to its legality; the intention of the knife wielder is also used to determine whether it is legal or illegal. There are certain knives, such as ballistic, throwing, and automatic knives, which are totally illegal. A person cannot, make, own, sell, or possess these knives while in Illinois. As stated above, the intention of the person carrying the weapon can determine its legality, *i.e.,* "carries or possesses with intent to use the same unlawfully against another."

A dagger carried harmlessly by one person could be considered legal, but on another person illegal, based on their intent to use it against another unlawfully. This distinction, if the intent can be proven, means that almost any knife can be considered illegal.

Additionally, knives that are over 3 inches in length are illegal on property which is even partially owned by the government.

> "Section 720 ILL. COMP. STAT. 33A-1, (a) Whoever possesses or stores any weapon enumerated in Section 720 ILL. COMP. STAT. 33A-1 in any building or on land supported in whole or part with public funds or in any building on such land without prior written permission from the chief security officer for such land or building commits a Class A misdemeanor. (b) The chief security officer must grant any reasonable request for permission under paragraph (a)."

The relevant definition of these weapons are as follows:

> "A category I weapon is a handgun, sawed-off shotgun, sawed-off rifle, any other firearm small enough to be concealed upon the person, semiautomatic firearm, or machine gun. A category II weapon is any other rifle, shotgun, spring gun, other firearm, stun gun or taser as defined in paragraph (a) of Section 24-1 of this Code, knife with a blade of at least 3 inches in length, dagger, dirk, switchblade knife, stiletto, axe, hatchet, or other deadly or dangerous weapon or instrument of like character. As used in this subsection."

In Illinois there are only a few types of knives which are outright banned. In addition there are only specific areas where knives longer than 3 inches in length may not be carried. The areas where these knives are banned is stated above (publicly funded properties). There is no difference in relation to legality whether the knife is carried open or concealed. If the knife is legal to possess than it does not matter how you carry, open or concealed.

Pocket knives

Pocket knives with a blade smaller than 3 inches have no legal restrictions. A person can own, purchase, trade, or carry them anywhere in the state. Remember, if the blade is over 3 inches then the public properties law comes into effect.

Butterfly knives

Butterfly knives are legal to own and carry, either openly or concealed, in Illinois. Again, the 3-inch rule will come into play if on public property.

Fixed blade knives

Typical fixed blade knives are legal in Illinois. Fixed blade knives can be carried openly or concealed. However, if they are part of any automatic knife, wherein a covering is automatically removed, then they are illegal. If over 3 inches in length and carried on public property, they are considered a dangerous weapon in Illinois.

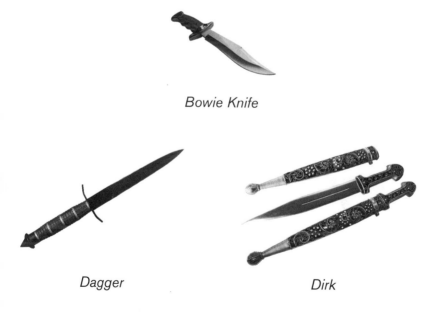

Bowie Knife

Dagger

Dirk

Automatic knives

All automatic knives are illegal in Illinois. They are completely banned and cannot be owned, sold, traded, made, or possessed while in Illinois.

Stiletto

B. Pepper spray

Pepper spray is legal to use and carry in Illinois for self-defense. You must be over 18-years-old to purchase, use, or carry pepper spray. In Chicago you cannot use pepper spray in an enclosed space with more than 20 people (like a bar). There are no restrictions in Illinois on pepper spray size, formula, strength, or canister style. 720 ILL. COMP. STAT. 5/24-1.

C. Batons

Although not specifically illegal in Illinois, you would need to have a legitimate reason to carry one. If you claim to be carrying for self-defense purposes, they are considered a weapon under Illinois law. 720 ILL. COMP. STAT. 5/24-1.

Blackjack   *Nightstick*

If you are a security guard on duty, or a store owner within your business, you should be alright. An ordinary citizen would need to show more than self-defense purposes. We may appear to be giving a vague answer, but under Illinois law, the purpose of carrying the baton is controlling in relation to its legality.

D. Knuckles

Not only is it illegal to possess brass knuckles in Illinois, it is also illegal to possess jewelry, or items that look similar to brass knuckles. Brass knuckles are considered a deadly weapon in Illinois. If you are found in possession of brass knuckles in Illinois you can be charged with Unlawful Use of a Weapon, a Class A misdemeanor. You can be charged with the more serious Class 4 felony if found in possession of brass knuckles in an establishment that sells alcohol, or any property that has received a government license to have a public gathering, or any place that charges people a fee. 720 ILL. COMP. STAT. 5/24.

Traditional "Brass Knuckles"

E. Tasers

In Illinois it is illegal to buy or possess a stun gun or taser without a valid Firearm Owner's Identification Card ("FOID"). The definition of a stun gun or taser in Illinois is, "any device which is powered by electrical charging units, such as batteries, and which fires one or several barbs attached to a length of wire which, upon hitting a human, can send out a current capable of disrupting a person's nervous system in such a manner as to render him incapable of normal functioning." 720 ILL. COMP. STAT. 5/24-1(8).

Handheld "Stun Gun"

Cartridge Taser

F. Other weapons

Pursuant to 720 ILL. COMP. STAT. 5/24-1(a)(2), almost any item can be considered a dangerous weapon if the requisite intent can be proven. The language, "Carries or possess with the intent to use the same unlawfully against another…" expands the law to include other items if being used unlawfully against another. The statute also includes the catchall language, "or deadly weapon or instrument of like character." The list is not all encompassing, but can include almost any item which could cause great bodily harm if being used unlawfully. Many everyday items can be considered illegal if the requisite intent can be proven.

Commercial "Fist Filler"

Roll of Coins

➤ CHAPTER FOURTEEN ◄

WHAT IS THE
NATIONAL FIREARMS ACT?
Silencers, Short-barreled Weapons, And Machine Guns

Can an individual in Illinois legally own a silencer or suppressor, short-barreled shotgun, short-barreled rifle, machine gun, or destructive device? NO. This chapter deals with the laws regarding the possession and use of firearms that are subject to the provisions of the National Firearms Act ("NFA") codified in 26 U.S.C. Chapter 53, specifically, silencers, short-barreled firearms, machine guns, and firearms that are otherwise illegal. Most of these firearms are illegal to purchase or possess even with the proper paperwork and a tax stamp. In this chapter, we will discuss the purpose behind the NFA, what firearms are regulated by the Act, as well as the process and procedure for legally possessing weapons that are subject to the Act's provisions.

I. INTRODUCTION AND OVERVIEW

The National Firearms Act was enacted in 1934 in response to gangster crimes. Prior to the Act's passage, any person could go to the local hardware store and purchase a Thompson Submachine Gun or shorten the barrel on their rifle or shotgun. President Roosevelt pushed for the passage of the NFA in an attempt to diminish a gangster's ability to possess and carry dangerous and/or easily concealable firearms, such as machine guns and short-barreled rifles and shotguns.

A. The NFA is a firearms regulation using a registration and tax stamp requirement

The NFA requires both the registration of and tax on the manufacture and transfer of certain firearms. The law created a tax of $200 on the transfer of the following firearms: short-barreled shotguns, short-barreled rifles, machine guns, silencers, and destructive devices. The tax is only $5 for transferring firearms that are classified as "Any Other Weapons" or AOWs. Back in 1934, a $200 tax was the approximate equivalent to about $3,500 today!

Five years after the NFA's passage, the Supreme Court held in *United States v. Miller* that the right to bear arms can be subject to federal regulation. Miller defended himself against the government stating that the NFA infringed upon his Constitutional right to bear arms under the Second Amendment. While the Court agreed that the Constitution does guarantee a right to bear arms, it held that the right does not extend to every firearm. *See United States v. Miller*, 307 U.S. 174 (1939).

II. WHAT FIREARMS DOES THE NFA REGULATE?

A. Short-barreled rifles and shotguns

What is a short-barreled shotgun? Under both federal and Illinois law, short-barreled shotguns have one or more barrels less than 18 inches in length and the overall length of the shotgun is less than 26 inches. What is a short-barreled rifle? It is any rifle with one or more barrels less than 16 inches in length, and the overall length of the rifle is less than 26 inches. 720 ILL. COMP. STAT. 5/24-1(a)(17). Short-barreled shotguns and rifles may not be purchased.

B. Stabilizing braces

The most common type of rifle that is manufactured or modified into a short-barreled rifle ("SBR") is the AR style sporting rifle. The AR can also be manufactured as a pistol. An AR-style SBR and an AR-style pistol appear very similar. The key difference between the two is that the SBR has a shoulder stock and the pistol does not. However, the AR pistol will have a "buffer tube" extending from the back of the receiver to compensate for the firearm's recoil. In recent years it has become a trend that some manufacturers and DIY firearm hobbyists will attach a device to this buffer tube, called an "arm brace" or "stabilizing brace." This is an accessory, typically made of plastic and Velcro, wraps around the shooter's forearm, enabling him or her to have better aim and recoil control. When the arm brace was first developed, it had the appearance of a telescoping shoulder stock. Attaching a shoulder stock to a traditional handgun or AR-style pistol with a barrel length under 16 inches turns the handgun into an NFA weapon which is only allowed upon the approval of a Form 1. Many manufacturers of these stabilizing braces have sought pre-approval from the ATF's Firearms Technology Industry Services Branch to confirm that their devices did not turn AR pistols into SBRs. In a somewhat confusing series of letters and statements, the ATF has taken the position that the stabilizing brace, when used as manufactured and intended, does not make an AR pistol into an SBR or AOW.

However, if an individual installing and using the brace made any alterations with the intent to use it as a shoulder stock, such as adding padding or taping the sides of the brace together, and they did not get approval with a Form 1 and pay the $200 tax, they could be subject to prosecution for illegally making an NFA weapon. Further, if a person does affix a stabilizing brace to a pistol, a vertical foregrip cannot be added because the ATF has determined that this addition alters the character of the firearm so that it is no longer a pistol (since it is not designed to be fired with one hand).

C. Personal defense firearms

Recently, a weapon came into the market that is designed as a personal defense firearm utilizing shotgun rounds. Mossberg was the first manufacturer to produce such a weapon, the Shockwave. This market now includes the Remington TAC-14 and the Black Aces Tactical Pro Series S Semiautomatic. These firearms have barrels that are shorter than the 18 inches required for a non-NFA shotgun. However, the ATF has determined that these firearms are not short-barreled shotguns (because of their "bird head" stocks which is not designed to be fired from the shoulder). As such, these firearms fall outside the NFA regulations. *See* Chapter 2.

D. Machine guns

Machine guns are illegal under federal and state law. First, what is a machine gun? Federal law defines a machine gun as "any weapon which shoots, is designed to shoot, or can be readily restored to shoot, automatically more than one shot, without manual reloading, by a single function of the trigger. The term shall also include the frame or receiver of any such weapon, any part designed and intended solely and exclusively, or combination of parts designed and intended, for use in converting a weapon into a machine gun, and any combination of parts from which a machine gun can be assembled if such parts are in the possession or under the control of a person." 27 CFR § 478.11. As a result of this definition, the individual metal components that make up a whole machine gun, such as a full-auto sear, individually meet the federal definition of machine gun. The parts for the machine gun do not have to be assembled.

Illinois law defines a machine gun as, "any weapon, which shoots, is designed to shoot, or can be readily restored to shoot, automatically more than one shot without manually reloading by a single function of the trigger, including the frame or receiver of any such weapon." There is no new manufacturing of machine guns for private ownership.

Bump stocks

Bump stocks are a rifle accessory that harnesses the energy of the recoil to assist the shooter in pulling the trigger as soon as it resets. This device does not alter the mechanical operation of the rifle; it still fires only one round for each trigger pull. The bump stock became controversial after the October 1, 2017 shooting at an outdoor concert in Las Vegas. Politicians and the media immediately declared that these devices allow a semi-automatic rifle to fire as rapidly as a machine gun. Many of them erroneously stated that a bump stock "turns a rifle into a machine gun." Bills were filed in Congress which did not pass, but ultimately in 2018, the Department of Justice, through the ATF, issued a final rule banning bump stocks by way of regulation. This was done in spite of an ATF determination in 2010 that bump stocks did not modify a semi-automatic rifle to make it an NFA-regulated machine gun. This new rule specifically defined bump stocks as "machine guns" under federal law. This effectively renders all such devices illegal to possess under federal law, since any lawful machine gun must have been in existence and properly registered under the National Firearms Act as of May 19, 1986, decades before the bump stock was invented. In crafting the new rule, the ATF reasoned that bump stocks allow the shooter to produce fully automatic fire while continuously applying pressure to the trigger. The new rule mandated that all bump stocks must be destroyed or surrendered to the ATF by March 26, 2019. Afterward, it became a federal felony to possess a bump stock. This crime is classified as a violation of 18 U.S.C. § 922(o)—illegal possession of a machine gun. If convicted of such a crime, you could face up to 10 years in federal prison and up to a $250,000 fine for each bump stock in your possession. Immediately following the passage of this rule, Second Amendment advocacy groups and individuals across the United States began litigation. However, no court has issued a nationwide preliminary injunction against the final rule going into effect while its constitutionality is litigated.

E. Firearm suppressors

What is a suppressor? It is just a muffler for a firearm and is legal if all NFA requirements are met. In legal terms, a firearm suppressor is defined in 27 CFR § 478.11 as "any device for silencing, muffling, or diminishing the report of a portable firearm, including any combination of parts, designed or redesigned, and intended for use in assembling or fabricating a firearm silencer or firearm muffler, and any part intended only for use in such assembly or fabrication." The Illinois definition is found in the Unlawful Use of Weapons statute, 720 ILL. COMP. STAT. 5/24(a)(6) "...any device or attachment of any kind designed, used or intended for use in silencing the report of any firearm."

Firearm suppressors are very practical instruments. They are great for hunting and recreational shooting not only because it suppresses gunshots in a way so as to not alarm other animals being hunted nearby, but also because it lessens the impact on the shooter's ears. However, firearms owners should be carefully aware that the definition of a suppressor is very broad whether under federal or Illinois law. Suppressors do not need to be items manufactured specifically for use as a suppressor. There are some ordinary, every-day items that could be easily converted into a suppressor such as a water bottle or an automotive oil filter. Possession of otherwise legal items when used or modified to be used as a suppressor is illegal. In 2017, the Hearing Protection Act which sought to remove silencers from regulation under the NFA and treat them as common firearms died in Congress. At the time of writing this book, this act has yet to be considered by either the House of Representatives or the Senate.

To further complicate matters, in 2019, in response to a mass shooting where a suppressor was used, a bill banning them was introduced in Congress.

F. Destructive devices

The term "destructive device" is a legal term given to certain firearms, objects, and munitions that are illegal under the NFA.

DESTRUCTIVE DEVICES – PART A
27 CFR § 478.11

Any explosive, incendiary, or poison gas (1) bomb, (2) grenade, (3) rocket having a propellant charge of more than 4 ounces, (4) missile having an explosive or incendiary charge of more than one-quarter ounce, (5) mine, or (6) device similar to any of the devices described in the preceding paragraphs of this definition.

DESTRUCTIVE DEVICES – PART B
27 CFR § 478.11

Any type of weapon (other than a shotgun or shotgun shell which the Director finds is generally recognized as particularly suitable for sporting purposes) by whatever name known which will, or which may be readily converted to, expel a projectile by the action of an explosive or other propellant, and which has any barrel with a bore of more than one-half inch in diameter.

DESTRUCTIVE DEVICES – PART C
27 CFR § 478.11

Any combination of parts either designed or intended for use in converting any destructive device described in [part] (A) and (B) of this section and from which a destructive device may be readily assembled.

The "destructive devices" as defined in the statute are effectively broken down into three categories: explosive devices, large caliber weapons, and parts easily convertible into a destructive device.

The first portion of the definition of a destructive device deals with explosive, incendiary, and poison gas munitions. The definition specifies that any explosive, incendiary, or poison gas bomb, grenade, mine, or similar device is a destructive device. In addition, the definition includes a rocket having a propellant charge of more than four ounces and a missile (projectile) having an explosive or incendiary charge of more than one-quarter ounce. These topics and the regulations thereof are beyond the scope of this book's discussion. The second section of the definition addresses large caliber weapons and states that any type of weapon that has a bore of more than one-half inch in diameter is a destructive device with the exception of shotguns (and shotgun shells) that are suitable for sporting purposes. Thus, any caliber in a rifle or handgun more than .50 inches or fifty caliber is classified as a destructive device. Shotguns are exempt from this prohibition on size unless the ATF rules it is not for sporting purposes. How do you know if a shotgun is suitable for sporting purposes? The ATF keeps a list, and has issued rulings classifying specific shotguns as destructive devices because they are not considered to be particularly "suitable for sporting purposes" including the USAS-12, Striker-12, Streetsweeper, and 37/38mm Beanbags. The ATF does not provide any specific definition of what constitutes being "suitable for sporting purposes" nor does it specify the methodology in which it determines what makes a particular shotgun suitable for sporting purposes. Ultimately, one will have to check with the ATF lists to see whether a particular shotgun with a larger bore-diameter is classified as a destructive device or not.

Finally, a destructive device does not need to be a completed and assembled product to fall under the federal definition and regulation under the NFA. Much like machine guns, if a person possesses parts that can be readily assembled into a destructive device, then whether or not the device has actually been constructed is irrelevant—by law it's already a destructive device.

Although these firearms, munitions, and devices are prohibited by the law on its face pursuant to the National Firearms Act, a person may nevertheless receive permission to possess them so long as they possess the correct legal authorization.

G. "Any Other Weapons" or AOWs

The AOW category under the NFA pertains to firearms and weapons that may not fit the traditional definition of some of the firearms discussed elsewhere in this book due to the way in which they are manufactured or modified. Under federal law, an AOW is "any weapon or device capable of being concealed on the person from which a shot can be discharged through the energy of an explosive, a pistol or revolver having a barrel with a smooth bore designed or redesigned to fire a fixed shotgun shell, weapons with combination shotgun and rifle barrels 12 inches or more, less than 18 inches in length, from which only a single discharge can be made from either barrel without manual reloading, and shall include any such weapon which may be readily restored to fire. Such term shall not include a pistol or a revolver having a rifled bore, or rifled bores, or weapons designed, made, or intended to be fired from the shoulder and not capable of firing fixed ammunition." 26 U.S.C. § 5845(e).

1. Concealable weapons and devices

Weapons which are capable of being concealed from which a shot can be discharged are AOWs. Large bore destructive devices and AOWs require a tax stamp from the ATF and proper approval, but are legal. 720 ILL. COMP. STAT. 5/24-2. The statute lists the individuals who have certain exemptions which make possessing these weapons legal with an ATF tax stamp and approval.

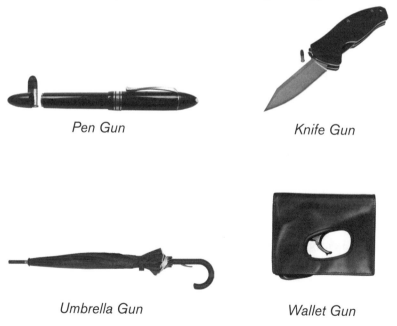

Pen Gun

Knife Gun

Umbrella Gun

Wallet Gun

2. Pistols and revolvers having a smooth-bore barrel for firing shotgun shells

Pistols and revolvers which have a smooth bore (no rifling) that are designed to shoot shotgun ammunition are defined as an AOW. The ATF cites firearms such as the H&R Handy Gun or the Ithaca Auto & Burglar Gun as firearms which fall under the AOW category.

Note: handguns with partially rifled barrels such as The Judge do not fall under this category due to the rifling of the barrel.

H&R Handy Gun   *Ithaca Auto & Burglar Gun*

3. Weapons with barrels 12 inches or longer and lengths 18 inches or shorter

The definition of AOW also includes any weapon which has a shotgun or rifle barrel of 12 inches or more but is 18 inches or less in overall length from which only a single discharge can be made from either barrel without manual reloading. The ATF identifies the "Marble Game Getter" as the firearm most commonly associated with this definition (excluding the model with an 18" barrel and folding shoulder stock).

4. Pistols and revolvers with vertical foregrips

If a pistol is modified with a vertical grip on the front, it will now be legally classified as an AOW and require registration and a paid tax. Note, vertical grips are readily available and are legal to own as long as they are not placed on a handgun. The definition of a handgun is a weapon which is intended to be fired by one hand, the addition of the vertical foregrip makes it so the weapon now is intended to be used with two hands to fire. This modification changes the weapon from a handgun to an AOW and is now a prohibited weapon without the proper documentation. It is not an SBR or a SBS because it cannot be fired from the shoulder. *See* 26 U.S.C. § 5845(e).

H. Antique firearms

Firearms that are defined by the NFA as "antique firearms" are not regulated by the NFA. The NFA definition of antique firearm is found in 26 U.S.C. § 5845(g) as "any firearm not designed or redesigned for using rim fire or conventional center fire ignition with fixed ammunition and manufactured in or before 1898 (including any matchlock, flintlock, percussion cap, or similar type of ignition system or replica thereof, whether actually manufactured before or after the year 1898) and also any firearm using fixed ammunition manufactured in or before 1898, for which ammunition is no longer manufactured in the United States and is not readily available in the ordinary channels of commercial trade." Under this statute and for NFA purposes, the only firearms that are antiques are firearms which were both actually manufactured in or before 1898 and ones for which fixed ammunition is no longer manufactured in the

United States and is not readily available in the ordinary channels of commercial trade.

With this in mind, the ATF states in its NFA guidebook that "it is important to note that a specific type of fixed ammunition that has been out of production for many years may again become available due to increasing interest in older firearms. Therefore, the classification of a specific NFA firearm as an antique can change if ammunition for the weapon becomes readily available in the ordinary channels of commerce."

I. NFA curio firearms and relics

Under federal law, curios or relics are defined in 27 CFR § 478.11 as "firearms which are of special interest to collectors by reason of some quality other than is associated with firearms intended for sporting use or as offensive or defensive weapons." Persons who collect curios or relics may do so with a special collector's license although one is not required. The impact of an NFA item being classified as a curio or relic, however, is that it allows the item to be transferred interstate to persons possessing a collector's license. The collector's license does not allow the individual to deal in curios or relics, nor does it allow the collector to obtain other firearms interstate as those transactions still require an FFL.

Some of the items regulated by the NFA simply don't make as much sense as the other things it regulates. Suppressors are really nothing more than mufflers for your firearm—they aren't really firearms themselves (notwithstanding the legal definition). Thinking about the utility of the suppressor, if the firearm was invented today, you can be sure that not only would the government not prohibit them, OSHA would probably require them for safety purposes! –Michael

To be classified as a curio or relic, federal law states that the firearm must fall into one of the following three categories:

1) firearms which were manufactured at least 50 years prior to the current date, but not including replicas thereof;

2) firearms which are certified by the curator of a municipal, State, or Federal museum which exhibits firearms to be curios or relics of museum interest; or

3) any other firearms which derive a substantial part of their monetary value from the fact that they are novel, rare, bizarre, or because of their association with some historical figure, period, or event.

See 27 CFR § 478.11.

The ATF maintains a list of firearms that are classified as curios or relics.

J. How can some after-market gun parts make your firearm illegal?

A number of companies manufacture and sell gun products or parts that alter the appearance or utility of a firearm (*i.e.* shoulder stocks, forward hand grips, *etc.*). However, some of these after-market products can actually change the firearm you possess from one type of a weapon to another type of weapon for legal purposes whether you realize it or not. As a result, many individuals make the modifications to their firearms thinking that because there was no special process for purchasing the accessory, any modification would be in compliance with the law. Unfortunately, this is not always the case. Consider the example of short-barreled uppers for AR-15s: selling, buying, or possessing AR-15 "uppers" with barrels less than 16 inches is legal. However, it is illegal to put the upper on a receiver of an AR-15 because this would be the act of manufacturing a short-barreled rifle and is legally prohibited. This is equally true of vertical foregrips on a handgun. Vertical foregrips are legal to buy or possess, however, if you actually install one on a handgun, you have manufactured an AOW, and it is illegal, unless registered and a tax paid.

III. PROCESS AND PROCEDURE FOR OBTAINING NFA FIREARMS
A. Who can own and possess an NFA firearm?

Any person may own and possess an NFA firearm as long as they are legally not disqualified to own or possess firearms and live in a state that allows possession of NFA items. (*See* Chapters 2 and 3). The ATF also allows for a non-person legal entity to own these items, such as corporations, partnerships, and trusts, *etc*. On July 13, 2016, a new rule went into effect modifying the process for filing for a transfer or manufacture of an NFA weapon.

B. What are the usual steps for buying or manufacturing NFA items?

Whether a person is buying or making (manufacturing) an NFA firearm, there are several steps in the process. The transfer or manufacture of an NFA firearm requires the filing of an appropriate form with the ATF, payment of any federally-mandated tax, approval of the transfer by the ATF, and registration of the firearm to the transferee. Only after these steps have occurred may a buyer legally take possession of the NFA item, or may a person legally assemble or manufacture the NFA item. In this section, we will walk through the process, step-by-step, of: (1) purchasing an NFA item that already exists; and (2) manufacturing an NFA firearm.

PRACTICAL LEGAL TIP

Even if you don't own a machine gun today, that doesn't mean you won't be the intended owner of one later. A person could always leave you their NFA items in a will. If this happens, you must file the appropriate paperwork with the ATF as soon as possible, or at least before probate is closed.
–Michael

Steps for buying an existing NFA item (for example, a suppressor):

1. select and purchase the item (suppressor) from a transferor who is usually an FFL dealer who is authorized to sell NFA weapons;

2. assemble appropriate paperwork: ATF Form 4 (*See* Appendix C), fingerprints on an FBI Form FD-258, a passport size photograph, and a payment for the tax of $200;

   a. if the buyer is an individual they must notify the Chief Law

Enforcement Officer of their city or county of residence by delivering the CLEO copy of ATF Form 4;

b. if the buyer is a corporation or trust, each "responsible person" of the corporation or trust must complete an ATF Form 5320.23 (*See* Appendix C), including fingerprints and a passport photograph, and must notify the Chief Law Enforcement Officer of their city or county of residence by delivering to them the CLEO copy of ATF Form 5320.23;

3. submit paperwork, fingerprints, and tax to the ATF for review and approval;

4. ATF sends approval (tax stamp affixed to Form 4) to the transferor; and then

5. transferor notifies the buyer to pick up the suppressor.

Steps for manufacturing an NFA item (such as a short-barreled rifle):

1. select the item to manufacture or modify, *i.e.*, short-barreled AR-15;

2. assemble appropriate paperwork: ATF Form 1 (*See* Appendix C), fingerprints on an FBI Form FD-258, a passport size photograph, and a payment for the tax ($200):

a. if the maker is an individual they must notify the Chief Law Enforcement Officer of the city or county of their residence by delivering the CLEO copy of ATF Form 1;

b. if the maker is a corporation or trust, each "responsible person" of the corporation or trust must complete an ATF Form 5320.23 (*See* Appendix C), including fingerprints and a passport photograph, and must notify the Chief Law Enforcement Officer of their city or county of residence by delivering to them the CLEO copy of ATF Form 5320.23;

3. the "Applicant" submits paperwork and tax to the ATF for review and approval;

4. ATF sends approval (tax stamp affixed to Form 1); and then

5. the short-barreled AR-15 may be legally assembled, *i.e.*, put upper with a barrel length of less than 16 inches on a lower receiver, *etc.* The item must now be engraved and identified.

When purchasing an NFA firearm from a dealer, the dealer is required to have the purchaser fill out ATF Form 4473 when the purchaser goes to pick up the item from the dealer.

C. How must an NFA item be engraved and identified if I make it myself?

Once you receive ATF approval to manufacture your own NFA item (such as the short-barreled AR-15 in the previous section), federal law requires that you engrave, cast, stamp, or otherwise conspicuously place or cause to be engraved, cast, stamped, or placed on the frame, receiver, or barrel of the NFA item the following information:

1. the item's serial number;

2. the item's model (if so designated);

3. caliber or gauge;

4. the name of the owner whether individual, corporation, or trust; and

5. the city and state where the item was made.

This information must be placed on the item with a minimum depth of .003 inch and in a print size no smaller than 1/16 inch. *See* 27 CFR § 479.102.

D. Which way should I own my NFA item? Paperwork requirements for individuals, trusts, or business entities to own NFA items

Form 4 and Form 1 are the appropriate paperwork that must be assembled and submitted to the ATF and varies depending on whether it is an individual, or a legal entity such as a trust, a corporation, or a partnership purchasing or manufacturing the NFA item. The paperwork generally starts either with an ATF Form 4 used for purchasing an existing NFA item, or an ATF Form 1 which is used if a person wishes to manufacture a new NFA item. All relevant portions of the forms must be completed. Both Form 4 and Form 1 have a requirement that a Chief Law Enforcement Officer for the city or county where the applicant lives must be given their copy of the ATF Form.

Who is a Chief Law Enforcement Officer who must be notified? For the purposes of ATF Form 4 or Form 1, and the responsible person questionnaire, ATF Form 5320.23, the Chief Law Enforcement Officer is considered to be the chief law enforcement officer who has jurisdiction where the transferor, the applicant, and any "responsible persons" are located. These persons include: "the Chief of Police; the Sheriff; the Head of the State Police; or a State or local district attorney or prosecutor."

Photograph and fingerprints are required for individual applicants and "responsible persons." If an individual is purchasing or manufacturing an NFA item, the applicant must submit an appropriate photograph and their fingerprints. An entity such as a trust or corporation must designate "responsible persons" who are allowed to have access to use and possess an NFA weapon. As of July 13, 2016, corporations and trusts must submit the appropriate documents showing its existence, such as the trust or corporate formation documents, the ATF responsible person questionnaire, fingerprints, and passport photographs of these persons.

Responsible persons of trusts, partnerships, associations, companies, or corporations, are defined as "any individual who possesses, directly or indirectly, the power or authority to direct the management and policies of the trust or entity to receive, possess, ship, transport, deliver, transfer or otherwise dispose of a firearm for, or on behalf of, the trust or legal entity." *See* ATF Form 1, Instructions. Further, with regard to NFA trusts, responsible persons are defined in the following way: "those persons with the power or authority to direct the management and policies of the trust includes any person who has the capability to exercise such power and possesses, directly or indirectly the power or authority under any trust instrument, or under State law, to receive, possess, ship, transport, deliver, transfer, or otherwise dispose of a firearm for, or on behalf of the trust." The ATF Form 5320.23 provides examples of responsible persons, including, "settlors/grantors, trustees, partners, members, officers, directors, board members, or owners." Persons who are not "responsible persons" are "the beneficiary of a trust, if the beneficiary does not have the capability to exercise the enumerated powers or authorities."

E. Why are trusts so popular to own NFA items?

There are three major reasons trusts are very popular to own NFA items: paperwork, control, and ease of ownership. A trust is a legal entity that can hold property.

A major reason for having a trust own an NFA item is that it makes owning and using the NFA item easier if more than one person wishes to use the item. If an individual owns the item, then only the individual can possess it. On the other hand, if the item is owned by a trust, all trustees, including co-trustees, are able to possess and use the items contained in the trust. Therefore, co-trustees may be added or removed as necessary.

Further, unlike other entities such as corporations, LLCs, *etc.*, a trust requires no filings with a government to create, which saves expenses. Further, these expense savings continue because there are no continuing government fees or compliance requirements. Thus, trusts are one of the best ways currently to own an NFA item.

F. The tax stamp

Once the ATF has an applicant's materials in hand, they will be reviewed and checked by NFA researchers and an examiner. The application will then either be approved or denied. A denial will be accompanied by an explanation of why the application was denied and how to remedy it, if possible. If the application is approved, the examiner will affix a tax stamp on one of the submitted Form 1 or Form 4 and send the newly-stamped form to the applicant.

This tax stamp on the appropriate form is a person's evidence of compliance with the NFA's requirements and is a very important document. A copy should always be kept with the NFA item.

G. What documents should I have with me when I am in actual possession of my suppressor, short-barreled firearm, or other NFA item?

If you have an NFA item, it is a good idea to have the proper documentation with you to prove that you legally possess the item. The law states it is a crime to be in possession of an unregistered NFA item which means the police officer will need reasonable suspicion of your failure to register in order to detain you to determine the status of your item. Reasonable suspicion is a very low standard to meet. It is good advice that if you are in possession of your suppressor, short-barreled firearm, destructive device, or if you are lucky enough, your machine gun—have your paperwork showing you are legal, or it may be a long day with law enforcement. To show you are legal, always keep a copy of your ATF Form 4 or Form 1 (whichever is applicable) with the tax stamp affixed for every NFA item in your possession, personal identification, and if the item is held in a trust or corporation, a copy of the trust or articles of incorporation, and the authorization for your possession. Care should be given to make sure these documents name the individual so as to show legal ownership, *i.e.*, trust and/or amendments showing the person is a co-trustee or an officer of the corporation.

Practically, individuals should not carry around the original documents as they could be destroyed by wear and tear, rain, or be misplaced, effectively destroying the required evidence of compliance. Photocopies of the stamp and any other pertinent documents are generally enough to satisfy inquisitive law enforcement officials. The more technologically advanced may take pictures on their phone or other mobile device, or even upload them to a cloud database. Keep in mind that if the phone dies or the cloud cannot be reached, and you have no way to access the documents, your proof is gone and you may have a very bad day ahead of you! We recommend keeping photocopies of the ATF Form with the tax stamp affixed and appropriate documents with the NFA weapon to avoid any problems with technology.

APPENDIX A:
Selected Illinois Statutes

ILLINOIS COMPILED STATUTES CHAPTER 720 CRIMINAL OFFENSES:

CRIMINAL CODE OF 2012.
ARTICLE 7. JUSTIFIABLE USE OF FORCE; EXONERATION

720 ILL. COMP. STAT. 5/7-1
SEC. 7-1. USE OF FORCE IN DEFENSE OF PERSON.

(a) A person is justified in the use of force against another when and to the extent that he reasonably believes that such conduct is necessary to defend himself or another against such other's imminent use of unlawful force. However, he is justified in the use of force which is intended or likely to cause death or great bodily harm only if he reasonably believes that such force is necessary to prevent imminent death or great bodily harm to himself or another, or the commission of a forcible felony.

(b) In no case shall any act involving the use of force justified under this Section give rise to any claim or liability brought by or on behalf of any person acting within the definition of "aggressor" set forth in Section 7-4 of this Article, or the estate, spouse, or other family member of such a person, against the person or estate of the person using such justified force, unless the use of force involves willful or wanton misconduct.
(Source: P.A. 93-832, eff. 7-28-04.)

720 ILL. COMP. STAT. 5/7-2
SEC. 7-2. USE OF FORCE IN DEFENSE OF DWELLING.

(a) A person is justified in the use of force against another when and to the extent that he reasonably believes that such conduct is necessary to prevent or terminate such other's unlawful entry into or attack upon a dwelling. However, he is justified in the use of force which is intended or likely to cause death or great bodily harm only if:

(1) The entry is made or attempted in a violent, riotous, or tumultuous manner, and he reasonably believes that such force is necessary to prevent an assault upon, or offer of personal violence to, him or another then in the dwelling, or

(2) He reasonably believes that such force is necessary to prevent the commission of a felony in the dwelling.

(b) In no case shall any act involving the use of force justified under this Section give rise to any claim or liability brought by or on behalf of any person acting within the definition of "aggressor" set forth in Section 7-4 of this Article, or the estate, spouse, or other family member of such a person, against the person or estate of the person using such justified force, unless the use of force involves willful or wanton misconduct.
(Source: P.A. 93-832, eff. 7-28-04.)

720 ILL. COMP. STAT. 5/7-3
SEC. 7-3. USE OF FORCE IN DEFENSE OF OTHER PROPERTY.

(a) A person is justified in the use of force against another when and to the extent that he reasonably believes that such conduct is necessary to prevent or terminate such other's trespass on or other tortious or criminal interference with either real property (other than a dwelling) or personal property, lawfully in his possession or in the possession of another who is a member of his immediate family or household or of a person whose property he has a legal duty to protect. However, he is justified in the use of force which is intended or likely to cause death or great bodily harm only if he reasonably believes that such force is necessary to prevent the commission of a forcible felony.

(b) In no case shall any act involving the use of force justified under this Section give rise to any claim or liability brought by or on behalf of any person acting within the definition of "aggressor" set forth in Section 7-4 of this Article, or the estate, spouse, or other family member of such a person, against the person or estate of the person using such justified force, unless the use of force involves willful or wanton misconduct.
(Source: P.A. 93-832, eff. 7-28-04.)

720 ILL. COMP. STAT. 5/7-4
SEC. 7-4. USE OF FORCE BY AGGRESSOR.

The justification described in the preceding Sections of this Article is not available to a person who:

(a) is attempting to commit, committing, or escaping after the commission of, a forcible felony; or

(b) initially provokes the use of force against himself, with the intent to use such force as an excuse to inflict bodily harm upon the assailant; or

(c) otherwise initially provokes the use of force against himself, unless:

    (1) such force is so great that he reasonably believes that he is in imminent danger of death or great bodily harm, and that he has exhausted every reasonable means to escape such danger other than the use of force which is likely to cause death or great bodily harm to the assailant; or

    (2) in good faith, he withdraws from physical contact with the assailant and indicates clearly to the assailant that he desires to withdraw and terminate the use of force, but the assailant continues or resumes the use of force.

(Source: Laws 1961, p. 1983.)

720 ILL. COMP. STAT. 5/7-5
SEC. 7-5. PEACE OFFICER'S USE OF FORCE IN MAKING ARREST.

(a) A peace officer, or any person whom he has summoned or directed to assist him, need not retreat or desist from efforts to make a lawful arrest because of resistance or threatened resistance to the arrest. He is justified in the use of any force which he reasonably believes to be necessary to effect the arrest and of any force which he reasonably believes to be necessary to defend himself or another from bodily harm while making the arrest. However, he is justified in using force likely to cause death or great bodily harm only when he reasonably believes that such force is necessary to prevent death or great bodily harm to himself or such other person, or when he reasonably believes both that:

    (1) Such force is necessary to prevent the arrest from being defeated by resistance or escape; and

(2) The person to be arrested has committed or attempted a forcible felony which involves the infliction or threatened infliction of great bodily harm or is attempting to escape by use of a deadly weapon, or otherwise indicates that he will endanger human life or inflict great bodily harm unless arrested without delay.

(b) A peace officer making an arrest pursuant to an invalid warrant is justified in the use of any force which he would be justified in using if the warrant were valid, unless he knows that the warrant is invalid.

(Source: P.A. 84-1426.)

---

720 ILL. COMP. STAT. 5/7-5.5
SEC. 7-5.5. PROHIBITED USE OF FORCE BY A PEACE OFFICER.

(a) A peace officer shall not use a chokehold in the performance of his or her duties, unless deadly force is justified under Article 7 of this Code.

(b) A peace officer shall not use a chokehold, or any lesser contact with the throat or neck area of another, in order to prevent the destruction of evidence by ingestion.

(c) As used in this Section, "chokehold" means applying any direct pressure to the throat, windpipe, or airway of another with the intent to reduce or prevent the intake of air. "Chokehold" does not include any holding involving contact with the neck that is not intended to reduce the intake of air.

(Source: P.A. 99-352, eff. 1-1-16; 99-642, eff. 7-28-16.)

720 ILL. COMP. STAT. 5/7-6
SEC. 7-6. PRIVATE PERSON'S USE OF FORCE IN MAKING ARREST.

(a) A private person who makes, or assists another private person in making a lawful arrest is justified in the use of any force which he would be justified in using if he were summoned or directed by a peace officer to make such arrest, except that he is justified in the use of force likely to cause death or great bodily harm only when he reasonably believes that such force is necessary to prevent death or great bodily harm to himself or another.

(b) A private person who is summoned or directed by a peace officer to assist in making an arrest which is unlawful, is justified in the use of any force which he would be justified in using if the arrest were lawful, unless he knows that the arrest is unlawful.
(Source: Laws 1961, p. 1983.)

720 ILL. COMP. STAT. 5/7-7
SEC. 7-7. PRIVATE PERSON'S USE OF FORCE IN RESISTING ARREST.

A person is not authorized to use force to resist an arrest which he knows is being made either by a peace officer or by a private person summoned and directed by a peace officer to make the arrest, even if he believes that the arrest is unlawful and the arrest in fact is unlawful.
(Source: P.A. 86-1475.)

720 ILL. COMP. STAT. 5/7-8
SEC. 7-8. FORCE LIKELY TO CAUSE DEATH OR GREAT BODILY HARM.

(a) Force which is likely to cause death or great bodily harm, within the meaning of Sections 7-5 and 7-6 includes:

(1) The firing of a firearm in the direction of the person to be arrested, even though no intent exists to kill or inflict great bodily harm; and

(2) The firing of a firearm at a vehicle in which the person to be arrested is riding.

(b) A peace officer's discharge of a firearm using ammunition designed to disable or control an individual without creating the likelihood of death or great bodily harm shall not be considered force likely to cause death or great bodily harm within the meaning of Sections 7-5 and 7-6.

(Source: P.A. 90-138, eff. 1-1-98.)

720 ILL. COMP. STAT. 5/7-9
SEC. 7-9. USE OF FORCE TO PREVENT ESCAPE.

(a) A peace officer or other person who has an arrested person in his custody is justified in the use of such force to prevent the escape of the arrested person from custody as he would be justified in using if he were arresting such person.

(b) A guard or other peace officer is justified in the use of force, including force likely to cause death or great bodily harm, which he reasonably believes to be necessary to prevent the escape from a penal institution of a person whom the officer reasonably believes to be lawfully detained in such institution under sentence for an offense or awaiting trial or commitment for an offense.

(Source: Laws 1961, p. 1983.)

720 ILL. COMP. STAT. 5/7-10
SEC. 7-10. EXECUTION OF DEATH SENTENCE.

A public officer who, in the exercise of his official duty, puts a

person to death pursuant to a sentence of a court of competent jurisdiction, is justified if he acts in accordance with the sentence pronounced and the law prescribing the procedure for execution of a death sentence.
(Source: Laws 1961, p. 1983.)

720 ILL. COMP. STAT. 5/7-11
SEC. 7-11. COMPULSION.

(a) A person is not guilty of an offense, other than an offense punishable with death, by reason of conduct that he or she performs under the compulsion of threat or menace of the imminent infliction of death or great bodily harm, if he or she reasonably believes death or great bodily harm will be inflicted upon him or her, or upon his or her spouse or child, if he or she does not perform that conduct.

(b) A married woman is not entitled, by reason of the presence of her husband, to any presumption of compulsion or to any defense of compulsion, except that stated in subsection (a).
(Source: P.A. 96-710, eff. 1-1-10.)

720 ILL. COMP. STAT. 5/7-12 SEC. 7-12. ENTRAPMENT.

A person is not guilty of an offense if his or her conduct is incited or induced by a public officer or employee, or agent of either, for the purpose of obtaining evidence for the prosecution of that person. However, this Section is inapplicable if the person was predisposed to commit the offense and the public officer or employee, or agent of either, merely affords to that person the opportunity or facility for committing an offense.
(Source: P.A. 89-332, eff. 1-1-96.)

720 ILL. COMP. STAT. 5/7-13
SEC. 7-13. NECESSITY.

Conduct which would otherwise be an offense is justifiable by reason of necessity if the accused was without blame in occasioning or developing the situation and reasonably believed such conduct was necessary to avoid a public or private injury greater than the injury which might reasonably result from his own conduct.
(Source: Laws 1961, p. 1983.)

720 ILL. COMP. STAT. 5/7-14
SEC. 7-14. AFFIRMATIVE DEFENSE.

A defense of justifiable use of force, or of exoneration, based on the provisions of this Article is an affirmative defense.
(Source: Laws 1961, p. 1983.)

720 ILL. COMP. STAT. 5/24-1
ARTICLE 24. DEADLY WEAPONS
(TEXT OF SECTION BEFORE AMENDMENT BY P.A. 101-223)
SEC. 24-1. UNLAWFUL USE OF WEAPONS.

(a) A person commits the offense of unlawful use of weapons when he knowingly:

  (1) Sells, manufactures, purchases, possesses or carries any bludgeon, black-jack, slung-shot, sand-club, sand-bag, metal knuckles or other knuckle weapon regardless of its composition, throwing star, or any knife, commonly referred to as a switchblade knife, which has a blade that opens automatically by hand pressure applied to a button, spring or other device in the handle of the knife, or a ballistic knife, which is a device that propels a knifelike blade as a projectile

by means of a coil spring, elastic material or compressed gas; or

(2) Carries or possesses with intent to use the same unlawfully against another, a dagger, dirk, billy, dangerous knife, razor, stiletto, broken bottle or other piece of glass, stun gun or taser or any other dangerous or deadly weapon or instrument of like character; or

(3) Carries on or about his person or in any vehicle, a tear gas gun projector or bomb or any object containing noxious liquid gas or substance, other than an object containing a non-lethal noxious liquid gas or substance designed solely for personal defense carried by a person 18 years of age or older; or

(4) Carries or possesses in any vehicle or concealed on or about his person except when on his land or in his own abode, legal dwelling, or fixed place of business, or on the land or in the legal dwelling of another person as an invitee with that person's permission, any pistol, revolver, stun gun or taser or other firearm, except that this subsection (a) (4) does not apply to or affect transportation of weapons that meet one of the following conditions:

    (i) are broken down in a non-functioning state; or

    (ii) are not immediately accessible; or

    (iii) are unloaded and enclosed in a case, firearm carrying box, shipping box, or other container by a person who has been issued a currently valid Firearm Owner's Identification Card; or

    (iv) are carried or possessed in accordance with the Firearm Concealed Carry Act by a person who has been issued a currently valid license under the Firearm Concealed Carry Act; or

(5) Sets a spring gun; or

(6) Possesses any device or attachment of any kind designed, used or intended for use in silencing the report of any firearm; or

(7) Sells, manufactures, purchases, possesses or carries:

(i) a machine gun, which shall be defined for the purposes of this subsection as any weapon, which shoots, is designed to shoot, or can be readily restored to shoot, automatically more than one shot without manually reloading by a single function of the trigger, including the frame or receiver of any such weapon, or sells, manufactures, purchases, possesses, or carries any combination of parts designed or intended for use in converting any weapon into a machine gun, or any combination or parts from which a machine gun can be assembled if such parts are in the possession or under the control of a person;

(ii) any rifle having one or more barrels less than 16 inches in length or a shotgun having one or more barrels less than 18 inches in length or any weapon made from a rifle or shotgun, whether by alteration, modification, or otherwise, if such a weapon as modified has an overall length of less than 26 inches; or

(iii) any bomb, bomb-shell, grenade, bottle or other container containing an explosive substance of over one-quarter ounce for like purposes, such as, but not limited to, black powder bombs and Molotov cocktails or artillery projectiles; or

(8) Carries or possesses any firearm, stun gun or taser or other deadly weapon in any place which is licensed to sell intoxicating beverages, or at any public gathering held pursuant to a license issued by any governmental body or any public gathering at which an admission is charged, excluding

a place where a showing, demonstration or lecture involving the exhibition of unloaded firearms is conducted.

This subsection (a)(8) does not apply to any auction or raffle of a firearm held pursuant to a license or permit issued by a governmental body, nor does it apply to persons engaged in firearm safety training courses; or

(9) Carries or possesses in a vehicle or on or about his person any pistol, revolver, stun gun or taser or firearm or ballistic knife, when he is hooded, robed or masked in such manner as to conceal his identity; or

(10) Carries or possesses on or about his person, upon any public street, alley, or other public lands within the corporate limits of a city, village or incorporated town, except when an invitee thereon or therein, for the purpose of the display of such weapon or the lawful commerce in weapons, or except when on his land or in his own abode, legal dwelling, or fixed place of business, or on the land or in the legal dwelling of another person as an invitee with that person's permission, any pistol, revolver, stun gun or taser or other firearm, except that this subsection (a) (10) does not apply to or affect transportation of weapons that meet one of the following conditions:

    (i) are broken down in a non-functioning state; or

    (ii) are not immediately accessible; or

    (iii) are unloaded and enclosed in a case, firearm carrying box, shipping box, or other container by a person who has been issued a currently valid Firearm Owner's Identification Card; or

    (iv) are carried or possessed in accordance with the Firearm Concealed Carry Act by a person who has been issued a currently valid license under the Firearm Concealed Carry Act.

A "stun gun or taser", as used in this paragraph (a) means (i) any device which is powered by electrical charging units, such as, batteries, and which fires one or several barbs attached to a length of wire and which, upon hitting a human, can send out a current capable of disrupting the person's nervous system in such a manner as to render him incapable of normal functioning or (ii) any device which is powered by electrical charging units, such as batteries, and which, upon contact with a human or clothing worn by a human, can send out current capable of disrupting the person's nervous system in such a manner as to render him incapable of normal functioning; or

(11) Sells, manufactures or purchases any explosive bullet. For purposes of this paragraph (a) "explosive bullet" means the projectile portion of an ammunition cartridge which contains or carries an explosive charge which will explode upon contact with the flesh of a human or an animal. "Cartridge" means a tubular metal case having a projectile affixed at the front thereof and a cap or primer at the rear end thereof, with the propellant contained in such tube between the projectile and the cap; or

(12) (Blank); or

(13) Carries or possesses on or about his or her person while in a building occupied by a unit of government, a billy club, other weapon of like character, or other instrument of like character intended for use as a weapon. For the purposes of this Section, "billy club" means a short stick or club commonly carried by police officers which is either telescopic or constructed of a solid piece of wood or other man-made material.

(b) Sentence. A person convicted of a violation of subsection 24-

1(a)(1) through (5), subsection 24-1(a)(10), subsection 24-1(a)(11), or subsection 24-1(a)(13) commits a Class A misdemeanor. A person convicted of a violation of subsection 24-1(a)(8) or 24-1(a)(9) commits a Class 4 felony; a person convicted of a violation of subsection 24-1(a)(6) or 24-1(a)(7)(ii) or (iii) commits a Class 3 felony. A person convicted of a violation of subsection 24-1(a)(7)(i) commits a Class 2 felony and shall be sentenced to a term of imprisonment of not less than 3 years and not more than 7 years, unless the weapon is possessed in the passenger compartment of a motor vehicle as defined in Section 1-146 of the Illinois Vehicle Code, or on the person, while the weapon is loaded, in which case it shall be a Class X felony. A person convicted of a second or subsequent violation of subsection 24-1(a)(4), 24-1(a)(8), 24-1(a)(9), or 24-1(a)(10) commits a Class 3 felony. The possession of each weapon in violation of this Section constitutes a single and separate violation.

(c) Violations in specific places.

(1) A person who violates subsection 24-1(a)(6) or 24-1(a)(7) in any school, regardless of the time of day or the time of year, in residential property owned, operated or managed by a public housing agency or leased by a public housing agency as part of a scattered site or mixed-income development, in a public park, in a courthouse, on the real property comprising any school, regardless of the time of day or the time of year, on residential property owned, operated or managed by a public housing agency or leased by a public housing agency as part of a scattered site or mixed-income development, on the real property comprising any public park, on the real property comprising any courthouse, in any conveyance owned, leased or contracted by a school to transport students to or from school or a school related activity, in any conveyance

owned, leased, or contracted by a public transportation agency, or on any public way within 1,000 feet of the real property comprising any school, public park, courthouse, public transportation facility, or residential property owned, operated, or managed by a public housing agency or leased by a public housing agency as part of a scattered site or mixed-income development commits a Class 2 felony and shall be sentenced to a term of imprisonment of not less than 3 years and not more than 7 years.

(1.5) A person who violates subsection 24-1(a)(4), 24-1(a)(9), or 24-1(a)(10) in any school, regardless of the time of day or the time of year, in residential property owned, operated, or managed by a public housing agency or leased by a public housing agency as part of a scattered site or mixed-income development, in a public park, in a courthouse, on the real property comprising any school, regardless of the time of day or the time of year, on residential property owned, operated, or managed by a public housing agency or leased by a public housing agency as part of a scattered site or mixed-income development, on the real property comprising any public park, on the real property comprising any courthouse, in any conveyance owned, leased, or contracted by a school to transport students to or from school or a school related activity, in any conveyance owned, leased, or contracted by a public transportation agency, or on any public way within 1,000 feet of the real property comprising any school, public park, courthouse, public transportation facility, or residential property owned, operated, or managed by a public housing agency or leased by a public housing agency as part of a scattered site or mixed-income development commits a Class 3 felony.

(2) A person who violates subsection 24-1(a)(1), 24-1(a)(2), or 24-1(a)(3) in any school, regardless of the time of day or the time of year, in residential property owned, operated or managed by a public housing agency or leased by a public housing agency as part of a scattered site or mixed-income development, in a public park, in a courthouse, on the real property comprising any school, regardless of the time of day or the time of year, on residential property owned, operated or managed by a public housing agency or leased by a public housing agency as part of a scattered site or mixed-income development, on the real property comprising any public park, on the real property comprising any courthouse, in any conveyance owned, leased or contracted by a school to transport students to or from school or a school related activity, in any conveyance owned, leased, or contracted by a public transportation agency, or on any public way within 1,000 feet of the real property comprising any school, public park, courthouse, public transportation facility, or residential property owned, operated, or managed by a public housing agency or leased by a public housing agency as part of a scattered site or mixed-income development commits a Class 4 felony. "Courthouse" means any building that is used by the Circuit, Appellate, or Supreme Court of this State for the conduct of official business.

(3) Paragraphs (1), (1.5), and (2) of this subsection (c) shall not apply to law enforcement officers or security officers of such school, college, or university or to students carrying or possessing firearms for use in training courses, parades, hunting, target shooting on school ranges, or otherwise with the consent of school authorities and which firearms are transported unloaded enclosed in a suitable case, box, or

transportation package.

(4) For the purposes of this subsection (c), "school" means any public or private elementary or secondary school, community college, college, or university.

(5) For the purposes of this subsection (c), "public transportation agency" means a public or private agency that provides for the transportation or conveyance of persons by means available to the general public, except for transportation by automobiles not used for conveyance of the general public as passengers; and "public transportation facility" means a terminal or other place where one may obtain public transportation.

(d) The presence in an automobile other than a public omnibus of any weapon, instrument or substance referred to in subsection (a)(7) is prima facie evidence that it is in the possession of, and is being carried by, all persons occupying such automobile at the time such weapon, instrument or substance is found, except under the following circumstances: (i) if such weapon, instrument or instrumentality is found upon the person of one of the occupants therein; or (ii) if such weapon, instrument or substance is found in an automobile operated for hire by a duly licensed driver in the due, lawful and proper pursuit of his trade, then such presumption shall not apply to the driver.

(e) Exemptions.

(1) Crossbows, Common or Compound bows and Underwater Spearguns are exempted from the definition of ballistic knife as defined in paragraph (1) of subsection (a) of this Section.

(2) The provision of paragraph (1) of subsection (a) of this Section prohibiting the sale, manufacture, purchase, possession, or carrying of any knife, commonly referred to as a switchblade knife, which has a blade that opens automatically by hand

pressure applied to a button, spring or other device in the handle of the knife, does not apply to a person who possesses a currently valid Firearm Owner's Identification Card previously issued in his or her name by the Department of State Police or to a person or an entity engaged in the business of selling or manufacturing switchblade knives.

(Source: P.A. 99-29, eff. 7-10-15; 100-82, eff. 8-11-17.)

(TEXT OF SECTION AFTER AMENDMENT BY P.A. 101-223)
SEC. 24-1. UNLAWFUL USE OF WEAPONS.

(a) A person commits the offense of unlawful use of weapons when he knowingly:

(1) Sells, manufactures, purchases, possesses or carries any bludgeon, black-jack, slung-shot, sand-club, sand-bag, metal knuckles or other knuckle weapon regardless of its composition, throwing star, or any knife, commonly referred to as a switchblade knife, which has a blade that opens automatically by hand pressure applied to a button, spring or other device in the handle of the knife, or a ballistic knife, which is a device that propels a knifelike blade as a projectile by means of a coil spring, elastic material or compressed gas; or

(2) Carries or possesses with intent to use the same unlawfully against another, a dagger, dirk, billy, dangerous knife, razor, stiletto, broken bottle or other piece of glass, stun gun or taser or any other dangerous or deadly weapon or instrument of like character; or

(2.5) Carries or possesses with intent to use the same unlawfully against another, any firearm in a church, synagogue, mosque, or other building, structure, or place used for religious worship; or

(3) Carries on or about his person or in any vehicle, a tear gas gun projector or bomb or any object containing noxious liquid gas or substance, other than an object containing a non-lethal noxious liquid gas or substance designed solely for personal defense carried by a person 18 years of age or older; or

(4) Carries or possesses in any vehicle or concealed on or about his person except when on his land or in his own abode, legal dwelling, or fixed place of business, or on the land or in the legal dwelling of another person as an invitee with that person's permission, any pistol, revolver, stun gun or taser or other firearm, except that this subsection (a) (4) does not apply to or affect transportation of weapons that meet one of the following conditions:

   (i) are broken down in a non-functioning state; or

   (ii) are not immediately accessible; or

   (iii) are unloaded and enclosed in a case, firearm carrying box, shipping box, or other container by a person who has been issued a currently valid Firearm Owner's Identification Card; or

   (iv) are carried or possessed in accordance with the Firearm Concealed Carry Act by a person who has been issued a currently valid license under the Firearm Concealed Carry Act; or

(5) Sets a spring gun; or

(6) Possesses any device or attachment of any kind designed, used or intended for use in silencing the report of any firearm; or

(7) Sells, manufactures, purchases, possesses or carries:

   (i) a machine gun, which shall be defined for the purposes of this subsection as any weapon, which shoots, is designed to shoot, or can be readily restored to shoot, automatically more than one shot without manually reloading by a single function of the trigger, including the frame or receiver of any such weapon, or sells, manufactures, purchases, possesses, or carries any combination of parts designed or intended for use in converting any weapon into a machine gun, or any combination or parts from which a machine gun can be assembled if such parts are in the possession or under the control of a person;

(ii) any rifle having one or more barrels less than 16 inches in length or a shotgun having one or more barrels less than 18 inches in length or any weapon made from a rifle or shotgun, whether by alteration, modification, or otherwise, if such a weapon as modified has an overall length of less than 26 inches; or

(iii) any bomb, bomb-shell, grenade, bottle or other container containing an explosive substance of over one-quarter ounce for like purposes, such as, but not limited to, black powder bombs and Molotov cocktails or artillery projectiles; or

(8) Carries or possesses any firearm, stun gun or taser or other deadly weapon in any place which is licensed to sell intoxicating beverages, or at any public gathering held pursuant to a license issued by any governmental body or any public gathering at which an admission is charged, excluding a place where a showing, demonstration or lecture involving the exhibition of unloaded firearms is conducted.

This subsection (a)(8) does not apply to any auction or raffle of a firearm held pursuant to a license or permit issued by a governmental body, nor does it apply to persons engaged in firearm safety training courses; or

(9) Carries or possesses in a vehicle or on or about his or her person any pistol, revolver, stun gun or taser or firearm or ballistic knife, when he or she is hooded, robed or masked in such manner as to conceal his or her identity; or

(10) Carries or possesses on or about his or her person, upon any public street, alley, or other public lands within the corporate limits of a city, village, or incorporated town, except when an invitee thereon or therein, for the purpose of the display of such weapon or the lawful commerce in weapons, or except when on his land or in his or her own abode, legal dwelling, or fixed place of business, or on the land or in the legal dwelling of another person as an invitee with that person's permission, any pistol, revolver, stun gun, or taser or other firearm, except that this subsection (a) (10) does not apply to or affect transportation of weapons that meet one of the following conditions:

   (i) are broken down in a non-functioning state; or

   (ii) are not immediately accessible; or

   (iii) are unloaded and enclosed in a case, firearm carrying box, shipping box, or other container by a person who has been issued a currently valid Firearm Owner's Identification Card; or

   (iv) are carried or possessed in accordance with the Firearm Concealed Carry Act by a person who has been issued a currently valid license under the Firearm Concealed Carry Act.

A "stun gun or taser", as used in this paragraph (a) means (i) any device which is powered by electrical charging units, such as, batteries, and which fires one or several barbs attached to a length of wire and which, upon hitting a human, can send out a current capable of disrupting the person's nervous system in such a manner as to render him incapable of normal functioning or (ii) any device which is powered by electrical charging units, such as batteries, and which, upon contact with a human or clothing worn by a human, can send out current capable of disrupting the person's nervous system in such a manner as to render him incapable of normal functioning; or

(11) Sells, manufactures, or purchases any explosive bullet. For purposes of this paragraph (a) "explosive bullet" means the projectile portion of an ammunition cartridge which contains or carries an explosive charge which will explode upon contact with the flesh of a human or an animal. "Cartridge" means a tubular metal case having a projectile affixed at the front thereof and a cap or primer at the rear end thereof, with the propellant contained in such tube between the projectile and the cap; or

(12) (Blank); or

(13) Carries or possesses on or about his or her person while in a building occupied by a unit of government, a billy club, other weapon of like character, or other instrument of like character intended for use as a weapon. For the purposes of this Section, "billy club" means a short stick or club commonly carried by police officers which is either telescopic or constructed of a solid piece of wood or other man-made material.

(b) Sentence. A person convicted of a violation of subsection 24-1(a)(1) through (5), subsection 24-1(a)(10), subsection 24-1(a)(11), or subsection 24-1(a)(13) commits a Class A misdemeanor. A person convicted of a violation of subsection 24-1(a)(8) or 24-1(a)(9) commits a Class 4 felony; a person convicted of a violation of subsection 24-1(a)(6) or 24-1(a)(7)(ii) or (iii) commits a Class 3 felony. A person convicted of a violation of subsection 24-1(a)(7)

(i) commits a Class 2 felony and shall be sentenced to a term of imprisonment of not less than 3 years and not more than 7 years, unless the weapon is possessed in the passenger compartment of a motor vehicle as defined in Section 1-146 of the Illinois Vehicle Code, or on the person, while the weapon is loaded, in which case it shall be a Class X felony. A person convicted of a second or subsequent violation of subsection 24-1(a)(4), 24-1(a)(8), 24-1(a)(9), or 24-1(a)(10) commits a Class 3 felony. A person convicted of a violation of subsection 24-1(a)(2.5) commits a Class 2 felony. The possession of each weapon in violation of this Section constitutes a single and separate violation.

(c) Violations in specific places.

  (1) A person who violates subsection 24-1(a)(6) or 24-1(a)(7) in any school, regardless of the time of day or the time of year, in residential property owned, operated or managed by a public housing agency or leased by a public housing agency as part of a scattered site or mixed-income development, in a public park, in a courthouse, on the real property comprising any school, regardless of the time of day or the time of year, on residential property owned, operated or managed by a public housing agency or leased by a public housing agency as part of a scattered site or mixed-income development, on the real property comprising any public park, on the real property comprising any courthouse, in any conveyance owned, leased or contracted by a school to transport students to or from school or a school related activity, in any conveyance owned, leased, or contracted by a public transportation agency, or on any public way within 1,000 feet of the real property comprising any school, public park, courthouse, public transportation facility, or residential property owned, operated, or managed by a public housing agency or leased

by a public housing agency as part of a scattered site or mixed-income development commits a Class 2 felony and shall be sentenced to a term of imprisonment of not less than 3 years and not more than 7 years.

(1.5) A person who violates subsection 24-1(a)(4), 24-1(a)(9), or 24-1(a)(10) in any school, regardless of the time of day or the time of year, in residential property owned, operated, or managed by a public housing agency or leased by a public housing agency as part of a scattered site or mixed-income development, in a public park, in a courthouse, on the real property comprising any school, regardless of the time of day or the time of year, on residential property owned, operated, or managed by a public housing agency or leased by a public housing agency as part of a scattered site or mixed-income development, on the real property comprising any public park, on the real property comprising any courthouse, in any conveyance owned, leased, or contracted by a school to transport students to or from school or a school related activity, in any conveyance owned, leased, or contracted by a public transportation agency, or on any public way within 1,000 feet of the real property comprising any school, public park, courthouse, public transportation facility, or residential property owned, operated, or managed by a public housing agency or leased by a public housing agency as part of a scattered site or mixed-income development commits a Class 3 felony.

(2) A person who violates subsection 24-1(a)(1), 24-1(a)(2), or 24-1(a)(3) in any school, regardless of the time of day or the time of year, in residential property owned, operated or managed by a public housing agency or leased by a public housing agency as part of a scattered site or mixed-income

development, in a public park, in a courthouse, on the real property comprising any school, regardless of the time of day or the time of year, on residential property owned, operated or managed by a public housing agency or leased by a public housing agency as part of a scattered site or mixed-income development, on the real property comprising any public park, on the real property comprising any courthouse, in any conveyance owned, leased or contracted by a school to transport students to or from school or a school related activity, in any conveyance owned, leased, or contracted by a public transportation agency, or on any public way within 1,000 feet of the real property comprising any school, public park, courthouse, public transportation facility, or residential property owned, operated, or managed by a public housing agency or leased by a public housing agency as part of a scattered site or mixed-income development commits a Class 4 felony. "Courthouse" means any building that is used by the Circuit, Appellate, or Supreme Court of this State for the conduct of official business.

(3) Paragraphs (1), (1.5), and (2) of this subsection (c) shall not apply to law enforcement officers or security officers of such school, college, or university or to students carrying or possessing firearms for use in training courses, parades, hunting, target shooting on school ranges, or otherwise with the consent of school authorities and which firearms are transported unloaded enclosed in a suitable case, box, or transportation package.

(4) For the purposes of this subsection (c), "school" means any public or private elementary or secondary school, community college, college, or university.

(5) For the purposes of this subsection (c), "public transportation

agency" means a public or private agency that provides for the transportation or conveyance of persons by means available to the general public, except for transportation by automobiles not used for conveyance of the general public as passengers; and "public transportation facility" means a terminal or other place where one may obtain public transportation.

(d) The presence in an automobile other than a public omnibus of any weapon, instrument or substance referred to in subsection (a)(7) is prima facie evidence that it is in the possession of, and is being carried by, all persons occupying such automobile at the time such weapon, instrument or substance is found, except under the following circumstances: (i) if such weapon, instrument or instrumentality is found upon the person of one of the occupants therein; or (ii) if such weapon, instrument or substance is found in an automobile operated for hire by a duly licensed driver in the due, lawful and proper pursuit of his or her trade, then such presumption shall not apply to the driver.

(e) Exemptions.

(1) Crossbows, Common or Compound bows and Underwater Spearguns are exempted from the definition of ballistic knife as defined in paragraph (1) of subsection (a) of this Section.

(2) The provision of paragraph (1) of subsection (a) of this Section prohibiting the sale, manufacture, purchase, possession, or carrying of any knife, commonly referred to as a switchblade knife, which has a blade that opens automatically by hand pressure applied to a button, spring or other device in the handle of the knife, does not apply to a person who possesses a currently valid Firearm Owner's Identification Card previously issued in his or her name by the Department of State Police or to a person or an entity engaged in the

business of selling or manufacturing switchblade knives.
(Source: P.A. 100-82, eff. 8-11-17; 101-223, eff. 1-1-20.)

ILLINOIS COMPILED STATUTES CHAPTER 430
PUBLIC SAFETY
430 ILL. COMP. STAT. 65/0.01 FIREARM OWNERS IDENTIFICATION CARD ACT
SEC. 0.01. SHORT TITLE.

This Act may be cited as the Firearm Owners Identification Card Act.
(Source: P.A. 86-1324.)

430 ILL. COMP. STAT. 65/1
SEC. 1.

It is hereby declared as a matter of legislative determination that in order to promote and protect the health, safety and welfare of the public, it is necessary and in the public interest to provide a system of identifying persons who are not qualified to acquire or possess firearms, firearm ammunition, stun guns, and tasers within the State of Illinois by the establishment of a system of Firearm Owner's Identification Cards, thereby establishing a practical and workable system by which law enforcement authorities will be afforded an opportunity to identify those persons who are prohibited by Section 24-3.1 of the Criminal Code of 2012, from acquiring or possessing firearms and firearm ammunition and who are prohibited by this Act from acquiring stun guns and tasers.
(Source: P.A. 97-1150, eff. 1-25-13.)

430 ILL. COMP. STAT. 65/1.1
SEC. 1.1.

For purposes of this Act:

"Addicted to narcotics" means a person who has been:

(1) convicted of an offense involving the use or possession of cannabis, a controlled substance, or methamphetamine within the past year; or

(2) determined by the Department of State Police to be addicted to narcotics based upon federal law or federal guidelines.

"Addicted to narcotics" does not include possession or use of a prescribed controlled substance under the direction and authority of a physician or other person authorized to prescribe the controlled substance when the controlled substance is used in the prescribed manner.

"Adjudicated as a person with a mental disability" means the person is the subject of a determination by a court, board, commission or other lawful authority that the person, as a result of marked subnormal intelligence, or mental illness, mental impairment, incompetency, condition, or disease:

(1) presents a clear and present danger to himself, herself, or to others;

(2) lacks the mental capacity to manage his or her own affairs or is adjudicated a person with a disability as defined in Section 11a-2 of the Probate Act of 1975;

(3) is not guilty in a criminal case by reason of insanity, mental disease or defect;

(3.5) is guilty but mentally ill, as provided in Section 5-2-6 of the Unified Code of Corrections;

(4) is incompetent to stand trial in a criminal case;

(5) is not guilty by reason of lack of mental responsibility under Articles 50a and 72b of the Uniform Code of Military Justice, 10 U.S.C. 850a, 876b;

(6) is a sexually violent person under subsection (f) of Section 5 of the Sexually Violent Persons Commitment Act;

(7) is a sexually dangerous person under the Sexually Dangerous Persons Act;

(8) is unfit to stand trial under the Juvenile Court Act of 1987;

(9) is not guilty by reason of insanity under the Juvenile Court Act of 1987;

(10) is subject to involuntary admission as an inpatient as defined in Section 1-119 of the Mental Health and Developmental Disabilities Code;

(11) is subject to involuntary admission as an outpatient as defined in Section 1-119.1 of the Mental Health and Developmental Disabilities Code;

(12) is subject to judicial admission as set forth in Section 4-500 of the Mental Health and Developmental Disabilities Code; or

(13) is subject to the provisions of the Interstate Agreements on Sexually Dangerous Persons Act.

"Clear and present danger" means a person who:

(1) communicates a serious threat of physical violence against a reasonably identifiable victim or poses a clear and imminent risk of serious physical injury to himself, herself, or another person as determined by a physician, clinical psychologist, or qualified examiner; or

(2) demonstrates threatening physical or verbal behavior, such as violent, suicidal, or assaultive threats, actions, or other behavior, as determined by a physician, clinical psychologist, qualified examiner, school administrator, or law enforcement official.

"Clinical psychologist" has the meaning provided in Section 1-103 of the Mental Health and Developmental Disabilities Code.

"Controlled substance" means a controlled substance or controlled substance analog as defined in the Illinois Controlled Substances Act.

"Counterfeit" means to copy or imitate, without legal authority, with intent to deceive.

"Federally licensed firearm dealer" means a person who is licensed as a federal firearms dealer under Section 923 of the federal Gun Control Act of 1968 (18 U.S.C. 923).

"Firearm" means any device, by whatever name known, which is designed to expel a projectile or projectiles by the action of an explosion, expansion of gas or escape of gas; excluding, however:

(1) any pneumatic gun, spring gun, paint ball gun, or B-B gun which expels a single globular projectile not exceeding .18 inch in diameter or which has a maximum muzzle velocity of less than 700 feet per second;

(1.1) any pneumatic gun, spring gun, paint ball gun, or B-B gun which expels breakable paint balls containing washable marking colors;

(2) any device used exclusively for signalling or safety and required or recommended by the United States Coast Guard or the Interstate Commerce Commission;

(3) any device used exclusively for the firing of stud cartridges, explosive rivets or similar industrial ammunition; and

(4) an antique firearm (other than a machine-gun) which, although designed as a weapon, the Department of State Police finds by reason of the date of its manufacture, value, design, and other characteristics is primarily a collector's item and is not likely to be used as a weapon.

"Firearm ammunition" means any self-contained cartridge or shotgun shell, by whatever name known, which is designed to be used or adaptable to use in a firearm; excluding, however:

(1) any ammunition exclusively designed for use with a device used exclusively for signalling or safety and required or recommended by the United States Coast Guard or the Interstate Commerce Commission; and

(2) any ammunition designed exclusively for use with a stud or rivet driver or other similar industrial ammunition.

"Gun show" means an event or function:

(1) at which the sale and transfer of firearms is the regular and normal course of business and where 50 or more firearms are displayed, offered, or exhibited for sale, transfer, or exchange; or

(2) at which not less than 10 gun show vendors display, offer, or exhibit for sale, sell, transfer, or exchange firearms.

"Gun show" includes the entire premises provided for an event or function, including parking areas for the event or function, that is sponsored to facilitate the purchase, sale, transfer, or exchange of firearms as described in this Section. Nothing in this definition shall be construed to exclude a gun show held in conjunction with competitive shooting events at the World Shooting Complex sanctioned by a national governing body in which the sale or transfer of firearms is authorized under subparagraph (5) of paragraph (g) of subsection (A) of Section 24-3 of the Criminal Code of 2012.

Unless otherwise expressly stated, "gun show" does not include training or safety classes, competitive shooting events, such as rifle, shotgun, or handgun matches, trap, skeet, or sporting clays shoots, dinners, banquets, raffles, or any other event where the sale or transfer of firearms is not the primary course of business.

"Gun show promoter" means a person who organizes or operates a gun show.

"Gun show vendor" means a person who exhibits, sells, offers for sale, transfers, or exchanges any firearms at a gun show, regardless of whether the person arranges with a gun show promoter for a fixed location from which to exhibit, sell, offer for sale, transfer, or exchange any firearm.

"Involuntarily admitted" has the meaning as prescribed in Sections 1-119 and 1-119.1 of the Mental Health and Developmental Disabilities Code.

"Mental health facility" means any licensed private hospital or hospital affiliate, institution, or facility, or part thereof, and any facility, or part thereof, operated by the State or a political subdivision thereof which provide treatment of persons with mental illness and includes all hospitals, institutions, clinics, evaluation facilities, mental health centers, colleges, universities, long-term care facilities, and nursing homes, or parts thereof, which provide treatment of persons with mental illness whether or not the primary purpose is to provide treatment of persons with mental illness.

"National governing body" means a group of persons who adopt rules and formulate policy on behalf of a national firearm sporting organization.

"Patient" means:

(1) a person who is admitted as an inpatient or resident of a public or private mental health facility for mental health treatment under Chapter III of the Mental Health and Developmental Disabilities Code as an informal admission, a voluntary admission, a minor admission, an emergency admission, or an involuntary admission, unless the treatment was solely for an alcohol abuse disorder; or

(2) a person who voluntarily or involuntarily receives mental health treatment as an out-patient or is otherwise provided services by a public or private mental health facility, and who poses a clear and present danger to himself, herself, or to others.

"Person with a developmental disability" means a person with a disability which is attributable to any other condition which results in impairment similar to that caused by an intellectual disability and which requires services similar to those required by persons with intellectual disabilities. The disability must originate before the age of 18 years, be expected to continue indefinitely, and constitute a substantial disability. This disability results, in the professional opinion of a physician, clinical psychologist, or qualified examiner, in significant functional limitations in 3 or more of the following areas of major life activity:

  (i) self-care;

  (ii) receptive and expressive language;

  (iii) learning;

  (iv) mobility; or

  (v) self-direction.

"Person with an intellectual disability" means a person with a significantly subaverage general intellectual functioning which exists concurrently with impairment in adaptive behavior and which originates before the age of 18 years.

"Physician" has the meaning as defined in Section 1-120 of the Mental Health and Developmental Disabilities Code.

"Qualified examiner" has the meaning provided in Section 1-122 of the Mental Health and Developmental Disabilities Code.

"Sanctioned competitive shooting event" means a shooting contest officially recognized by a national or state shooting sport association, and includes any sight-in or practice conducted in conjunction with the event.

"School administrator" means the person required to report under the School Administrator Reporting of Mental Health Clear and Present Danger Determinations Law.

"Stun gun or taser" has the meaning ascribed to it in Section 24-1 of the Criminal Code of 2012.

(Source: P.A. 99-29, eff. 7-10-15; 99-143, eff. 7-27-15; 99-642, eff. 7-28-16; 100-906, eff. 1-1-19.)

430 ILL. COMP. STAT. 65/2
SEC. 2. FIREARM OWNER'S IDENTIFICATION CARD REQUIRED; EXCEPTIONS.

(a)

    (1) No person may acquire or possess any firearm, stun gun, or taser within this State without having in his or her possession a Firearm Owner's Identification Card previously issued in his or her name by the Department of State Police under the provisions of this Act.

    (2) No person may acquire or possess firearm ammunition within this State without having in his or her possession a Firearm Owner's Identification Card previously issued in his or her name by the Department of State Police under the provisions of this Act.

(b) The provisions of this Section regarding the possession of firearms, firearm ammunition, stun guns, and tasers do not apply to:

    (1) United States Marshals, while engaged in the operation of their official duties;

    (2) Members of the Armed Forces of the United States or the National Guard, while engaged in the operation of their official duties;

    (3) Federal officials required to carry firearms, while engaged in the operation of their official duties;

    (4) Members of bona fide veterans organizations which receive firearms directly from the armed forces of the United States, while using the firearms for ceremonial purposes with blank ammunition;

(5) Nonresident hunters during hunting season, with valid nonresident hunting licenses and while in an area where hunting is permitted; however, at all other times and in all other places these persons must have their firearms unloaded and enclosed in a case;

(6) Those hunters exempt from obtaining a hunting license who are required to submit their Firearm Owner's Identification Card when hunting on Department of Natural Resources owned or managed sites;

(7) Nonresidents while on a firing or shooting range recognized by the Department of State Police; however, these persons must at all other times and in all other places have their firearms unloaded and enclosed in a case;

(8) Nonresidents while at a firearm showing or display recognized by the Department of State Police; however, at all other times and in all other places these persons must have their firearms unloaded and enclosed in a case;

(9) Nonresidents whose firearms are unloaded and enclosed in a case;

(10) Nonresidents who are currently licensed or registered to possess a firearm in their resident state;

(11) Unemancipated minors while in the custody and immediate control of their parent or legal guardian or other person in loco parentis to the minor if the parent or legal guardian or other person in loco parentis to the minor has a currently valid Firearm Owner's Identification Card;

(12) Color guards of bona fide veterans organizations or members of bona fide American Legion bands while using firearms for ceremonial purposes with blank ammunition;

(13) Nonresident hunters whose state of residence does not require them to be licensed or registered to possess a firearm

and only during hunting season, with valid hunting licenses, while accompanied by, and using a firearm owned by, a person who possesses a valid Firearm Owner's Identification Card and while in an area within a commercial club licensed under the Wildlife Code where hunting is permitted and controlled, but in no instance upon sites owned or managed by the Department of Natural Resources;

(14) Resident hunters who are properly authorized to hunt and, while accompanied by a person who possesses a valid Firearm Owner's Identification Card, hunt in an area within a commercial club licensed under the Wildlife Code where hunting is permitted and controlled;

(15) A person who is otherwise eligible to obtain a Firearm Owner's Identification Card under this Act and is under the direct supervision of a holder of a Firearm Owner's Identification Card who is 21 years of age or older while the person is on a firing or shooting range or is a participant in a firearms safety and training course recognized by a law enforcement agency or a national, statewide shooting sports organization; and

(16) Competitive shooting athletes whose competition firearms are sanctioned by the International Olympic Committee, the International Paralympic Committee, the International Shooting Sport Federation, or USA Shooting in connection with such athletes' training for and participation in shooting competitions at the 2016 Olympic and Paralympic Games and sanctioned test events leading up to the 2016 Olympic and Paralympic Games.

(c) The provisions of this Section regarding the acquisition and possession of firearms, firearm ammunition, stun guns, and tasers do not apply to law enforcement officials of this or any other jurisdiction, while engaged in the operation of their official duties.

(c-5) The provisions of paragraphs (1) and (2) of subsection (a) of this Section regarding the possession of firearms and firearm ammunition do not apply to the holder of a valid concealed carry license issued under the Firearm Concealed Carry Act who is in physical possession of the concealed carry license.

(d) Any person who becomes a resident of this State, who is not otherwise prohibited from obtaining, possessing, or using a firearm or firearm ammunition, shall not be required to have a Firearm Owner's Identification Card to possess firearms or firearms ammunition until 60 calendar days after he or she obtains an Illinois driver's license or Illinois Identification Card.

(Source: P.A. 99-29, eff. 7-10-15.)

430 ILL. COMP. STAT. 65/3
SEC. 3.

(a) Except as provided in Section 3a, no person may knowingly transfer, or cause to be transferred, any firearm, firearm ammunition, stun gun, or taser to any person within this State unless the transferee with whom he deals displays either: (1) a currently valid Firearm Owner's Identification Card which has previously been issued in his or her name by the Department of State Police under the provisions of this Act; or (2) a currently valid license to carry a concealed firearm which has previously been issued in his or her name by the Department of State Police under the Firearm Concealed Carry Act. In addition, all firearm, stun gun, and taser transfers by federally licensed firearm dealers are subject to Section 3.1.

(a-5)   Any person who is not a federally licensed firearm dealer and who desires to transfer or sell a firearm while that person is on the grounds of a gun show must, before selling or transferring the firearm, request the Department of State Police to conduct a background check on the prospective recipient of the firearm in accordance with Section 3.1.

(a-10) Notwithstanding item (2) of subsection (a) of this Section, any person who is not a federally licensed firearm dealer and who desires to transfer or sell a firearm or firearms to any person who is not a federally licensed firearm dealer shall, before selling or transferring the firearms, contact the Department of State Police with the transferee's or purchaser's Firearm Owner's Identification Card number to determine the validity of the transferee's or purchaser's Firearm Owner's Identification Card. This subsection shall not be effective until January 1, 2014. The Department of State Police may adopt rules concerning the implementation of this subsection. The Department of State Police shall provide the seller or transferor an approval number if the purchaser's Firearm Owner's Identification Card is valid. Approvals issued by the Department for the purchase of a firearm pursuant to this subsection are valid for 30 days from the date of issue.

(a-15) The provisions of subsection (a-10) of this Section do not apply to:

(1) transfers that occur at the place of business of a federally licensed firearm dealer, if the federally licensed firearm dealer conducts a background check on the prospective recipient of the firearm in accordance with Section 3.1 of this Act and follows all other applicable federal, State, and local laws as if he or she were the seller or transferor of the firearm, although the dealer is not required to accept the firearm into his or her inventory. The purchaser or transferee may be required by the federally licensed firearm dealer to pay a fee not to exceed $10 per firearm, which the dealer may retain as compensation for performing the functions required

under this paragraph, plus the applicable fees authorized by Section 3.1;

(2) transfers as a bona fide gift to the transferor's husband, wife, son, daughter, stepson, stepdaughter, father, mother, stepfather, stepmother, brother, sister, nephew, niece, uncle, aunt, grandfather, grandmother, grandson, granddaughter, father-in-law, mother-in-law, son-in-law, or daughter-in-law;

(3) transfers by persons acting pursuant to operation of law or a court order;

(4) transfers on the grounds of a gun show under subsection (a-5) of this Section;

(5) the delivery of a firearm by its owner to a gunsmith for service or repair, the return of the firearm to its owner by the gunsmith, or the delivery of a firearm by a gunsmith to a federally licensed firearms dealer for service or repair and the return of the firearm to the gunsmith;

(6) temporary transfers that occur while in the home of the unlicensed transferee, if the unlicensed transferee is not otherwise prohibited from possessing firearms and the unlicensed transferee reasonably believes that possession of the firearm is necessary to prevent imminent death or great bodily harm to the unlicensed transferee;

(7) transfers to a law enforcement or corrections agency or a law enforcement or corrections officer acting within the course and scope of his or her official duties;

(8) transfers of firearms that have been rendered permanently inoperable to a nonprofit historical society, museum, or institutional collection; and

(9) transfers to a person who is exempt from the requirement of possessing a Firearm Owner's Identification Card under Section 2 of this Act.

(a-20) The Department of State Police shall develop an Internet-based system for individuals to determine the validity of a Firearm Owner's Identification Card prior to the sale or transfer of a firearm. The Department shall have the Internet-based system completed and available for use by July 1, 2015. The Department shall adopt rules not inconsistent with this Section to implement this system.

(b) Any person within this State who transfers or causes to be transferred any firearm, stun gun, or taser shall keep a record of such transfer for a period of 10 years from the date of transfer. Such record shall contain the date of the transfer; the description, serial number or other information identifying the firearm, stun gun, or taser if no serial number is available; and, if the transfer was completed within this State, the transferee's Firearm Owner's Identification Card number and any approval number or documentation provided by the Department of State Police pursuant to subsection (a-10) of this Section; if the transfer was not completed within this State, the record shall contain the name and address of the transferee. On or after January 1, 2006, the record shall contain the date of application for transfer of the firearm. On demand of a peace officer such transferor shall produce for inspection such record of transfer. If the transfer or sale took place at a gun show, the record shall include the unique identification number. Failure to record the unique identification number or approval number is a petty offense. For transfers of a firearm, stun gun, or taser made on or after the effective date of this amendatory Act of the 100th General Assembly, failure by the private seller to maintain the transfer records in accordance with this Section is a Class A misdemeanor for the first offense and a Class 4 felony for a second or subsequent offense. A transferee shall not be criminally liable under this Section provided that he or she provides the Department of State Police with the transfer records in accordance with procedures established by the Department. The Department shall establish, by rule, a standard form on its website.

(b-5) Any resident may purchase ammunition from a person within or outside of Illinois if shipment is by United States mail or by a private express carrier authorized by federal law to ship ammunition. Any resident purchasing ammunition within or outside the State of Illinois must provide the seller with a copy of his or her valid Firearm Owner's Identification Card or valid concealed carry license and either his or her Illinois driver's license or Illinois State Identification Card prior to the shipment of the ammunition. The ammunition may be shipped only to an address on either of those 2 documents.

(c) The provisions of this Section regarding the transfer of firearm ammunition shall not apply to those persons specified in paragraph (b) of Section 2 of this Act.

(Source: P.A. 99-29, eff. 7-10-15; 100-1178, eff. 1-18-19.)

---

430 ILL. COMP. STAT. 65/3A
SEC. 3A.

(a) Any resident of Illinois who has obtained a firearm owner's identification card pursuant to this Act and who is not otherwise prohibited from obtaining, possessing or using a firearm may purchase or obtain a rifle or shotgun or ammunition for a rifle or shotgun in Iowa, Missouri, Indiana, Wisconsin or Kentucky.

(b) Any resident of Iowa, Missouri, Indiana, Wisconsin or Kentucky or a non-resident with a valid non-resident hunting license, who is 18 years of age or older and who is not prohibited by the laws of Illinois, the state of his domicile, or the United States from obtaining, possessing or using a firearm, may purchase or obtain a rifle, shotgun or ammunition for a rifle or shotgun in Illinois.

(b-5)   Any non-resident who is participating in a sanctioned competitive shooting event, who is 18 years of age or older and who is not prohibited by the laws of Illinois, the state of his or her domicile, or the United States from obtaining, possessing, or using a firearm, may purchase or obtain a shotgun or shotgun ammunition in Illinois for the purpose of participating in that event. A person may purchase or obtain a shotgun or shotgun ammunition under this subsection only at the site where the sanctioned competitive shooting event is being held.

(b-10) Any non-resident registered competitor or attendee of a competitive shooting event held at the World Shooting Complex sanctioned by a national governing body, who is not prohibited by the laws of Illinois, the state of his or her domicile, or the United States from obtaining, possessing, or using a firearm may purchase or obtain a rifle, shotgun, or other long gun or ammunition for a rifle, shotgun, or other long gun at the competitive shooting event. The sanctioning body shall provide a list of registered competitors and attendees as required under subparagraph (5) of paragraph (g) of subsection (A) of Section 24-3 of the Criminal Code of 2012. A competitor or attendee of a competitive shooting event who does not wish to purchase a firearm at the event is not required to register or have his or her name appear on a list of registered competitors and attendees provided to the Department of State Police by the sanctioning body.

(c)   Any transaction under this Section is subject to the provisions of the Gun Control Act of 1968 (18 U.S.C. 922 (b)(3)).

(Source: P.A. 99-29, eff. 7-10-15.)

430 ILL. COMP. STAT. 65/3.1
SEC. 3.1. DIAL UP SYSTEM.

(a) The Department of State Police shall provide a dial up telephone system or utilize other existing technology which shall be used by any federally licensed firearm dealer, gun show promoter, or gun show vendor who is to transfer a firearm, stun gun, or taser under the provisions of this Act. The Department of State Police may utilize existing technology which allows the caller to be charged a fee not to exceed $2. Fees collected by the Department of State Police shall be deposited in the State Police Services Fund and used to provide the service.

(b) Upon receiving a request from a federally licensed firearm dealer, gun show promoter, or gun show vendor, the Department of State Police shall immediately approve, or within the time period established by Section 24-3 of the Criminal Code of 2012 regarding the delivery of firearms, stun guns, and tasers notify the inquiring dealer, gun show promoter, or gun show vendor of any objection that would disqualify the transferee from acquiring or possessing a firearm, stun gun, or taser. In conducting the inquiry, the Department of State Police shall initiate and complete an automated search of its criminal history record information files and those of the Federal Bureau of Investigation, including the National Instant Criminal Background Check System, and of the files of the Department of Human Services relating to mental health and developmental disabilities to obtain any felony conviction or patient hospitalization information which would disqualify a person from obtaining or require revocation of a currently valid Firearm Owner's Identification Card.

(c) If receipt of a firearm would not violate Section 24-3 of the Criminal Code of 2012, federal law, or this Act the Department of State Police shall:

(1) assign a unique identification number to the transfer; and

(2) provide the licensee, gun show promoter, or gun show vendor with the number.

(d) Approvals issued by the Department of State Police for the purchase of a firearm are valid for 30 days from the date of issue.

(e)

(1) The Department of State Police must act as the Illinois Point of Contact for the National Instant Criminal Background Check System.

(2) The Department of State Police and the Department of Human Services shall, in accordance with State and federal law regarding confidentiality, enter into a memorandum of understanding with the Federal Bureau of Investigation for the purpose of implementing the National Instant Criminal Background Check System in the State. The Department of State Police shall report the name, date of birth, and physical description of any person prohibited from possessing a firearm pursuant to the Firearm Owners Identification Card Act or 18 U.S.C. 922(g) and (n) to the National Instant Criminal Background Check System Index, Denied Persons Files.

(3) The Department of State Police shall provide notice of the disqualification of a person under subsection (b) of this Section or the revocation of a person's Firearm Owner's Identification Card under Section 8 or Section 8.2 of this Act, and the reason for the disqualification or revocation, to all law enforcement agencies with jurisdiction to assist with the seizure of the person's Firearm Owner's Identification Card.

(f) The Department of State Police shall adopt rules not inconsistent with this Section to implement this system.

(Source: P.A. 98-63, eff. 7-9-13; 99-787, eff. 1-1-17.)

430 ILL. COMP. STAT. 65/3.2
SEC. 3.2. LIST OF PROHIBITED PROJECTILES; NOTICE TO DEALERS.

Prior to January 1, 2002, the Department of State Police shall list on the Department's World Wide Web site all firearm projectiles that are prohibited under Sections 24-2.1, 24-2.2, and 24-3.2 of the Criminal Code of 2012, together with a statement setting forth the sentence that may be imposed for violating those Sections. The Department of State Police shall, prior to January 1, 2002, send a list of all firearm projectiles that are prohibited under Sections 24-2.1, 24-2.2, and 24-3.2 of the Criminal Code of 2012 to each federally licensed firearm dealer in Illinois registered with the Department. (Source: P.A. 97-1150, eff. 1-25-13.)

430 ILL. COMP. STAT. 65/3.3
SEC. 3.3. REPORT TO THE LOCAL LAW ENFORCEMENT AGENCY.

The Department of State Police must report the name and address of a person to the local law enforcement agency where the person resides if the person attempting to purchase a firearm is disqualified from purchasing a firearm because of information obtained under subsection (a-10) of Section 3 or Section 3.1 that would disqualify the person from obtaining a Firearm Owner's Identification Card under any of subsections (c) through (n) of Section 8 of this Act. (Source: P.A. 98-508, eff. 8-19-13.)

430 ILL. COMP. STAT. 65/4
SEC. 4. APPLICATION FOR FIREARM OWNER'S IDENTIFICATION CARDS.

(a) Each applicant for a Firearm Owner's Identification Card must:

(1) Make application on blank forms prepared and furnished at convenient locations throughout the State by the Department of State Police, or by electronic means, if and when made available by the Department of State Police; and

(2) Submit evidence to the Department of State Police that:

(i) This subparagraph (i) applies through the 180th day following the effective date of this amendatory Act of the 101st General Assembly. He or she is 21 years of age or over, or if he or she is under 21 years of age that he or she has the written consent of his or her parent or legal guardian to possess and acquire firearms and firearm ammunition and that he or she has never been convicted of a misdemeanor other than a traffic offense or adjudged delinquent, provided, however, that such parent or legal guardian is not an individual prohibited from having a Firearm Owner's Identification Card and files an affidavit with the Department as prescribed by the Department stating that he or she is not an individual prohibited from having a Card;

(i-5) This subparagraph (i-5) applies on and after the 181st day following the effective date of this amendatory Act of the 101st General Assembly. He or she is 21 years of age or over, or if he or she is under 21 years of age that he or she has never been convicted of a misdemeanor other than a traffic offense or adjudged delinquent and is an active duty member of the United States Armed Forces or has the written consent of his or her parent or legal guardian to possess and acquire firearms and firearm ammunition, provided, however, that such parent or legal guardian is not an individual prohibited from having a Firearm Owner's Identification Card and files an affidavit with the Department as prescribed by the Department stating that he or she is not an individual prohibited from having a Card or the active duty member of the United States Armed Forces under 21 years of age annually submits proof to the Department of State Police, in a manner prescribed by the Department;

(ii) He or she has not been convicted of a felony under the laws of this or any other jurisdiction;

(iii) He or she is not addicted to narcotics;

(iv) He or she has not been a patient in a mental health facility within the past 5 years or, if he or she has been a patient in a mental health facility more than 5 years ago submit the certification required under subsection (u) of Section 8 of this Act;

(v) He or she is not a person with an intellectual disability;

(vi) He or she is not an alien who is unlawfully present in the United States under the laws of the United States;

(vii) He or she is not subject to an existing order of protection prohibiting him or her from possessing a firearm;

(viii) He or she has not been convicted within the past 5 years of battery, assault, aggravated assault, violation of an order of protection, or a substantially similar offense in another jurisdiction, in which a firearm was used or possessed;

(ix) He or she has not been convicted of domestic battery, aggravated domestic battery, or a substantially similar offense in another jurisdiction committed before, on or after January 1, 2012 (the effective date of Public Act 97-158). If the applicant knowingly and intelligently waives the right to have an offense described in this clause (ix) tried by a jury, and by guilty plea or otherwise, results in a conviction for an offense in which a domestic relationship is not a required element of the offense but in which a determination of the applicability of 18 U.S.C. 922(g)(9) is made under Section 112A-11.1 of the Code of Criminal Procedure of 1963, an entry by the court of a judgment of conviction for that offense shall be grounds for denying the issuance of a Firearm Owner's Identification Card under this Section;

(x) (Blank);

(xi) He or she is not an alien who has been admitted to the United States under a non-immigrant visa (as that term is defined in Section 101(a)(26) of the Immigration and Nationality Act (8 U.S.C. 1101(a)(26))), or that he or she is an alien who has been lawfully admitted to the United States under a non-immigrant visa if that alien is:

(1) admitted to the United States for lawful hunting or sporting purposes;

(2) an official representative of a foreign government who is:

(A) accredited to the United States Government or the Government's mission to an international organization having its headquarters in the United States; or

(B) en route to or from another country to which that alien is accredited;

(3) an official of a foreign government or distinguished foreign visitor who has been so designated by the Department of State;

(4) a foreign law enforcement officer of a friendly foreign government entering the United States on

official business; or

(5) one who has received a waiver from the Attorney General of the United States pursuant to 18 U.S.C. 922(y)(3);

(xii) He or she is not a minor subject to a petition filed under Section 5-520 of the Juvenile Court Act of 1987 alleging that the minor is a delinquent minor for the commission of an offense that if committed by an adult would be a felony;

(xiii) He or she is not an adult who had been adjudicated a delinquent minor under the Juvenile Court Act of 1987 for the commission of an offense that if committed by an adult would be a felony;

(xiv) He or she is a resident of the State of Illinois;

(xv) He or she has not been adjudicated as a person with a mental disability;

(xvi) He or she has not been involuntarily admitted into a mental health facility; and

(xvii) He or she is not a person with a developmental disability; and

(3) Upon request by the Department of State Police, sign a release on a form prescribed by the Department of State Police waiving any right to confidentiality and requesting the disclosure to the Department of State Police of limited mental health institution admission information from another state, the District of Columbia, any other territory of the United States, or a foreign nation concerning the applicant for the sole purpose of determining whether the applicant is or was a patient in a mental health institution and disqualified because of that status from receiving a Firearm Owner's Identification Card. No mental health care or treatment records may be

requested. The information received shall be destroyed within one year of receipt.

(a-5) Each applicant for a Firearm Owner's Identification Card who is over the age of 18 shall furnish to the Department of State Police either his or her Illinois driver's license number or Illinois Identification Card number, except as provided in subsection (a-10).

(a-10) Each applicant for a Firearm Owner's Identification Card, who is employed as a law enforcement officer, an armed security officer in Illinois, or by the United States Military permanently assigned in Illinois and who is not an Illinois resident, shall furnish to the Department of State Police his or her driver's license number or state identification card number from his or her state of residence. The Department of State Police may adopt rules to enforce the provisions of this subsection (a-10).

(a-15) If an applicant applying for a Firearm Owner's Identification Card moves from the residence address named in the application, he or she shall immediately notify in a form and manner prescribed by the Department of State Police of that change of address.

(a-20) Each applicant for a Firearm Owner's Identification Card shall furnish to the Department of State Police his or her photograph. An applicant who is 21 years of age or older seeking a religious exemption to the photograph requirement must furnish with the application an approved copy of United States Department of the Treasury Internal Revenue Service Form 4029. In lieu of a photograph, an applicant regardless of age seeking a religious exemption to the photograph requirement shall submit fingerprints on a form and manner prescribed by the Department with his or her application.

(b) Each application form shall include the following statement printed in bold type: "Warning: Entering false information on an application for a Firearm Owner's Identification Card is punishable as a Class 2 felony in accordance with subsection (d-5) of Section 14 of the Firearm Owners Identification Card Act.".

(c) Upon such written consent, pursuant to Section 4, paragraph (a) (2)(i), the parent or legal guardian giving the consent shall be liable for any damages resulting from the applicant's use of firearms or firearm ammunition.

(Source: P.A. 101-80, eff. 7-12-19.)

430 ILL. COMP. STAT. 65/5
SEC. 5. APPLICATION AND RENEWAL.

(a)   The Department of State Police shall either approve or deny all applications within 30 days from the date they are received, except as provided in subsection (b) of this Section, and every applicant found qualified under Section 8 of this Act by the Department shall be entitled to a Firearm Owner's Identification Card upon the payment of a $10 fee. Any applicant who is an active duty member of the Armed Forces of the United States, a member of the Illinois National Guard, or a member of the Reserve Forces of the United States is exempt from the application fee. $6 of each fee derived from the issuance of Firearm Owner's Identification Cards, or renewals thereof, shall be deposited in the Wildlife and Fish Fund in the State Treasury; $1 of the fee shall be deposited in the State Police Services Fund and $3 of the fee shall be deposited in the State Police Firearm Services Fund.

(b)   Renewal applications shall be approved or denied within 60 business days, provided the applicant submitted his or her renewal application prior to the expiration of his or her Firearm Owner's Identification Card. If a renewal application has been submitted prior to the expiration date of the applicant's Firearm Owner's

Identification Card, the Firearm Owner's Identification Card shall remain valid while the Department processes the application, unless the person is subject to or becomes subject to revocation under this Act. The cost for a renewal application shall be $10 which shall be deposited into the State Police Firearm Services Fund.
(Source: P.A. 100-906, eff. 1-1-19.)

430 ILL. COMP. STAT. 65/5.1
SEC. 5.1. STATE POLICE FIREARM SERVICES FUND.

All moneys remaining in the Firearm Owner's Notification Fund on the effective date of this amendatory Act of the 98th General Assembly shall be transferred into the State Police Firearm Services Fund, a special fund created in the State treasury, to be expended by the Department of State Police, for the purposes specified in this Act and Section 2605-595 of the Department of State Police Law of the Civil Administrative Code of Illinois.
(Source: P.A. 98-63, eff. 7-9-13.)

430 ILL. COMP. STAT. 65/6
SEC. 6. CONTENTS OF FIREARM OWNER'S IDENTIFICATION CARD.

(a) A Firearm Owner's Identification Card, issued by the Department of State Police at such places as the Director of the Department shall specify, shall contain the applicant's name, residence, date of birth, sex, physical description, recent photograph, except as provided in subsection (c-5), and signature. Each Firearm Owner's Identification Card must have the expiration date boldly and conspicuously displayed on the face of the card. Each Firearm Owner's Identification Card must have printed on it the following: "CAUTION - This card does not permit bearer to UNLAWFULLY carry or use firearms." Before December 1, 2002, the Department may use a person's digital photograph and signature from his or her Illinois driver's license or Illinois Identification Card, if available. On and after December 1, 2002, the Department shall use a person's digital photograph and signature from his or her Illinois driver's license or Illinois Identification Card, if available. The Department shall decline to use a person's digital photograph or signature if the digital photograph or signature is the result of or associated with fraudulent or erroneous data, unless otherwise provided by law.

(b) A person applying for a Firearm Owner's Identification Card shall consent to the Department of State Police using the applicant's digital driver's license or Illinois Identification Card photograph, if available, and signature on the applicant's Firearm Owner's Identification Card. The Secretary of State shall allow the Department of State Police access to the photograph and signature for the purpose of identifying the applicant and issuing to the applicant a Firearm Owner's Identification Card.

(c) The Secretary of State shall conduct a study to determine the cost and feasibility of creating a method of adding an identifiable code, background, or other means on the driver's license or Illinois Identification Card to show that an individual is not disqualified from owning or possessing a firearm under State or federal law. The Secretary shall report the findings of this study 12 months after the effective date of this amendatory Act of the 92nd General Assembly.

(c-5) If a person qualifies for a photograph exemption, in lieu of a photograph, the Firearm Owner's Identification Card shall contain a copy of the card holder's fingerprints. Each Firearm Owner's Identification Card described in this subsection (c-5) must have printed on it the following: "This card is only valid for firearm purchases through a federally licensed firearms dealer

when presented with photographic identification, as prescribed by 18 U.S.C. 922(t)(1)(C)."
(Source: P.A. 97-1131, eff. 1-1-13.)

---

430 ILL. COMP. STAT. 65/6.1
SEC. 6.1. ALTERED, FORGED OR COUNTERFEIT FIREARM OWNER'S IDENTIFICATION CARDS.

(a) Any person who forges or materially alters a Firearm Owner's Identification Card or who counterfeits a Firearm Owner's Identification Card commits a Class 2 felony.

(b) Any person who knowingly possesses a forged or materially altered Firearm Owner's Identification Card with the intent to use it commits a Class 2 felony. A person who possesses a Firearm Owner's Identification Card with knowledge that it is counterfeit commits a Class 2 felony.
(Source: P.A. 92-414, eff. 1-1-02.)

---

430 ILL. COMP. STAT. 65/7
SEC. 7. VALIDITY OF FIREARM OWNER'S IDENTIFICATION CARD.

(a) Except as provided in Section 8 of this Act or subsection (b) of this Section, a Firearm Owner's Identification Card issued under the provisions of this Act shall be valid for the person to whom it is issued for a period of 10 years from the date of issuance.

(b) If a renewal application is submitted to the Department before the expiration date of the applicant's current Firearm Owner's Identification Card, the Firearm Owner's Identification Card shall remain valid for a period of 60 business days, unless the person is subject to or becomes subject to revocation under this Act.
(Source: P.A. 100-906, eff. 1-1-19.)

430 ILL. COMP. STAT. 65/8
SEC. 8. GROUNDS FOR DENIAL AND REVOCATION.

The Department of State Police has authority to deny an application for or to revoke and seize a Firearm Owner's Identification Card previously issued under this Act only if the Department finds that the applicant or the person to whom such card was issued is or was at the time of issuance:

(a) A person under 21 years of age who has been convicted of a misdemeanor other than a traffic offense or adjudged delinquent;

(b) This subsection (b) applies through the 180th day following the effective date of this amendatory Act of the 101st General Assembly. A person under 21 years of age who does not have the written consent of his parent or guardian to acquire and possess firearms and firearm ammunition, or whose parent or guardian has revoked such written consent, or where such parent or guardian does not qualify to have a Firearm Owner's Identification Card;

(b-5) This subsection (b-5) applies on and after the 181st day following the effective date of this amendatory Act of the 101st General Assembly. A person under 21 years of age who is not an active duty member of the United States Armed Forces and does not have the written consent of his or her parent or guardian to acquire and possess firearms and firearm ammunition, or whose parent or guardian has revoked such written consent, or where such parent or guardian does not qualify to have a Firearm Owner's Identification Card;

(c) A person convicted of a felony under the laws of this or any other jurisdiction;

(d) A person addicted to narcotics;

(e) A person who has been a patient of a mental health facility within the past 5 years or a person who has been a patient in a mental health facility more than 5 years ago who has not received the certification required under subsection (u) of this Section. An active law enforcement officer employed by a unit of government who is denied, revoked, or has his or her Firearm Owner's Identification Card seized under this subsection (e) may obtain relief as described in subsection (c-5) of Section 10 of this Act if the officer did not act in a manner threatening to the officer, another person, or the public as determined by the treating clinical psychologist or physician, and the officer seeks mental health treatment;

(f)   A person whose mental condition is of such a nature that it poses a clear and present danger to the applicant, any other person or persons or the community;

(g)   A person who has an intellectual disability;

(h)   A person who intentionally makes a false statement in the Firearm Owner's Identification Card application;

(i)   An alien who is unlawfully present in the United States under the laws of the United States;

(i-5)   An alien who has been admitted to the United States under a non-immigrant visa (as that term is defined in Section 101(a)(26) of the Immigration and Nationality Act (8 U.S.C. 1101(a)(26))), except that this subsection (i-5) does not apply to any alien who has been lawfully admitted to the United States under a non-immigrant visa if that alien is:

(1)   admitted to the United States for lawful hunting or sporting purposes;

(2)   an official representative of a foreign government who is:
(A)   accredited to the United States Government or the Government's mission to an international organization having its headquarters in the United States; or
(B)   en route to or from another country to which that alien is accredited;

(3)   an official of a foreign government or distinguished foreign

visitor who has been so designated by the Department of State;

(4) a foreign law enforcement officer of a friendly foreign government entering the United States on official business; or

(5) one who has received a waiver from the Attorney General of the United States pursuant to 18 U.S.C. 922(y)(3);

(j) (Blank);

(k) A person who has been convicted within the past 5 years of battery, assault, aggravated assault, violation of an order of protection, or a substantially similar offense in another jurisdiction, in which a firearm was used or possessed;

(l) A person who has been convicted of domestic battery, aggravated domestic battery, or a substantially similar offense in another jurisdiction committed before, on or after January 1, 2012 (the effective date of Public Act 97-158). If the applicant or person who has been previously issued a Firearm Owner's Identification Card under this Act knowingly and intelligently waives the right to have an offense described in this paragraph (l) tried by a jury, and by guilty plea or otherwise, results in a conviction for an offense in which a domestic relationship is not a required element of the offense but in which a determination of the applicability of 18 U.S.C. 922(g)(9) is made under Section 112A-11.1 of the Code of Criminal Procedure of 1963, an entry by the court of a judgment of conviction for that offense shall be grounds for denying an application for and for revoking and seizing a Firearm Owner's Identification Card previously issued to the person under this Act;

(m) (Blank);

(n) A person who is prohibited from acquiring or possessing firearms or firearm ammunition by any Illinois State statute or by federal law;

(o) A minor subject to a petition filed under Section 5-520 of the

Juvenile Court Act of 1987 alleging that the minor is a delinquent minor for the commission of an offense that if committed by an adult would be a felony;

(p) An adult who had been adjudicated a delinquent minor under the Juvenile Court Act of 1987 for the commission of an offense that if committed by an adult would be a felony;

(q) A person who is not a resident of the State of Illinois, except as provided in subsection (a-10) of Section 4;

(r) A person who has been adjudicated as a person with a mental disability;

(s) A person who has been found to have a developmental disability;

(t) A person involuntarily admitted into a mental health facility; or

(u) A person who has had his or her Firearm Owner's Identification Card revoked or denied under subsection (e) of this Section or item (iv) of paragraph (2) of subsection (a) of Section 4 of this Act because he or she was a patient in a mental health facility as provided in subsection (e) of this Section, shall not be permitted to obtain a Firearm Owner's Identification Card, after the 5-year period has lapsed, unless he or she has received a mental health evaluation by a physician, clinical psychologist, or qualified examiner as those terms are defined in the Mental Health and Developmental Disabilities Code, and has received a certification that he or she is not a clear and present danger to himself, herself, or others. The physician, clinical psychologist, or qualified examiner making the certification and his or her employer shall not be held criminally, civilly, or professionally liable for making or not making the certification required under this subsection, except for willful or wanton misconduct. This subsection does not apply to a person whose firearm possession rights have been restored through

administrative or judicial action under Section 10 or 11 of this Act. Upon revocation of a person's Firearm Owner's Identification Card, the Department of State Police shall provide notice to the person and the person shall comply with Section 9.5 of this Act.
(Source: P.A. 101-80, eff. 7-12-19.)

430 ILL. COMP. STAT. 65/8.1

SEC. 8.1. NOTIFICATIONS TO THE DEPARTMENT OF STATE POLICE.

(a) The Circuit Clerk shall, in the form and manner required by the Supreme Court, notify the Department of State Police of all final dispositions of cases for which the Department has received information reported to it under Sections 2.1 and 2.2 of the Criminal Identification Act.

(b) Upon adjudication of any individual as a person with a mental disability as defined in Section 1.1 of this Act or a finding that a person has been involuntarily admitted, the court shall direct the circuit court clerk to immediately notify the Department of State Police, Firearm Owner's Identification (FOID) department, and shall forward a copy of the court order to the Department.

(b-1) Beginning July 1, 2016, and each July 1 and December 30 of every year thereafter, the circuit court clerk shall, in the form and manner prescribed by the Department of State Police, notify the Department of State Police, Firearm Owner's Identification (FOID) department if the court has not directed the circuit court clerk to notify the Department of State Police, Firearm Owner's Identification (FOID) department under subsection (b) of this Section, within the preceding 6 months, because no person has been adjudicated as a person with a mental disability by the court as defined in Section 1.1 of this Act or if no person has been involuntarily admitted. The Supreme Court may adopt any orders or rules necessary to identify the persons who shall be reported to the Department of State Police under subsection (b), or any other orders or rules necessary to implement the requirements of this Act.

(c) The Department of Human Services shall, in the form and manner prescribed by the Department of State Police, report all information collected under subsection (b) of Section 12 of the Mental Health and Developmental Disabilities Confidentiality Act for the purpose of determining whether a person who may be or may have been a patient in a mental health facility is disqualified under State or federal law from receiving or retaining a Firearm Owner's Identification Card, or purchasing a weapon.

(d) If a person is determined to pose a clear and present danger to himself, herself, or to others:

  (1) by a physician, clinical psychologist, or qualified examiner, or is determined to have a developmental disability by a physician, clinical psychologist, or qualified examiner, whether employed by the State or privately, then the physician, clinical psychologist, or qualified examiner shall, within 24 hours of making the determination, notify the Department of Human Services that the person poses a clear and present danger or has a developmental disability; or

  (2) by a law enforcement official or school administrator, then the law enforcement official or school administrator shall, within 24 hours of making the determination, notify the Department of State Police that the person poses a clear and present danger.

The Department of Human Services shall immediately update its records and information relating to mental health and developmental disabilities, and if appropriate, shall notify the Department of State Police in a form and manner prescribed by the Department of State Police. The Department of State Police shall determine whether to revoke the person's Firearm Owner's Identification Card under Section 8 of this Act. Any information disclosed under this subsection shall remain privileged and confidential, and shall not be redisclosed, except as required under subsection (e) of Section 3.1 of this Act, nor used for any other purpose. The method of providing this information shall guarantee that the information is not released beyond what is necessary for the purpose of this Section and shall be provided by rule by the Department of Human Services. The identity of the person reporting under this Section shall not be disclosed to the subject of the report. The physician, clinical psychologist, qualified examiner, law enforcement official, or school administrator making the determination and his or her employer shall not be held criminally, civilly, or professionally liable for making or not making the notification required under this subsection, except for willful or wanton misconduct.

(e)   The Department of State Police shall adopt rules to implement this Section.

(Source: P.A. 98-63, eff. 7-9-13; 98-600, eff. 12-6-13; 99-143, eff. 7-27-15; 99-696, eff. 7-29-16.)

430 ILL. COMP. STAT. 65/8.2
SEC. 8.2. FIREARM OWNER'S IDENTIFICATION CARD DENIAL OR REVOCATION.

The Department of State Police shall deny an application or shall revoke and seize a Firearm Owner's Identification Card previously issued under this Act if the Department finds that the applicant or person to whom such card was issued is or was at the time of issuance subject to an existing order of protection or firearms restraining order.

(Source: P.A. 100-607, eff. 1-1-19.)

430 ILL. COMP. STAT. 65/8.3
SEC. 8.3. SUSPENSION OF FIREARM OWNER'S IDENTIFICATION CARD.

The Department of State Police may, by rule in a manner consistent with the Department's rules concerning revocation, provide for the suspension of the Firearm Owner's Identification Card of a person whose Firearm Owner's Identification Card is subject to revocation and seizure under this Act for the duration of the disqualification if the disqualification is not a permanent grounds for revocation of a Firearm Owner's Identification Card under this Act.
(Source: P.A. 100-607, eff. 1-1-19; 100-906, eff. 1-1-19.)

430 ILL. COMP. STAT. 65/9
SEC. 9.

Every person whose application for a Firearm Owner's Identification Card is denied, and every holder of such a Card whose Card is revoked or seized, shall receive a written notice from the Department of State Police stating specifically the grounds upon which his application has been denied or upon which his Identification Card has been revoked. The written notice shall include the requirements of Section 9.5 of this Act and the person's right to administrative or judicial review under Section 10 and 11 of this Act. A copy of the written notice shall be provided to the sheriff and law enforcement agency where the person resides.
(Source: P.A. 100-201, eff. 8-18-17.)

430 ILL. COMP. STAT. 65/9.5

SEC. 9.5. REVOCATION OF FIREARM OWNER'S IDENTIFICATION CARD.

(a) A person who receives a revocation notice under Section 9 of this Act shall, within 48 hours of receiving notice of the revocation:

 (1) surrender his or her Firearm Owner's Identification Card to the local law enforcement agency where the person resides. The local law enforcement agency shall provide the person a receipt and transmit the Firearm Owner's Identification Card to the Department of State Police; and

 (2) complete a Firearm Disposition Record on a form prescribed by the Department of State Police and place his or her firearms in the location or with the person reported in the Firearm Disposition Record. The form shall require the person to disclose:

   (A) the make, model, and serial number of each firearm owned by or under the custody and control of the revoked person;

   (B) the location where each firearm will be maintained during the prohibited term; and

   (C) if any firearm will be transferred to the custody of another person, the name, address and Firearm Owner's Identification Card number of the transferee.

(b) The local law enforcement agency shall provide a copy of the Firearm Disposition Record to the person whose Firearm Owner's Identification Card has been revoked and to the Department of State Police.

(c) If the person whose Firearm Owner's Identification Card has been revoked fails to comply with the requirements of this Section, the sheriff or law enforcement agency where the person resides may petition the circuit court to issue a warrant to search for and seize the Firearm Owner's Identification Card and firearms in the possession or under the custody or control of the person whose Firearm Owner's Identification Card has been revoked.

(d) A violation of subsection (a) of this Section is a Class A misdemeanor.

(e) The observation of a Firearm Owner's Identification Card in the possession of a person whose Firearm Owner's Identification Card has been revoked constitutes a sufficient basis for the arrest of that person for violation of this Section.

(f) Within 30 days after the effective date of this amendatory Act of the 98th General Assembly, the Department of State Police shall provide written notice of the requirements of this Section to persons whose Firearm Owner's Identification Cards have been revoked, suspended, or expired and who have failed to surrender their cards to the Department.

(g) A person whose Firearm Owner's Identification Card has been revoked and who received notice under subsection (f) shall comply with the requirements of this Section within 48 hours of receiving notice.

(Source: P.A. 98-63, eff. 7-9-13.)

430 ILL. COMP. STAT. 65/10

SEC. 10. APPEAL TO DIRECTOR; HEARING; RELIEF FROM FIREARM PROHIBITIONS.

(a) Whenever an application for a Firearm Owner's Identification Card is denied, whenever the Department fails to act on an application within 30 days of its receipt, or whenever such a Card is revoked or seized as provided for in Section 8 of this Act, the aggrieved party may appeal to the Director of State Police for a hearing upon such denial, revocation or seizure, unless the denial, revocation, or seizure was based upon a forcible felony, stalking, aggravated stalking, domestic battery, any violation of the Illinois Controlled Substances Act, the Methamphetamine Control and Community Protection Act, or the Cannabis Control Act that is classified as a Class 2 or greater felony, any felony violation of Article 24 of the Criminal Code of 1961 or the Criminal Code of 2012, or any adjudication as a delinquent minor for the commission of an offense that if committed by an adult would be a felony, in which case the aggrieved party may petition the circuit court in writing in the county of his or her residence for a hearing upon such denial, revocation, or seizure.

(b) At least 30 days before any hearing in the circuit court, the petitioner shall serve the relevant State's Attorney with a copy of the petition. The State's Attorney may object to the petition and present evidence. At the hearing the court shall determine whether substantial justice has been done. Should the court determine that substantial justice has not been done, the court shall issue an order directing the Department of State Police to issue a Card. However, the court shall not issue the order if the petitioner is otherwise prohibited from obtaining, possessing, or using a firearm under federal law.

(c) Any person prohibited from possessing a firearm under Sections 24-1.1 or 24-3.1 of the Criminal Code of 2012 or acquiring a Firearm Owner's Identification Card under Section 8 of this Act may apply to the Director of State Police or petition the circuit court in the county where the petitioner resides, whichever is applicable in accordance with subsection (a) of this Section, requesting relief from such prohibition and the Director or court may grant such relief if it is established by the applicant to the court's or Director's satisfaction that:

(0.05) when in the circuit court, the State's Attorney has been served with a written copy of the petition at least 30 days before any such hearing in the circuit court and at the hearing the State's Attorney was afforded an opportunity to present evidence and object to the petition;

(1) the applicant has not been convicted of a forcible felony under the laws of this State or any other jurisdiction within 20 years of the applicant's application for a Firearm Owner's Identification Card, or at least 20 years have passed since the end of any period of imprisonment imposed in relation to that conviction;

(2) the circumstances regarding a criminal conviction, where applicable, the applicant's criminal history and his reputation are such that the applicant will not be likely to act in a manner dangerous to public safety;

(3) granting relief would not be contrary to the public interest; and

(4) granting relief would not be contrary to federal law.

(c-5)

(1) An active law enforcement officer employed by a unit of government, who is denied, revoked, or has his or her Firearm Owner's Identification Card seized under subsection (e) of Section 8 of this Act may apply to the Director of State Police requesting relief if the officer did not act in a manner threatening to the officer, another person, or the public as determined by the treating clinical psychologist or physician, and as a result of his or her work is referred by the employer for or voluntarily seeks mental health evaluation or treatment by a licensed clinical psychologist, psychiatrist, or qualified examiner, and:

(A) the officer has not received treatment involuntarily at a mental health facility, regardless of the length of admission; or has not been voluntarily admitted to a mental health facility for more than 30 days and not for more than one incident within the past 5 years; and

(B) the officer has not left the mental institution against medical advice.

(2) The Director of State Police shall grant expedited relief to active law enforcement officers described in paragraph (1) of this subsection (c-5) upon a determination by the Director that the officer's possession of a firearm does not present a threat to themselves, others, or public safety. The Director shall act on the request for relief within 30 business days of receipt of:

(A) a notarized statement from the officer in the form prescribed by the Director detailing the circumstances that led to the hospitalization;

(B) all documentation regarding the admission, evaluation, treatment and discharge from the treating licensed clinical psychologist or psychiatrist of the officer;

(C) a psychological fitness for duty evaluation of the person completed after the time of discharge; and

(D) written confirmation in the form prescribed by the Director from the treating licensed clinical psychologist or psychiatrist that the provisions set forth in paragraph (1) of this subsection (c-5) have been met, the person successfully completed treatment, and their professional opinion regarding the person's ability to possess firearms.

(3) Officers eligible for the expedited relief in paragraph (2) of this subsection (c-5) have the burden of proof on eligibility and must provide all information required. The Director may not consider granting expedited relief until the proof and information is received.

(4) "Clinical psychologist", "psychiatrist", and "qualified examiner" shall have the same meaning as provided in Chapter I of the Mental Health and Developmental Disabilities Code.

(c-10)

(1) An applicant, who is denied, revoked, or has his or her Firearm Owner's Identification Card seized under subsection (e) of Section 8 of this Act based upon a determination of a developmental disability or an intellectual disability may apply to the Director of State Police requesting relief.

(2) The Director shall act on the request for relief within 60 business days of receipt of written certification, in the form prescribed by the Director, from a physician or clinical psychologist, or qualified examiner, that the aggrieved party's developmental disability or intellectual disability condition is determined by a physician, clinical psychologist, or qualified to be mild. If a fact-finding conference is scheduled to obtain additional information concerning the circumstances of the denial or revocation, the 60 business days the Director has to act shall be tolled until the completion of the fact-finding conference.

(3) The Director may grant relief if the aggrieved party's developmental disability or intellectual disability is mild as determined by a physician, clinical psychologist, or qualified examiner and it is established by the applicant to the Director's satisfaction that:

(A) granting relief would not be contrary to the public interest; and

(B) granting relief would not be contrary to federal law.

(4) The Director may not grant relief if the condition is determined by a physician, clinical psychologist, or qualified examiner to be moderate, severe, or profound.

(5) The changes made to this Section by this amendatory Act of the 99th General Assembly apply to requests for relief pending on or before the effective date of this amendatory Act, except that the 60-day period for the Director to act on requests pending before the effective date shall begin on the effective date of this amendatory Act.

(d) When a minor is adjudicated delinquent for an offense which if committed by an adult would be a felony, the court shall notify the Department of State Police.

(e) The court shall review the denial of an application or the revocation of a Firearm Owner's Identification Card of a person who has been adjudicated delinquent for an offense that if committed by an adult would be a felony if an application for relief has been filed at least 10 years after the adjudication of delinquency and the court determines that the applicant should be granted relief from disability to obtain a Firearm Owner's Identification Card. If the court grants relief, the court shall notify the Department of State Police that the disability has been removed and that the applicant is eligible to obtain a Firearm Owner's Identification Card.

(f) Any person who is subject to the disabilities of 18 U.S.C. 922(d)(4) and 922(g)(4) of the federal Gun Control Act of 1968 because of an adjudication or commitment that occurred under the laws of this State or who was determined to be subject to the provisions of subsections (e), (f), or (g) of Section 8 of this Act may apply to the Department of State Police requesting relief from that prohibition. The Director shall grant the relief if it is established by a preponderance of the evidence that the person will not be likely to act in a manner dangerous to public safety and that granting relief would not be contrary to the public interest. In making this determination, the Director shall receive evidence concerning (i)

the circumstances regarding the firearms disabilities from which relief is sought; (ii) the petitioner's mental health and criminal history records, if any; (iii) the petitioner's reputation, developed at a minimum through character witness statements, testimony, or other character evidence; and (iv) changes in the petitioner's condition or circumstances since the disqualifying events relevant to the relief sought. If relief is granted under this subsection or by order of a court under this Section, the Director shall as soon as practicable but in no case later than 15 business days, update, correct, modify, or remove the person's record in any database that the Department of State Police makes available to the National Instant Criminal Background Check System and notify the United States Attorney General that the basis for the record being made available no longer applies. The Department of State Police shall adopt rules for the administration of this Section.
(Source: P.A. 98-63, eff. 7-9-13; 99-29, eff. 7-10-15; 99-78, eff. 7-20-15.)

430 ILL. COMP. STAT. 65/11
SEC. 11. JUDICIAL REVIEW OF FINAL ADMINISTRATIVE DECISIONS.

(a) All final administrative decisions of the Department under this Act, except final administrative decisions of the Director of State Police to deny a person's application for relief under subsection (f) of Section 10 of this Act, shall be subject to judicial review under the provisions of the Administrative Review Law, and all amendments and modifications thereof, and the rules adopted pursuant thereto. The term "administrative decision" is defined as in Section 3-101 of the Code of Civil Procedure.

(b) Any final administrative decision by the Director of State

Police to deny a person's application for relief under subsection (f) of Section 10 of this Act is subject to de novo judicial review by the circuit court, and any party may offer evidence that is otherwise proper and admissible without regard to whether that evidence is part of the administrative record.

(c) The Director of State Police shall submit a report to the General Assembly on March 1 of each year, beginning March 1, 1991, listing all final decisions by a court of this State upholding, reversing, or reversing in part any administrative decision made by the Department of State Police.

(Source: P.A. 97-1131, eff. 1-1-13.)

430 ILL. COMP. STAT. 65/12
SEC. 12.

The provisions of this Act shall not apply to the passing or transfer of any firearm or firearm ammunition upon the death of the owner thereof to his heir or legatee or to the passing or transfer of any firearm or firearm ammunition incident to any legal proceeding or action until 60 days after such passing or transfer.

(Source: Laws 1967, p. 2600.)

430 ILL. COMP. STAT. 65/13
SEC. 13.

Nothing in this Act shall make lawful the acquisition or possession of firearms or firearm ammunition which is otherwise prohibited by law.

(Source: Laws 1967, p. 2600.)

430 ILL. COMP. STAT. 65/13.1
SEC. 13.1. PREEMPTION.

(a) Except as otherwise provided in the Firearm Concealed Carry Act and subsections (b) and (c) of this Section, the provisions of any ordinance enacted by any municipality which requires registration or imposes greater restrictions or limitations on the acquisition, possession and transfer of firearms than are imposed by this Act, are not invalidated or affected by this Act.

(b) Notwithstanding subsection (a) of this Section, the regulation, licensing, possession, and registration of handguns and ammunition for a handgun, and the transportation of any firearm and ammunition by a holder of a valid Firearm Owner's Identification Card issued by the Department of State Police under this Act are exclusive powers and functions of this State. Any ordinance or regulation, or portion of that ordinance or regulation, enacted on or before the effective date of this amendatory Act of the 98th General Assembly that purports to impose regulations or restrictions on a holder of a valid Firearm Owner's Identification Card issued by the Department of State Police under this Act in a manner that is inconsistent with this Act, on the effective date of this amendatory Act of the 98th General Assembly, shall be invalid in its application to a holder of a valid Firearm Owner's Identification Card issued by the Department of State Police under this Act.

(c) Notwithstanding subsection (a) of this Section, the regulation of the possession or ownership of assault weapons are exclusive powers and functions of this State. Any ordinance or regulation, or portion of that ordinance or regulation, that purports to regulate the possession or ownership of assault weapons in a manner that is inconsistent with this Act, shall be invalid unless the ordinance or regulation is enacted on, before, or within 10 days after the effective date of this amendatory Act of the 98th General Assembly. Any ordinance or regulation described in this subsection (c) enacted more than 10 days after the effective date of this amendatory Act of the 98th General Assembly is invalid. An ordinance enacted on, before, or within 10 days after the effective date of this amendatory Act of the 98th General Assembly may be amended. The enactment or amendment of ordinances under this subsection (c) are subject to the submission requirements of Section 13.3. For the purposes of this subsection, "assault weapons" means firearms designated by either make or model or by a test or list of cosmetic features that cumulatively would place the firearm into a definition of "assault weapon" under the ordinance.

(d) For the purposes of this Section, "handgun" has the meaning ascribed to it in Section 5 of the Firearm Concealed Carry Act.

(e) This Section is a denial and limitation of home rule powers and functions under subsection (h) of Section 6 of Article VII of the Illinois Constitution.

(Source: P.A. 98-63, eff. 7-9-13.)

430 ILL. COMP. STAT. 65/13.2
SEC. 13.2. RENEWAL; NAME OR ADDRESS CHANGE; REPLACEMENT CARD.

The Department of State Police shall, 60 days prior to the expiration of a Firearm Owner's Identification Card, forward by first class mail to each person whose card is to expire a notification of the expiration of the card and instructions for renewal. It is the obligation of the holder of a Firearm Owner's Identification Card to notify the Department of State Police of any address change since the issuance of the Firearm Owner's Identification Card. Whenever any person moves from the residence address named on his or her card, the person shall within 21 calendar days thereafter notify in

a form and manner prescribed by the Department of his or her old and new residence addresses and the card number held by him or her. Any person whose legal name has changed from the name on the card that he or she has been previously issued must apply for a corrected card within 30 calendar days after the change. The cost for a corrected card shall be $5. The cost for replacement of a card which has been lost, destroyed, or stolen shall be $5 if the loss, destruction, or theft of the card is reported to the Department of State Police. The fees collected under this Section shall be deposited into the State Police Firearm Services Fund.
(Source: P.A. 100-906, eff. 1-1-19.)

430 ILL. COMP. STAT. 65/13.3
SEC. 13.3. MUNICIPAL ORDINANCE SUBMISSION.

Within 6 months after the effective date of this amendatory Act of the 92nd General Assembly, every municipality must submit to the Department of State Police a copy of every ordinance adopted by the municipality that regulates the acquisition, possession, sale, or transfer of firearms within the municipality and must submit, 30 days after adoption, every such ordinance adopted after its initial submission of ordinances under this Section. The Department of State Police shall compile these ordinances and publish them in a form available to the public free of charge and shall periodically update this compilation of ordinances in a manner prescribed by the Director of State Police.
(Source: P.A. 92-238, eff. 8-3-01.)

430 ILL. COMP. STAT. 65/14
SEC. 14. SENTENCE.

(a) Except as provided in subsection (a-5), a violation of

paragraph (1) of subsection (a) of Section 2, when the person's Firearm Owner's Identification Card is expired but the person is not otherwise disqualified from renewing the card, is a Class A misdemeanor.

(a-5)   A violation of paragraph (1) of subsection (a) of Section 2, when the person's Firearm Owner's Identification Card is expired but the person is not otherwise disqualified from owning, purchasing, or possessing firearms, is a petty offense if the card was expired for 6 months or less from the date of expiration.

(b) Except as provided in subsection (a) with respect to an expired card, a violation of paragraph (1) of subsection (a) of Section 2 is a Class A misdemeanor when the person does not possess a currently valid Firearm Owner's Identification Card, but is otherwise eligible under this Act. A second or subsequent violation is a Class 4 felony.

(c) A violation of paragraph (1) of subsection (a) of Section 2 is a Class 3 felony when:

  (1) the person's Firearm Owner's Identification Card is revoked or subject to revocation under Section 8; or

  (2) the person's Firearm Owner's Identification Card is expired and not otherwise eligible for renewal under this Act; or

  (3) the person does not possess a currently valid Firearm Owner's Identification Card, and the person is not otherwise eligible under this Act.

(d) A violation of subsection (a) of Section 3 is a Class 4 felony. A third or subsequent conviction is a Class 1 felony.

(d-5)   Any person who knowingly enters false information on an application for a Firearm Owner's Identification Card, who knowingly gives a false answer to any question on the application, or who knowingly submits false evidence in connection with an application is guilty of a Class 2 felony.

(e) Except as provided by Section 6.1 of this Act, any other

violation of this Act is a Class A misdemeanor.
(Source: P.A. 97-1131, eff. 1-1-13.)

430 ILL. COMP. STAT. 65/15
SEC. 15.

If any provision of this Act or application thereof to any person or circumstance is held invalid, such invalidity does not affect other provisions or applications of this Act which can be given effect without the invalid application or provision, and to this end the provisions of this Act are declared to be severable.
(Source: Laws 1967, p. 2600.)

430 ILL. COMP. STAT. 65/15A
SEC. 15A.

When this amendatory Act enacted by the Seventy-Sixth General Assembly takes effect the records of the Department of Public Safety relating to the administration of the Act amended shall be transferred to the Department of State Police. All Firearm Owner's Identification Cards issued by the Department of Public Safety shall be valid for the period for which they were issued unless revoked or seized in the manner provided in the Act amended. The Department of State Police as the successor to the Department of Public Safety shall have the rights, powers and duties provided in, and be subject to the provisions of Sections 5-95, 5-700, and 5-705 of the Departments of State Government Law (20 ILL. COMP. STAT. 5/5-95, 5/5-700, and 5/5-705).
(Source: P.A. 91-239, eff. 1-1-00.)

430 ILL. COMP. STAT. 65/15B
SEC. 15B. CERTIFIED ABSTRACTS.

Any certified abstract issued by the Director of State Police or transmitted electronically by the Director of State Police under this Section to a court or on request of a law enforcement agency for the record of a named person as to the status of the person's Firearm Owner's Identification Card is prima facie evidence of the facts stated in the certified abstract and if the name appearing in the abstract is the same as that of a person named in an information or warrant, the abstract is prima facie evidence that the person named in the information or warrant is the same person as the person named in the abstract and is admissible for any prosecution under this Act or any other applicable violation of law and may be admitted as proof of any prior conviction or proof of records, notices, or orders recorded on individual Firearm Owner's Identification Card records maintained by the Department of State Police.
(Source: P.A. 92-839, eff. 8-22-02.)

430 ILL. COMP. STAT. 65/16
SEC. 16.

When 2% of the number of registered voters in the State desire to pass upon the question of whether the General Assembly should repeal this Act regulating the acquisition, possession and transfer of firearms and firearm ammunition, they shall, at least 78 days before a regular election to be held throughout the State, file in the office of the State Board of Elections, a petition directed to the Board in accordance with the general election law. The petition shall be composed of county petitions from each of the counties throughout the State and each county petition shall contain the signatures of at least 2% of the number of registered voters in the county. The petition shall request that the question "Should the General Assembly repeal the Act entitled 'An Act relating to the acquisition, possession and transfer of firearms and firearm ammunition, to provide a penalty for the violation thereof and to make an appropriation in connection therewith,' approved August 3, 1967, as amended?" be submitted to the voters of the State at the next ensuing State-wide election at which such question may be acted upon.

(Source: P.A. 81-1489.)

430 ILL. COMP. STAT. 65/16.1
SEC. 16.1.

A petition for the submission of the proposition shall be in substantially the following form:

> To the State Board of Elections
>
> The undersigned, residents and registered voters of the State of Illinois, respectfully petition that you cause to be submitted, in the manner provided by the general election law to the voters of the State of Illinois, at the next State-wide election, the proposition "Should the General Assembly repeal an Act entitled 'An Act relating to the acquisition, possession and transfer of firearms and firearm ammunition, to provide a penalty for the violation thereof and to make an appropriation in connection therewith', approved August 3, 1967, as amended?"

Such petition shall conform to the requirements of the general election law. The Board shall certify the question to the proper election officials who shall submit the question at an election in accordance with the general election law. Upon request of any

citizen for a reproduced copy of the petition and paying or tendering to the State Board of Elections the costs of making the copy, the Board shall immediately make, or cause to be made a reproduced copy of such petition. The Board shall also deliver to such person his official certification that such copy is a true copy of the original, stating the day when such original was filed in its office.
(Source: P.A. 81-1489.)

430 ILL. COMP. STAT. 65/16-3
SEC. 16-3.

The Secretary of State shall cause the question to be plainly printed upon separate ballots as follows:

> Should the General Assembly repeal the Act entitled "An Act relating to the acquisition, possession and transfer of firearms and firearm ammunition, to provide a penalty for the violation thereof and to make an appropriation in connection therewith", approved August 3, 1967, as amended?

(Source: P.A. 77-1819.)

430 ILL. COMP. STAT. 66/ FIREARM CONCEALED CARRY ACT.
430 ILL. COMP. STAT. 66/1
SEC. 1. SHORT TITLE.

This Act may be cited as the Firearm Concealed Carry Act.
(Source: P.A. 98-63, eff. 7-9-13.)

430 ILL. COMP. STAT. 66/5
SEC. 5. DEFINITIONS.

As used in this Act:

"Applicant" means a person who is applying for a license to carry a concealed firearm under this Act.

"Board" means the Concealed Carry Licensing Review Board.

"Concealed firearm" means a loaded or unloaded handgun carried on or about a person completely or mostly concealed from view of the public or on or about a person within a vehicle.

"Department" means the Department of State Police.

"Director" means the Director of State Police.

"Handgun" means any device which is designed to expel a projectile or projectiles by the action of an explosion, expansion of gas, or escape of gas that is designed to be held and fired by the use of a single hand. "Handgun" does not include:

(1) a stun gun or taser;

(2) a machine gun as defined in item (i) of paragraph (7) of subsection (a) of Section 24-1 of the Criminal Code of 2012;

(3) a short-barreled rifle or shotgun as defined in item (ii) of paragraph (7) of subsection (a) of Section 24-1 of the Criminal Code of 2012; or

(4) any pneumatic gun, spring gun, paint ball gun, or B-B gun which expels a single globular projectile not exceeding .18 inch in diameter, or which has a maximum muzzle velocity of less than 700 feet per second, or which expels breakable paint balls containing washable marking colors.

"Law enforcement agency" means any federal, State, or local law enforcement agency, including offices of State's Attorneys and the Office of the Attorney General.

"License" means a license issued by the Department of State Police to carry a concealed handgun.

"Licensee" means a person issued a license to carry a concealed handgun.

"Municipality" has the meaning ascribed to it in Section 1 of Article VII of the Illinois Constitution.

"Unit of local government" has the meaning ascribed to it in Section 1 of Article VII of the Illinois Constitution.

(Source: P.A. 98-63, eff. 7-9-13.)

---

430 ILL. COMP. STAT. 66/10

SEC. 10. ISSUANCE OF LICENSES TO CARRY A CONCEALED FIREARM.

(a) The Department shall issue a license to carry a concealed firearm under this Act to an applicant who:

  (1) meets the qualifications of Section 25 of this Act;

  (2) has provided the application and documentation required in Section 30 of this Act;

  (3) has submitted the requisite fees; and

  (4) does not pose a danger to himself, herself, or others, or a threat to public safety as determined by the Concealed Carry Licensing Review Board in accordance with Section 20.

(b) The Department shall issue a renewal, corrected, or duplicate license as provided in this Act.

(c) A license shall be valid throughout the State for a period of 5 years from the date of issuance. A license shall permit the licensee to:

  (1) carry a loaded or unloaded concealed firearm, fully concealed or partially concealed, on or about his or her person; and

  (2) keep or carry a loaded or unloaded concealed tfirearm on or about his or her person within a vehicle.

(d) The Department shall make applications for a license available no later than 180 days after the effective date of this Act. The

Department shall establish rules for the availability and submission of applications in accordance with this Act.

(e) An application for a license submitted to the Department that contains all the information and materials required by this Act, including the requisite fee, shall be deemed completed. Except as otherwise provided in this Act, no later than 90 days after receipt of a completed application, the Department shall issue or deny the applicant a license.

(f) The Department shall deny the applicant a license if the applicant fails to meet the requirements under this Act or the Department receives a determination from the Board that the applicant is ineligible for a license. The Department must notify the applicant stating the grounds for the denial. The notice of denial must inform the applicant of his or her right to an appeal through administrative and judicial review.

(g) A licensee shall possess a license at all times the licensee carries a concealed firearm except:

(1) when the licensee is carrying or possessing a concealed firearm on his or her land or in his or her abode, legal dwelling, or fixed place of business, or on the land or in the legal dwelling of another person as an invitee with that person's permission;

(2) when the person is authorized to carry a firearm under Section 24-2 of the Criminal Code of 2012, except subsection (a-5) of that Section; or

(3) when the handgun is broken down in a non-functioning state, is not immediately accessible, or is unloaded and enclosed in a case.

(h) If an officer of a law enforcement agency initiates an investigative stop, including but not limited to a traffic stop, of a licensee or a non-resident carrying a concealed firearm under subsection (e) of Section 40 of this Act, upon the request of the officer the licensee or non-resident shall disclose to the officer that he or she is in possession of a concealed firearm under this Act, or present the license upon the request of the officer if he or she is a licensee or present upon the request of the officer evidence under paragraph (2) of subsection (e) of Section 40 of this Act that he or she is a non-resident qualified to carry under that subsection. The disclosure requirement under this subsection (h) is satisfied if the licensee presents his or her license to the officer or the non-resident presents to the officer evidence under paragraph (2) of subsection (e) of Section 40 of this Act that he or she is qualified to carry under that subsection. Upon the request of the officer, the licensee or non-resident shall also identify the location of the concealed firearm and permit the officer to safely secure the firearm for the duration of the investigative stop. During a traffic stop, any passenger within the vehicle who is a licensee or a non-resident carrying under subsection (e) of Section 40 of this Act must comply with the requirements of this subsection (h).

(h-1)   If a licensee carrying a firearm or a non-resident carrying a firearm in a vehicle under subsection (e) of Section 40 of this Act is contacted by a law enforcement officer or emergency services personnel, the law enforcement officer or emergency services personnel may secure the firearm or direct that it be secured during the duration of the contact if the law enforcement officer or emergency services personnel determines that it is necessary for the safety of any person present, including the law enforcement officer or emergency services personnel. The licensee or nonresident shall submit to the order to secure the firearm. When the law enforcement officer or emergency services personnel have determined that the licensee or non-resident is not a threat to the safety of any person present, including the law enforcement officer or emergency services personnel, and if the licensee or non-resident is physically and mentally capable of possessing the firearm, the law enforcement officer or emergency services personnel shall return the firearm to the licensee or non-resident before releasing him or her from the scene and breaking contact. If the licensee or non-resident is transported for treatment to another location, the firearm shall be turned over to any peace officer. The peace officer shall provide a receipt which includes the make, model, caliber, and serial number of the firearm.

(i) The Department shall maintain a database of license applicants and licensees. The database shall be available to all federal, State, and local law enforcement agencies, State's Attorneys, the Attorney General, and authorized court personnel. Within 180 days after the effective date of this Act, the database shall be searchable and provide all information included in the application, including the applicant's previous addresses within the 10 years prior to the license application and any information related to violations of this Act. No law enforcement agency, State's Attorney, Attorney General, or member or staff of the judiciary shall provide any information to a requester who is not entitled to it by law.

(j) No later than 10 days after receipt of a completed application, the Department shall enter the relevant information about the applicant into the database under subsection (i) of this Section which is accessible by law enforcement agencies.

(Source: P.A. 98-63, eff. 7-9-13; 98-600, eff. 12-6-13; 99-29, eff. 7-10-15.)

---

430 ILL. COMP. STAT. 66/15

SEC. 15. OBJECTIONS BY LAW ENFORCEMENT AGENCIES.

(a) Any law enforcement agency may submit an objection to a

license applicant based upon a reasonable suspicion that the applicant is a danger to himself or herself or others, or a threat to public safety. The objection shall be made by the chief law enforcement officer of the law enforcement agency, or his or her designee, and must include any information relevant to the objection. If a law enforcement agency submits an objection within 30 days after the entry of an applicant into the database, the Department shall submit the objection and all information available to the Board under State and federal law related to the application to the Board within 10 days of completing all necessary background checks.

(b) If an applicant has 5 or more arrests for any reason, that have been entered into the Criminal History Records Information (CHRI) System, within the 7 years preceding the date of application for a license, or has 3 or more arrests within the 7 years preceding the date of application for a license for any combination of gang-related offenses, the Department shall object and submit the applicant's arrest record to the extent the Board is allowed to receive that information under State and federal law, the application materials, and any additional information submitted by a law enforcement agency to the Board. For purposes of this subsection, "gang-related offense" is an offense described in Section 12-6.4, Section 24-1.8, Section 25-5, Section 33-4, or Section 33G-4, or in paragraph (1) of subsection (a) of Section 12-6.2, paragraph (2) of subsection (b) of Section 16-30, paragraph (2) of subsection (b) of Section 31-4, or item (iii) of paragraph (1.5) of subsection (i) of Section 48-1 of the Criminal Code of 2012.

(c) The referral of an objection under this Section to the Board shall toll the 90-day period for the Department to issue or deny the applicant a license under subsection (e) of Section 10 of this Act, during the period of review and until the Board issues its decision.

(d) If no objection is made by a law enforcement agency or the

Department under this Section, the Department shall process the application in accordance with this Act.

(Source: P.A. 98-63, eff. 7-9-13; 98-600, eff. 12-6-13.)

---

430 ILL. COMP. STAT. 66/20

SEC. 20. CONCEALED CARRY LICENSING REVIEW BOARD.

(a) There is hereby created within the Department of State Police a Concealed Carry Licensing Review Board to consider any objection to an applicant's eligibility to obtain a license under this Act submitted by a law enforcement agency or the Department under Section 15 of this Act. The Board shall consist of 7 commissioners to be appointed by the Governor, with the advice and consent of the Senate, with 3 commissioners residing within the First Judicial District and one commissioner residing within each of the 4 remaining Judicial Districts. No more than 4 commissioners shall be members of the same political party. The Governor shall designate one commissioner as the Chairperson. The Board shall consist of:

(1) one commissioner with at least 5 years of service as a federal judge;

(2) 2 commissioners with at least 5 years of experience serving as an attorney with the United States Department of Justice;

(3) 3 commissioners with at least 5 years of experience as a federal agent or employee with investigative experience or duties related to criminal justice under the United States Department of Justice, Drug Enforcement Administration, Department of Homeland Security, or Federal Bureau of Investigation; and

(4) one member with at least 5 years of experience as a licensed physician or clinical psychologist with expertise in the

diagnosis and treatment of mental illness.

(b) The initial terms of the commissioners shall end on January 12, 2015. Thereafter, the commissioners shall hold office for 4 years, with terms expiring on the second Monday in January of the fourth year. Commissioners may be reappointed. Vacancies in the office of commissioner shall be filled in the same manner as the original appointment, for the remainder of the unexpired term. The Governor may remove a commissioner for incompetence, neglect of duty, malfeasance, or inability to serve. Commissioners shall receive compensation in an amount equal to the compensation of members of the Executive Ethics Commission and may be reimbursed for reasonable expenses actually incurred in the performance of their Board duties, from funds appropriated for that purpose.

(c) The Board shall meet at the call of the chairperson as often as necessary to consider objections to applications for a license under this Act. If necessary to ensure the participation of a commissioner, the Board shall allow a commissioner to participate in a Board meeting by electronic communication. Any commissioner participating electronically shall be deemed present for purposes of establishing a quorum and voting.

(d) The Board shall adopt rules for the review of objections and the conduct of hearings. The Board shall maintain a record of its decisions and all materials considered in making its decisions. All Board decisions and voting records shall be kept confidential and all materials considered by the Board shall be exempt from inspection except upon order of a court.

(e) In considering an objection of a law enforcement agency or the Department, the Board shall review the materials received with the objection from the law enforcement agency or the Department. By a vote of at least 4 commissioners, the Board may request additional information from the law enforcement agency, Department, or the applicant, or the testimony of the law enforcement agency, Department, or the applicant. The Board may require that the applicant submit electronic fingerprints to the Department for an updated background check where the Board determines it lacks sufficient information to determine eligibility. The Board may only consider information submitted by the Department, a law enforcement agency, or the applicant. The Board shall review each objection and determine by a majority of commissioners whether an applicant is eligible for a license.

(f) The Board shall issue a decision within 30 days of receipt of the objection from the Department. However, the Board need not issue a decision within 30 days if:

(1) the Board requests information from the applicant, including but not limited to electronic fingerprints to be submitted to the Department, in accordance with subsection (e) of this Section, in which case the Board shall make a decision within 30 days of receipt of the required information from the applicant;

(2) the applicant agrees, in writing, to allow the Board additional time to consider an objection; or

(3) the Board notifies the applicant and the Department that the Board needs an additional 30 days to issue a decision.

(g) If the Board determines by a preponderance of the evidence that the applicant poses a danger to himself or herself or others, or is a threat to public safety, then the Board shall affirm the objection of the law enforcement agency or the Department and shall notify the Department that the applicant is ineligible for a license. If the Board does not determine by a preponderance of the evidence that the applicant poses a danger to himself or herself or others, or is a threat to public safety, then the Board shall notify the Department that the applicant is eligible for a license.

(h)   Meetings of the Board shall not be subject to the Open Meetings Act and records of the Board shall not be subject to the Freedom of Information Act.

(i)   The Board shall report monthly to the Governor and the General Assembly on the number of objections received and provide details of the circumstances in which the Board has determined to deny licensure based on law enforcement or Department objections under Section 15 of this Act. The report shall not contain any identifying information about the applicants.

(Source: P.A. 98-63, eff. 7-9-13; 98-600, eff. 12-6-13.)

430 ILL. COMP. STAT. 66/25
SEC. 25. QUALIFICATIONS FOR A LICENSE.

The Department shall issue a license to an applicant completing an application in accordance with Section 30 of this Act if the person:

(1)   is at least 21 years of age;

(2)   has a currently valid Firearm Owner's Identification Card and at the time of application meets the requirements for the issuance of a Firearm Owner's Identification Card and is not prohibited under the Firearm Owners Identification Card Act or federal law from possessing or receiving a firearm;

(3)   has not been convicted or found guilty in this State or in any other state of:

   (A)   a misdemeanor involving the use or threat of physical force or violence to any person within the 5 years preceding the date of the license application; or

   (B)   2 or more violations related to driving while under the influence of alcohol, other drug or drugs, intoxicating compound or compounds, or any combination thereof, within the 5 years preceding the date of the license application;

(4) is not the subject of a pending arrest warrant, prosecution, or proceeding for an offense or action that could lead to disqualification to own or possess a firearm;

(5) has not been in residential or court-ordered treatment for alcoholism, alcohol detoxification, or drug treatment within the 5 years immediately preceding the date of the license application; and

(6) has completed firearms training and any education component required under Section 75 of this Act.

(Source: P.A. 98-63, eff. 7-9-13; 98-756, eff. 7-16-14.)

---

430 ILL. COMP. STAT. 66/30
SEC. 30. CONTENTS OF LICENSE APPLICATION.

(a) The license application shall be in writing, under penalty of perjury, on a standard form adopted by the Department and shall be accompanied by the documentation required in this Section and the applicable fee. Each application form shall include the following statement printed in bold type: "Warning: Entering false information on this form is punishable as perjury under Section 32-2 of the Criminal Code of 2012."

(b) The application shall contain the following:

(1) the applicant's name, current address, date and year of birth, place of birth, height, weight, hair color, eye color, maiden name or any other name the applicant has used or identified with, and any address where the applicant resided for more than 30 days within the 10 years preceding the date of the license application;

(2) the applicant's valid driver's license number or valid state identification card number;

(3) a waiver of the applicant's privacy and confidentiality rights and privileges under all federal and state laws, including those limiting access to juvenile court, criminal justice, psychological, or psychiatric records or records relating to any institutionalization of the applicant, and an affirmative request that a person having custody of any of these records provide it or information concerning it to the Department. The waiver only applies to records sought in connection with determining whether the applicant qualifies for a license to carry a concealed firearm under this Act, or whether the applicant remains in compliance with the Firearm Owners Identification Card Act;

(4) an affirmation that the applicant possesses a currently valid Firearm Owner's Identification Card and card number if possessed or notice the applicant is applying for a Firearm Owner's Identification Card in conjunction with the license application;

(5) an affirmation that the applicant has not been convicted or found guilty of:

(A) a felony;

(B) a misdemeanor involving the use or threat of physical force or violence to any person within the 5 years preceding the date of the application; or

(C) 2 or more violations related to driving while under the influence of alcohol, other drug or drugs, intoxicating compound or compounds, or any combination thereof, within the 5 years preceding the date of the license application; and

(6) whether the applicant has failed a drug test for a drug for which the applicant did not have a prescription, within the previous year, and if so, the provider of the test, the specific

substance involved, and the date of the test;

(7) written consent for the Department to review and use the applicant's Illinois digital driver's license or Illinois identification card photograph and signature;

(8) a full set of fingerprints submitted to the Department in electronic format, provided the Department may accept an application submitted without a set of fingerprints in which case the Department shall be granted 30 days in addition to the 90 days provided under subsection (e) of Section 10 of this Act to issue or deny a license;

(9) a head and shoulder color photograph in a size specified by the Department taken within the 30 days preceding the date of the license application; and

(10) a photocopy of any certificates or other evidence of compliance with the training requirements under this Act.

(Source: P.A. 98-63, eff. 7-9-13; 99-29, eff. 7-10-15.)

---

430 ILL. COMP. STAT. 66/35
SEC. 35. INVESTIGATION OF THE APPLICANT.

The Department shall conduct a background check of the applicant to ensure compliance with the requirements of this Act and all federal, State, and local laws. The background check shall include a search of the following:

(1) the National Instant Criminal Background Check System of the Federal Bureau of Investigation;

(2) all available state and local criminal history record information files, including records of juvenile adjudications;

(3) all available federal, state, and local records regarding wanted persons;

(4) all available federal, state, and local records of domestic

violence restraining and protective orders;

(5) the files of the Department of Human Services relating to mental health and developmental disabilities; and

(6) all other available records of a federal, state, or local agency or other public entity in any jurisdiction likely to contain information relevant to whether the applicant is prohibited from purchasing, possessing, or carrying a firearm under federal, state, or local law.

Fingerprints collected under Section 30 shall be checked against the Department of State Police and Federal Bureau of Investigation criminal history record databases now and hereafter filed. The Department shall charge applicants a fee for conducting the criminal history records check, which shall be deposited in the State Police Services Fund and shall not exceed the actual cost of the records check.

(Source: P.A. 98-63, eff. 7-9-13; 98-756, eff. 7-16-14.)

---

430 ILL. COMP. STAT. 66/40
SEC. 40. NON-RESIDENT LICENSE APPLICATIONS.

(a) For the purposes of this Section, "non-resident" means a person who has not resided within this State for more than 30 days and resides in another state or territory.

(b) The Department shall by rule allow for non-resident license applications from any state or territory of the United States with laws related to firearm ownership, possession, and carrying, that are substantially similar to the requirements to obtain a license under this Act.

(c) A resident of a state or territory approved by the Department under subsection (b) of this Section may apply for a non-resident license. The applicant shall apply to the Department and must meet all of the qualifications established in Section 25 of this Act, except for the Illinois residency requirement in item (xiv) of paragraph (2) of subsection (a) of Section 4 of the Firearm Owners Identification Card Act. The applicant shall submit:

(1) the application and documentation required under Section 30 of this Act and the applicable fee;

(2) a notarized document stating that the applicant:

(A) is eligible under federal law and the laws of his or her state or territory of residence to own or possess a firearm;

(B) if applicable, has a license or permit to carry a firearm or concealed firearm issued by his or her state or territory of residence and attach a copy of the license or permit to the application;

(C) understands Illinois laws pertaining to the possession and transport of firearms; and

(D) acknowledges that the applicant is subject to the jurisdiction of the Department and Illinois courts for any violation of this Act;

(3) a photocopy of any certificates or other evidence of compliance with the training requirements under Section 75 of this Act; and

(4) a head and shoulder color photograph in a size specified by the Department taken within the 30 days preceding the date of the application.

(d) In lieu of an Illinois driver's license or Illinois identification card, a non-resident applicant shall provide similar documentation from his or her state or territory of residence. In lieu of a valid Firearm Owner's Identification Card, the applicant shall submit documentation and information required by the Department to obtain a Firearm Owner's Identification Card, including an affidavit that the non-resident meets the mental health standards to obtain a firearm under Illinois law, and the Department shall ensure that the applicant would meet the eligibility criteria to obtain a Firearm Owner's Identification card if he or she was a resident of this State. (e) Nothing in this Act shall prohibit a non-resident from transporting a concealed firearm within his or her vehicle in Illinois, if the concealed firearm remains within his or her vehicle and the non-resident:

(1) is not prohibited from owning or possessing a firearm under federal law;

(2) is eligible to carry a firearm in public under the laws of his or her state or territory of residence, as evidenced by the possession of a concealed carry license or permit issued by his or her state of residence, if applicable; and

(3) is not in possession of a license under this Act.

If the non-resident leaves his or her vehicle unattended, he or she shall store the firearm within a locked vehicle or locked container within the vehicle in accordance with subsection (b) of Section 65 of this Act.

(Source: P.A. 98-63, eff. 7-9-13; 98-600, eff. 12-6-13; 99-78, eff. 7-20-15.)

430 ILL. COMP. STAT. 66/45
SEC. 45. CIVIL IMMUNITY; BOARD, EMPLOYEES, AND AGENTS.

The Board, Department, local law enforcement agency, or the employees and agents of the Board, Department, or local law enforcement agency participating in the licensing process under this Act shall not be held liable for damages in any civil action arising from alleged wrongful or improper granting, denying,

renewing, revoking, suspending, or failing to grant, deny, renew, revoke, or suspend a license under this Act, except for willful or wanton misconduct.
(Source: P.A. 98-63, eff. 7-9-13.)

430 ILL. COMP. STAT. 66/50
SEC. 50. LICENSE RENEWAL.

(a) This subsection (a) applies through the 180th day following the effective date of this amendatory Act of the 101st General Assembly. Applications for renewal of a license shall be made to the Department. A license shall be renewed for a period of 5 years upon receipt of a completed renewal application, completion of 3 hours of training required under Section 75 of this Act, payment of the applicable renewal fee, and completion of an investigation under Section 35 of this Act. The renewal application shall contain the information required in Section 30 of this Act, except that the applicant need not resubmit a full set of fingerprints.

(b) This subsection (b) applies on and after the 181st day following the effective date of this amendatory Act of the 101st General Assembly. Applications for renewal of a license shall be made to the Department. A license shall be renewed for a period of 5 years from the date of expiration on the applicant's current license upon the receipt of a completed renewal application, completion of 3 hours of training required under Section 75 of this Act, payment of the applicable renewal fee, and completion of an investigation under Section 35 of this Act. The renewal application shall contain the information required in Section 30 of this Act, except that the applicant need not resubmit a full set of fingerprints.
(Source: P.A. 101-80, eff. 7-12-19.)

430 ILL. COMP. STAT. 66/55

SEC. 55. CHANGE OF ADDRESS OR NAME; LOST, DESTROYED, OR STOLEN LICENSES.

(a) A licensee shall notify the Department within 30 days of moving or changing residence or any change of name. The licensee shall submit the requisite fee and the Department may require a notarized statement that the licensee has changed his or her residence or his or her name, including the prior and current address or name and the date the applicant moved or changed his or her name.

(b) A licensee shall notify the Department within 10 days of discovering that a license has been lost, destroyed, or stolen. A lost, destroyed, or stolen license is invalid. To request a replacement license, the licensee shall submit:

  (1) a notarized statement that the licensee no longer possesses the license, and that it was lost, destroyed, or stolen;

  (2) if applicable, a copy of a police report stating that the license was stolen; and

  (3) the requisite fee.

(c) A violation of this Section is a petty offense with a fine of $150 which shall be deposited into the Mental Health Reporting Fund.
(Source: P.A. 98-63, eff. 7-9-13; 99-29, eff. 7-10-15.)

---

430 ILL. COMP. STAT. 66/60

SEC. 60. FEES.

(a) All fees collected under this Act shall be deposited as provided in this Section. Application, renewal, and replacement fees shall be non-refundable.

(b) An applicant for a new license or a renewal shall submit $150 with the application, of which $120 shall be apportioned to the State Police Firearm Services Fund, $20 shall be apportioned to the

Mental Health Reporting Fund, and $10 shall be apportioned to the State Crime Laboratory Fund.

(c) A non-resident applicant for a new license or renewal shall submit $300 with the application, of which $250 shall be apportioned to the State Police Firearm Services Fund, $40 shall be apportioned to the Mental Health Reporting Fund, and $10 shall be apportioned to the State Crime Laboratory Fund.

(d) A licensee requesting a new license in accordance with Section 55 shall submit $75, of which $60 shall be apportioned to the State Police Firearm Services Fund, $5 shall be apportioned to the Mental Health Reporting Fund, and $10 shall be apportioned to the State Crime Laboratory Fund.

(Source: P.A. 98-63, eff. 7-9-13.)

430 ILL. COMP. STAT. 66/65
SEC. 65. PROHIBITED AREAS.

(a) A licensee under this Act shall not knowingly carry a firearm on or into:

(1) Any building, real property, and parking area under the control of a public or private elementary or secondary school.

(2) Any building, real property, and parking area under the control of a pre-school or child care facility, including any room or portion of a building under the control of a pre-school or child care facility. Nothing in this paragraph shall prevent the operator of a child care facility in a family home from owning or possessing a firearm in the home or license under this Act, if no child under child care at the home is present in the home or the firearm in the home is stored in a locked container when a child under child care at the home is present in the home.

(3) Any building, parking area, or portion of a building under the control of an officer of the executive or legislative branch of government, provided that nothing in this paragraph shall prohibit a licensee from carrying a concealed firearm onto the real property, bikeway, or trail in a park regulated by the Department of Natural Resources or any other designated public hunting area or building where firearm possession is permitted as established by the Department of Natural Resources under Section 1.8 of the Wildlife Code.

(4) Any building designated for matters before a circuit court, appellate court, or the Supreme Court, or any building or portion of a building under the control of the Supreme Court.

(5) Any building or portion of a building under the control of a unit of local government.

(6) Any building, real property, and parking area under the control of an adult or juvenile detention or correctional institution, prison, or jail.

(7) Any building, real property, and parking area under the control of a public or private hospital or hospital affiliate, mental health facility, or nursing home.

(8) Any bus, train, or form of transportation paid for in whole or in part with public funds, and any building, real property, and parking area under the control of a public transportation facility paid for in whole or in part with public funds.

(9) Any building, real property, and parking area under the control of an establishment that serves alcohol on its premises, if more than 50% of the establishment's gross receipts within the prior 3 months is from the sale of alcohol. The owner of an establishment who knowingly fails to prohibit concealed firearms on its premises as provided in this paragraph or who knowingly makes a false statement or record to avoid the

prohibition on concealed firearms under this paragraph is subject to the penalty under subsection (c-5) of Section 10-1 of the Liquor Control Act of 1934.

(10) Any public gathering or special event conducted on property open to the public that requires the issuance of a permit from the unit of local government, provided this prohibition shall not apply to a licensee who must walk through a public gathering in order to access his or her residence, place of business, or vehicle.

(11) Any building or real property that has been issued a Special Event Retailer's license as defined in Section 1-3.17.1 of the Liquor Control Act during the time designated for the sale of alcohol by the Special Event Retailer's license, or a Special use permit license as defined in subsection (q) of Section 5-1 of the Liquor Control Act during the time designated for the sale of alcohol by the Special use permit license.

(12) Any public playground.

(13) Any public park, athletic area, or athletic facility under the control of a municipality or park district, provided nothing in this Section shall prohibit a licensee from carrying a concealed firearm while on a trail or bikeway if only a portion of the trail or bikeway includes a public park.

(14) Any real property under the control of the Cook County Forest Preserve District.

(15) Any building, classroom, laboratory, medical clinic, hospital, artistic venue, athletic venue, entertainment venue, officially recognized university-related organization property, whether owned or leased, and any real property, including parking areas, sidewalks, and common areas under the control of a public or private community college, college, or university.

(16) Any building, real property, or parking area under the control

of a gaming facility licensed under the Illinois Gambling Act or the Illinois Horse Racing Act of 1975, including an inter-track wagering location licensee.

(17) Any stadium, arena, or the real property or parking area under the control of a stadium, arena, or any collegiate or professional sporting event.

(18) Any building, real property, or parking area under the control of a public library.

(19) Any building, real property, or parking area under the control of an airport.

(20) Any building, real property, or parking area under the control of an amusement park.

(21) Any building, real property, or parking area under the control of a zoo or museum.

(22) Any street, driveway, parking area, property, building, or facility, owned, leased, controlled, or used by a nuclear energy, storage, weapons, or development site or facility regulated by the federal Nuclear Regulatory Commission. The licensee shall not under any circumstance store a firearm or ammunition in his or her vehicle or in a compartment or container within a vehicle located anywhere in or on the street, driveway, parking area, property, building, or facility described in this paragraph.

(23) Any area where firearms are prohibited under federal law.

(a-5) Nothing in this Act shall prohibit a public or private community college, college, or university from:

(1) prohibiting persons from carrying a firearm within a vehicle owned, leased, or controlled by the college or university;

(2) developing resolutions, regulations, or policies regarding student, employee, or visitor misconduct and discipline, including suspension and expulsion;

(3) developing resolutions, regulations, or policies regarding the storage or maintenance of firearms, which must include designated areas where persons can park vehicles that carry firearms; and

(4) permitting the carrying or use of firearms for the purpose of instruction and curriculum of officially recognized programs, including but not limited to military science and law enforcement training programs, or in any designated area used for hunting purposes or target shooting.

(a-10) The owner of private real property of any type may prohibit the carrying of concealed firearms on the property under his or her control. The owner must post a sign in accordance with subsection (d) of this Section indicating that firearms are prohibited on the property, unless the property is a private residence.

(b) Notwithstanding subsections (a), (a-5), and (a-10) of this Section except under paragraph (22) or (23) of subsection (a), any licensee prohibited from carrying a concealed firearm into the parking area of a prohibited location specified in subsection (a), (a-5), or (a-10) of this Section shall be permitted to carry a concealed firearm on or about his or her person within a vehicle into the parking area and may store a firearm or ammunition concealed in a case within a locked vehicle or locked container out of plain view within the vehicle in the parking area. A licensee may carry a concealed firearm in the immediate area surrounding his or her vehicle within a prohibited parking lot area only for the limited purpose of storing or retrieving a firearm within the vehicle's trunk. For purposes of this subsection, "case" includes a glove compartment or console that completely encloses the concealed firearm or ammunition, the trunk of the vehicle, or a firearm carrying box, shipping box, or other container.

(c) A licensee shall not be in violation of this Section while he or she is traveling along a public right of way that touches or crosses any of the premises under subsection (a), (a-5), or (a-10) of this Section if the concealed firearm is carried on his or her person in accordance with the provisions of this Act or is being transported in a vehicle by the licensee in accordance with all other applicable provisions of law.

(d) Signs stating that the carrying of firearms is prohibited shall be clearly and conspicuously posted at the entrance of a building, premises, or real property specified in this Section as a prohibited area, unless the building or premises is a private residence. Signs shall be of a uniform design as established by the Department and shall be 4 inches by 6 inches in size. The Department shall adopt rules for standardized signs to be used under this subsection.

(Source: P.A. 101-31, eff. 6-28-19.)

430 ILL. COMP. STAT. 66/70
SEC. 70. VIOLATIONS.

(a) A license issued or renewed under this Act shall be revoked if, at any time, the licensee is found to be ineligible for a license under this Act or the licensee no longer meets the eligibility requirements of the Firearm Owners Identification Card Act.

(b) A license shall be suspended if an order of protection, including an emergency order of protection, plenary order of protection, or interim order of protection under Article 112A of the Code of Criminal Procedure of 1963 or under the Illinois Domestic Violence Act of 1986, or if a firearms restraining order, including an emergency firearms restraining order, under the Firearms Restraining Order Act, is issued against a licensee for the duration of the order, or if the Department is made aware of a similar order issued against the licensee in any other jurisdiction. If an order of protection is issued against a licensee, the licensee shall surrender the license, as applicable, to the court at the time the order is entered or to the law enforcement agency or entity serving process at the time the licensee is served the order. The court, law enforcement agency, or entity responsible for serving the order of protection shall notify the Department within 7 days and transmit the license to the Department.

(c) A license is invalid upon expiration of the license, unless the licensee has submitted an application to renew the license, and the applicant is otherwise eligible to possess a license under this Act.

(d) A licensee shall not carry a concealed firearm while under the influence of alcohol, other drug or drugs, intoxicating compound or combination of compounds, or any combination thereof, under the standards set forth in subsection (a) of Section 11-501 of the Illinois Vehicle Code.

A licensee in violation of this subsection (d) shall be guilty of a Class A misdemeanor for a first or second violation and a Class 4 felony for a third violation. The Department may suspend a license for up to 6 months for a second violation and shall permanently revoke a license for a third violation.

(e) Except as otherwise provided, a licensee in violation of this Act shall be guilty of a Class B misdemeanor. A second or subsequent violation is a Class A misdemeanor. The Department may suspend a license for up to 6 months for a second violation and shall permanently revoke a license for 3 or more violations of Section 65 of this Act. Any person convicted of a violation under this Section shall pay a $150 fee to be deposited into the Mental Health Reporting Fund, plus any applicable court costs or fees.

(f) A licensee convicted or found guilty of a violation of this

Act who has a valid license and is otherwise eligible to carry a concealed firearm shall only be subject to the penalties under this Section and shall not be subject to the penalties under Section 21-6, paragraph (4), (8), or (10) of subsection (a) of Section 24-1, or subparagraph (A-5) or (B-5) of paragraph (3) of subsection (a) of Section 24-1.6 of the Criminal Code of 2012. Except as otherwise provided in this subsection, nothing in this subsection prohibits the licensee from being subjected to penalties for violations other than those specified in this Act.

(g) A licensee whose license is revoked, suspended, or denied shall, within 48 hours of receiving notice of the revocation, suspension, or denial, surrender his or her concealed carry license to the local law enforcement agency where the person resides. The local law enforcement agency shall provide the licensee a receipt and transmit the concealed carry license to the Department of State Police. If the licensee whose concealed carry license has been revoked, suspended, or denied fails to comply with the requirements of this subsection, the law enforcement agency where the person resides may petition the circuit court to issue a warrant to search for and seize the concealed carry license in the possession and under the custody or control of the licensee whose concealed carry license has been revoked, suspended, or denied. The observation of a concealed carry license in the possession of a person whose license has been revoked, suspended, or denied constitutes a sufficient basis for the arrest of that person for violation of this subsection. A violation of this subsection is a Class A misdemeanor.

(h) A license issued or renewed under this Act shall be revoked if, at any time, the licensee is found ineligible for a Firearm Owner's Identification Card, or the licensee no longer possesses a valid Firearm Owner's Identification Card. A licensee whose license is revoked under this subsection (h) shall surrender his or her concealed carry license as provided for in subsection (g) of this Section.

This subsection shall not apply to a person who has filed an application with the State Police for renewal of a Firearm Owner's Identification Card and who is not otherwise ineligible to obtain a Firearm Owner's Identification Card.

(i) A certified firearms instructor who knowingly provides or offers to provide a false certification that an applicant has completed firearms training as required under this Act is guilty of a Class A misdemeanor. A person guilty of a violation of this subsection (i) is not eligible for court supervision. The Department shall permanently revoke the firearms instructor certification of a person convicted under this subsection (i).

(Source: P.A. 100-607, eff. 1-1-19.)

430 ILL. COMP. STAT. 66/75
SEC. 75. APPLICANT FIREARM TRAINING.

(a) Within 60 days of the effective date of this Act, the Department shall begin approval of firearm training courses and shall make a list of approved courses available on the Department's website.

(b) An applicant for a new license shall provide proof of completion of a firearms training course or combination of courses approved by the Department of at least 16 hours, which includes range qualification time under subsection (c) of this Section, that covers the following:

  (1) firearm safety;
  (2) the basic principles of marksmanship;
  (3) care, cleaning, loading, and unloading of a concealable firearm;
  (4) all applicable State and federal laws relating to the ownership,

storage, carry, and transportation of a firearm; and

(5) instruction on the appropriate and lawful interaction with law enforcement while transporting or carrying a concealed firearm.

(c) An applicant for a new license shall provide proof of certification by a certified instructor that the applicant passed a live fire exercise with a concealable firearm consisting of:

(1) a minimum of 30 rounds; and

(2) 10 rounds from a distance of 5 yards; 10 rounds from a distance of 7 yards; and 10 rounds from a distance of 10 yards at a B-27 silhouette target approved by the Department.

(d) An applicant for renewal of a license shall provide proof of completion of a firearms training course or combination of courses approved by the Department of at least 3 hours.

(e) A certificate of completion for an applicant's firearm training course shall not be issued to a student who:

(1) does not follow the orders of the certified firearms instructor;

(2) in the judgment of the certified instructor, handles a firearm in a manner that poses a danger to the student or to others; or

(3) during the range firing portion of testing fails to hit the target with 70% of the rounds fired.

(f) An instructor shall maintain a record of each student's performance for at least 5 years, and shall make all records available upon demand of authorized personnel of the Department.

(g) The Department and certified firearms instructors shall recognize up to 8 hours of training already completed toward the 16 hour training requirement under this Section if the training course is submitted to and approved by the Department. Any remaining hours that the applicant completes must at least cover the classroom subject matter of paragraph (4) of subsection (b) of this Section, and the range qualification in subsection (c) of this Section.

(h) A person who has qualified to carry a firearm as an active law enforcement or corrections officer, who has successfully completed firearms training as required by his or her law enforcement agency and is authorized by his or her agency to carry a firearm; a person currently certified as a firearms instructor by this Act or by the Illinois Law Enforcement Training Standards Board; or a person who has completed the required training and has been issued a firearm control card by the Department of Financial and Professional Regulation shall be exempt from the requirements of this Section.

(i) The Department and certified firearms instructors shall recognize 8 hours of training as completed toward the 16 hour training requirement under this Section, if the applicant is an active, retired, or honorably discharged member of the United States Armed Forces. Any remaining hours that the applicant completes must at least cover the classroom subject matter of paragraph (4) of subsection (b) of this Section, and the range qualification in subsection (c) of this Section.

(j) The Department and certified firearms instructors shall recognize up to 8 hours of training already completed toward the 16 hour training requirement under this Section if the training course is approved by the Department and was completed in connection with the applicant's previous employment as a law enforcement or corrections officer. Any remaining hours that the applicant completes must at least cover the classroom subject matter of paragraph (4) of subsection (b) of this Section, and the range qualification in subsection (c) of this Section. A former law enforcement or corrections officer seeking credit under this subsection (j) shall provide evidence that he or she separated from employment in good standing from each law enforcement agency where he or she was employed. An applicant who was discharged from a law enforcement agency for misconduct or disciplinary reasons is not eligible for credit under this subsection (j).

(Source: P.A. 98-63, eff. 7-9-13; 98-600, eff. 12-6-13.)

430 ILL. COMP. STAT. 66/80
SEC. 80. CERTIFIED FIREARMS INSTRUCTORS.

(a) Within 60 days of the effective date of this Act, the Department shall begin approval of certified firearms instructors and enter certified firearms instructors into an online registry on the Department's website.

(b) A person who is not a certified firearms instructor shall not teach applicant training courses or advertise or otherwise represent courses they teach as qualifying their students to meet the requirements to receive a license under this Act. Each violation of this subsection is a business offense with a fine of at least $1,000 per violation.

(c) A person seeking to become a certified firearms instructor shall:

 (1) be at least 21 years of age;

 (2) be a legal resident of the United States; and

 (3) meet the requirements of Section 25 of this Act, except for the Illinois residency requirement in item (xiv) of paragraph (2) of subsection (a) of Section 4 of the Firearm Owners Identification Card Act; and any additional uniformly applied requirements established by the Department.

(d) A person seeking to become a certified firearms instructor, in addition to the requirements of subsection (c) of this Section, shall:

 (1) possess a high school diploma or high school equivalency certificate; and

(2) have at least one of the following valid firearms instructor certifications:

(A) certification from a law enforcement agency;

(B) certification from a firearm instructor course offered by a State or federal governmental agency;

(C) certification from a firearm instructor qualification course offered by the Illinois Law Enforcement Training Standards Board; or

(D) certification from an entity approved by the Department that offers firearm instructor education and training in the use and safety of firearms.

(e) A person may have his or her firearms instructor certification denied or revoked if he or she does not meet the requirements to obtain a license under this Act, provides false or misleading information to the Department, or has had a prior instructor certification revoked or denied by the Department.

(Source: P.A. 98-63, eff. 7-9-13; 98-600, eff. 12-6-13; 98-718, eff. 1-1-15.)

---

430 ILL. COMP. STAT. 66/85
SEC. 85. BACKGROUND CHECKS FOR SALES.

A license to carry a concealed firearm issued by this State shall not exempt the licensee from the requirements of a background check, including a check of the National Instant Criminal Background Check System, upon purchase or transfer of a firearm.

(Source: P.A. 98-63, eff. 7-9-13.)

---

430 ILL. COMP. STAT. 66/87
SEC. 87. ADMINISTRATIVE AND JUDICIAL REVIEW.

(a) Whenever an application for a concealed carry license is denied, whenever the Department fails to act on an application within 90 days of its receipt, or whenever a license is revoked or suspended as provided in this Act, the aggrieved party may appeal to the Director for a hearing upon the denial, revocation, suspension, or failure to act on the application, unless the denial was made by the Concealed Carry Licensing Review Board, in which case the aggrieved party may petition the circuit court in writing in the county of his or her residence for a hearing upon the denial.

(b) All final administrative decisions of the Department or the Concealed Carry Licensing Review Board under this Act shall be subject to judicial review under the provisions of the Administrative Review Law. The term "administrative decision" is defined as in Section 3-101 of the Code of Civil Procedure.

(Source: P.A. 98-63, eff. 7-9-13.)

430 ILL. COMP. STAT. 66/90
SEC. 90. PREEMPTION.

The regulation, licensing, possession, registration, and transportation of handguns and ammunition for handguns by licensees are exclusive powers and functions of the State. Any ordinance or regulation, or portion thereof, enacted on or before the effective date of this Act that purports to impose regulations or restrictions on licensees or handguns and ammunition for handguns in a manner inconsistent with this Act shall be invalid in its application to licensees under this Act on the effective date of this Act. This Section is a denial and limitation of home rule powers and functions under subsection (h) of Section 6 of Article VII of the Illinois Constitution.

(Source: P.A. 98-63, eff. 7-9-13.)

430 ILL. COMP. STAT. 66/92
SEC. 92. (REPEALED).
(Source: P.A. 98-63, eff. 7-9-13. Repealed internally, eff. 3-2-14.)

---

430 ILL. COMP. STAT. 66/95
SEC. 95. PROCUREMENT; RULEMAKING.
(a) The Department of State Police, in consultation with and subject to the approval of the Chief Procurement Officer, may procure a single contract or multiple contracts to implement the provisions of this Act. A contract or contracts under this paragraph are not subject to the provisions of the Illinois Procurement Code, except for Sections 20-60, 20-65, 20-70, and 20-160 and Article 50 of that Code, provided that the Chief Procurement Officer may, in writing with justification, waive any certification required under Article 50. This exemption shall be repealed one year from the effective date of this Act.

(b) The Department shall adopt rules to implement the provisions of this Act. The Department may adopt rules necessary to implement the provisions of this Act through the use of emergency rulemaking in accordance with Section 5-45 of the Illinois Administrative Procedure Act for a period not to exceed 180 days after the effective date of this Act.
(Source: P.A. 98-63, eff. 7-9-13.)

(430 ILL. COMP. STAT. 66/100)
SEC. 100.
Short title. Sections 100 through 110 may be cited as the School Administrator Reporting of Mental Health Clear and Present Danger Determinations Law.
(Source: P.A. 98-63, eff. 7-9-13.)

430 ILL. COMP. STAT. 66/105
SEC. 105. DUTY OF SCHOOL ADMINISTRATOR.

It is the duty of the principal of a public elementary or secondary school, or his or her designee, and the chief administrative officer of a private elementary or secondary school or a public or private community college, college, or university, or his or her designee, to report to the Department of State Police when a student is determined to pose a clear and present danger to himself, herself, or to others, within 24 hours of the determination as provided in Section 6-103.3 of the Mental Health and Developmental Disabilities Code. "Clear and present danger" has the meaning as provided in paragraph (2) of the definition of "clear and present danger" in Section 1.1 of the Firearm Owners Identification Card Act.

(Source: P.A. 98-63, eff. 7-9-13.)

430 ILL. COMP. STAT. 66/110
SEC. 110. IMMUNITY.

A principal or chief administrative officer, or the designee of a principal or chief administrative officer, making the determination and reporting under Section 105 of this Law shall not be held criminally, civilly, or professionally liable, except for willful or wanton misconduct.

(Source: P.A. 98-63, eff. 7-9-13.)

430 ILL. COMP. STAT. 66/195
SEC. 195. NO ACCELERATION OR DELAY.

Where this Act makes changes in a statute that is represented in this Act by text that is not yet or no longer in effect (for example, a Section represented by multiple versions), the use of that text does not accelerate or delay the taking effect of (i) the changes made by this Act or (ii) provisions derived from any other Public Act. (Source: P.A. 98-63, eff. 7-9-13.)

APPENDIX B:
Federal Law

18 U.S.C. § 922.

UNLAWFUL ACTS

(a) It shall be unlawful—

    (1) for any person—

        (A) except a licensed importer, licensed manufacturer, or licensed dealer, to engage in the business of importing, manufacturing, or dealing in firearms, or in the course of such business to ship, transport, or receive any firearm in interstate or foreign commerce; or

        (B) except a licensed importer or licensed manufacturer, to engage in the business of importing or manufacturing ammunition, or in the course of such business, to ship, transport, or receive any ammunition in interstate or foreign commerce;

    (2) for any importer, manufacturer, dealer, or collector licensed under the provisions of this chapter to ship or transport in interstate or foreign commerce any firearm

to any person other than a licensed importer, licensed manufacturer, licensed dealer, or licensed collector, except that—

(A) this paragraph and subsection (b)(3) shall not be held to preclude a licensed importer, licensed manufacturer, licensed dealer, or licensed collector from returning a firearm or replacement firearm of the same kind and type to a person from whom it was received; and this paragraph shall not be held to preclude an individual from mailing a firearm owned in compliance with Federal, State, and local law to a licensed importer, licensed manufacturer, licensed dealer, or licensed collector;

(B) this paragraph shall not be held to preclude a licensed importer, licensed manufacturer, or licensed dealer from depositing a firearm for conveyance in the mails to any officer, employee, agent, or watchman who, pursuant to the provisions of section 1715 of this title, is eligible to receive through the mails pistols, revolvers, and other firearms capable of being concealed on the person, for use in connection with his official duty; and

(C) nothing in this paragraph shall be construed as applying in any manner in the District of Columbia, the Commonwealth of Puerto Rico, or any possession of the United States differently than it would apply if the District of Columbia, the Commonwealth of Puerto Rico, or the possession were in fact a State of the United States;

(3) for any person, other than a licensed importer, licensed manufacturer, licensed dealer, or licensed collector to transport into or receive in the State where he resides (or if the person is a corporation or other business entity, the State where it maintains a place of business) any firearm purchased or otherwise obtained by such person outside that State, except that this paragraph (A) shall not preclude any person who lawfully acquires a firearm by bequest or intestate succession in a State other than his State of residence from transporting the firearm into or receiving it in that State, if it is lawful for such person to purchase or possess such firearm in that State, (B) shall not apply to the transportation or receipt of a firearm obtained in conformity with subsection (b)(3) of this section, and (C) shall not apply to the transportation of any firearm acquired in any State prior to the effective date of this chapter;

(4) for any person, other than a licensed importer, licensed manufacturer, licensed dealer, or licensed collector, to transport in interstate or foreign commerce any destructive device, machinegun (as defined in section 5845 of the Internal Revenue Code of 1986), short-barreled shotgun, or short-barreled rifle, except as specifically authorized by the Attorney General consistent with public safety and necessity;

(5) for any person (other than a licensed importer, licensed manufacturer, licensed dealer, or licensed collector) to transfer, sell, trade, give, transport, or deliver any firearm to any person (other than a licensed importer,

licensed manufacturer, licensed dealer, or licensed collector) who the transferor knows or has reasonable cause to believe does not reside in (or if the person is a corporation or other business entity, does not maintain a place of business in) the State in which the transferor resides; except that this paragraph shall not apply to (A) the transfer, transportation, or delivery of a firearm made to carry out a bequest of a firearm to, or an acquisition by intestate succession of a firearm by, a person who is permitted to acquire or possess a firearm under the laws of the State of his residence, and (B) the loan or rental of a firearm to any person for temporary use for lawful sporting purposes;

(6) for any person in connection with the acquisition or attempted acquisition of any firearm or ammunition from a licensed importer, licensed manufacturer, licensed dealer, or licensed collector, knowingly to make any false or fictitious oral or written statement or to furnish or exhibit any false, fictitious, or misrepresented identification, intended or likely to deceive such importer, manufacturer, dealer, or collector with respect to any fact material to the lawfulness of the sale or other disposition of such firearm or ammunition under the provisions of this chapter;

(7) for any person to manufacture or import armor piercing ammunition, unless—

(A) the manufacture of such ammunition is for the use of the United States, any department or agency of the United States, any State, or any department, agency, or political subdivision of a State;

(B) the manufacture of such ammunition is for the purpose of exportation; or

(C) the manufacture or importation of such ammunition is for the purpose of testing or experimentation and has been authorized by the Attorney General;

(8) for any manufacturer or importer to sell or deliver armor piercing ammunition, unless such sale or delivery—

(A) is for the use of the United States, any department or agency of the United States, any State, or any department, agency, or political subdivision of a State;

(B) is for the purpose of exportation; or

(C) is for the purpose of testing or experimentation and has been authorized by the Attorney General; and

(9) or any person, other than a licensed importer, licensed manufacturer, licensed dealer, or licensed collector, who does not reside in any State to receive any firearms unless such receipt is for lawful sporting purposes.

(b) It shall be unlawful for any licensed importer, licensed manufacturer, licensed dealer, or licensed collector to sell or deliver—

(1) any firearm or ammunition to any individual who the licensee knows or has reasonable cause to believe is less than eighteen years of age, and, if the firearm, or ammunition is other than a shotgun or rifle, or ammunition for a shotgun or rifle, to any individual who the licensee knows or has reasonable cause to believe is less than twenty-one years of age;

(2) any firearm to any person in any State where the purchase or possession by such person of such firearm would be

in violation of any State law or any published ordinance applicable at the place of sale, delivery or other disposition, unless the licensee knows or has reasonable cause to believe that the purchase or possession would not be in violation of such State law or such published ordinance;

(3) any firearm to any person who the licensee knows or has reasonable cause to believe does not reside in (or if the person is a corporation or other business entity, does not maintain a place of business in) the State in which the licensee's place of business is located, except that this paragraph (A) shall not apply to the sale or delivery of any rifle or shotgun to a resident of a State other than a State in which the licensee's place of business is located if the transferee meets in person with the transferor to accomplish the transfer, and the sale, delivery, and receipt fully comply with the legal conditions of sale in both such States (and any licensed manufacturer, importer or dealer shall be presumed, for purposes of this subparagraph, in the absence of evidence to the contrary, to have had actual knowledge of the State laws and published ordinances of both States), and (B) shall not apply to the loan or rental of a firearm to any person for temporary use for lawful sporting purposes;

(4) to any person any destructive device, machinegun (as defined in section 5845 of the Internal Revenue Code of 1986), short-barreled shotgun, or short-barreled rifle, except as specifically authorized by the Attorney General consistent with public safety and necessity; and

(5) any firearm or armor-piercing ammunition to any person unless the licensee notes in his records, required

to be kept pursuant to section 923 of this chapter, the name, age, and place of residence of such person if the person is an individual, or the identity and principal and local places of business of such person if the person is a corporation or other business entity.

Paragraphs (1), (2), (3), and (4) of this subsection shall not apply to transactions between licensed importers, licensed manufacturers, licensed dealers, and licensed collectors. Paragraph (4) of this subsection shall not apply to a sale or delivery to any research organization designated by the Attorney General.

(c) In any case not otherwise prohibited by this chapter, a licensed importer, licensed manufacturer, or licensed dealer may sell a firearm to a person who does not appear in person at the licensee's business premises (other than another licensed importer, manufacturer, or dealer) only if–

(1) the transferee submits to the transferor a sworn statement in the following form:

"Subject to penalties provided by law, I swear that, in the case of any firearm other than a shotgun or a rifle, I am twenty-one years or more of age, or that, in the case of a shotgun or a rifle, I am eighteen years or more of age; that I am not prohibited by the provisions of chapter 44 of Title 18, United States Code, from receiving a firearm in interstate or foreign commerce; and that my receipt of this firearm will not be in violation of any statute of the State and published ordinance applicable to the locality in which I reside. Further, the true title, name, and address of the principal law enforcement officer of the locality to which the firearm will be delivered is _____

_____

Signature _____ Date _____."

and containing blank spaces for the attachment of a true copy of any permit or other information required pursuant to such statute or published ordinance;

(2) the transferor has, prior to the shipment or delivery of the firearm, forwarded by registered or certified mail (return receipt requested) a copy of the sworn statement, together with a description of the firearm, in a form prescribed by the Attorney General, to the chief law enforcement officer of the transferee's place of residence, and has received a return receipt evidencing delivery of the statement or has had the statement returned due to the refusal of the named addressee to accept such letter in accordance with United States Post Office Department regulations; and

(3) the transferor has delayed shipment or delivery for a period of at least seven days following receipt of the notification of the acceptance or refusal of delivery of the statement.

A copy of the sworn statement and a copy of the notification to the local law enforcement officer, together with evidence of receipt or rejection of that notification shall be retained by the licensee as a part of the records required to be kept under section 923(g).

(d) It shall be unlawful for any person to sell or otherwise dispose of any firearm or ammunition to any person knowing or having reasonable cause to believe that such person–

(1) is under indictment for, or has been convicted in any court of, a crime punishable by imprisonment for a term exceeding one year;

(2) is a fugitive from justice;

(3) is an unlawful user of or addicted to any controlled substance (as defined in section 102 of the Controlled Substances Act (21 U.S.C. 802));

(4) has been adjudicated as a mentally defective or has been committed to any mental institution;

(5) who, being an alien–

    (A) is illegally or unlawfully in the United States; or

    (B) except as provided in subsection (y)(2), has been admitted to the United States under a nonimmigrant visa (as that term is defined in section 101(a)(26) of the Immigration and Nationality Act (8 U.S.C. 1101(a)(26)));

(6) who has been discharged from the Armed Forces under dishonorable conditions;

(7) who, having been a citizen of the United States, has renounced their citizenship;

(8) is subject to a court order that restrains such person from harassing, stalking, or threatening an intimate partner of such person or child of such intimate partner or person, or engaging in other conduct that would place an intimate partner in reasonable fear of bodily injury to the partner or child, except that this paragraph shall only apply to a court order that–

    (A) was issued after a hearing of which such person received actual notice, and at which such person had the opportunity to participate; and

    (B)

        (i) includes a finding that such person represents a credible threat to the physical safety of such intimate partner or child; or

(ii) by its terms explicitly prohibits the use, attempted use, or threatened use of physical force against such intimate partner or child that would reasonably be expected to cause bodily injury.

(9) has been convicted in any court of a misdemeanor crime of domestic violence.

This subsection shall not apply with respect to the sale or disposition of a firearm or ammunition to a licensed importer, licensed manufacturer, licensed dealer, or licensed collector who pursuant to subsection (b) of section 925 of this chapter is not precluded from dealing in firearms or ammunition, or to a person who has been granted relief from disabilities pursuant to subsection (c) of section 925 of this chapter.

(e) It shall be unlawful for any person knowingly to deliver or cause to be delivered to any common or contract carrier for transportation or shipment in interstate or foreign commerce, to persons other than licensed importers, licensed manufacturers, licensed dealers, or licensed collectors, any package or other container in which there is any firearm or ammunition without written notice to the carrier that such firearm or ammunition is being transported or shipped; except that any passenger who owns or legally possesses a firearm or ammunition being transported aboard any common or contract carrier for movement with the passenger in interstate or foreign commerce may deliver said firearm or ammunition into the custody of the pilot, captain, conductor or operator of such common or contract carrier for the duration of the trip without violating any of the provisions of this chapter. No common or contract carrier shall require or cause any label, tag, or other written notice to be placed on the outside of any package, luggage, or other container that such package, luggage, or other container contains a firearm.

(f)

(1) It shall be unlawful for any common or contract carrier to transport or deliver in interstate or foreign commerce any firearm or ammunition with knowledge or reasonable cause to believe that the shipment, transportation, or receipt thereof would be in violation of the provisions of this chapter.

(2) It shall be unlawful for any common or contract carrier to deliver in interstate or foreign commerce any firearm without obtaining written acknowledgement of receipt from the recipient of the package or other container in which there is a firearm.

(g) It shall be unlawful for any person–

(1) who has been convicted in any court of, a crime punishable by imprisonment for a term exceeding one year;

(2) who is a fugitive from justice;

(3) who is an unlawful user of or addicted to any controlled substance (as defined in section 102 of the Controlled Substances Act (21 U.S.C. 802));

(4) who has been adjudicated as a mental defective or who has been committed to a mental institution;

(5) who, being an alien–

(A) is illegally or unlawfully in the United States; or

(B) except as provided in subsection (y)(2), has been admitted to the United States under a nonimmigrant visa (as that term is defined in section 101(a)(26) of the Immigration and

Nationality Act (8 U.S.C. 1101(a)(26)));

(6) who has been discharged from the Armed Forces under dishonorable conditions;

(7) who, having been a citizen of the United States, has renounced his citizenship;

(8) who is subject to a court order that–

    (A) was issued after a hearing of which such person received actual notice, and at which such person had an opportunity to participate;

    (B) restrains such person from harassing, stalking, or threatening an intimate partner of such person or child of such intimate partner or person, or engaging in other conduct that would place an intimate partner in reasonable fear of bodily injury to the partner or child; and

    (C)

        (i) includes a finding that such person represents a credible threat to the physical safety of such intimate partner or child; or

        (ii) by its terms explicitly prohibits the use, attempted use, or threatened use of physical force against such intimate partner or child that would reasonably be expected to cause bodily injury; or

(9) who has been convicted in any court of a misdemeanor crime of domestic violence, to ship or transport in interstate or foreign commerce, or possess in or affecting commerce, any firearm or ammunition; or to receive any firearm or ammunition which has been shipped or transported in interstate or foreign commerce.

(h) It shall be unlawful for any individual, who to that individual's knowledge and while being employed for any person described in any paragraph of subsection (g) of this section, in the course of such employment–

  (1) to receive, possess, or transport any firearm or ammunition in or affecting interstate or foreign commerce; or

  (2) to receive any firearm or ammunition which has been shipped or transported in interstate or foreign commerce.

(i) It shall be unlawful for any person to transport or ship in interstate or foreign commerce, any stolen firearm or stolen ammunition, knowing or having reasonable cause to believe that the firearm or ammunition was stolen.

(j) It shall be unlawful for any person to receive, possess, conceal, store, barter, sell, or dispose of any stolen firearm or stolen ammunition, or pledge or accept as security for a loan any stolen firearm or stolen ammunition, which is moving as, which is a part of, which constitutes, or which has been shipped or transported in, interstate or foreign commerce, either before or after it was stolen, knowing or having reasonable cause to believe that the firearm or ammunition was stolen.

(k) It shall be unlawful for any person knowingly to transport, ship, or receive, in interstate or foreign commerce, any firearm which has had the importer's or manufacturer's serial number removed, obliterated, or altered or to possess or receive any firearm which has had the importer's or manufacturer's serial number removed, obliterated, or altered and has, at any time, been shipped or transported in interstate or foreign commerce.

(l) Except as provided in section 925(d) of this chapter, it shall be unlawful for any person knowingly to import or bring into the United States or any possession thereof any firearm or ammunition; and it shall be unlawful for any person knowingly to receive any firearm or ammunition which has been imported or brought into the United States or any possession thereof in violation of the provisions of this chapter.

(m) It shall be unlawful for any licensed importer, licensed manufacturer, licensed dealer, or licensed collector knowingly to make any false entry in, to fail to make appropriate entry in, or to fail to properly maintain, any record which he is required to keep pursuant to section 923 of this chapter or regulations promulgated thereunder.

(n) It shall be unlawful for any person who is under indictment for a crime punishable by imprisonment for a term exceeding one year to ship or transport in interstate or foreign commerce any firearm or ammunition or receive any firearm or ammunition which has been shipped or transported in interstate or foreign commerce.

(o)

(1) Except as provided in paragraph (2), it shall be unlawful for any person to transfer or possess a machinegun.

(2) This subsection does not apply with respect to—

(A) a transfer to or by, or possession by or under the authority of, the United States or any department or agency thereof or a State, or a department, agency, or political subdivision thereof; or

(B) any lawful transfer or lawful possession of a machinegun that was lawfully possessed before the date this subsection takes effect.

(p)

(1) It shall be unlawful for any person to manufacture, import, sell, ship, deliver, possess, transfer, or receive any firearm—

(A) that, after removal of grips, stocks, and magazines, is not as detectable as the Security Exemplar, by walk-through metal detectors calibrated and operated to detect the Security Exemplar; or

(B) any major component of which, when subjected to inspection by the types of x-ray machines commonly used at airports, does not generate an image that accurately depicts the shape of the component. Barium sulfate or other compounds may be used in the fabrication of the component.

(2) For purposes of this subsection–

(A) the term "firearm" does not include the frame or receiver of any such weapon;

(B) the term "major component" means, with respect to a firearm, the barrel, the slide or cylinder, or the frame or receiver of the firearm; and

(C) the term "Security Exemplar" means an object, to be fabricated at the direction of the Attorney General, that is–

(i) constructed of, during the 12-month period beginning on the date of the enactment of this subsection, 3.7 ounces of material type 17–4 PH stainless steel in a shape resembling a handgun; and

(ii) suitable for testing and calibrating metal detectors:

Provided, however, That at the close of such 12-month period, and at appropriate times thereafter the Attorney General shall promulgate regulations to permit the manufacture, importation, sale, shipment, delivery, possession, transfer, or receipt of firearms previously prohibited under this subparagraph that are as detectable as a "Security Exemplar" which contains 3.7 ounces of material type 17–4 PH stainless steel, in a shape resembling a handgun, or such lesser amount as is detectable in view of advances in state-of-the-art developments in weapons detection technology.

(3) Under such rules and regulations as the Attorney General shall prescribe, this subsection shall not apply to the manufacture, possession, transfer, receipt, shipment, or delivery of a firearm by a licensed manufacturer or any person acting pursuant to a contract with a licensed manufacturer, for the purpose of examining and testing such firearm to determine whether paragraph (1) applies to such firearm. The Attorney General shall ensure that rules and regulations adopted pursuant to this paragraph do not impair the manufacture of prototype firearms or the development of new technology.

(4) The Attorney General shall permit the conditional importation of a firearm by a licensed importer or licensed manufacturer, for examination and testing to determine whether or not the unconditional importation of such firearm would violate this subsection.

(5) This subsection shall not apply to any firearm which–

(A) has been certified by the Secretary of Defense or the Director of Central Intelligence, after consultation with the Attorney General and the Administrator of the Federal Aviation Administration, as necessary for military or intelligence applications; and

(B) is manufactured for and sold exclusively

to military or intelligence agencies of the United States.

(6) This subsection shall not apply with respect to any firearm manufactured in, imported into, or possessed in the United States before the date of the enactment of the Undetectable Firearms Act of 1988.

(q)

(1) The Congress finds and declares that—

    (A) crime, particularly crime involving drugs and guns, is a pervasive, nationwide problem;

    (B) crime at the local level is exacerbated by the interstate movement of drugs, guns, and criminal gangs;

    (C) firearms and ammunition move easily in interstate commerce and have been found in increasing numbers in and around schools, as documented in numerous hearings in both the Committee on the Judiciary 3 the House of Representatives and the Committee on the Judiciary of the Senate;

    (D) in fact, even before the sale of a firearm, the gun, its component parts, ammunition, and the raw materials from which they are made have considerably moved in interstate commerce;

    (E) while criminals freely move from State to State, ordinary citizens and foreign visitors may fear to travel to or through certain parts of the country due to concern about violent crime and gun violence, and parents may decline to send their children to school for the same reason;

    (F) the occurrence of violent crime in school

zones has resulted in a decline in the quality of education in our country;

(G) this decline in the quality of education has an adverse impact on interstate commerce and the foreign commerce of the United States;

(H) States, localities, and school systems find it almost impossible to handle gun-related crime by themselves-even States, localities, and school systems that have made strong efforts to prevent, detect, and punish gun-related crime find their efforts unavailing due in part to the failure or inability of other States or localities to take strong measures; and

(I) the Congress has the power, under the interstate commerce clause and other provisions of the Constitution, to enact measures to ensure the integrity and safety of the Nation's schools by enactment of this subsection.

(2)

(A) It shall be unlawful for any individual knowingly to possess a firearm that has moved in or that otherwise affects interstate or foreign commerce at a place that the individual knows, or has reasonable cause to believe, is a school zone.

(B) Subparagraph (A) does not apply to the possession of a firearm—

(i) on private property not part of school grounds;

(ii) if the individual possessing the firearm is licensed to do so by the State in which the school zone is located or a political subdivision of the State, and the law of the State or political subdivision requires that, before an individual obtains such a license, the law enforcement authorities of the State or political subdivision verify that the individual is qualified under law to receive the license;

(iii) that is–

(I) not loaded; and

(II) in a locked container, or a locked firearms rack that is on a motor vehicle;

(iv) by an individual for use in a program approved by a school in the school zone;

(v) by an individual in accordance with a contract entered into between a school in the school zone and the individual or an employer of the individual;

(vi) by a law enforcement officer acting in his or her official capacity; or

(vii) that is unloaded and is possessed by an individual while traversing school premises for the purpose of gaining access to public or private lands open to hunting, if the entry on school premises is authorized by school authorities.

(3)

(A) Except as provided in subparagraph (B), it shall be unlawful for any person, knowingly or with reckless disregard for the safety of another, to discharge or attempt to discharge a firearm that has moved in or that otherwise affects interstate or foreign commerce at a place that the person knows is a school zone.

(B) Subparagraph (A) does not apply to the discharge of a firearm –

    (i) on private property not part of school grounds;

    (ii) as part of a program approved by a school in the school zone, by an individual who is participating in the program;

    (iii) by an individual in accordance with a contract entered into between a school in a school zone and the individual or an employer of the individual; or

    (iv) by a law enforcement officer acting in his or her official capacity.

(4) Nothing in this subsection shall be construed as preempting or preventing a State or local government from enacting a statute establishing gun free school zones as provided in this subsection.

(r) It shall be unlawful for any person to assemble from imported parts any semiautomatic rifle or any shotgun which is identical to any rifle or shotgun prohibited from importation under section 925(d)(3) of this chapter as not being particularly suitable for or readily adaptable to sporting purposes except that this subsection shall not apply to –

(1) the assembly of any such rifle or shotgun for sale or distribution by a licensed manufacturer to the United States or any department or agency thereof or to any State or any department, agency, or political subdivision

thereof; or

(2) the assembly of any such rifle or shotgun for the purposes of testing or experimentation authorized by the Attorney General.

(s)

(1) Beginning on the date that is 90 days after the date of enactment of this subsection and ending on the day before the date that is 60 months after such date of enactment, it shall be unlawful for any licensed importer, licensed manufacturer, or licensed dealer to sell, deliver, or transfer a handgun (other than the return of a handgun to the person from whom it was received) to an individual who is not licensed under section 923, unless –

    (A) after the most recent proposal of such transfer by the transferee –

        (i) the transferor has –

            (I) received from the transferee a statement of the transferee containing the information described in paragraph (3);

            (II) verified the identity of the transferee by examining the identification document presented;

            (III) within 1 day after the transferee furnishes the statement, provided notice of the contents of the statement to the chief law enforcement officer of the place of residence of the transferee; and

            (IV) within 1 day after the transferee

furnishes the statement, transmitted a copy of the statement to the chief law enforcement officer of the place of residence of the transferee; and

(ii)

(I) 5 business days (meaning days on which State offices are open) have elapsed from the date the transferor furnished notice of the contents of the statement to the chief law enforcement officer, during which period the transferor has not received information from the chief law enforcement officer that receipt or possession of the handgun by the transferee would be in violation of Federal, State, or local law; or

(II) the transferor has received notice from the chief law enforcement officer that the officer has no information indicating that receipt or possession of the handgun by the transferee would violate Federal, State, or local law;

(B) the transferee has presented to the transferor a written statement, issued by the chief law enforcement officer of the place of residence of the transferee during the 10-day period ending on the date of the most recent proposal of such transfer by the transferee, stating that the transferee requires access to a handgun because of a threat to the life of the transferee or of any member of the household of the transferee;

(C)
    (i) the transferee has presented to the transferor a permit that–
        (I) allows the transferee to possess or acquire a handgun; and
        (II) was issued not more than 5 years earlier by the State in which the transfer is to take place; and
    (ii) the law of the State provides that such a permit is to be issued only after an authorized government official has verified that the information available to such official does not indicate that possession of a handgun by the transferee would be in violation of the law;

(D) the law of the State requires that, before any licensed importer, licensed manufacturer, or licensed dealer completes the transfer of a handgun to an individual who is not licensed under section 923, an authorized government official verify that the information available to such official does not indicate that possession of a handgun by the transferee would be in violation of law;

(E) the Attorney General has approved the transfer

under section 5812 of the Internal Revenue Code of 1986; or

(F) on application of the transferor, the Attorney General has certified that compliance with subparagraph (A)(i)(III) is impracticable because—

(i) the ratio of the number of law enforcement officers of the State in which the transfer is to occur to the number of square miles of land area of the State does not exceed 0.0025;

(ii) the business premises of the transferor at which the transfer is to occur are extremely remote in relation to the chief law enforcement officer; and

(iii) there is an absence of telecommunications facilities in the geographical area in which the business premises are located.

(2) A chief law enforcement officer to whom a transferor has provided notice pursuant to paragraph (1)(A)(i) (III) shall make a reasonable effort to ascertain within 5 business days whether receipt or possession would be in violation of the law, including research in whatever State and local recordkeeping systems are available and in a national system designated by the Attorney General.

(3) The statement referred to in paragraph (1)(A)(i)(I) shall contain only—

(A) the name, address, and date of birth appearing on a valid identification document (as defined in section 1028(d)(1) 4) of the transferee containing a photograph of the transferee and a description of the identification used;

(B) a statement that the transferee—

(i) is not under indictment for, and has not been convicted in any court of, a crime punishable by imprisonment for a term exceeding 1 year, and has not been convicted in any court of a misdemeanor crime of domestic violence;

(ii) is not a fugitive from justice;

(iii) is not an unlawful user of or addicted to any controlled substance (as defined in section 102 of the Controlled Substances Act);

(iv) has not been adjudicated as a mental defective or been committed to a mental institution;

(v) is not an alien who—

(I) is illegally or unlawfully in the United States; or

(II) subject to subsection (y)(2), has been admitted to the United States under a nonimmigrant visa (as that term is defined in section 101(a)(26) of the Immigration and Nationality Act (8 U.S.C. 1101(a)(26)));

(vi) has not been discharged from the Armed Forces under dishonorable conditions; and

(vii) is not a person who, having been a citizen of the United States, has renounced such citizenship;

(C) the date the statement is made; and

(D) notice that the transferee intends to obtain a handgun from the transferor.

(4) Any transferor of a handgun who, after such transfer, receives a report from a chief law enforcement officer containing information that receipt or possession of the handgun by the transferee violates Federal, State, or local law shall, within 1 business day after receipt of such request, communicate any information related to the transfer that the transferor has about the transfer and the transferee to—

(A) the chief law enforcement officer of the place of business of the transferor; and

(B) the chief law enforcement officer of the place of residence of the transferee.

(5) Any transferor who receives information, not otherwise available to the public, in a report under this subsection shall not disclose such information except to the transferee, to law enforcement authorities, or pursuant to the direction of a court of law.

(6)

(A) Any transferor who sells, delivers, or otherwise transfers a handgun to a transferee shall retain the copy of the statement of the transferee with respect to the handgun transaction, and shall retain evidence that the transferor has complied with subclauses (III) and (IV) of paragraph (1) (A)(i) with respect to the statement.

(B) Unless the chief law enforcement officer to whom a statement is transmitted under paragraph (1)

(A)(i)(IV) determines that a transaction would violate Federal, State, or local law—

   (i) the officer shall, within 20 business days after the date the transferee made the statement on the basis of which the notice was provided, destroy the statement, any record containing information derived from the statement, and any record created as a result of the notice required by paragraph (1)(A)(i)(III);

   (ii) the information contained in the statement shall not be conveyed to any person except a person who has a need to know in order to carry out this subsection; and

   (iii) the information contained in the statement shall not be used for any purpose other than to carry out this subsection.

(C) If a chief law enforcement officer determines that an individual is ineligible to receive a handgun and the individual requests the officer to provide the reason for such determination, the officer shall provide such reasons to the individual in writing within 20 business days after receipt of the request.

(7) A chief law enforcement officer or other person responsible for providing criminal history background information pursuant to this subsection shall not be liable in an action at law for damages—

   (A) for failure to prevent the sale or transfer of a handgun to a person whose receipt or possession of the handgun is unlawful under this section; or

(B) for preventing such a sale or transfer to a person who may lawfully receive or possess a handgun.

(8) For purposes of this subsection, the term "chief law enforcement officer" means the chief of police, the sheriff, or an equivalent officer or the designee of any such individual.

(9) The Attorney General shall take necessary actions to ensure that the provisions of this subsection are published and disseminated to licensed dealers, law enforcement officials, and the public.

(t)

(1) Beginning on the date that is 30 days after the Attorney General notifies licensees under section 103(d) of the Brady Handgun Violence Prevention Act that the national instant criminal background check system is established, a licensed importer, licensed manufacturer, or licensed dealer shall not transfer a firearm to any other person who is not licensed under this chapter, unless—

(A) before the completion of the transfer, the licensee contacts the national instant criminal background check system established under section 103 of that Act;

(B)

(i) the system provides the licensee with a unique identification number; or

(ii) 3 business days (meaning a day on which State offices are open) have elapsed since the licensee contacted the system, and the system has not notified the licensee that the receipt of a firearm by such other person would violate subsection (g) or

(n) of this section; and

(C) the transferor has verified the identity of the transferee by examining a valid identification document (as defined in section 1028(d) of this title) of the transferee containing a photograph of the transferee.

(2) If receipt of a firearm would not violate subsection (g) or (n) or State law, the system shall—

(A) assign a unique identification number to the transfer;

(B) provide the licensee with the number; and

(C) destroy all records of the system with respect to the call (other than the identifying number and the date the number was assigned) and all records of the system relating to the person or the transfer.

(3) Paragraph (1) shall not apply to a firearm transfer between a licensee and another person if—

(A)

(i) such other person has presented to the licensee a permit that—

(I) allows such other person to possess or acquire a firearm; and

(II) was issued not more than 5 years earlier by the State in which the transfer is to take place; and

(ii) the law of the State provides that such a permit is to be issued only after an authorized government official has verified that the information available to such official does not indicate that possession of a firearm by such other person would be in violation of law;

(B) the Attorney General has approved the transfer under section 5812 of the Internal Revenue Code of 1986; or

(C) on application of the transferor, the Attorney General has certified that compliance with paragraph (1)(A) is impracticable because –

　(i) the ratio of the number of law enforcement officers of the State in which the transfer is to occur to the number of square miles of land area of the State does not exceed 0.0025;

　(ii) the business premises of the licensee at which the transfer is to occur are extremely remote in relation to the chief law enforcement officer (as defined in subsection (s)(8)); and

　(iii) there is an absence of telecommunications facilities in the geographical area in which the business premises are located.

(4) If the national instant criminal background check system notifies the licensee that the information available to the system does not demonstrate that the receipt of a firearm by such other person would violate subsection (g) or (n) or State law, and the licensee transfers a firearm to such other person, the licensee shall include in the record of the transfer the unique identification number provided by the system with respect to the transfer.

(5) If the licensee knowingly transfers a firearm to such other

person and knowingly fails to comply with paragraph (1) of this subsection with respect to the transfer and, at the time such other person most recently proposed the transfer, the national instant criminal background check system was operating and information was available to the system demonstrating that receipt of a firearm by such other person would violate subsection (g) or (n) of this section or State law, the Attorney General may, after notice and opportunity for a hearing, suspend for not more than 6 months or revoke any license issued to the licensee under section 923, and may impose on the licensee a civil fine of not more than $5,000.

(6) Neither a local government nor an employee of the Federal Government or of any State or local government, responsible for providing information to the national instant criminal background check system shall be liable in an action at law for damages–

    (A) for failure to prevent the sale or transfer of a firearm to a person whose receipt or possession of the firearm is unlawful under this section; or

    (B) for preventing such a sale or transfer to a person who may lawfully receive or possess a firearm.

(u) It shall be unlawful for a person to steal or unlawfully take or carry away from the person or the premises of a person who is licensed to engage in the business of importing, manufacturing, or dealing in firearms, any firearm in the licensee's business inventory that has been shipped or transported in interstate or foreign commerce.

(v), (w) Repealed. Pub. L. 103–322, title XI, §110105(2), Sept. 13, 1994, 108 Stat. 2000.

(x)

(1) It shall be unlawful for a person to sell, deliver, or otherwise transfer to a person who the transferor knows or has reasonable cause to believe is a juvenile–

    (A) a handgun; or

    (B) ammunition that is suitable for use only in a handgun.

(2) It shall be unlawful for any person who is a juvenile to knowingly possess–

    (A) a handgun; or

    (B) ammunition that is suitable for use only in a handgun.

(3) This subsection does not apply to–

    (A) a temporary transfer of a handgun or ammunition to a juvenile or to the possession or use of a handgun or ammunition by a juvenile if the handgun and ammunition are possessed and used by the juvenile–

        (i) in the course of employment, in the course of ranching or farming related to activities at the residence of the juvenile (or on property used for ranching or farming at which the juvenile, with the permission of the property owner or lessee, is performing activities related to the operation of the farm or ranch), target practice, hunting, or a course of instruction in the safe and lawful use of a handgun;

        (ii) with the prior written consent of the juvenile's parent or guardian who is not prohibited by Federal, State, or local law from possessing a firearm, except–

(I) during transportation by the juvenile of an unloaded handgun in a locked container directly from the place of transfer to a place at which an activity described in clause (i) is to take place and transportation by the juvenile of that handgun, unloaded and in a locked container, directly from the place at which such an activity took place to the transferor; or

(II) with respect to ranching or farming activities as described in clause (i), a juvenile may possess and use a handgun or ammunition with the prior written approval of the juvenile's parent or legal guardian and at the direction of an adult who is not prohibited by Federal, State or local law from possessing a firearm;

(iii) the juvenile has the prior written consent in the juvenile's possession at all times when a handgun is in the possession of the juvenile; and

(iv) in accordance with State and local law;

(B) a juvenile who is a member of the Armed Forces of the United States or the National Guard who possesses or is armed with a handgun in the line of duty;

(C) a transfer by inheritance of title (but not possession) of a handgun or ammunition to a juvenile; or

(D) the possession of a handgun or ammunition by a juvenile taken in defense of the juvenile or other persons against an intruder into the residence of the juvenile or a residence in which the juvenile is an invited guest.

(4) A handgun or ammunition, the possession of which is transferred to a juvenile in circumstances in which the transferor is not in violation of this subsection shall not be subject to permanent confiscation by the Government if its possession by the juvenile subsequently becomes unlawful because of the conduct of the juvenile, but shall be returned to the lawful owner when such handgun or ammunition is no longer required by the Government for the purposes of investigation or prosecution.

(5) For purposes of this subsection, the term "juvenile" means a person who is less than 18 years of age.

(6)

(A) In a prosecution of a violation of this subsection, the court shall require the presence of a juvenile defendant's parent or legal guardian at all proceedings.

(B) The court may use the contempt power to enforce subparagraph (A).

(C) The court may excuse attendance of a parent or legal guardian of a juvenile defendant at a proceeding in a prosecution of a violation of this subsection for good cause shown.

(y) Provisions Relating to Aliens Admitted Under Nonimmigrant Visas.–

    (1) Definitions.– In this subsection –

        (A) the term "alien" has the same meaning as in section 101(a)(3) of the Immigration and Nationality Act (8 U.S.C. 1101(a)(3)); and

        (B) the term "nonimmigrant visa" has the same meaning as in section 101(a)(26) of the Immigration and Nationality Act (8 U.S.C. 1101(a)(26)).

    (2) Exceptions.– Subsections (d)(5)(B), (g)(5)(B), and (s)(3)(B)(v)(II) do not apply to any alien who has been lawfully admitted to the United States under a nonimmigrant visa, if that alien is–

        (A) admitted to the United States for lawful hunting or sporting purposes or is in possession of a hunting license or permit lawfully issued in the United States;

        (B) an official representative of a foreign government who is–

            (i) accredited to the United States Government or the Government's mission to an international organization having its headquarters in the United States; or

            (ii) en route to or from another country to which that alien is accredited;

        (C) an official of a foreign government or a distinguished foreign visitor who has been so designated by the Department of State; or

(D) a foreign law enforcement officer of a friendly foreign government entering the United States on official law enforcement business.

(3) Waiver.–

(A) Conditions for waiver.–Any individual who has been admitted to the United States under a nonimmigrant visa may receive a waiver from the requirements of subsection (g)(5), if–

(i) the individual submits to the Attorney General a petition that meets the requirements of subparagraph (C); and

(ii) the Attorney General approves the petition.

(B) Petition.–Each petition under subparagraph (B) shall–

(i) demonstrate that the petitioner has resided in the United States for a continuous period of not less than 180 days before the date on which the petition is submitted under this paragraph; and

(ii) include a written statement from the embassy or consulate of the petitioner, authorizing the petitioner to acquire a firearm or ammunition and certifying that the alien would not, absent the application of subsection (g)(5)(B), otherwise be prohibited from such acquisition under subsection (g).

(C) Approval of petition.–The Attorney General shall approve a petition submitted in accordance with this paragraph, if the Attorney General determines that waiving the requirements of subsection (g)(5)(B) with respect to the petitioner–

> (i) would be in the interests of justice; and
>
> (ii) would not jeopardize the public safety.

(z) Secure Gun Storage or Safety Device.–

(1) In general.–Except as provided under paragraph (2), it shall be unlawful for any licensed importer, licensed manufacturer, or licensed dealer to sell, deliver, or transfer any handgun to any person other than any person licensed under this chapter, unless the transferee is provided with a secure gun storage or safety device (as defined in section 921(a)(34)) for that handgun.

(2) Exceptions.–Paragraph (1) shall not apply to–

(A)

> (i) the manufacture for, transfer to, or possession by, the United States, a department or agency of the United States, a State, or a department, agency, or political subdivision of a State, of a handgun; or
>
> (ii) the transfer to, or possession by, a law enforcement officer employed by an entity referred to in clause (i) of a handgun for law enforcement purposes (whether on or off duty); or

(B) the transfer to, or possession by, a rail police officer directly employed by or contracted by a rail carrier and certified or commissioned as a police officer under the laws of a State of

a handgun for purposes of law enforcement (whether on or off duty);

(C) the transfer to any person of a handgun listed as a curio or relic by the Secretary pursuant to section 921(a)(13); or

(D) the transfer to any person of a handgun for which a secure gun storage or safety device is temporarily unavailable for the reasons described in the exceptions stated in section 923(e), if the licensed manufacturer, licensed importer, or licensed dealer delivers to the transferee within 10 calendar days from the date of the delivery of the handgun to the transferee a secure gun storage or safety device for the handgun.

(3) Liability for use.–

(A) In general.–Notwithstanding any other provision of law, a person who has lawful possession and control of a handgun, and who uses a secure gun storage or safety device with the handgun, shall be entitled to immunity from a qualified civil liability action.

(B) Prospective actions.–A qualified civil liability action may not be brought in any Federal or State court.

(C) Defined term.–As used in this paragraph, the term "qualified civil liability action"–

(i) means a civil action brought by any person against a person described in subparagraph (A) for damages resulting from the criminal or unlawful misuse of the handgun by a third party, if–

(I) the handgun was accessed by another person who did not have the permission or authorization of the person having lawful possession and control of the handgun to have access to it; and

(II) at the time access was gained by the person not so authorized, the handgun had been made inoperable by use of a secure gun storage or safety device; and

(ii) shall not include an action brought against the person having lawful possession and control of the handgun for negligent entrustment or negligence per se.

[Appendix A repealed]

APPENDIX C:
Selected Federal Forms

U.S. Department of Justice
Bureau of Alcohol, Tobacco, Firearms and Explosives

OMB No. 1140-0011 (06/30/2019)

Application to Make and Register a Firearm

ATF Control Number

To: National Firearms Act Division, Bureau of Alcohol, Tobacco, Firearms and Explosives, P.O. Box 5015, Portland, OR 97208-5015

(Submit in duplicate. Please do not staple documents. See instructions attached.)

As required by Sections 5821 (b), 5822, and 5841 of the National Firearms Act, Title 26 U.S.C., Chapter 53, the undersigned hereby submits application to make and register the firearm described below.

2. Application is made by:

☐ INDIVIDUAL ☐ TRUST or LEGAL ENTITY ☐ GOVERNMENT ENTITY

3a. Trade name *(If any)*

3b. Applicant's name and mailing address *(Type or print below) (see instruction 2d)*

3d. County

3e. Telephone Number

3f. E-mail address *(optional)*

3c. If P.O. Box is shown above, street address must be given here

1. Type of Application *(check one)*

☐ a. Tax Paid. Submit your tax payment of $200 with the application. The tax may be paid by credit or debit card, check, or money order. Please complete item 17. Upon approval of the application, we will affix and cancel the required National Firearms Act Stamp. *(See instruction 2c and 3)*

☐ b. Tax Exempt because firearm is being made on behalf of the United States, or any department, independent establishment, or agency thereof.

☐ c. Tax Exempt because firearm is being made by or on behalf of any State or possession of the United States, or any political subdivision thereof, or any official police organization of such a government entity engaged in criminal investigations.

4. Description of Firearm *(complete items a through k) (See instruction 2i)*

a. Name and Address of Original Manufacturer and/or Importer of Firearm *(if any)*	b. Type of Firearm to be made *(See definition 1c)* *If a destructive device, complete item 4j*	c. Caliber or Gauge *(Specify one)*	d. Model *(as marked on firearm)*
			e. Barrel length: / f. Overall length:
			g. Serial Number

h. Additional Description *(Indicate required maker's markings to include maker's name (as registered), city and state as each will appear on firearm)*

i. Specify Why You Intend To Make Firearm *(Use additional sheet if necessary)*

j. Type of destructive device (check one box): ☐ Firearm ☐ Explosives *(If the Explosives box is checked, complete item 5 and see instruction 2l)*

If an explosive type destructive device, identify the type of explosive(s): _____

k. Is this firearm being reactivated? ☐ Yes ☐ No *(See definition 1k)*

5. Applicant's Federal Firearms License *(if any)* or Explosives License or Permit Number	6. Special *(Occupational)* Tax Status *(if applicable) (See definitions)*	
(Give complete 15-digit Number)	a. Employer Identification Number	b. Class

Under Penalties of Perjury, I Declare that I have examined this application, including accompanying documents, and to the best of my knowledge and belief it is true, accurate and complete and the making and possession of the firearm described above would not constitute a violation of Title 18, U.S.C., Chapter 44, Title 26, U.S.C., Chapter 53; or any provisions of State or local law.

7. Signature of Applicant	8. Name and Title of Authorized Official	9. Date

The space below is for the use of the Bureau of Alcohol, Tobacco, Firearms and Explosives

By authority of the Director, Bureau of Alcohol, Tobacco, Firearms and Explosives, this application has been examined and the applicant's making and registration of the firearm described above is:

☐ Approved *(With the following conditions, if any)*

☐ Disapproved *(For the following reasons)*

Authorized ATF Official	Date

Previous Editions Are Obsolete

ATF Copy

ATF E-Form 1 (5320.1)
Revised November 2018

ATF Form 1 Page 2

10. **Law Enforcement Notification** *(See instruction 2g)*

Each applicant is to provide notification of the proposed making and possession of the firearm described on this Form 1 by providing a copy of the completed form to the chief law enforcement officer in the agency identified below:

Agency or Department Name   Name and Title of Official

Address (Street address or P.O. Box, City, State and Zip Code) to which sent (mailed or delivered)

Information for the Chief Law Enforcement Officer

This form provides notification of the applicant's intent to make and register a National Firearms Act (NFA) firearm. No action on your part is required. However, should you have information that may disqualify this person from making or possessing a firearm, please contact the NFA Division at (304) 616-4500 or NFA@atf.gov. A "Yes" answer to items 11.a. through 11.h. or 13.b. or 13.c. could disqualify a person from acquiring or possessing a firearm. Also, ATF will not approve an application if the making or possession of the firearm is in violation of State or local law.

Maker's Questions *(complete only when the maker is an individual)*

A maker who is an individual must complete this Section.

11. Answer questions 11.a. through 11.h. Answer questions 13 and 14, if applicable. For any "Yes" answer the applicant shall provide details on a separate sheet. *(See instruction 7c and definitions)*

	Yes	No
a. Are you under indictment or information in any court for a felony, or any other crime, for which the judge could imprison you for more than one year? *(See definition 1n)*		
b. Have you ever been convicted in any court for a felony, or any other crime, for which the judge could have imprisoned you for more than one year, even if you received a shorter sentence including probation? *(See definition 1n)*		
c. Are you a fugitive from justice? *(See definition 1t)*		
d. Are you an unlawful user of, or addicted to, marijuana or any depressant, stimulant, narcotic drug, or any other controlled substance? **Warning: The use or possession of marijuana remains unlawful under Federal law regardless of whether it has been legalized or decriminalized for medicinal or recreational purposes in the state where you reside.**		
e. Have you ever been adjudicated as a mental defective OR have you ever been committed to a mental institution? *(See definition 1o and 1p)*		
f. Have you been discharged from the Armed Forces under **dishonorable** conditions?		
g. Are you subject to a court order restraining you from harassing, stalking, or threatening your child or an intimate partner or child of such partner? *(See definition 1q)*		
h. Have you ever been convicted in any court of a misdemeanor crime of domestic violence? *(See definition 1r)*		

13a. Country of Citizenship: *(Check/List more than one, if applicable. Nationals of the United States may check U.S.A.) (See definition 1s)*

☐ United States of America   ☐ Other Country/Countries *(specify)*: _____

	Yes	No
b. Have you ever renounced your United States citizenship?		
c. Are you an alien illegally or unlawfully in the United States?		
d.1. Are you an alien who has been admitted to the United States under a nonimmigrant visa?		
d.2. If "yes", do you fall within any of the exceptions stated in the instructions? Attach the documentation to the application ☐ N/A		

14. If you are an alien, record your U.S.-Issued Alien or Admission number (AR#, USCIS#, or 194#): _____

12. Photograph

**Affix a 2" x 2" Photograph Here
No Stapling. Please Tape
Sides of Photo to the Application.**

1. Photo must have been taken within the last year.

2. Photo must have been taken in full face view without a hat or head covering that obscures the hair or hairline.

3. On back of photograph print full name, last 4 of SSN, and business address.

CERTIFICATION: Under penalties imposed by 18 U.S.C. § 924 and 26 U.S.C. § 5861, I certify that, upon submission of this form to ATF, a completed copy of this form will be directed to the chief law enforcement officer (CLEO) shown in item 10, that the statements, as applicable, contained in this certification, and any attached documents in support thereof, are true and correct to the best of my knowledge and belief. NOTE: See instructions 2.d(2) and 2.d(3) for the items to be completed depending on the type of applicant.

Signature of Maker   Date

ATF Form 1 Page 3

15. Number of Responsible Persons *(see definitions)* associated with the applicant trust or legal entity _____

16. Provide the full name (printed or typed) below for each Responsible Person associated with the applicant trust or legal entity *(if there are more Responsible Persons than can be listed on the form, attach a separate sheet listing the additional Responsible Person(s))*. Please note that a completed Form 5320.23, National Firearms Act (NFA) Responsible Person Questionnaire, must be submitted with the Form 1 application for each Responsible Person.

Full Name   Full Name

_____   _____

_____   _____

_____   _____

17. **Method of Payment** *(Check one) (See instruction 2h) (if paying by credit/debit card, complete the sections below)*

| ☐ Check *(Enclosed)* | ☐ Cashier's Check or Money Order *(Enclosed)* | ☐ Visa | ☐ Mastercard | ☐ American Express | ☐ Discover | ☐ Diners Club |

Credit/Debit Card Number *(No dashes)* | Name as Printed on the Credit/Debit Card | Expiration Date *(Month & year)*

| Credit/Debit Card Billing Address: | Address: | | | |
| | City: | State: | | Zip Code: |

Tax Amount:
$

I Authorize ATF to Charge my Credit/Debit Card the Above Amount.

_____   _____
Signature of Cardholder   Date

Your credit/debit card will be charged the above stated amount upon receipt of your application. The charge will be reflected on your credit/debit card statement. In the event your application is NOT approved, the above amount will be credited to the credit/debit card noted above.

Important Information for Currently Registered Firearms

If you are the current registrant of the firearm described on this form, please note the following information.

Estate Procedures: For procedures regarding the transfer of firearms in an estate resulting from the death of the registrant identified in item 3b, the executor should contact the NFA Division, Bureau of ATF, 244 Needy Road, Martinsburg, WV 25405.

Interstate Movement: If the firearm identified in item 4 is a **machinegun, short-barreled rifle, short-barreled shotgun, or destructive device**, the registrant may be required by 18 U.S.C. § 922(a)(4) to obtain permission from ATF prior to any transportation in interstate or foreign commerce. ATF Form 5320.20 can be used to request this permission.

Change of Description or Address: The registrant shall notify the NFA Division, Bureau of Alcohol, Tobacco, Firearms and Explosives, 244 Needy Road, Martinsburg, WV 25405, in writing, of any change to the description of the firearm in item 4, or any change to the address of the registrant.

Restrictions on Possession: Any restriction *(see approval block on face of form)* on the possession of the firearm identified in item 4 continues with the further transfer of the firearm.

Persons Prohibited from Possessing Firearms: If the registrant becomes prohibited from possessing a firearm, please contact the NFA Division for procedures on how to dispose of the firearm.

Proof of Registration: A person possessing a firearm registered as required by the NFA shall retain proof of registration which shall be made available to any ATF officer upon request.

Paperwork Reduction Act Notice

This form is in accordance with the Paperwork Reduction Act of 1995. The information you provide is used to establish that the applicant's making and possession of the firearm would be in conformance with Federal, State, and local law. The data is used as proof of lawful registration of a firearm to the manufacturer. The furnishing of this information is mandatory *(26 U.S.C. § 5822)*.

The estimated average burden associated with this collection of information is 4.0 hours per respondent or recordkeeper, depending on individual circumstances. Comments concerning the accuracy of this burden estimate and suggestion for reducing this burden should be addressed to Reports Management Officer, Information Technology Coordination Staff, Bureau of Alcohol, Tobacco, Firearms and Explosives, Washington, DC 20226.

An agency may not conduct or sponsor, and a person is not required to respond to, a collection of information unless it displays a currently valid OMB control number.

ATF Copy

ATF E-Form 1 (5320.1)
Revised November 2018

ATF Form 4 Page 1

OMB No. 1140-0014 (06/30/2019)

U.S. Department of Justice
Bureau of Alcohol, Tobacco, Firearms and Explosives

Application for Tax Paid Transfer and Registration of Firearm

ATF Control Number

SUBMIT in DUPLICATE to: **National Firearms Act Division**
Bureau of Alcohol, Tobacco, Firearms and Explosives, P.O. Box 5015, Portland, OR 97208-5015

1. Type of Transfer *(Check one)*	2a. Transferee's Name and Address *(Include trade name, if any) (See instruction 2d)*	
☐ $5 ☐ $200		
Submit the appropriate tax payment with the application. The tax may be paid by credit or debit card, check, or money **order. Please complete item 20. Upon approval of** the application, we will affix and cancel the required National Firearms Act stamp. *(See instructions 2b, 2i and 3)*	☐ **INDIVIDUAL** ☐ **TRUST or LEGAL ENTITY**	2b. County

3a. Transferor's Name and Address *(Include trade name, if any)* *(Executors: see instruction 2k)*	3b. e-mail address *(optional)*	3c. Transferor's Telephone *(Area Code and Number)*
	3d. If Applicable: Decedent's Name, Address, and Date of Death	
	3e. Number, Street, City, State and Zip Code of Residence *(or Firearms Business Premises)* **If Different from Item 3a.**	

The above-named and undersigned transferor hereby makes application as required by Section 5812 of the National Firearms Act to transfer and register the firearm described below to the transferee.

4. Description of Firearm *(Complete items a through h) (See instruction 2m)*

a. Name and Address of Maker Manufacturer and/or Importer of Firearm	b. Type of Firearm *(see definitions)*	c. Caliber or Gauge	d. Model
			e. Of Barrel Length: f. Overall Length:
			g. Serial Number

h. Additional Description or Data Appearing on Firearm *(Attach additional sheet if necessary)*

5. Transferee's Federal Firearms License *(If any)*				6. Transferee's Special (Occupational) Tax Status *(If any)*	
(Give complete 15-digit number) (See instruction 2c)				**a. Employer Identification Number**	b. Class
First 6 digits	2 digits	2 digits	5 digits		

7. Transferor's Federal Firearms License *(If any)*				8. Transferor's Special (Occupational) Tax Status *(If any)*	
First 6 digits	2 digits	2 digits	5 digits	**a. Employer Identification Number**	b. Class

Under Penalties of Perjury, I Declare that I have examined this application, and to the best of my knowledge and belief it is true, correct and complete, and that the transfer of the described firearm to the transferee and receipt and possession of it by the transferee are not prohibited by the provisions of Title 18, United States Code; Chap 44; Title 26, United States Code; Chap 53; or any provisions of State or local law.

9. Signature of Transferor *(Or authorized official)*	10. Name and Title of Authorized Official *(Print or type)*	11. Date

The Space Below is for the use of the Bureau of Alcohol, Tobacco, Firearms and Explosives

By Authority of The Director, This Application Has Been Examined, and the Transfer and Registration of the Firearm Described Herein and the Interstate Movement of that Firearm, When Applicable, to the Transferee are:	Stamp Denomination
☐ Approved *(With the following conditions, if any)* ☐ Disapproved *(For the following reasons)*	

Signature of Authorized ATF Official	Date

Previous Editions Are Obsolete

ATF Copy

ATF E-Form 4 (5320.4)
Revised November 2018

ATF Form 4 Page 2

Transferee Certification

12. Law Enforcement Notification *(See instruction 2f)*

The transferee is to provide notification of the proposed acquisition and possession of the firearm described on this Form 4 by providing a copy of the completed form to the chief law enforcement officer in the agency identified below:

Agency or Department Name

Name and Title of Official

Address (Street address or P.O. Box, City, State and Zip Code) to which sent (mailed or delivered))

Information for the Chief Law Enforcement Officer

This form provides notification of the transferee's intent to acquire and possess a National Firearms Act (NFA) firearm. No action on your part is required. However, should you have information that may disqualify this person from acquiring or possessing a firearm, please contact the NFA Division at (304) 616-4500 or NFA@atf.gov. A "Yes" answer to items 14.a. through 14.h. or 16.b. or 16.c. could disqualify a person from acquiring or possessing a firearm. Also, ATF will not approve an application if the transfer or possession of the firearm is in violation of State or local law.

13. Transferee Necessity Statement *(See instruction 2e)*

I, _____ , have a reasonable necessity to possess the machinegun, short-barreled rifle,
(Name and Title of Transferee)
short-barreled shotgun, or destructive device described on this application for the following reason(s) _____

and my possession of the device or weapon would be consistent with public safety (18 U.S.C. § 922(b) (4) and 27 CFR § 478.98).

Transferee Questions *(Complete Only When Transferee is An Individual)*

14. Answer questions 14.a. through 14.h. Answer questions 16 and 17, if applicable. For any "Yes" answer the transferee shall provide details on a separate sheet. *(See instruction 7b and definitions)*

		Yes	No
a.	Are you under indictment or information in any court for a felony, or any other crime, for which the judge could imprison you for more than one year? *(See definition 1m)*		
b.	Have you ever been convicted in any court for a felony, or any other crime, for which the judge could have imprisoned you for more than one year, even if you received a shorter sentence including probation? *(See definition 1m)*		
c.	Are you a fugitive from justice? *(See definition 1x)*		
d.	Are you an unlawful user of, or addicted to, marijuana or any depressant, stimulant, narcotic drug, or any other controlled substance? **Warning: The use or possession of marijuana remains unlawful under Federal law regardless of whether it has been legalized or decriminalized for medicinal or recreational purposes in the state where you reside.**		
e.	Have you ever been adjudicated as a mental defective OR have you ever been committed to a mental institution? *(See definitions 1n and 1o)*		
f.	Have you been discharged from the Armed Forces under dishonorable conditions?		
g.	Are you subject to a court order restraining you from harassing, stalking, or threatening your child or an intimate partner or child of such partner? *(See definition 1p)*		
h.	Have you ever been convicted in any court of a misdemeanor crime of domestic violence? *(See definition 1q)*		

15. Photograph

Affix a 2" x 2" Photograph here.
No Stapling. Tape Sides of Photo to the Application.

1. Photo must have been taken within the last year.

2. Photo must have been taken in full face view without a hat or head covering that obscures the hair or hairline.

3. On back of photograph print full name, last 4 of SSN, and business address.

16a. Country of Citizenship: *(Check/List more than one, if applicable. Nationals of the United States may check U.S.A.) (See definition 1r)*

☐ United States of America   ☐ Other Country/Countries *(specify)*: _____

		Yes	No
b.	Have you ever renounced your United States citizenship?		
c.	Are you an alien illegally or unlawfully in the United States?		
d.1.	Are you an alien who has been admitted to the United States under a nonimmigrant visa?		
d.2.	If "yes", do you fall within any of the exceptions stated in the instructions? Attach the documentation to the application	☐ N/A	

17. If you are an alien, record your U.S.-Issued Alien or Admission number (AR#, USCIS#, or 194#): _____

CERTIFICATION: Under penalties imposed by 18 U.S.C. § 924 and 26 U.S.C. § 5861, I certify that, upon submission of this form to ATF, a completed copy of this form will **be directed to the chief law enforcement officer (CLEO)** shown in item 12, that the statements, **as applicable, contained in this certification, and any attached documents in support** thereof, are true and correct to the best of my knowledge and belief. NOTE: See instructions 2.d(2) and 2.d(3) for the items to be completed depending on the type of transferee.

Signature of Transferee   Date

ATF Copy

ATF E-Form 4 (5320.4)
Revised November 2018

ATF Form 4 Page 3

18. Number of Responsible Persons *(see definitions)* associated with the transferee trust or legal entity_____

19. Provide the full name (printed or typed) below for each Responsible Person associated with the applicant trust or legal entity (if there are more Responsible Persons than can be listed on the form, attach a separate sheet listing the additional Responsible Person(s)). Please note that a completed Form 5320.23, National Firearms Act (NFA) Responsible Person Questionnaire, must be submitted with the Form 4 application for each Responsible Person.

Full Name   Full Name

_____   _____

_____   _____

_____   _____

20. Method of Payment *(Check one) (See instruction 2i)* (if paying by credit/debit card, complete the section below)

☐ Check *(Enclosed)*   ☐ Cashier's Check or   ☐ Visa   ☐ Mastercard   ☐ American   ☐ Discover   ☐ Diners Club
                         Money Order *(Enclosed)*   Express

Credit/Debit Card Number *(No dashes)*		Name as Printed on the Credit/Debit Card	Expiration Date *(Month & year)*

Credit/Debit Card Billing Address:	Address:			
	City:	State:	Zip Code:	
			Tax Amount:$	

I Authorize ATF to Charge my Credit/Debit Card the Tax Amount.

_____   _____
Signature of Cardholder   Date

Your credit/debit card will be charged the above stated amount upon receipt of the application. The charge will be reflected on your credit/debit card statement. In the event your application is NOT approved, the above amount will be credited to the credit/debit card noted above.

Important Information for Currently Registered Firearms

If you are the current registrant of the firearm described on this form, please note the following information.

Estate Procedures: For procedures regarding the transfer of firearms in an estate resulting from the death of the registrant identified in item 2a, the executor should contact the NFA Division, Bureau of Alcohol, Tobacco, Firearms and Explosives, 244 Needy Road, Martinsburg, WV 25405.

Change of Address: Unless currently licensed under the Gun Control Act, the registrant shall notify the NFA Division, Bureau of Alcohol, Tobacco, Firearms and Explosives, 244 Needy Road, Martinsburg, WV 25405, in writing, of any change to the address in item 2a.

Change of Description: The registrant shall notify the NFA Division, Bureau of Alcohol, Tobacco, Firearms and Explosives, 244 Needy Road, Martinsburg, WV 25405, in writing, of any change to the description of the firearm(s) in item 4.

Interstate Movement: If the firearm identified in item 4 is a **machinegun, short-barreled rifle, short-barreled shotgun,** or **destructive device**, the registrant may be required by 18 U.S.C. § 922(a)(4) to obtain permission from ATF prior to any transportation in interstate or foreign commerce. ATF Form 5320. 20 can be used to request this permission.

Restrictions on Possession: Any restriction *(see approval block on face of form)* on the possession of the firearm identified in item 4 continues with the further transfer of the firearm.

Persons Prohibited from Possessing Firearms: If the registrant becomes prohibited from possessing a firearm, please contact the NFA Division for procedures on how to dispose of the firearm.

Proof of Registration: A person possessing a firearm registered as required by the NFA shall retain proof of registration which shall be made available to any ATF officer upon request.

Paperwork Reduction Act Notice

This form meets the clearance requirements of the Paperwork Reduction Act of 1995. The information you provide is used in applying to transfer serviceable firearms taxpaid. Data is used to identify transferor, transferee, and firearm, and to ensure legality for transfer under Federal, State and local laws. The furnishing of this information is mandatory (26 U.S.C. § 5812).

The estimated average burden associated with this collection of information is 3.78 hours per respondent or recordkeeper, depending on individual circumstances. Comments concerning the accuracy of this burden estimate and suggestion for reducing this burden should be addressed to Reports Management Officer, Information Technology Coordination Staff, Bureau of Alcohol, Tobacco, Firearms and Explosives, Washington, DC 20226.

An agency may not conduct or sponsor, and a person is not required to respond to, a collection of information unless it displays a currently valid OMB control number.

ATF E-Form 4 (5320.4)
Revised November 2018

ATF Copy

ATF Form 4473 Page 1

Note: At the time of publishing, this is the current version of the ATF Form. However, this form will be updated at the end of July 2020.

U.S. Department of Justice
Bureau of Alcohol, Tobacco, Firearms and Explosives

OMB No. 1140-0020

Firearms Transaction Record

	Transferor's/ Seller's Transaction Serial Number *(If any)*
WARNING: You may not receive a firearm if prohibited by Federal or State law. The information you provide will be used to determine whether you are prohibited from receiving a firearm. Certain violations of the Gun Control Act, 18 U.S.C. 921 et. seq., are punishable by up to 10 years imprisonment and/or up to a $250,000 fine. Read the Notices, Instructions, and Definitions on this form. Prepare in original only at the licensed premises *("licensed premises" includes business temporarily conducted from a qualifying gun show or event in the same State in which the licensed premises is located)* unless the transaction qualifies under 18 U.S.C. 922(c). All entries must be handwritten in ink. **"PLEASE PRINT."**	

Section A - Must Be Completed Personally By Transferee/Buyer

1. Transferee's/Buyer's Full Name *(If legal name contain an initial only, record "IO" after the initial. If no middle initial or name, record "NMN".)*

Last Name *(Including suffix (e.g., Jr, Sr, II, III))*	First Name	Middle Name

2. Current State of Residence and Address **(U.S. Postal abbreviations are acceptable. Cannot be a post office box.)**

Number and Street Address	City	County	State	ZIP Code

3. Place of Birth U.S. City and State -OR- Foreign Country	4. Height Ft. ___ In. ___	5. Weight *(LBs.)*	6. Sex ☐ Male ☐ Female	7. Birth Date Month Day Year

8. Social Security Number *(Optional, but will help prevent misidentification)*	9. Unique Personal Identification Number *(UPIN)* if applicable *(See Instructions for Question 9.)*

10.a. Ethnicity ☐ Hispanic or Latino ☐ Not Hispanic or Latino	10.b. Race **(In addition to ethnicity, select one or more race in 10.b. Both 10.a. and 10.b. must be answered.)** ☐ American Indian or Alaska Native ☐ Black or African American ☐ White ☐ Asian ☐ Native Hawaiian or Other Pacific Islander

11. Answer the following questions by checking or marking *"yes"* or *"no"* in the boxes to the right of the questions.

	Yes	No
a. Are you the actual transferee/buyer of the firearm(s) listed on this form? **Warning: You are not the actual transferee/buyer if you are acquiring the firearm(s) on behalf of another person. If you are not the actual transferee/buyer, the licensee cannot transfer the firearm(s) to you.** *Exception: If you are picking up a repaired firearm(s) for another person, you are not required to answer 11.a. and may proceed to question 11.b. (See Instructions for Question 11.a.)*	☐	☐
b. Are you under indictment or information in any court for a **felony**, or any other crime for which the judge could imprison you for more than one year? *(See Instructions for Question 11.b.)*	☐	☐
c. Have you ever been convicted in any court of a **felony**, or any other crime for which the judge could have imprisoned you for more than one year, even if you received a shorter sentence including probation? *(See Instructions for Question 11.c.)*	☐	☐
d. Are you a fugitive from justice? *(See Instructions for Question 11.d.)*	☐	☐
e. Are you an unlawful user of, or addicted to, marijuana or any depressant, stimulant, narcotic drug, or any other controlled substance? **Warning: The use or possession of marijuana remains unlawful under Federal law regardless of whether it has been legalized or decriminalized for medicinal or recreational purposes in the state where you reside.**	☐	☐
f. Have you ever been adjudicated as a mental defective **OR** have you ever been committed to a mental institution? *(See Instructions for Question 11.f.)*	☐	☐
g. Have you been discharged from the Armed Forces under **dishonorable** conditions?	☐	☐
h. Are you subject to a court order restraining you from harassing, stalking, or threatening your child or an intimate partner or child of such partner? *(See Instructions for Question 11.h.)*	☐	☐
i. Have you ever been **convicted** in any court of a misdemeanor crime of domestic violence? *(See Instructions for Question 11.i.)*	☐	☐

12.a. Country of Citizenship: *(Check/List more than one, if applicable. Nationals of the United States may check U.S.A.)*
☐ United States of America *(U.S.A.)*   ☐ Other Country/Countries *(Specify)*

	Yes	No
12.b. Have you ever renounced your United States citizenship?	☐	☐
12.c. Are you an alien **illegally** or **unlawfully** in the United States?	☐	☐
12.d.1. Are you an alien who has been admitted to the United States under a nonimmigrant visa? *(See Instructions for Question 12.d.)*	☐	☐
12.d.2. If "yes", do you fall within any of the exceptions stated in the instructions? ☐ N/A	☐	☐

13. If you are an alien, record your U.S.-Issued Alien or Admission number *(AR#, USCIS#, or I94#)*:

Previous Editions Are Obsolete

Transferee/Buyer Continue to Next Page
STAPLE IF PAGES BECOME SEPARATED

Page 1 of 6

ATF E-Form 4473 (5300.9)
Revised October 2016

ATF Form 4473 Page 2

Note: At the time of publishing, this is the current version of the ATF Form. However, this form will be updated at the end of July 2020.

I certify that my answers in Section A are true, correct, and complete. I have read and understand the Notices, Instructions, and Definitions on ATF Form 4473. I understand that answering "yes" to question 11.a. if I am not the actual transferee/buyer is a crime punishable as a felony under Federal law, and may also violate State and/or local law. I understand that a person who answers "yes" to any of the questions 11.b. through 11.i and/or 12.b. through 12.c. is prohibited from purchasing or receiving a firearm. I understand that a person who answers "yes" to question 12.d.1. is prohibited from receiving or possessing a firearm, unless the person answers "yes" to question 12.d.2. and provides the documentation required in 18.c. I also understand that making any false oral or written statement, or exhibiting any false or misrepresented identification with respect to this transaction, is a crime punishable as a felony under Federal law, and may also violate State and/or local law. I further understand that the repetitive purchase of firearms for the purpose of resale for livelihood and profit without a Federal firearms license is a violation of Federal law. *(See Instructions for Question 14.)*

14. Transferee's/Buyer's Signature	15. Certification Date

Section B - Must Be Completed By Transferor/Seller

16. Type of firearm(s) to be transferred *(check or mark all that apply)*:

☐ Handgun ☐ Long Gun *(rifles or shotguns)* ☐ Other Firearm *(frame, receiver, etc, See Instructions for Question 16.)*

17. If transfer is at a qualifying gun show or event:

Name of Function: _____

City, State: _____

18.a. Identification *(e.g., Virginia Driver's license (VA DL) or other valid government-issued photo identification.) (See Instructions for Question 18.a.)*

Issuing Authority and Type of Identification	Number on Identification	Expiration Date of Identification *(if any)*		
		Month	Day	Year

18.b. Supplemental Government Issued Documentation *(if identification document does not show current residence address) (See Instructions for Question 18.b.)*

18.c. Exception to the Nonimmigrant Alien Prohibition: If the transferee/buyer answered "YES" to 12.d.2. the transferor/seller must record the type of documentation showing the exception to the prohibition and attach a copy to this ATF Form 4473. *(See Instructions for Question 18.c.)*

Questions 19, 20, or 21 Must Be Completed Prior To The Transfer Of The Firearm(s) *(See Instructions for Questions 19, 20 and 21.)*

19.a. Date the transferee's/buyer's identifying information in Section A was transmitted to NICS or the appropriate State agency:

Month	Day	Year

19.b. The NICS or State transaction number *(if provided)* was:

19.c. The response initially (first) provided by NICS or the appropriate State agency was:

☐ Proceed ☐ Delayed
☐ Denied   *[The firearm(s) may be transferred on*
☐ Cancelled   _____ *if State law permits (optional)]*

19.d. The following response(s) was/were later received from NICS or the appropriate State agency:

☐ Proceed _____ *(date)* ☐ Overturned
☐ Denied _____ *(date)*
☐ Cancelled _____ *(date)*
☐ No response was provided within 3 business days.

19.e. *(Complete if applicable.)* After the firearm was transferred, the following response was received from NICS or the appropriate State agency on:

_____ *(date).* ☐ Proceed ☐ Denied ☐ Cancelled

19.f. The name and Brady identification number of the NICS examiner. *(Optional)*	19.g. Name of FFL Employee Completing NICS check. *(Optional)*
(name) *(number)*	

20. ☐ No NICS check was required because a background check was completed during the NFA approval process on the individual who will receive the NFA firearm(s), as reflected on the approved NFA application. *(See Instructions for Question 20.)*

21. ☐ No NICS check was required because the transferee/buyer has a valid permit from the Sate where the transfer is to take place, which qualifies as an exemption to NICS. *(See Instructions for Question 21.)*

Issuing State and Permit Type	Date of Issuance *(if any)*	Expiration Date *(if any)*	Permit Number *(if any)*

Section C - Must Be Completed Personally By Transferee/Buyer

If the transfer of the firearm(s) takes place on a different day from the date that the transferee/buyer signed Section A, the transferee/buyer must complete Section C immediately prior to the transfer of the firearm(s). *(See Instructions for Question 22 and 23.)*

I certify that my answers to the questions in Section A of this form are still true, correct, and complete.

22. Transferee's/Buyer's Signature	23. Recertification Date

Transferor/Seller Continue to Next Page
STAPLE IF PAGES BECOME SEPARATED

ATF E-Form 4473 (5300.9)
Revised October 2016

ATF Form 4473 Page 3

Note: At the time of publishing, this is the current version of the ATF Form. However, this form will be updated at the end of July 2020.

Section D - Must Be Completed By Transferor/Seller Even If The Firearm(s) is Not Transferred

24. Manufacturer and Importer *(If any) (If the manufacturer and importer are different, the FFL must include both.)*	25. Model *(If Designated)*	26. Serial Number	27. Type *(See Instructions for Question 27.)*	28. Caliber or Gauge
1.				
2.				
3.				
4.				

REMINDER - By the Close of Business Complete ATF Form 3310.4 For Multiple Purchases of Handguns Within 5 Consecutive Business Days

29. Total Number of Firearms Transferred *(Please handwrite by printing e.g., zero, one, two, three, etc. Do not use numerals.)*

30. Check if any part of this transaction is a pawn redemption.
☐ Line Number(s) From Question 24 Above:

31. For Use by Licensee *(See Instructions for Question 31.)*

32. Check if this transaction is to facilitate a private part transfer.
☐ *(See Instructions for Question 32.)*

33. Trade/corporate name and address of transferor/seller and Federal Firearm License Number *(Must contain at least first three and last five digits of FFL Number X-XX-XXXXX.) (Hand stamp may be used.)*

The Person Transferring The Firearm(s) Must Complete Questions 34-37.
For Denied/Cancelled Transactions, the Person Who Completed Section B Must Complete Questions 34-36.

I certify that: (1) I have read and understand the Notices, Instructions, and Definitions on this ATF Form 4473; (2) the information recorded in Sections B and D is true, correct, and complete; and (3) this entire transaction record has been completed at my licensed business premises ("licensed premises" includes business temporarily conducted from a qualifying gun show or event in the same State in which the licensed premises is located) unless this transaction has met the requirements of 18 U.S.C. 922(c). Unless this transaction has been denied or cancelled, I further certify on the basis of — (1) the transferee's/buyer's responses in Section A (and Section C, if applicable); (2) my verification of the identification recorded in question 18 (and my re-verification at the time of transfer, *if Section C was completed*); and (3) State or local law applicable to the firearms business — it is my belief that it is not unlawful for me to sell, deliver, transport, or otherwise dispose of the firearm(s) listed on this form to the person identified in Section A.

34. Transferor's/Seller's Name *(Please print)*	35. Transferor's/Seller's Signature	36. Transferor's/Seller's Title	37. Date Transferred

NOTICES, INSTRUCTIONS, AND DEFINITIONS

Purpose of the Form: The information and certification on this form are designed so that a person licensed under 18 U.S.C. 923 may determine if he/she may lawfully sell or deliver a firearm to the person identified in Section A, and to alert the transferee/buyer of certain restrictions on the receipt and possession of firearms. The transferor/seller of a firearm must determine the lawfulness of the transaction and maintain proper records of the transaction. Consequently, the transferor/seller must be familiar with the provisions of 18 U.S.C. 921-931 and the regulations in 27 CFR Parts 478 and 479. In determining the lawfulness of the sale or delivery of a rifle or shotgun to a resident of another State, the transferor's/seller's is presumed to know the applicable State laws and published ordinances in both the transferor's/seller's State and the transferee's/buyer's State. *(See ATF Publication 5300.5, State Laws and Published Ordinances.)*

Generally, ATF Form 4473 must be completed at the licensed business premises when a firearm is transferred over-the-counter. Federal law, 18 U.S.C. 922(c), allows a licensed importer, manufacturer, or dealer to sell a firearm to a nonlicensee who does not appear in person at the licensee's business premises only if the transferee/buyer meets certain requirements. These requirements are set forth in section 922(c), 27 CFR 478.96(b), and ATF Procedure 2013-2.

After the transferor/seller has completed the firearms transaction, he/she must make the completed, original ATF Form 4473 *(which includes the Notices, General Instructions, and Definitions)*, and any supporting documents, part of his/her permanent records. Such Forms 4473 must be retained for at least 20 years and after that period may be submitted to ATF. Filing may be chronological *(by date of disposition)*, alphabetical *(by name of purchaser)*, or numerical *(by transaction serial number)*, as long as all of the transferor's/seller's completed Forms 4473 are filed in the same manner.

FORMS 4473 FOR DENIED/CANCELLED TRANSFERS MUST BE RETAINED: If the transfer of a firearm is denied/cancelled by NICS, or if for any other reason the transfer is not completed after a NICS check is initiated, the licensee must retain the ATF Form 4473 in his/her records for at least 5 years. Forms 4473 with respect to which a sale, delivery, or transfer did not take place shall be separately retained in alphabetical *(by name of transferee)* or chronological *(by date of transferee's certification)* order.

If the transferor/seller or the transferee/buyer discovers that an ATF Form 4473 is incomplete or improperly completed after the firearm has been transferred, and the transferor/seller or the transferee/buyer wishes to correct the omission(s) or error(s), photocopy the inaccurate form and make any necessary additions or revisions to the photocopy. The transferor/seller should only make changes to Sections B and D. The transferee/buyer should only make changes to Section A and C. Whenever made the changes should initial and date the changes. The corrected photocopy should be attached to the original Form 4473 and retained as part of the transferor's/seller's permanent records.

Exportation of Firearms: The State or Commerce Departments may require a firearms exporter to obtain a license prior to export. **Warning:** Any person who exports a firearm without proper authorization may be fined not more than $1,000,000 and/or imprisoned for not more than 20 years. See 22 U.S.C. 2778(c).

Section A

The transferee/buyer must personally complete Section A of this form and certify *(sign)* that the answers are true, correct, and complete. However, if the transferee/buyer is unable to read and write, the answers *(other than the signature)* may be completed by another person, excluding the transferor/seller. Two persons *(other than the transferor/seller)* must then sign as witnesses to the transferee's/buyer's answers and signature/certification in question 14.

ATF E-Form 4473 (5300.9)
Revised October 2016

ATF Form 5320.23 Page 1

U.S. Department of Justice
Bureau of Alcohol, Tobacco, Firearms and Explosives

OMB No. 1140-0107 (06/30/2019)

National Firearms Act *(NFA)*
Responsible Person Questionnaire

Complete the form in duplicate. The ATF copy of the form, with fingerprints on Form FD-258 and photograph, will be submitted with the ATF Form 1, 4, or 5 (to the address shown on the specific form) and the other copy will be directed to the responsible person's chief law enforcement officer. *(See Instructions)*

1. Please check the appropriate box to indicate with which ATF form this questionnaire will be submitted.

  ☐ ATF Form 1 ☐ ATF Form 4 ☐ ATF Form 5

2. Name and Address of Applicant or Transferee *(as shown on the ATF Form 1, 4 or 5) (see instruction 2)*

3a. Name and Home Address of Responsible Person	3b. Telephone *(Area code and Number)*
	3c. e-mail address *(optional)*
	3d. Other names used *(including maiden name)*

4a. Type of Firearm *(see definition 5)*	3e. Photograph
4b. Name and Address of Maker, Manufacturer and/or Importer of Firearm	Affix recent Photograph Here *(Approximately 2" x 2")* *(See instruction 3b)*

4c. Firearm Model	4d. Caliber or Gauge	4e. Firearm Serial Number	

5. Law Enforcement Notification *(See instruction 5)*

As a responsible person (see definition 4) of the trust or legal entity identified in Item 2 of this form, I am required to provide notification of the proposed making or acquisition and possession of the firearm described in item 4 of this form by providing a copy of the completed form to the chief law enforcement officer (CLEO) in the agency identified below:

Agency or Department Name   Name and Title of Official

Address (Street address or P.O. Box, City, State and Zip Code) to which sent (mailed or delivered)

Information for the Chief Law Enforcement Officer

This form provides notification of the maker or transferee's intent to make or acquire and possess a National Firearms Act (NFA) firearm. No action on your part is required. However, should you have information that may disqualify this person from making or possessing a firearm, please contact the NFA Branch at (304) 616-4500 or NFA@atf.gov. A "Yes" answer to items 6h or item 7b or 7c could disqualify a person from acquiring or possessing a firearm. Also, ATF may not approve an application if the transfer or possession of the firearm would be in violation of State or local law.

ATF Copy

ATF E-Form 5320.23
Revised May 2016

6. Answer questions 6.a through 6.h. Answer questions 7 and 8 if applicable. For any "Yes" answer the transferee shall provide details on a separate sheet. *(See definitions 8-12)*

	Yes	No
a. Are you under indictment or information in any court for a felony, or any other crime, for which the judge could imprison you for more than one year? *(See definition 8)*		
b. Have you ever been convicted in any court for a felony, or any other crime, for which the judge could have imprisoned you for more than one year, even if you received a shorter sentence including probation? *(See definition 8)*		
c. Are you a fugitive from justice? *(See definition 13)*		
d. Are you an unlawful user of, or addicted to, marijuana or any depressant, stimulant, narcotic drug, or any other controlled substance? **Warning: The use or possession of marijuana remains unlawful under Federal law regardless of whether is has been legalized or decriminalized for medicinal or recreational purposes in the state where you reside.**		
e. Have you ever been adjudicated as a mental defective OR have you ever been committed to a mental institution? *(See definitions 9 and 10)*		
f. Have you been discharged from the Armed Forces under **dishonorable** conditions?		
g. Are you subject to a court order restraining you from harassing, stalking, or threatening your child or an intimate partner or child of such partner? *(See definition 11)*		
h. Have you ever been convicted in any court of a misdemeanor crime of domestic violence? *(See definition 14)*		

7a. Country of Citizenship: *(Check/List more than one, if applicable. Nationals of the United States may check U.S.A.) (See definition 12)*

☐ United States of America ☐ Other Country/Countries (specify): _____

	Yes	No
b. Have you ever renounced your United States citizenship?		
c. Are you an alien illegally or unlawfully in the United States?		
d.1. Are you an alien who has been admitted to the United States under a nonimmigrant visa?		
d.2. If "yes", do you fall within any of the exceptions stated in the instructions? Attach the documentation to the questionnaire ☐ N/A		

8. If you are an alien, record your U.S.-Issued Alien or Admission number (AR#, USCIS#, or 194#): _____

CERTIFICATION: Under penalties imposed by 18 U.S.C. § 924 and 26 U.S.C. § 5861, I certify that, upon submission of this form to ATF, a completed copy of this form will be directed to the chief law enforcement officer (CLEO) shown in item 5, that the statements contained in this certification, and any attached documents in support thereof, are true and correct to the best of my knowledge and belief.

_____
Signature of Responsible Person

_____
Date

Instructions

1. Completion: Each responsible person (see definition 4) of a trust or legal entity seeking to make or acquire a National Firearms Act *(NFA)* firearm shall complete this form in duplicate. (see instruction 9)
   a. Each responsible person must submit his/her fingerprints and photograph with this form *(see below)*.
   b. Please note that this form is not required when the applicant on Form 1, 4 or 5 is an individual.
2. Item 2- Enter the name, trade name *(if any)* and address of the trust or legal entity identified on the Form 1 (items 3a and b); Form 4 *(item 2a)*; or Form 5 *(item 2a)*
3. Item 3- Responsible Person information
   a. Provide the information for the responsible person in items 3a through 3e.
   b. Item 3e - Photograph: The responsible person shall attach, in item 3e on the ATF copy of the form only, a 2-inch by 2-inch frontal view photograph taken within one year prior to the date of the filing of the form. Item 3c is obscured on the CLEO copy.
4. Firearm information
   a. Type of NFA firearm: see definition 5 and as identified in item 4b of Form 1, 4, or 5
   b. Name of maker, manufacturer and/or importer: as identified in item 4a of Form 1, 4, or 5
   c. Firearm Model: identified in item 4d of Form 1, 4, or 5
   d. Caliber or Gauge: identified in item 4c of Form 1, 4 or 5
   e. Firearm Serial Number: identified in item 4e of Form 1, 4 or 5. Item 4e is obscured on the CLEO copy.
5. Item 5- Law Enforcement Notification: Each responsible person must provide a notification on this form of the proposed making or acquisition of an NFA firearm to his/her chief law enforcement officer having jurisdiction where the responsible person is located. The chief law enforcement officer is considered to be the Chief of Police; the Sheriff; the Head of the State Police; or a State or local district attorney or prosecutor.
6. Complete items 6 through 8
7. Fingerprints: The responsible person shall submit, in duplicate with the ATF copy of this form, his or her fingerprints on FBI Form FD-258 and the fingerprints must be clear for accurate classification and taken by someone properly equipped to take them. No fingerprints are required with the copy of the form sent to the chief law enforcement officer.
8. State or Local Permit: If the State in which the responsible person resides requires the responsible person to have a State or Local permit or licensee, a copy of the permit or license must be submitted with this form.
9. Disposition: The ATF copy of the form, with the fingerprints and photograph, shall be submitted with the ATF Form 1, 4 or 5. The other copy shall be directed to the responsible person's chief law enforcement officer identified in item 5 of this form.
10. Sign and date the form. The signature must be original.

ATF Copy

ATF E-Form 5320.23
Revised May 2016

ATF Form 5320.23 Page 3

U.S. Department of Justice
Bureau of Alcohol, Tobacco, Firearms and Explosives

OMB No. 1140-0107 (06/30/2019)

National Firearms Act *(NFA)*
Responsible Person Questionnaire

Complete the form in duplicate. The ATF copy of the form, with fingerprints on Form FD-258 and photograph, will be submitted with the ATF Form 1, 4, or 5 (to the address shown on the specific form) and the other copy will be directed to the responsible person's chief law enforcement officer. *(See Instructions)*

1. Please check the appropriate box to indicate with which ATF form this questionnaire will be submitted.

☐ ATF Form 1 ☐ ATF Form 4 ☐ ATF Form 5

2. Name and Address of Applicant or Transferee *(as shown on the ATF Form 1, 4 or 5) (see instruction 2)*

3a. Name and Home Address of Responsible Person	3b. Telephone *(Area code and Number)*
	3c. e-mail address *(optional)*
	3d. Other names used *(including maiden name)*

4a. Type of Firearm *(see definition 5)*

4b. Name and Address of Maker, Manufacturer and/or Importer of Firearm

4c. Firearm Model	4d. Caliber or Gauge

5. Law Enforcement Notification *(See instruction 5)*

As a responsible person (see definition 4) of the trust or legal entity identified in Item 2 of this form, I am required to provide notification of the proposed making or acquisition and possession of the firearm described in item 4 of this form by providing a copy of the completed form to the chief law enforcement officer (CLEO) in the agency identified below:

Agency or Department Name

Name and Title of Official

Address (Street address or P.O. Box, City, State and Zip Code) to which sent (mailed or delivered)

Information for the Chief Law Enforcement Officer

This form provides notification of the maker or transferee's intent to make or acquire and possess a National Firearms Act (NFA) firearm. No action on your part is required. However, should you have information that may disqualify this person from making or possessing a firearm, please contact the NFA Branch at (304) 616-4500 or NFA@atf.gov. A "Yes" answer to items 6h or item 7b or 7c could disqualify a person from acquiring or possessing a firearm. Also, ATF may not approve an application if the transfer or possession of the firearm would be in violation of State or local law.

6. Answer questions 6.a through 6.h. Answer questions 7 and 8 if applicable. For any "Yes" answer the transferee shall provide details on a separate sheet. *(See definitions 8-12)*

	Yes	No
a. Are you under indictment or information in any court for a felony, or any other crime, for which the judge could imprison you for more than one year? *(See definition 8)*		
b. Have you ever been convicted in any court for a felony, or any other crime, for which the judge could have imprisoned you for more than one year, even if you received a shorter sentence including probation? *(See definition 8)*		
c. Are you a fugitive from justice? *(See definition 13)*		
d. Are you an unlawful user of, or addicted to, marijuana or any depressant, stimulant, narcotic drug, or any other controlled substance? **Warning: The use or possession of marijuana remains unlawful under Federal law regardless of whether is has been legalized or decriminalized for medicinal or recreational purposes in the state where you reside.**		
e. Have you ever been adjudicated as a mental defective **OR** have you ever been committed to a mental institution? *(See definitions 9 and 10)*		
f. Have you been discharged from the Armed Forces under **dishonorable** conditions?		
g. Are you subject to a court order restraining you from harassing, stalking, or threatening your child or an intimate partner or child of such partner? *(See definition 11)*		
h. Have you ever been convicted in any court of a misdemeanor crime of domestic violence? *(See definition 14)*		

7a. Country of Citizenship: *(Check/List more than one, if applicable. Nationals of the United States may check U.S.A.) (See definition 12)*

☐ United States of America   ☐ Other Country/Countries (specify): _____

	Yes	No
b. Have you ever renounced your United States citizenship?		
c. Are you an alien illegally or unlawfully in the United States?		
d.1. Are you an alien who has been admitted to the United States under a nonimmigrant visa?		
d.2. If "yes", do you fall within any of the exceptions stated in the instructions? Attach the documentation to the questionnaire ☐ N/A		

8. If you are an alien, record your U.S. -Issued Alien or Admission number (AR#, USCIS#, or 194#): _____

CERTIFICATION: Under penalties imposed by 18 U.S.C. § 924 and 26 U.S.C. § 5861, I certify that, upon submission of this form to ATF, a completed copy of this form will be directed to the chief law enforcement officer (CLEO) shown in item 5, that the statements contained in this certification, and any attached documents in support thereof, are true and correct to the best of my knowledge and belief.

Signature of Responsible Person _____   Date _____

Instructions

1. Completion: Each responsible person (see definition 4) of a trust or legal entity seeking to make or acquire a National Firearms Act *(NFA)* firearm shall complete this form in duplicate. (see instruction 9)
   a. Each responsible person must submit his/her fingerprints and photograph with this form *(see below)*.
   b. Please note that this form is not required when the applicant on Form 1, 4 or 5 is an individual.
2. Item 2- Enter the name, trade name *(if any)* and address of the trust or legal entity identified on the Form 1 (items 3a and b); Form 4 *(item 2a)*; or Form 5 *(item 2a)*
3. Item 3- Responsible Person information
   a. Provide the information for the responsible person in items 3a through 3e.
   b. Item 3e - Photograph: The responsible person shall attach, in item 3e on the ATF copy of the form only, a 2-inch by 2-inch frontal view photograph taken within one year prior to the date of the filing of the form. Item 3c is obscured on the CLEO copy.
4. Firearm information
   a. Type of NFA firearm: see definition 5 and as identified in item 4b of Form 1, 4, or 5
   b. Name of maker, manufacturer and/or importer: as identified in item 4a of Form 1, 4, or 5
   c. Firearm Model: identified in item 4d of Form 1, 4, or 5
   d. Caliber or Gauge: identified in item 4c of Form 1, 4 or 5
   e. Firearm Serial Number: identified in item 4g of Form 1, 4, or 5. Item 4e is obscured on the CLEO copy.
5. Item 5- Law Enforcement Notification: Each responsible person must provide a notification on this form of the proposed making or acquisition of an NFA firearm to his/her chief law enforcement officer having jurisdiction where the responsible person is located. The chief law enforcement officer is considered to be the Chief of Police; the Sheriff; the Head of the State Police; or a State or local district attorney or prosecutor.
6. Complete items 6 through 8
7. Fingerprints: The responsible person shall submit, in duplicate with the ATF copy of this form, his or her fingerprints on FBI Form FD-258 and the fingerprints must be clear for accurate classification and taken by someone properly equipped to take them. No fingerprints are required with the copy of the form sent to the chief law enforcement officer.
8. State or Local Permit: If the State in which the responsible person resides requires the responsible person to have a State or Local permit or licensee, a copy of the permit or license must be submitted with this form.
9. Disposition: The ATF copy of the form, with the fingerprints and photograph, shall be submitted with the ATF Form 1, 4 or 5. The other copy shall be directed to the responsible person's chief law enforcement officer identified in item 5 of this form.
10. Sign and date the form. The signature must be original.

CLEO Copy

ATF E-Form 5320.23
Revised May 2016

➤ ABOUT THE ◄
ATTORNEY AUTHOR

MICHAEL A. JOHNSON
AUTHOR

Mike is an independent firearms program attorney for U.S. and Texas LawShield in Illinois. Mike was born and raised in Chicago and has been actively representing citizens in Illinois and throughout the country for over 37 years. Mike has a reputation for making himself available to people who may find themselves in need day or night. He has handled in excess of 200 homicide cases and been retained to represent folks in both state and federal court, as well as military court. He has successfully argued before Appellate Courts as well as the Illinois Supreme Court. Mike has been sought after by many other firms to represent clients in jurisdictions such as,

Laredo, Texas; Owensboro, Kentucky; Miami, Florida; Nashville, Tennessee; Fort Rucker, Alabama; and Duluth, Minnesota; just to name a few. He has been recognized by legal organizations as one of the top trial lawyers in the country.

Mike has been lecturing to gun owners over the past several years since Illinois passed their Conceal Carry laws in 2013. His emphasis is to familiarize them with the laws in Illinois in relation to justified use of force, self-defense, as well as current laws regarding when and where you can carry your weapon.

Mike's other passions include spending time at his lake home in Northern Minnesota with family and his dogs, Beau and Teddy.

The U.S. LawShield® Legal Defense for Self Defense® Program is dedicated to preserving its members' fundamental and Constitutional right to self-defense through zealous legal representation by Independent Program Attorneys experienced in self-defense and gun laws. A cornerstone of the U.S. LawShield program is legal education.

U.S. LawShield boasts hundreds of thousands of members, including civilians, law enforcement and security officers, and military personnel. U.S. LawShield is honored to be affiliated with thousands of gun ranges, gun stores, FFL dealers, instructors, educators, and other firearms experts and professionals. U.S. LawShield is one of the largest civilian repositories of state-specific self-defense and gun law legal information available anywhere.

For more information about the U.S. LawShield Legal Defense for Self Defense Program, visit www.uslawshield.com.

Michael A. Johnson is an Independent Program Attorney for U.S. LawShield with the law firm of Michael A. Johnson and Associates. This publication is not an endorsement or solicitation for any product or service. The content in Illinois Gun Law: Armed And Educated was produced for educational purposes only as a general legal overview of the law in Illinois. No legal advice is being provided and no attorney-client relationship is being created. This publication is not a substitute for legal advice. You should contact an attorney regarding your specific legal circumstances.